The Ultimate His
Fast Bikes

The Ultimate History of
Fast Bikes

Roland Brown

p

This is a Parragon Book
This edition published in 2005

Parragon
Queen Street House
4 Queen Street
Bath BA1 1HE, UK

Copyright © Parragon 2002

Designed, produced and packaged by
Stonecastle Graphics Limited

Text by Roland Brown
Edited by Philip de Ste. Croix
Designed by Paul Turner and Sue Pressley

ISBN 1-40545-362-1

Printed in China

Photographic credits:

(l) = left, (c) = centre, (r) = right, (t) = top, (b) = below.

Ray Archer/R Brown: pages 9(b), 277(t).

Kevin Ash (© Roland Brown): pages 126, 127(t), 128(br).

Graeme Bell (© Roland Brown): page 247(cr).

© Roland Brown: pages 6, 8, 35(t), 65(t), 78-79, 82, 83(tr), 83(b), 91, 100, 103(t), 106(b), 107, 110-111, 114, 115(b), 117(b), 130, 131(tl), 140(b), 141, 142-143, 144-145, 146-147, 152, 153(t), 154-155, 160-161, 166-167, 168, 169(tl), 169(b), 176(b), 177(t), 178-179, 198(t), 199(l), 205(b), 206(b), 207(l), 222, 223(t), 229(bl), 230, 232, 233(tl), 233(b), 234, 235(br), 237(b), 239(r), 242, 243(c), 247(b), 251(l), 252, 253(tl), 253(b), 254-255, 257(cr), 258(b), 259, 260, 261(r), 265(r), 268, 269(l), 271(tr), 272, 273(tl), 273(cr), 275, 276, 277(b), 278-279, 280, 281(tl), 282-283, 288-289, 290(b), 291, 293(t), 294-295, 297(br), 298, 299(b), 302, 304, 305(l), 306, 307(tl), 307(cr), 308, 309(l), 313(cl), 313(tr), 316-317.

Paul Bryant/R Brown: pages 243(t), 243(b).

Jean-Pierre Bulmet/R Brown: page 281(b).

Jack Burnicle (© Roland Brown): pages 108(t), 134-135, 136, 137(bl), 149(r), 156-157.

Jason Critchell/R Brown: pages 273(b), 290(t), 292, 293(bl), 293(br).

Patrick Curtet/R Brown: page 258(t).

Richard Francis/R Brown: page 216(t).

David Goldman (© Roland Brown): pages 125(l), 162-163, 186-187, 202-203, 204, 205(tl), 205(tr), 210, 211, 212(b), 213(tl), 213(b), 246, 247(tl), 249(t).

Gold & Goose (© Roland Brown): pages 31(b), 67(cr), 77(br), 98-99, 233(cr), 309(r).

© Gold & Goose: pages 3, 172-173, 189(t), 192, 192(l), 198(b), 200-201, 208-209, 212(t), 214-215, 216(b), 217, 218-219, 228, 229(t), 229(br), 235(bl), 238, 239(l), 251(r), 261(l), 264, 265(l), 274, 303(l).

Patrick Gosling (© Roland Brown): pages 37(r), 109(r).

© Mac McDiarmid: pages 42-43, 92-93, 104-105, 112-113, 117(t), 118-119.

Mac McDiarmid (© Roland Brown): pages 124, 125(r), 310-311.

Phil Masters (© Roland Brown): pages 1, 17(cr), 56, 57(tl), 57(b), 58-59, 64, 65(bl), 65(br), 68-69, 70-71, 72-73, 80-81, 83(tl), 84(t), 88-89, 90(t), 96-97, 102, 103(b), 115(t), 122-123, 128-129, 132-133, 137(cr), 148, 149(l), 153(b), 175(t), 190-191, 196, 197(cr), 197(b), 199(r), 206(t), 213(cr), 220, 221(l), 223(b), 224-225, 226, 227(b), 235(t), 236, 237(tl), 250, 253(tr), 262-263, 266-267, 270, 271(tl), 271(b), 284-285, 286-287, 296, 297(bl), 300-301, 307(b).

Wout Meppelink/R Brown: page 299(t).

© Andrew Morland: pages 7(tr), 12, 13(tl), 13(b), 16, 17(tr), 17(b), 18-19, 22-23, 32, 33(b), 36, 37(l), 40, 41(t), 41(b), 46-47, 48-49, 50-51, 54-55, 62, 63(tr), 63(cl), 76(b), 77(bl), 84(b), 85, 108(b), 109(l).

© Don Morley: pages 10-11, 14-15, 169(cr), 170-171.

Kenny P (© Roland Brown): pages 244, 245(tl), 245(tr).

© Colin Schiller: page 9(t), 176(t), 177(bl), 177(br), 180-181, 182-183, 185(tl), 185(b), 188, 189(b), 197(t).

© Garry Stuart: pages 7(tl), 7(b), 13(tr), 20-21, 24-25, 26-27, 28-29, 30, 31(tl), 31(tr), 33(t), 34, 35(b), 38, 39(t), 44-45, 52, 53(t), 57(cr), 63(bl), 76(t), 90(b), 94-95, 101, 150, 151(t), 151(bl).

Oli Tennent/R Brown: pages 312, 313(b).

Oli Tennent (© Roland Brown): pages 2, 39(b), 41(cr), 53(b), 60-61, 66, 67(tl), 67(b), 74-75, 86-87, 106(t), 116, 117(cr), 120-121, 127(cr), 131(cr), 131(b), 138-139, 140(t), 151(br), 158-159, 164-165, 174, 175(b), 184, 185(tr), 193(r), 194-195, 207(r), 221(r), 227(t), 231, 237(cr), 240-241, 248, 249(bl), 249(br), 256, 257(tl), 257(b), 303(r), 314, 315.

Mark Wernham/R Brown: page 305(r).

Contents

Introduction

Below left: The world's first production motorcycle was the Hildebrand and Wolfmüller, a 1500cc twin whose output of about 2.5 horsepower at 240rpm gave a top speed of 25mph (40km/h). A total of about 1000 were produced, both at the firm's base in Munich and also under licence in France.

Below right: Although steam-powered bicycles were built as early as the 1860s, the first true motorcycle was Gottlieb Daimler's Einspur of 1885. The wooden bike's 264cc four-stroke single engine ran on either petrol or coal gas, at a speed of 800rpm. Daimler soon turned his attention to cars.

The essential thrill of riding a fast motorbike has changed very little in more than a century. In that time the bikes themselves have evolved from simple, single-cylinder machines to ultra-sophisticated devices capable of almost 200mph (322km/h). Yet the feeling that comes from gripping a pair of handlebars and winding the throttle back to its stop is much the same, whether you're aboard the latest superbike or a big V-twin from the early years of the last century.

The raw, simple appeal of a fast bike comes from a combination of many sensations: satisfaction of being in control, freedom, exposure to nature, a hint of danger, not to mention the surge of acceleration possible on a machine with a power-to-weight ratio that other road users can only dream about. That was true 100 years ago, when someone might ride a bike as an alternative form of transport to the horse. And it remains true today of those who ride simply for fun or to escape from the pressures of the modern world.

Speed and excitement are by no means the only reasons why people ride motorcycles. Demands for style, convenience and long-distance comfort have led designers to produce a wide variety of bikes over the years, many of them combining all of those qualities. But performance has been an essential part of the motorcycle's appeal since its

earliest days, and most of the outstanding machines since then fully justify the description 'fast'.

That certainly applies to those selected for this book, which range from early V-twins from Indian and Flying Merkel to Harley-Davidson's recent V-Rod; and from fours such as the Henderson and Belgian-built FN to the latest Yamaha YZF-R1 and Suzuki GSX-R1000. In between are singles, twins of various engine layouts, triples, and sixes. It's a formidable and varied lineup that traces the story of the development of two-wheeled motoring through the fastest and best bikes ever produced.

Early speed machines

'Fast' is of course a relative concept, and few people would use the word today about a bike that could manage only 25mph (40km/h). But that was the top speed of the world's first production motorcycle, built by Messrs Hildebrand and Wolfmüller in Germany in 1894. And given that the 1500cc, liquid-cooled twin's rear brake was simply a metal bar that dragged on the ground, even that speed probably felt quite fast enough.

The Hildebrand and Wolfmüller was certainly an advance on the first ever motorbike, the wooden, 265cc single-cylinder Einspur ('One track') that another German, Gottlieb Daimler, had built nine years earlier. But it was arguably not until 1901 that the motorcycle as we know it today was

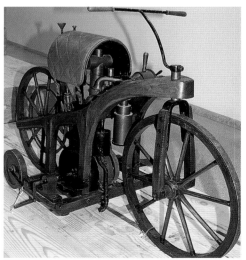

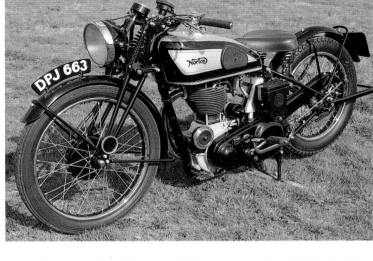

created. It was in that year that the Werner brothers of France, whose firm was one of many building bikes with a wide variety of engine positions, moved their machine's single-cylinder unit from above the front wheel to between the wheels, in a triangular-shaped frame.

The resultant 'New Werner' handled much better, due to its lower centre of gravity, and set the layout that motorcycles, with some notable exceptions, have followed ever since. Progress from then on was swift. American firm Indian built its first model in that same year of 1901, followed three years later by Harley-Davidson. As the demand for personal transport escalated on both sides of the Atlantic, a growing number of firms set up to build bikes with a wide variety of engine configurations.

Above left: American firm Flying Merkel was one of the most innovative of early manufacturers, producing rapid V-twins that were normally finished in bright orange paintwork. This is a racebike with dropped handlebars and short, unsilenced exhaust pipes.

Above right: Norton's 500cc International, introduced in 1932, was one of the best and most famous single-cylinder models of the era dominated by British manufacturers. High-performance rivals included BSA's Gold Star.

Left: Brough Superior was arguably the most glamorous marque before the Second World War. George Brough's V-twins were fast, stylish and superbly engineered. But it was a very different British bike, Triumph's Speed Twin, that did most to shape motorcycling in the post-war period.

Below: Kawasaki's 903cc Z1 arrived in 1973, in the wheel-tracks of Honda's CB750 four, to set a new standard for superbike performance. With 82bhp and a top speed of over 130mph (209km/h), the Z1 established the twin-cam, transverse four-cylinder layout that would still be dominating motorcycling – albeit refined with liquid cooling and four or five valves per cylinder – three decades later.

Increasing power and speed by doubling the number of cylinders to produce a large-capacity V-twin was a logical move that became very popular, especially in America. Refinements soon followed, with Harley's fully mechanically operated valves being followed by Cyclone's overhead camshafts. In 1914 came French firm Peugeot's racer with twin cams and four-valve heads. Others took a different approach, notably Britain's Scott, which by 1910 was producing a rapid liquid-cooled, two-stroke parallel twin that featured telescopic forks, a kickstarter and chain final drive.

Most of the American firms went bust in the years following the First World War, hit by the arrival of Ford's mass-produced Model T car. But motorcycling thrived in Europe, where high-performance machines included the incomparable Brough Superior V-twin and Ariel's luxurious but flawed Square Four. Triumph's Speed Twin, its name as inspired as its parallel twin engine format, arrived in 1937 to popularize the layout with which British marques including BSA and Norton would dominate motorcycling for three decades.

By the late 1960s speeds had risen, and a Triumph Bonneville or Norton Commando twin was capable of well over 100mph (161km/h). Those bikes also had good handling from a chassis combining a tubular steel frame with telescopic forks and twin rear shocks, in place of the old girder forks and either 'hard-tail' rear ends or crude plunger rear suspension systems. (In today's politically correct climate, with 'fast' so often a dirty word, it should be emphasized that it is the increasing speed of bikes that has inspired the dramatic improvements in handling, roadholding and braking performance...)

The next big advance came from Japan. Honda's CB750, launched in 1969, was no faster or better-handling than the Triumph Trident 750cc triple that had been introduced a few months earlier, but the Japanese bike's disc brake, electric starter and reliable four-cylinder engine put it in a different league. Kawasaki's 903cc Z1, Suzuki's GS1000 and others moved on the four-cylinder Japanese format, lifting top speeds towards 140mph (225km/h). Italian marques fought back with distinctive superbikes such as Ducati's 900SS and Moto Guzzi's Le Mans, whose fine handling forced the Japanese to improve their own chassis to new levels in order to compete.

Left: Honda's VF1000R was a state-of-the-art superbike in 1984. Its liquid-cooled V4 engine produced 122bhp, which was enough to send the sleek, fully-faired Honda to 150mph (241km/h). But it was a less expensive straight four, Kawasaki's GPZ900R, that was much more influential.

Below: Suzuki's GSX1300R Hayabusa was arguably the fastest standard production superbike of the 20th century. Its 190mph (306km/h) top speed was the product of rigorous wind-tunnel development as well as a mighty 173bhp four-cylinder engine.

Race-replicas arrive

By the mid 1980s, Japanese fours such as Kawasaki's GPZ900R and Honda's VF1000R had added liquid cooling, full fairings and 150mph (241km/h) top speed to the superbike rider's list of requirements. Suzuki's GSX-R750 pioneered the race-replica trend with its aggressive styling, aluminium frame and no-compromise personality. Honda's CBR900RR and Yamaha's YZF-R1 raised the speeds to 170mph (274km/h) as they fought the battle for power and light weight through the 1990s, while Ducati's 916 and its derivatives, with their V-twin engines and tubular steel frames, led a thrillingly fast and varied opposition to the Japanese fours.

Ironically the current millennium began with the performance of bikes including Kawasaki's ZX-12R and Suzuki's Hayabusa being limited to 186mph (300km/h) by their manufacturers, for fear that their awesome performance would trigger more severe government restrictions. Modern superbikes, it seems, are quite fast enough for modern roads and traffic conditions. But with riders increasingly taking to racetracks to use their bikes to the full in relative safety, and the machines regularly being updated with more power and less weight, it's clear that the definitive history of fast motorbikes is not yet completed – and hopefully never will be.

1900-1940
Evolution of the Iron Horse

Motorcycle designers did not take long to make big advances on the simple, single-cylinder machines of the 19th century. Powerful twins and smooth-running fours were being built by many firms before the First World War, as growing numbers of people discovered the excitement and practicality of the motorbike.

Increasingly fast and sophisticated singles remained popular through the 1920s and 1930s, while twin-cylinder machines such as Triumph's Speed Twin and the Brough Superior, with its top speed of 100mph (161km/h), arrived to give high-performance motorcycling a new dimension.

FN Four

Top speed
40mph
64km/h

Right: FN designer Paul Kelecom's sophisticated four-cylinder engines caused a sensation when introduced early in the last century. Capacity increased from the original 362cc to a limit of 748cc.

Below: This FN Four dates from 1922, and is one of the last 748cc models built before the shaft final drive was changed to a chain. Telescopic forks were used from the earliest model.

The four-cylinder machines built by Belgian firm FN were not the fastest bikes of motorcycling's early years, but they were certainly among the smoothest and most sophisticated. Introduced in 1904, the FN Four caused a sensation with its advanced specification, which included shaft final drive and a simple but light and efficient chassis. The Four was a commercial success too, remaining in production for more than two decades, and benefiting from several increases in capacity.

FN was originally an armaments manufacturer, having been founded at Herstal, south of Liège, in 1899 under the name Fabrique Nationale d'Armes de Guerre. The firm started producing bicycles in 1901, and in the following year added motorcycles, initially with single-cylinder engines of 225 and 286cc capacity.

The Four was conceived by FN designer Paul Kelecom, who had previously designed and manufactured engines under his own name. These had powered the London-built Ormonde bikes, one of which had taken part in the prestigious Paris-Madrid race in 1903. From this experience Kelecom knew the problems of early singles, which included slipping drive belts as well as engine vibration and the stress that this passed to the chassis often resulting in unreliability.

Kelecom's response was to design an in-line four-cylinder motor of 362cc, which ran very smoothly because its inner and outer pairs of cylinders moved in opposite directions, cancelling primary vibration. The four cylinders were separate

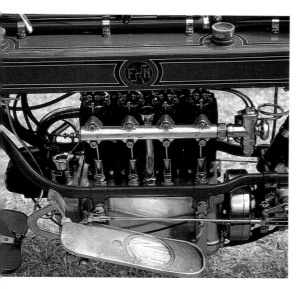

Pierce Arrow – First American Four

Percy Pierce, who ran the two-wheeled side of his father's car and bicycle firm in Buffalo, New York, built the first American four in 1909 after returning from Europe with an FN. The Belgian bike's influence was clear, but the Pierce Arrow was no copy. Its larger 696cc engine was a side-valve design, complete with FN-style shaft drive. And the frame consisted of large-diameter steel tubes which also held fuel and oil. The Arrow was smooth, good for over 50mph (80km/h), and reliable enough to win several endurance events. But the exotic four could not be produced profitably, and Pierce called a halt in 1913.

castings, with non-detachable cylinder heads. In contemporary fashion the FN's exhaust valves were operated by cams, but its inlet valves were 'automatic', opened by piston suction and closed by a light spring.

Shaft final drive

Much less familiar were the FN unit's long one-piece crankshaft with its five main bearings; and the cast iron crankcase, which featured four small mica windows through which the rider could check that oil was reaching the big-end bearings. Transmission was single-speed until 1908, when a two-speed gearbox and clutch were introduced, but even the earliest Four featured final drive by a shaft that was neatly enclosed in a frame tube.

The frame was a twin-loop design, with tubes running to each side of the engine. There was no rear suspension, but up front the FN featured one of the first telescopic forks, in a system combined with a parallelogram linkage. The front wheel had no brake but the rear had two: a drum that was operated by the rider pedalling backwards, and a hand-operated contracting band acting on the outside of the drum.

Some people considered the FN too strange and complex to succeed, but Kelecom's creation proved them wrong. Its engine capacity grew to 412cc and then to 491cc in 1911, increasing top speed to about 40mph (64km/h). The Four was updated and its engine enlarged again to 748cc just before the First World War, during which the occupied factory

produced bikes for the Germany army. After the war its popularity faded and production ended in 1926, three years after a final redesign that included replacing the shaft final drive with a chain.

Above left: FN increased the engine's capacity and incorporated improvements which included a clutch and two-speed gearbox during the Four's lifespan of more than 20 years.

Left: The Belgian marque's background was in armaments and bicycles. FN produced motorcycles until 1957, when it gave up the struggle to compete for sales with cheap cars.

Specification	FN Four (1906)
Engine	Air-cooled inlet-over-exhaust eight-valve in-line four
Capacity	412cc (48 x 57mm)
Maximum power	4bhp
Transmission	Single-speed, shaft final drive
Frame	Steel twin downtube
Suspension	Telescopic front; rigid rear
Brakes	None front; drum and contracting band rear
Weight	165lb (75kg)
Top speed	40mph (64km/h)

Scott Two-speed

**Top speed
50mph**
80km/h

*Below: This 450cc Scott
was very advanced when
it was produced in 1910,
with features including a
kickstart, two-speed
gearbox, and chain final
drive. The cylindrical fuel
tank beneath the seat was a
distinctive feature of the
Yorkshire firm's bikes for
many years. Telescopic fork
front suspension of this
type was produced from
1908 to 1930.*

The bikes built by Alfred Angas Scott and his Yorkshire-based firm were some of the most innovative and brilliantly engineered of motorcycling's early years – and also among the fastest. Scott's two-stoke parallel twins looked, sounded and performed like nothing else on two wheels. They proved their speed on numerous occasions, not least when winning the Isle of Man Senior TT in both 1912 and 1913.

Alfred Scott was a true one-off. One of 12 brothers, he was a visionary engineer who began experimenting with powered bicycles in 1901, and three years later produced his first air-cooled two-stroke twin. By 1908 he had found premises in Bradford and had begun production of a bike based on a 333cc version of the two-stroke motor, now with its cylinder heads cooled by water.

The parallel twin engine featured a central flywheel, set between two independent crankcases. Scott had devised a simple but efficient two-speed gearbox, and also the first kickstart ever seen on a motorbike. And this extraordinary engine had a distinctive two-stroke sound, its muted purr turning

to a high-rev yowl that was very much part of the unique Scott riding experience.

Hillclimb success

Scott made a stunning competition debut in the summer of 1908, when he arrived at the year's most prestigious hillclimb at Newnham in the English Midlands with his little 333cc twin. After starting the bike with a prod of its rear-mounted kickstart (everyone else had to run-and-bump), he used the two-stroke's superior acceleration to win three events.

His rivals were so taken aback that they campaigned to get the two-stroke handicapped (by multiplying its capacity by 1.32) on the grounds that its additional firing impulses gave an unfair advantage. Scott used this to advantage in his advertising, and his bikes continued to win many hillclimbs. He also increased the actual capacity of the engine, raising it first to 486cc and then to 532cc in 1912, by which time the twin was capable of 50mph (80km/h).

Scott's chassis was every bit as unusual and

impressive as his engine. He designed an open duplex frame of straight, triangulated steel tubes, which used the engine as a stressed member. The twins' legendary roadholding was thanks to the rigidity and low centre of gravity of this arrangement, plus the advantages of telescopic forks of which Scott was also a pioneer. Swept-back handlebars and a barrel-shaped fuel tank, normally painted in the factory's characteristic purple colour with two silver bands, made the bikes even more distinctive.

The two-stroke's profile was boosted by its terrific performance in the 1912 Isle of Man Senior TT, in which Frank Applebee led from start to finish on a twin equipped with another innovation, a rotary inlet valve. Applebee lapped at almost 50mph (80km/h) and won by more than six minutes. Further success came a year later at the TT, this time factory mechanic Tim Wood taking the victory after Applebee had gone out of the race while leading.

Wood was set to make it three wins in a row for Scott in the 1914 event when he hit mechanical problems. Even so, Scott had proved his bikes' ability and the distinctive two-strokes became very popular, especially, as a later report put it, with the professional classes who 'appreciated sophistication, refinement and the finer things in motorcycling', as well as excellent performance.

Part of the appeal was that Scott's production machines were very similar to the racers, except that they were not fitted with the rotary induction valve. The Squirrel sportster, launched in 1922, was a great success, as was the Super Squirrel of three years later, still with the trademark 'biscuit tin' fuel tank.

Specification	Scott Two-Speed (1912)
Engine	Liquid-cooled two-stroke parallel twin
Capacity	532cc (73 x 63.5mm)
Maximum power	3bhp approx
Transmission	Two-speed, chain final drive
Frame	Steel twin cradle
Suspension	Telescopic front; none rear
Brakes	Stirrup front; shoe-on-sprocket rear
Weight	200lb (91kg)
Top speed	50mph (80km/h)

Left: This front view shows the liquid-cooled two-stroke's radiator on this most distinctive of bikes. Exceptional straight-line performance was backed-up by sound handling that helped keep the twins competitive and popular during the 1920s.

Above: Scott's motor featured angled-forward twin cylinders with a central flywheel, forming a stressed member of the tubular steel frame. This 1912 engine was rated at 3.75hp.

Left: This 600cc Scott dates from 1928 and features a hand-operated 'gate' gearchange. The bike's large so-called 'biscuit tin' fuel tank is finished in the firm's traditional colours of purple with silver bands.

Williamson Flat Twin

**Top speed
55mph**
88km/h

*Right: The 964cc flat twin
engine was built by
Douglas in Bristol before
being transported to
Williamson's Coventry base.
Although designed for a
cyclecar, it was well suited
to two-wheeled use.*

*Below: The Williamson was
not the fastest of large-
capacity bikes, but its 50mph
(80km/h) plus performance
and basic brake system
ensured excitement.*

The bikes that Billy Williamson built
were some of the most distinctive and
unusual in the years before the First
World War, if not the most successful. The small
firm from Coventry in the English Midlands
assembled big 964cc flat twins, powered by an
engine that the better-known Douglas firm of
Bristol had originally developed for use in a four-
wheeled cyclecar.

Williamson was a larger-than-life character who
had been managing director of the Rex firm, before
resigning in 1911 along with his brother Harold,
who had been the sales manager. Harold went to
work for Singer but Billy set up on his own, backed
by William Douglas, whose firm specialized in
building 350cc flat twins with cylinders running
along the line of the bike. Douglas had also
developed the larger, liquid-cooled flat twin engine
for the cyclecar, and was keen to recoup some of
the development costs by seeing it used in a
motorbike too.

FH 540

Crank-start arrangement

Douglas built the engines and dispatched them to Coventry, where Billy Williamson was based. He was soon joined by Harold as a test rider. The engine was a side-valve unit whose cyclecar origins were revealed by its starting arrangement, which was not a kickstarter but a protruding dog to which a detachable crank handle was fitted. The two-speed Douglas gearbox was operated by a hand lever, in conjunction with a foot clutch.

The Williamson was a fairly stylish and well-built machine whose twin-downtube frame held a Douglas-Druid front suspension arrangement with twin springs held in tension. Elsewhere the chassis was rather basic, with no rear suspension and a brake system that comprised no more than a simple, bicycle-style front stirrup, with blocks pressing on the wheel rim, and at the rear a contracting band worked by a heel pedal.

Williamson improved the bike in the couple of years following its introduction in 1912, notably by adding a kickstarter and an optional three-speed gearbox. The firm also developed an air-cooled version of the twin, which sold for £75, a saving of £7 over the liquid-cooled model. But the start of the First World War saw the demise of the Williamson Flat Twin, because production was stopped; after the war the Douglas engine was no longer available.

Billy Williamson did not give up, and redesigned the bike to take a 980cc side-valve V-twin engine from JAP of north London. The new bike was due to enter production in 1920, but then Billy Williamson suffered a fatal heart attack, after which the firm closed down. One of the British bike industry's great early characters had gone, and with him his dream of a new generation of Coventry-built machines.

Douglas – The Flat Twin Firm

Bristol-based Douglas, the company that provided the 964cc liquid-cooled engine for the Williamson, was known for its smaller flat twins, 350cc air-cooled units that also had cylinders in line with the bike. These side-valve motors produced only a few horsepower, but the Douglas performed well, partly due to its light weight of less than 175lb (79kg). In 1912 the firm finished first and second in the Isle of Man Junior TT, and won the 350cc class at the Spanish Grand Prix.

Douglas had begun building flat twins in 1906, after acquiring the right to manufacture bikes build under the Fairy name. Production continued until the late 1920s with few changes, although an optional two-speed gearbox was offered from 1911, and later a clutch too. The Douglas was popular with First World War despatch riders, because of its lightness and agility in bad conditions. Douglas continued with flat twins and introduced the stylish 350cc Dragonfly in 1955, but production ended two years later.

Above left: Williamson built a cheaper air-cooled version of the twin as well as this original liquid-cooled model.

Left: Production ended with founder Billy Williamson's death in 1920.

Specification	Williamson Flat Twin (1913)
Engine	Liquid-cooled side-valve four-valve flat twin
Capacity	964cc (85 x 85mm)
Maximum power	Not known
Transmission	Two-speed, chain final drive
Frame	Steel twin cradle
Suspension	Girder front; rigid rear
Brakes	Stirrup front; contracting band rear
Weight	300lb (136kg)
Top speed	55mph (88km/h)

Zenith Gradua V-Twin

**Top speed
50mph**
80km/h

*Right: Zenith's Gradua
system was used by the
Surrey firm to improve the
performance of a long
series of machines, many
powered by JAP V-twin
engines. This bike is a
550cc model from 1914.*

*Below: This 678cc JAP-
engined Zenith was raced at
Brooklands' famous banked
circuit close to the firm's
Weybridge base. The Gradua
system's key features are the
vertical 'coffee grinder'
handle and horizontal rod
linking the crankshaft
pulley and rear wheel.*

Zenith's Gradua will long be remembered
for two reasons: the pioneering Gradua
gear system itself, and the clever
marketing campaign inspired by the Zenith's all-
conquering performance. So dominant was Zenith's
Freddie Barnes in 1911, riding a Gradua against
single-speed opposition, that he won no fewer than
53 hillclimbs that year, after which the organizing
Auto-Cycle Union barred the Gradua from entering
many events.

Zenith's management seized the opportunity to
emphasize that the Gradua had been banned
because of its superior performance. The firm from
Surrey produced a new badge, featuring the word
'Barred' and a motorcycle behind the bars of a jail.
The logo was used not only on the Gradua, but also
on other Zenith models long after the Gradua
system had been superseded.

Until Barnes invented the Gradua system in
1908, the only way of adjusting the gearing of the
belt-drive bikes of the day was by changing the
position of the crankshaft pulley that took the
engine's drive to the rear wheel. The problem with
this system was that if belt tension was correct in
high gear, it was too slack in low.

Barnes' patent system overcame this problem
by means a long handle, nicknamed the 'coffee
grinder', which ran vertically up one side of the
engine. The bottom of the shaft was connected to
both the crankshaft pulley and the rear wheel.
When the rider turned the coffee-grinder, both the
pulley and the spindle moved simultaneously, so

the gearing could be altered while the drive belt remained in tension.

Barnes was the driving force and engineering genius behind Zenith, having founded the firm at Weybridge in 1905 to build a curious two-wheeled machine called the Tooley's Bicar. This housed a 3hp Fafnir engine in a novel frame consisting of twin tubes joined by springs. One set of tubes held the rider and engine; the other set supported the wheels, with steering achieved via a complex car-type hub-centre arrangement.

Many a slip...

The Bicar and subsequent Zenette models were short-lived, but Barnes had much more success with conventional motorcycles fitted with the Gradua system. The system had its drawbacks, notably that the belt was prone to slip in some gear positions, especially in wet weather. The efficiency of the rear brake also varied with the position of the wheel. But most of the time the Gradua gave a big advantage over fixed gearing. *Motor Cycle* magazine's tester was hugely impressed to find that the Zenith could restart and accelerate up the one-in-nine gradient of London's Muswell Hill.

Zenith retained a reputation for performance long after the Gradua system had been superseded by Rudge's Multi (which used a similar variable belt system without needing to move the rear wheel) and, later, by more sophisticated countershaft gearboxes and chain final drive. The firm's range grew in the 1920s, until in 1928 it comprised nine models, three of them 680cc JAP-engined V-twins of which the fastest was the Super-Eight Sports.

The famous banked track at nearby Brooklands was ideal for performance testing and record attempts. Zenith riders Oliver Baldwin and Joe Wright jointly held the track record at 113.45mph (182.58km/h) aboard JAP-engined V-twins, before Wright lifted it to 118.86mph (191.28km/h). But the firm hit problems and closed down in 1930. Zenith dealer Writers of Kensington bought the marque name and restarted production. But JAP stopped building engines after the Second World War. After Writers' stock of 750cc V-twins had been used up, Zenith faded away.

Below left: Zenith's 'barred' tank logo, behind the famous 'coffee grinder', was a reference to the impressive performance that had led to the marque being banned from many events against single-speed opposition.

Below right: The Zenith name was famous in the 1920s, when the firm produced a variety of rapid JAP-powered twins and also competed successfully in race events, especially at Brooklands.

Specification	Zenith Gradua V-Twin (1914)
Engine	Air-cooled side-valve four-valve V-twin
Capacity	550cc
Maximum power	6bhp approx
Transmission	Gradua system; belt final drive
Frame	Steel single downtube
Suspension	Girder front; rigid rear
Brakes	Stirrup front; contracting band rear
Weight	Not known
Top speed	50mph (80km/h)

Pope V-Twin

**Top speed
70mph**
113km/h

*Right: Pope's big 999cc
V-twin engine, with its
overhead valvegear, was
one of motorcycling's most
sophisticated and powerful
units when it was
introduced in 1912.*

*Below: As well as handsome
looks, the Pope featured a
high quality chassis with
leaf-spring front suspension
and an advanced plunger
system at the rear.*

Pope built its big 1000cc V-twins for only seven years from 1912, but during that time they were among America's most sophisticated bikes, and some of the fastest too. The firm from Westfield in Massachusetts equipped its flagship with overhead valvegear, plus suspension at both front and rear. Few rival bikes could match that specification, and Pope riders had some notable racing successes.

Albert Pope was first a military man, serving as a lieutenant colonel in the Union Army during America's Civil War, and was then a leading figure in the country's transportation industry. In the 1870s he began by importing and then manufacturing bicycles, and progressed to automobile production before the turn of the century. His American Cycle Manufacturing Company then turned to making motorcycles, which initially followed the bicycles by being marketed using a variety of brand names including Columbia, American and Monarch.

Motorcycles were first built under the Pope name in 1911 (Pope himself had died in 1909), at which time they were fairly humble single-cylinder machines with conventional inlet-over-exhaust valvegear and leaf-spring front suspension. But the following year the firm uprated the single with pushrod-operated overhead valvegear, and also doubled up the cylinders to create a powerful 1000cc V-twin.

success. The Pope Motorcycle Division remained a part of the Pope automotive group, which was one of the American industry's largest. The parent company had been beneficial in providing cash for the bike firm's short-lived racing campaign.

However, this also meant that the fortunes of Pope motorcycles were dependent on the fluctuating financial health of the automotive group. Some improvements were made to the V-twin in the years from 1913, but Pope lacked the investment to compete during a period of rapid advance by the 'Big Three' of Harley, Indian and Excelsior. By 1918, a new Schebler carburettor had helped increase the V-twin's performance, but financial problems forced an end to Pope's motorcycle production.

Left: A sprung saddle was a typical feature of the day, and in the Pope's case gave a notably comfortable ride with the added assistance of the plunger rear suspension system.

Below: The Pope was a fast and comfortable roadster with a top speed of about 70mph (113km/h), and also enjoyed a brief success on the racetrack before the advanced valve system gave problems.

Fast enough to race

This was an important development, because at the time the only other American firm with overhead-valve engines was Indian, and these were limited to the exotic four-valve singles and eight-valve V-twin racers. The production Pope was so fast that some hard-riding owners were competitive against professional riders in local race meetings. In 1913, Pope riders scored some notable successes against established marques such as Indian and Excelsior.

Pope's management was encouraged by this, and created a factory team for the following year's high-profile events. But their hopes were dashed, because the bikes' supposed main asset, their overhead valvegear, turned out to be the weak link. Problems, including broken rocker arms, put out all of the Pope factory riders at the 1914 season's big 300-mile (483km) events at Venice, California and Dodge City, after which the firm was not seen again in major competition.

The big Pope was an impressively fast and capable roadster, even so. In standard form the V-twin was capable of well over 60mph (97km/h), and its sophisticated features included two-speed transmission and a shaft-driven Bosch magneto. The chassis was also cleverly designed. The frame's front section was a simple single downtube that bolted to the motor, and held leaf-spring front suspension. But the Pope was far ahead of its time in having a version of the plunger-type rear suspension that would be commonly adopted more than 20 years later.

This gave the Pope a comfortable ride, in conjunction with the conventional sprung saddle, but was not enough to ensure the machine's lasting

Specification	Pope V-Twin (1914)
Engine	Air-cooled ohv pushrod four-valve V-twin
Capacity	999cc (84.5 x 89mm)
Maximum power	12bhp
Transmission	Three-speed, chain final drive
Frame	Steel single downtube
Suspension	Leaf spring front; plunger rear
Brakes	None front; drum rear
Weight	305lb (138kg)
Top speed	70mph (113km/h)

Harley-Davidson Model 11F

**Top speed
60mph**
97km/h

*Right: Like several other
American manufacturers in
motorcycling's early years,
Harley-Davidson decided
that two single-cylinder
engines would make a
useful twin, especially if set
at 45 degrees apart.*

*Below: The Model 11F's
performance was often
exciting, especially given
the fact that the bike had no
front brake and only a crude
expanding band system on
the rear wheel.*

 The Model 11F of 1915 proved that Harley-Davidson's founders learned fast when it came to building V-twin motorbikes. The 11F was a good-looking, efficient and deservedly popular machine. Its 989cc V-twin engine produced about 10bhp, good for a top speed of about 60mph (97km/h), and the bike came with up-to-date features including footboards and chain final drive.

Yet the Milwaukee firm's founders, William Harley and the three Davidson brothers (Arthur, Walter and William), had suffered a serious setback six years earlier when, encouraged by the success of their pioneering single-cylinder models, they had introduced their first V-twin. The Model 5D of 1909 had an 811cc engine, with cylinders set at the 45-degree angle that would become a Harley trademark. It produced about 7hp, twice as much as the firm's single. But the 5D was hard to start, suffered from technical problems including a slipping drive belt, and was promptly withdrawn from the market.

This did not deter William Harley and the Davidsons, whose robust single-cylinder models were increasingly in demand. The quartet had founded the firm in 1903, in a small shed in the Davidsons' yard. Their early single became known as the Silent Grey Fellow, due to its colour and

efficient exhaust muffler. Production rose dramatically, from just 49 bikes in 1906 to more than 3000 in 1910 – by which time the firm had moved to larger premises in what would become Juneau Avenue, still the current address.

The next year, Harley-Davidson reintroduced the V-twin as the Model 7D. (H-D regarded 1904 as year zero, so 1911 was the seventh model year.) It featured an improved valve system, still with the original inlet-over-exhaust layout, plus a tensioner for the drive belt. It also had a new, stronger frame. This was a much improved bike, but William Harley, the firm's chief engineer, did not rest on his laurels. During the next few years he introduced a host of improvements that established Harley-Davidson as one of America's leading manufacturers.

'Ful Floteing' system

For 1912 the V-twin was made available with a larger 989cc engine, developing 8bhp, and could be ordered with the option of a clutch (in the rear wheel hub), and with chain instead of belt final drive. Further improvements included a more sophisticated lubrication system, a new frame that gave a lower seat, and a sprung seat post – the curiously named 'Ful Floteing' system – for added comfort. Two years later came more advances: footboards, enclosed valve springs, a kickstarter and two-speed transmission.

By 1915, when the Model 11F was introduced, Harley had established a V-twin format that would hold the firm in good stead for the next 15 years. Although other refinements would soon be added,

notably with the three-speed Model J, Harley had produced a big V-twin whose performance and strength would win many admirers, until it was replaced by the side-valve V Series in 1930.

For Harley, 1915 was memorable for another reason too: the firm's first competition success. After initial resistance to racing at the Milwaukee factory, ex-racer Bill Ottaway had been hired to run a factory team, and had developed a tuned and lightened version of the V-twin, the 11K. After breakdowns in its first season, the 100mph (161km/h) 11K took its rider Otto Walker to victory, against factory opposition, in two prestigious 300-mile (483km) races. Harley's hard-riding 'Wrecking Crew' would have many more wins in the years to come, many of them on powerful, purpose-built, eight-valve V-twins.

Below: The 11F's two-speed gearbox was operated by hand using a lever to the left of the tank. Another job for the rider was to lubricate the motor using a hand-operated oil pump.

Bottom left: Although some rival firms including Indian offered a basic form of rear suspension, Harley stuck to a 'hard-tail' frame, and improved the rider's comfort with a sprung saddle and 'Ful Floteing' seat post design.

Specification	Harley-Davidson Model 11F (1915)
Engine	Air-cooled four-valve inlet-over-exhaust 45-degree V-twin
Capacity	989cc (84 x 88.9mm)
Maximum power	10bhp
Transmission	Two-speed, chain or belt final drive
Frame	Steel single downtube
Suspension	Girder forks; rigid rear
Brakes	None front; expanding band rear
Weight	310lb (141kg)
Top speed	60mph (97km/h)

Flying Merkel V-Twin

**Top speed
60mph**
97km/h

*Below: This Flying Merkel,
finished in the firm's
traditional orange
paintwork, is a 1910 racer
that has been restored for
display in a museum in
California, USA. In that
year Merkel rider Fred
Whittler defeated Indian
star Jake de Rosier in
several races over the Los
Angeles Coliseum boards,
at a record average speed
of over 74mph (119km/h).*

Joseph Merkel's cleverly engineered V-twins were as notable for their performance as for their bright orange paintwork. Merkel began building bikes in 1902, in Milwaukee, initially with a single-cylinder engine of his own design. Like machines from several other manufacturers, the early Merkels used the frame's front downtube as part of the exhaust system.

In 1909, Merkel's firm was bought by the Light Motor Company, which had been producing bikes closely modelled on existing Indians. Joe Merkel moved to the Pottstown, Pennsylvania headquarters of the firm, which was renamed the Merkel-Light Motor Co, and began to improve its bikes. He invented a cantilever rear suspension system, similar to that later used by Vincent, and a compact sprung front fork arrangement that further improved the bikes' ride and handling.

From 1910 onwards the bikes were known as Flying Merkels, and a 1000cc V-twin was produced. The following year, the firm was bought by the Miami Cycle Company, which transferred production to its base at Middletown, Ohio. Although Merkel had no official competition department, employees who raced were sometimes given support by the factory.

Most famous of the Merkel riders was Maldwyn Jones, originally a promising racer who had been given a job testing engines in the firm's repair department. In 1910, Jones acquired an old Merkel single-cylinder racer that had been unsuccessful because oil from its 'ported' cylinder had made the drive belt slip. He resurrected the bike, made a shield to protect the belt from oil, and entered a big 4th July race meeting at Hamilton, Ohio, winning the 10-mile (16km) event.

Racing success

In the main, pursuit-style race, Jones faced opposition from the legendary Indian star Erwin 'Cannonball' Baker. Having eliminated all the other riders, the duo were neck and neck on opposite sides of the track, with neither gaining an advantage, when the Merkel ran out of fuel, leaving Baker to win. Later the same year, Jones made an impressive professional debut on a Flying Merkel single that had also been salvaged from the factory, winning three of his four events.

Merkel was one of the most innovative and bold of manufacturers, and introduced numerous technical features in following years. By 1913, the chassis had been modified with an integral seat post and oil tank, the engine's intake valves were mechanically operated (instead of simply by air pressure), and there was the option of final drive by chain instead of belt. In 1915 a kickstarter was fitted. The V-twin roadster was available in either 885 or 1000cc capacity, with optional two-speed transmission. The larger motor produced 9bhp and had a top speed of about 60mph (97km/h).

Maldwyn Jones' racing exploits ensured that Flying Merkel maintained a high profile. For the 1913 season he had built a special half-mile machine using a Jefferson overhead-valve cylinder head plus camshafts of his own design. This gave a substantial increase in speed, especially when Jones fitted special low, braced handlebars, also his own work. During the next three seasons he won 24 of the 42 races he entered, also taking ten second and three third places.

'If it passes you, it's a Flying Merkel,' boasted the firm's advertisements, but Merkel sales did not match Jones' results on the track. Joe Merkel had left the company in 1913, and the American motorcycle market had contracted. The firm had also introduced a disastrously unsuccessful spring-

Specification	Flying Merkel V-Twin (1915)
Engine	Air-cooled four-valve inlet-over-exhaust 45-degree V-twin
Capacity	998cc
Maximum power	9bhp
Transmission	Chain final drive
Frame	Steel loop
Suspension	Sprung fork front; single spring rear
Brakes	None front; drum rear
Weight	280lb (127kg)
Top speed	60mph (97km/h)

Left: Merkel's 45-degree V-twin engine used intake valves that were opened automatically (by piston suction). The firm's full involvement in racing and record setting lasted only from 1909 to 1911.

Below: Joe Merkel designed a compact telescopic front suspension system that was later used by other makes of bike. But in the style of early American racers, the Merkel had no brakes at all.

powered self-starter on its 1914 touring bikes, which had resulted in large service and legal costs. Flying Merkel production was halted at the end of 1915 and never restarted.

Cyclone V-Twin

**Top speed
85mph**
137km/h

Right: Cyclone's overhead camshaft V-twin was by far the most technically advanced motorcycle unit ever seen in America, and was arguably the most powerful engine of its size in the world.

Below: Cyclones were known for their speed, their advanced but not always reliable engine design, and their bright yellow paintwork. The 996cc V-twin engine was held in a U-shaped frame whose top tubes ran above and below the fuel tank.

If Cyclone's lean and powerful V-twins could have added reliability to their undoubted speed, they might have become a huge success. Built at St. Paul, Minnesota by the Joerns Motor Manufacturing Company, the bikes were produced for only a few years from 1913 but made an impact out of all proportion to their lifespan.

The key to the performance of Cyclone's 996cc, 45-degree V-twin engine, designed by Andrew Strand, was its single overhead camshaft layout, a rarity at the time. The cams were driven by bevel shaft. Another shaft worked the magneto at the front of the cylinders. The rest of the motor was packed with state-of-the-art engineering: roller bearing crankshaft, lightweight conrods, and forged steel flywheels in a spoked style.

Most roadgoing Cyclones were fitted with leaf-spring suspension at front and rear, giving reasonable comfort as well as excellent performance. Racing versions generally matched their highly tuned engines with distinctive bright yellow paintwork and no suspension. Other parts such as handlebars were also varied but the tubular steel frame, which held the fuel tank between its

twin top tubes, and cradled the engine in its U-shaped main section, was common to both.

During Cyclone's short life the marque generated a great amount of interest. This was due to the bikes' speed and technical specification, and also to the hard-riding style of factory pilot Don Johns. He was particularly impressive because, in the fashion of the era, Cyclone's racing V-twin four-stroke engines were 'ported' – vented to the open air through rectangular ports which opened when the pistons neared bottom-dead-centre. The theory was that this increased power by allowing rapid expulsion of exhaust gas, though in fact the boost is now thought to be due to a crude supercharging effect.

The result of porting was that the Cyclones were literally fire-breathing devices, belching smoke, noise and, in night races, blue flames that flickered around the motor and riders' legs. Porting prevented proper control of intake air, so riders including Johns had to control their speeding bikes using an ignition kill-switch on the handlebar, resulting in spectacular wheelspin on the dirt-tracks and sometimes in big crashes.

Suspiciously fast

Cyclone's reputation was boosted when in 1913 factory rider JA McNeil lapped the Omaha, Nebraska board track at 111.1mph (178.8km/h), a speed more than 10mph (16km/h) in excess of both the recognized world and American records. So big was this margin that the authorities were suspicious and refused to ratify the achievement.

The factory's status continued to grow following a string of wins in the 1915 season, although some of these were in second-rate races in

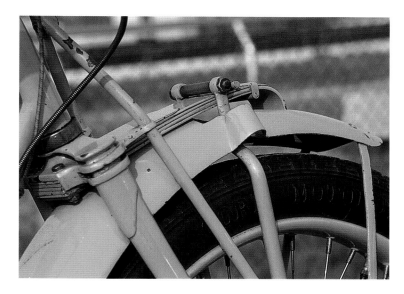

Illinois and Ohio. Less welcome was a succession of mechanical problems that would dog Cyclone throughout the marque's life. The ohc motor's failings included piston and valve problems. The two-part camshaft drive towers were also reported to have a tendency to stretch and flex at high revs.

Typical of the marque's fortunes was its experience at the prestigious 300-mile (483km) National championship race at Dodge City, Kansas. Against factory opposition from the 'Big Three' of Indian, Excelsior and Harley-Davidson, Cyclone rider Dave Kinney qualified fastest, at 88.5mph (142km/h), and Johns led the early stages of the race. But before one-third distance, both Cyclone riders had retired with machine problems.

Johns left to ride for Indian at the end of the season and, although Kinney won some races for Cyclone in 1916, Joerns Manufacturing could not sell enough roadsters to pay for further machine development and to hire top quality riders. The Minnesota firm folded at the end of that season.

Above: Roadgoing and racing Cyclones were similar in most respects, the roadster's most obvious difference being its front and rear leafspring suspension. With comfort to match its performance, the Cyclone would have been an outstanding roadster had reliability problems been successfully overcome.

Below left: Cyclones were produced by the Joerns Motor Manufacturing Company of St. Paul, Minnesota. Although built for only four years from 1913, their technology and speed were impressive.

Specification	Cyclone V-Twin (1916)
Engine	Air-cooled sohc four-valve 45-degree V-twin
Capacity	996cc
Maximum power	25bhp @ 5000rpm
Transmission	Chain final drive
Frame	Steel single downtube
Suspension	Leaf spring front and rear
Brakes	None front; drum rear
Weight	280lb (127kg)
Top speed	85mph (137km/h)

Indian Powerplus

**Top speed
65mph**
105km/h

Indian was the biggest American manufacturer in motorcycling's early years, producing large numbers of V-twins from its sprawling factory, known as the Wigwam, in Springfield, Massachusetts. Indians were fast, in every sense. They won races on board tracks, dirt tracks and even at the Isle of Man TT (where Indian took first, second and third in 1911). They set top speed records and posted quickest ever times for coast-to-coast trips across America.

Among the best and most influential of the early Indians was the Powerplus, which was introduced in 1916. As its name suggested, its engine was a more powerful version of Indian's existing unit, a 42-degree V-twin. The Powerplus had a side-valve layout in place of the traditional F-head (or inlet-over-exhaust) design that had been Indian's mainstay since the firm's first twin-cylinder model of 1907.

Ironically, Indian's best days were already in the past when the Powerplus arrived. The firm had been set up in 1901 by George Hendee and Oscar Hedstrom, two former bicycle racers, and had grown quickly. Production reached almost 5000

bikes in 1909, and by 1913 was over 32,000. But the following year Henry Ford set up his first car assembly line, and the US motorcycle market took a sharp downturn. Indian would never sell as many bikes again.

Co-founder and chief engineer Oscar Hedstrom retired in 1913. The Powerplus was designed by Charles Gustafson Snr., who had previously worked for Reading Standard, which had built America's first side-valve bikes. The new machine met with resistance from some Indian owners loyal to Hedstrom's F-head machines. But one ride normally won them over, because the Powerplus lived up to its name by delivering considerable extra performance.

Its 998cc long-stroke engine produced a claimed 18bhp, well up on the previous Big Twin, and gave the Powerplus a top speed of over 60mph (97km/h). The new motor was also cleaner and quieter, due to its enclosed valvegear. It had a three-speed gearbox with a hand change and foot clutch. There was also a back-up hand clutch lever, located to the right of the fuel tank because Indian's throttle was on the left.

Below: Finished in Indian's traditional maroon, the Powerplus lived up to its name by delivering plenty of performance with its 18bhp, 42-degree side-valve V-twin engine. Long-distance ace Cannonball Baker's string of high-speed record runs helped make the model popular, and it remained in production for almost a decade with few changes.

The Powerplus chassis was similar to that of the old model – understandably, because Indian was already offering optional leaf-spring rear suspension, years before most manufacturers would do so. A leaf-spring design was also used for the front suspension. Controls were via a complex system of rods and linkages until 1918, when cables were introduced.

Record-breaking performance

Long-distance legend Erwin 'Cannonball' Baker gave the Powerplus the perfect introduction in late 1915, when he used a pre-production bike to set a new Canada-to-Mexico Three Flags record – covering the 1655.5 miles (2664.2km) in 3 days, 9 hours and 15 minutes. The following year, he set a 24-hour record of 1018.7 miles (1639.4km) in Australia, despite hazards including giant parakeets and driving rain. And in 1917, Baker rode a

Specification	Indian Powerplus (1918)
Engine	Air-cooled four-valve side-valve 42-degree V-twin
Capacity	998cc (79.4 x 100.8mm)
Maximum power	18bhp
Transmission	Three-speed, chain final drive
Frame	Steel single downtube
Suspension	Leaf-spring front and (optional) rear
Brakes	None front; drum rear
Weight	410lb (186kg)
Top speed	65mph (105km/h)

Powerplus to another 24-hour record of 1534.7 miles (2469.8km) on the Cincinnati board track.

The Powerplus itself also proved impressively long-lasting, remaining in production until 1924 with few changes. It did, however, gain a new name in its old age. Following the Chief's introduction in 1922, the Powerplus was restyled the Standard to avoid overshadowing the new model.

Below left: Indian's left-hand throttle control meant that levers for compression release and gearshift, along with the back-up clutch operation, were located on the right side of the Powerplus fuel tank.

Indian's Eight-valve Heroes

Indian gained considerable publicity from the exploits of its racers, notably the daring board-track stars including Jake de Rosier, Charles 'Fearless' Balke and Eddie Hasha. They rode tuned, stripped-down V-twins which diced at well over 100mph (161km/h) on the steep boards. But the sport went into decline following the deaths of Hasha, Johnnie Albright another Indian pilot and six spectators at a New Jersey track in 1912. De Rosier, winner of over 900 races and the holder of many speed records, left Indian for Excelsior. He died of racing injuries in 1913.

Above: Indian's board-race bikes were powered by fire-breathing eight-valve V-twin engines with open exhausts. Low handlebars gave racers a streamlined riding position.

Left: This bike's leaf-spring rear suspension was a factory optional extra. Indian's leaf-spring front suspension system was used for racing and hillclimb bikes, as well as roadsters.

Excelsior V-Twin

**Top speed
80mph**
129km/h

*Below: This 992cc
Excelsior dates from 1919
and is finished in the olive
paintwork typical of the
year. It has a three-speed
gearbox, operated by the
large lever to the left of the
fuel tank, and a foot clutch.
The smaller hand lever at
the side of the tank adjusts
the timing of the magneto
ignition.*

Excelsior was the third of the 'Big Three'
American marques which early in the last
century were building sophisticated
roadsters plus race bikes that often got the better of
main rivals Indian and Harley-Davidson. The
Excelsior Supply Company began building bikes in
Chicago in 1907, with a simple 438cc, 3.25hp
single, and three years later introduced an 820cc V-
twin model with cylinders spaced at 45 degrees. In
1911, the year that Excelsior was taken over by
bicycle maker Ignaz Schwinn, this was followed by
a 1000cc model.

The big Excelsior twin was an impressive
machine that was gradually developed in following
years. Racing was valuable for development and
publicity. Stars including Joe Wolters and Jake de
Rosier scored numerous wins on the Chicago-made
bikes, and the firm gained publicity in 1913, when
Lee Humiston recorded the first official 100mph
(161km/h) lap, at a boardtrack in Los Angeles.

Excelsior's big V-twin used an F-head (or inlet-
over-exhaust) valve layout, and produced about
20bhp; good for a top speed of roughly 80mph
(129km/h). Lubrication of the front cylinder was by
a pipe leading to its base. This was required
because, unlike the rear cylinder, the front one was
not sufficiently well lubricated by oil thrown from
the crankshaft and conrod assemblies.

Restyled and improved

Schwinn introduced numerous improvements,
notably in 1915 when the twin was restyled and
gained a three-speed gearbox. By 1919 the Excelsior
typically featured leaf-spring front suspension,
sprung saddle, footboards, and olive drab
paintwork (a legacy of the First World War). Lights
were available at extra cost; some bikes featured
twin rear drum brakes but none on the front wheel.

In 1917, Schwinn formed Excelsior-Henderson
after buying the Henderson company, manufacturer
of sophisticated in-line fours. The firm's Chicago
factory was the largest motorcycle facility in the
world, famous for its rooftop test-track. After
America entered the First World War, the big

factories agreed to refrain from racing. But Excelsior rider Wells Bennett gave the firm a boost with a series of record runs between cities, notably averaging 42.3mph (68km/h) for the 300-mile (483km) desert crossing from Los Angeles to Needles, California in 1918.

Arguably Excelsior's most famous model was the Super-X, which was launched in 1925 and featured the novelty of a 750cc V-twin powerplant with unit-construction engine and gearbox. Its chassis featured a twin cradle frame and leading-link forks. The light Super-X was immediately competitive against larger-engined rivals in hillclimbing and oval racing, and sparked the rise of 750cc Class C competition when Indian and Harley built '45s' of their own.

In 1929 the Super-X was restyled with Excelsior-Henderson's 'Streamline' look, and was a notably refined machine with a central instrument panel set into its fuel tank. But the Depression of the early 1930s hit sales, as did the growing popularity of cheap cars such as the Model T Ford. In 1931 owner Ignaz Schwinn, who was 70 years old, stunned the industry when he abruptly halted motorcycle production and retired.

Above left and above: The V-twin had cylinders spaced at the common 45-degree angle, and F-head valve arrangement. An oil tank below the seat provided front cylinder lubrication.

Specification	Excelsior V-Twin (1918)
Engine	Air-cooled four-valve inlet-over-exhaust 45-degree V-twin
Capacity	992cc
Maximum power	20bhp
Transmission	Three-speed, chain final drive
Frame	Steel single downtube
Suspension	Leaf spring front; rigid rear
Brakes	None front; drum rear
Weight	500lb (227kg)
Top speed	80mph (129km/h)

Brief Revival – The New Super-X

The Excelsior name returned more than 60 years later when brothers Dave and Dan Hanlon bought the name Excelsior-Henderson from the Schwinn company and used it for a V-twin cruiser named the Super-X. The bike incorporated old-style Super-X touches including exposed fork springs, and was powered by a 1386cc, 50-degree V-twin that featured dohc, eight valves and produced 65bhp. Production began in 1999, in a $30 million, purpose-built factory at Belle Plaine, Minnesota. The Super-X was fast for a cruiser, but it was expensive and sold poorly. Excelsior-Henderson ceased production later the same year after only 2000 bikes had been built.

Brough Superior SS100

**Top speed
100mph**
161km/h

There is not much doubt about which was the fastest and most glamorous of pre-Second World War roadsters. The Brough Superior SS100 was a big, handsome, high-performance V-twin which, in the words of its creator, George Brough, was 'made up to an ideal and not down to a price'. Fewer than 400 examples of the SS100 were built between 1925 and 1940. For most of that time, there was nothing on two wheels that could match it.

George Brough was a master publicist. He summed up the SS100's appeal when he wrote in a 1926 catalogue that it 'is a machine made essentially for an experienced motorcyclist who realises that just as a racehorse needs more attention than a hunter, so an SS100, with its colossal output of power, requires more attention than the average sports machine. Give it the necessary attention and you have a machine that can always be relied upon to show its back number plate to anything on wheels likely to be met on the roads.'

Below: This 1932-model SS100 was owned by George Brough's most famous customer, Lawrence of Arabia. After Lawrence's first ride, he wrote to Brough: 'It is the silkiest thing I have ever ridden… I think this is going to be a very excellent bike… I am very grateful to you and everybody for the care taken to make her perfect.'

Signed guarantee

Brough, the son of a motorcycle manufacturer, assembled his bikes with the assistance of a small team of enthusiasts at a workshop in Haydn Road, Nottingham. He called his first big twin the SS80, after its top speed of 80mph (129km/h). The SS100 was the logical and even faster follow-up, and was delivered with a signed guarantee that the machine had been timed at over 100mph (161km/h) for a quarter of a mile.

The precise specification of Brough's bikes varied considerably, with even the engine of the SS100 being changed over the years. Initial models used a 988cc JAP V-twin unit that produced over 40bhp; the final 100 machines were powered by a similar-capacity V-twin from AMC (Matchless). What did not change was George Brough's refusal to accept anything less than the best. Manufacturers including JAP-built 'Special for Brough' parts; many components were returned to their makers to be redesigned and improved.

Left: Relaxed high-speed cruising was the Brough forte, and few contemporary bikes could come close to matching it. Handling was also exceptional by the standards of the day, leading Brough to boast of 'hands-off stability' at high speed. The reputation and rarity of both SS80 and SS100 models ensure that they are now far more valuable than most modern superbikes.

Hard-riding Brough and his fellow Superior riders, including notables such as Freddie Dixon, Eric Fernihough and Bert Le Vack, took the Nottingham-built machines to a string of victories in races, hillclimbs and sprints. This fuelled Brough's talent for publicity, which had revealed itself when he had coined the name Superior, prompting his father's reply: 'I suppose that makes mine the Inferior?'

'The Rolls-Royce of Motorcycles'

Brough's SS100 brochure promised 'hands-off stability at 95mph' (153km/h), but it was George's slogan 'The Rolls-Royce of Motorcycles' that made most impact. Adapted from a line in a magazine test of a Brough, the phrase initially displeased bosses at the luxury car firm. But after a Rolls executive had arrived at Haydn Road to find Brough workers wearing white gloves – to avoid marking the show bikes they were assembling – all objections were dropped.

The most famous Superior enthusiast was T.E. Lawrence (Lawrence of Arabia), who owned a special stainless steel petrol tank which he fitted to his series of Broughs. Lawrence wrote of his love of high-speed travel aboard his Superiors, but he died after a crash while riding one, probably following a collision with a cyclist.

George Brough was never content with the SS100's performance, and produced various special models, notably the Alpine Grand Sports, which

was intended for rapid touring. Fastest of all was the legendary SS100 Pendine, named after the long beach in south Wales where many speed records were set. With its low bars, rearset footrests and high-compression engine, the Pendine was good for a genuine 110mph (177km/h). Brough production stopped when the Second World War began, and did not restart afterwards.

Left: Lawrence's SS100 is powered by a 998cc V-twin engine from JAP of north London. A horizontal spring of the Bentley and Draper rear suspension system is visible below the saddle. The system worked well but required regular maintenance of bushes to ensure good handling.

Specification	Brough Superior SS100 (1925)
Engine	Air-cooled ohv four-valve pushrod 50-degree V-twin
Capacity	988cc (85.5 x 86mm)
Maximum power	45bhp @ 5000rpm
Transmission	Four-speed, chain final drive
Frame	Steel single downtube
Suspension	Girder forks; twin springs rear
Brakes	Drum front and rear
Weight	396lb (180kg)
Top speed	100mph (161km/h)

Henderson KJ

**Top speed
100mph**
161km/h

*Below: Fast, stylish and
sophisticated, the
Henderson KJ or
'Streamline' was one of the
world's finest bikes in the
late 1920s. Features
included drum brakes,
three-speed gearbox with
hand change, and an
illuminated instrument
console set into the fuel
tank. But despite its high
price, the exotic four-
cylinder machine could not
be built and sold at a profit.*

 Henderson's sophisticated Fours were among the fastest and most luxurious bikes on the road for almost 20 years. Brothers Tom and William Henderson built their first bike at Detroit in 1912, combining an in-line four-cylinder engine with a long chassis that placed the pillion seat in front of the rider's. This was changed to a conventional layout the following year, when the Henderson's 965cc engine, with inlet-over-exhaust valvegear, produced 7bhp. Although designed more for touring than speed, the Four was good for 60mph (97km/h).

In 1913, Carl Stevens Clancy put Henderson on the map when he became the first motorcyclist to circumnavigate the world. The Hendersons repeatedly refined the Four in subsequent years, while retaining its upmarket image. In 1915 they introduced the Model E, a more manageable machine whose 58.5in (1486mm) wheelbase was fully seven inches (178mm) shorter than that of the previous Model D. By 1917 the longer model had been dropped, and power of the Model G was up to 12bhp, giving a top speed of 75mph (121km/h).

Good enough for Henry Ford

There was no doubting the Henderson's performance and quality. That year, Alan Bedell crossed America in a time of 7 days and 16 hours, beating Indian ace Cannonball Baker's record by almost four days. Another Henderson rider, Ray Artley, took almost nine hours off Baker's Three-Flags record from Canada to Mexico, making the journey in 72 hours and 25 minutes. Henry Ford was sufficiently impressed to order an electrically equipped Henderson at the full price of $370, having been refused a discount.

But by this time Henderson had already justified a price rise by admitting that 'it would be impossible to continue production on the present high standard without an actual loss on every machine'. In late 1917 the firm was taken over by Excelsior boss Ignaz Schwinn, and production moved to Excelsior's plant in Chicago. Both Henderson brothers left in 1919, but development of the Four continued with the addition of features including side-valve cylinders, pressurized lubrication and heavier frames.

Faster Four – The Mighty Ace

When Bill Henderson left Excelsior-Henderson in 1919, he moved to Philadelphia and began production of a new four-cylinder machine, the Ace. In 1922 Henderson was killed after colliding with a car while testing his latest model. Following this, engineer Arthur Lemon and test rider Charles 'Red' Wolverton left Excelsior to continue Henderson's work at Ace. Their most famous creation was the XP4: a highly tuned, specially built 1262cc four that produced 45bhp and weighed less than 300lb (136kg). Wolverton rode it to a record 129mph (208km/h) in 1922, after which Ace advertising boasted of the 'Fastest Motorcycle in the World'. But the Ace, like the Henderson, was too costly to produce. The firm went into liquidation in 1924 and its assets were bought by Indian, which restarted production under the Indian name.

Above left: Henderson's 1301cc in-line four-cylinder engine was upgraded for KJ use with a number of modifications including a new Schebler carburettor and inlet manifold, plus a stronger crankshaft with five bearings instead of the previous three.

Left: The Streamline was a handsome machine that earned its nickname through sleek new styling, incorporating big fenders plus a new gas tank that covered the previously exposed upper frame tubes.

Record-breaking riders

Henderson's record-breaking resumed, notably with star rider Wells Bennett. In 1922 on the boardtrack at Tacoma, Washington, he roared 1562.54 miles (2514.6km) in 24 hours at an average speed of over 65mph (104km/h), setting a record that would last for 15 years. A few months later Bennett regained the transcontinental record for Henderson, and the following year he lowered the Three-Flags record to 42 hours, 24 minutes.

Henderson's roadsters became ever more sophisticated during the 1920s, and reached new heights with the Model KJ, known as the 'Streamline'. This had a 1301cc engine with improved cooling and a 40bhp peak output. The Streamline was good for 100mph (161km/h) and incorporated features including leading-link forks and an illuminated speedometer set into the fuel tank. But the exotic Four was too expensive to be commercially viable during America's Depression, and Schwinn halted production in 1931.

Specification	Henderson KJ (1929)
Engine	Air-cooled eight-valve inlet-over-exhaust in-line four
Capacity	1301cc
Maximum power	40bhp
Transmission	Three-speed, chain final drive
Frame	Steel twin cradle
Suspension	Girder front; none rear
Brakes	Drum front and rear
Weight	495lb (225kg)
Top speed	100mph (161km/h)

Norton International

**Top speed
90mph**
145km/h

*Right: The CS1, predecessor
of the International, became
an instant hit when it took
the race win and lap record
at the 1937 Senior TT.*

*Below: Similar silver and
black Norton paintwork for
the International, easily
distinguishable because its
exhaust pipe is on the right
instead of the left.*

Norton established such a mighty reputation in motorcycling's early years, most notably with a string of Isle of Man TT victories, that when the Birmingham firm added the prefix 'Unapproachable' to its name in its advertising, few people complained. That reputation began with the early singles and twins that had side-valve or pushrod-operated overhead-valve engine layouts. But it was Norton's later pair of overhead-cam singles, the CS1 and especially the International, that made the biggest impact.

The CS1 (short for Cam Shaft 1) was much needed when it was introduced in 1927, because Norton's future did not look bright. Founder James Lansdowne 'Pa' Norton had died two years earlier, aged 56, following a history of heart problems. There had been no Isle of Man victory that year, and only the riding ability of new star Stanley Woods had earned a win in the Senior TT in 1926. The days of Norton's pushrod single seemed numbered and a replacement was needed.

Blaze of glory

Enter Walter Moore, Norton's race team manager and development engineer, who redesigned the pushrod engine with overhead-camshaft valvegear to create the CS1. Moore did the design work for the 'cammy' engine at home, before offering it to Norton. The 490cc unit featured a vertical camshaft tower, and traditional long-stroke dimensions of 79

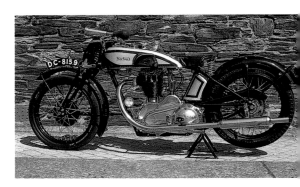

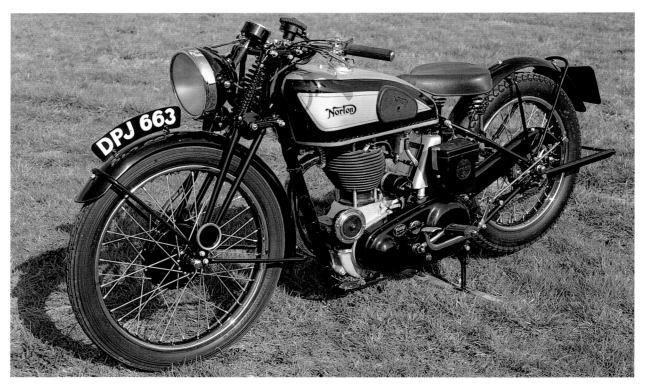

Racing Single – The Mighty Manx

Norton's dominance of Isle of Man TT racing in the 1930s led to the racing version of the International being christened the Manx. The single was updated many times, notably in 1937 with a dohc valve design. In 1950, Irish brothers Rex and Cromie McCandless produced an innovative tubular steel frame, the Featherbed. It gained this name because of racer Harold Daniell's comment that riding the new bike was like sitting on a feather bed. Geoff Duke won 500 and 350cc world championships on the Manx in 1951, retaining the 350 title in '52. Although the single was eventually outgunned by more powerful Italian fours, a Manx ridden by Godfrey Nash won the Yugoslavian GP in 1969.

x 100mm. The CS1 arrived in a blaze of glory when Alec Bennett won the 1927 Senior TT, with Woods breaking the lap record on a similar bike.

Norton was back, and in the following year the CS1 was made available as a super-sports roadster. But the next two seasons were disappointing for the team from Norton's Bracebridge Street factory, made worse when Moore accepted a lucrative offer from German firm NSU – and took his engine design with him. NSU's subsequent 500SS was so similar to the CS1 that Norton workers joked that the initials stood for Norton Spares Used.

Norton needed a new engine, and got one in 1931 when Arthur Carroll redesigned the CS1, under the direction of race boss Joe Craig. Carroll's design had identical cylinder dimensions, but the camshaft drive was new, and the exhaust pipe exited on the right instead of the left. The new engine's 30bhp output gave a top speed of over 100mph (161km/h) in racing trim, and triggered great success for Norton, whose works team dominated the Continental grands prix and took first, second and third in the Senior TT.

Norton produced a similar model for sale in 1932, calling it the International in recognition of the previous season's success. Customers could opt

Specification	Norton International (1932)
Engine	Air-cooled sohc two-valve single
Capacity	490cc (79 x 100mm)
Maximum power	29bhp @ 5500rpm
Transmission	Four-speed, chain final drive
Frame	Steel cradle
Suspension	Girder front; rigid rear
Brakes	Drum front and rear
Weight	355lb (161kg)
Top speed (road trim)	90mph (145km/h)

for road or track specification, and initially there were few differences, apart from a silencer that reduced top speed to about 90mph (145km/h). The Inter's impressive specification included Amal TT carburettor, four-speed gearbox, and Webb competition girder forks. The model remained popular throughout the 1930s, and survived in various forms well into the 1950s.

Above left: Arthur Carroll's second-generation 'cammy' single-cylinder engine shared the CS1's dimensions of 79 x 100mm but, as well as its right-sided exhaust pipe, had a redesigned camshaft bevel-drive system.

Indian Sport Scout

**Top speed
80mph**
129km/h

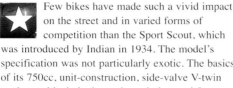

Few bikes have made such a vivid impact on the street and in varied forms of competition than the Sport Scout, which was introduced by Indian in 1934. The model's specification was not particularly exotic. The basics of its 750cc, unit-construction, side-valve V-twin engine and its bolted-together tubular steel frame (called 'keystone' by the factory) had been used by previous Indian machines.

But the Sport Scout combined fine handling with lively acceleration to a top speed of about 80mph (129km/h), and equally importantly it responded well to tuning. Before long, Sports were taking on allcomers on the road, and being stripped for competition in TT races, hillclimbs, endurance events and the increasingly popular production-based Class C dirt-track events.

A string of high-profile successes established the Sport Scout's reputation. In 1937, Californian hard man Ed Kretz won the inaugural Daytona 200-mile (322km) race on one; and Rollie Free, another

legendary Indian star, was timed at 111mph (179km/h) on the Daytona beach. The following year, Kretz used his same Sport Scout to win the first TT at Laconia, New Hampshire.

These were troubled times for Indian, with sales low following the Depression. Kretz, in particular, gave the firm a huge boost with his racing exploits. Although he did not win Daytona again, the Californian was America's most successful racer. That was as much due to his hard riding as to the superiority of his tuned and lightened Sport Scout, which by 1938 produced 35bhp, compared to the standard 22bhp. It was good for about 105mph (169km/h) and weighed just 320lb (145kg), some 120lb (54kg) less than the roadster.

The Sport Scout was the most famous of a long line of Scout models that began with Charles B Franklin's 615cc model, introduced in 1919. From those earliest days, Indian's mid-sized V-twin earned a reputation for speed and reliability. In 1920 a Scout covered 1114 miles (1793km) to break the

Below: Huge 'skirted' fenders became an Indian trademark following their introduction in 1940, but hardly fitted the Sport Scout's tradition of lively performance. Rear suspension was fitted for the first time in 1941, improving ride comfort but adding weight at the same time. Front suspension was by girder forks, as before.

Right: Early Scouts were successful in a wide variety of official and unofficial competition, and many are still ridden hard today. This is Indian rider Butch Baer in action at Daytona, where Scouts are still successful in vintage events. Racing now takes place at Daytona's banked Speedway, not the beach where Ed Kretz scored his famous victory in 1937.

24-hour world long-distance record by more than 250 miles (402km). In 1927 the engine gained power with a capacity increase to the familiar 750cc.

Built to last

Best of the early models was the 101 Scout, launched in 1928, which combined a long wheelbase and low seating position to give outstanding handling. Its 42-degree side-valve V-twin engine featured unit construction, and was strong enough to justify the Indian advertising line: 'You can't wear out an Indian Scout'. Other innovations included a drum front brake, plus new carburettor and oil pump designs.

Not all Scouts were as successful as the 101 and Sport. The Standard Scout, introduced in 1932, was heavier than its 101 predecessor, and was dismissed by many enthusiasts as not sporty enough. The Scout Pony of the same era was a 500cc lightweight, intended as an entry-level machine, but was too slow to be a hit. And its successor the Motoplane, essentially a Pony enlarged to 750cc, was another flop because its power was too much for the unchanged transmission and chassis.

The Sport Scout soon arrived to salvage Indian's reputation, though, and remained successful long after its production had ended in 1942, winning Class C races as late as 1956. The last production Sport Scouts looked very different to their predecessors because, like all Indian's range from 1940, they were equipped with the big 'skirted' fenders that helped increase weight to 485lb (220kg). The final Sport Scout hardly lived

Specification	Indian Sport Scout (1934)
Engine	Air-cooled four-valve side-valve 42-degree V-twin
Capacity	744cc (73 x 89mm)
Maximum power	22bhp
Transmission	Three-speed, chain final drive
Frame	Steel twin downtube
Suspension	Girder front; none rear
Brakes	Drum front and rear
Weight	450lb (204kg)
Top speed	80mph (129km/h)

up to its name in standard form, but many owners boosted its performance by enlarging the engine and chopping the fenders.

Above: This 1941 model Sport Scout is a handsome bike, if not a particularly sporty one. Power output was up slightly, to about 25bhp, but the Scout's skirted fenders and a number of other changes increased weight to a hefty 485lb (220kg), to the detriment of acceleration.

Left: One variant of the Sport Scout was the Model 741 military machine, whose V-twin engine was reduced in capacity from 750 to 500cc . The US military preferred Harley 45s, but the Model 741 was sold to many Allied forces.

Velocette KSS

**Top speed
75mph**
121km/h

Below: This 1934 KSS incorporates classical Velocette features of black and gold paintwork, single-cylinder engine and fish-tail silencer. The tank logo highlights the firm's trio of Isle of Man TT victories between 1929 and '29. This model incorporates the saddle tank, uprated electrics and four-speed, foot-change gearbox that had made the KSS more sophisticated but heavier following the model's introduction in 1925.

Velocette's 350cc overhead camshaft single of the mid-1920s was one of the most successful designs the motorcycle world had seen. Percy Goodman's creation, introduced by the Birmingham based Veloce Ltd as the Model K in 1925, not only performed brilliantly on the racetrack for more than 20 years, but formed the basis of sporting roadsters that were sold in large numbers for a similar period.

The 'cammy' (overhead-cam) Velocette's initial impact came in competition at the Isle of Man TT, where in 1926 Alec Bennett crashed on the last lap but still won the 350cc Junior TT by more than ten minutes, at a 66.7mph (107.3km/h) average speed that would have given him second place in the 500cc Senior race. Velocette followed this with a second place in the Junior the following year, and two more wins in 1928 and '29, with Bennett and Freddie Hicks.

Bennett's TT winner was a lightly modified version of the original Model K production bike. This was followed late in 1925 by a new model, the KSS – standing for camshaft super sports. Like its predecessor the KSS featured a single overhead camshaft, driven by shaft and bevel gears. It

produced 18bhp, was good for 80mph (129km/h), and had excellent acceleration partly because it weighed just 220lb (100kg) without lights.

In subsequent years the KSS was repeatedly updated, gaining refinements including a speedometer, larger saddle-style fuel tank, plus dynamo and battery electrics. It was also updated with a four-speed gearbox instead of the original three-speeder, plus the positive stop, foot-controlled gearchange that had been invented by Velocette development engineer Harold Wills, and introduced on the works racebikes in 1929.

Manx Grand Prix wins

In that year Velocette also broke new ground by introducing the KTT: another cammy 350, but an 'over-the-counter' production racer closely based on the works bike. It made a big impact, taking the first eight places in the following year's Manx Grand Prix. Even more impressively, its descendent the KTT Mk VIII was still competitive two decades later. Freddie Frith and Bob Foster proved that in 1949 and '50 by winning 350cc world titles on works double-overhead-cam ('double-knocker', in Harold Wills' colourful parlance) versions of the single.

Left: Velocette's choice of the KSS name stood for camshaft super sports, the use of K instead of C reflecting the Goodman family's German origins.

***Below left:** Percy Goodman's 349cc single-cylinder engine used bevel drive to its single overhead camshaft, and produced 18bhp. Harold Willis's positive-stop, four-speed gearbox was introduced to the KSS in 1932.*

While the KTT got faster, the KSS, in becoming better equipped and more refined over the years, also became heavier and slower. In 1935 production was halted while the factory completed development of a KSS Mk II, which was released the following year. This had an aluminium cylinder head with fully-enclosed valvegear, plus an uprated lubrication system and new chassis.

The KSS was a more sophisticated bike but its weight had grown to 340lb (154kg) and power output was unchanged at 18bhp. By this time Velocette's simpler, pushrod-operated singles offered comparable power for less money, and the days of the KSS were numbered. After the Second World War, Velocette briefly built a KSS updated with telescopic forks instead of girders, but discontinued it in 1948.

The MAC – 350cc Velo for the Masses

The KSS was a hit on road and track, but the 350cc single that made most profit for Veloce Ltd was its humbler pushrod-operated cousin, the MAC. Launched in 1933 as the 250cc MOV ('OV' standing for overhead valve), and enlarged to 349cc to create the MAC the following year, designer Charles Udall's pushrod single was much less expensive to produce, and became the mainstay of the range. The MAC remained in production until 1960, gaining telescopic forks, aluminium barrels and finally a twin-shock frame along the way. In 1935 it was joined by a 500cc version, the MSS.

Specification	Velocette KSS (1934)
Engine	Air-cooled sohc two-valve single
Capacity	349cc (74 x 81mm)
Maximum power	18bhp @ 5800rpm
Transmission	Four-speed, chain final drive
Frame	Steel cradle
Suspension	Girder front; rigid rear
Brakes	Drum front and rear
Weight	320lb (145kg)
Top speed (road trim)	75mph (121km/h)

Rudge Ulster

**Top speed
93mph**
150km/h

*Right: The heart of the
production Ulster model
was its powerful and
refined four-valve single
engine, which was
developed from Rudge's
successful racing machines
of the early 1930s.*

*Below: This Ulster dates
from 1935 and features a
hand-operated gearchange,
as well as Rudge's
innovative brake system.
This linked the front and
rear drums, in the style of
some modern disc systems,
and was highly regarded by
many riders.*

Rudge will long be remembered for its four-valve singles, and most of all for the succession of 500cc Ulster models that were the Coventry firm's flagship sportsters throughout the 1930s. The name came from the Ulster Grand Prix where, in 1928, Rudge factory ace Graham Walker had won a famous victory on a new bike whose engine featured four valves per cylinder, grouped round a central spark plug.

Walker's win at that event in Northern Ireland was the first ever in a road race at an average speed of over 80mph (129km/h). The victory was a perfect marketing opportunity for Rudge, whose policy was to adapt successful racing innovations to the following year's production machines. In 1929 the firm launched a four-valve single with the Ulster name, after receiving a further boost when Ernie Nott raised the world two-hour record to an average speed of just over 100mph (161km/h), including stops for refuelling.

Rudge followed this with a second-generation engine that arranged its four valves radially, and was even more powerful. This layout made a stunning debut in 1930, when Rudge took the first three places in the Isle of Man Junior TT.

Subsequently the production Ulster model had a semi-radial valve layout, and was good for over 90mph (145km/h). Rudge also produced a 500 Special whose four valves were arranged in pairs rather than radially. It was less powerful than the Ulster, but cheaper and easier to maintain.

There was more to the Rudge Ulster than its engine, too. The model was one of the first to be fitted with a four-speed gearbox, and also featured Rudge's innovative linked brake system. The foot-pedal operated both front and rear drums, with the hand lever also working the front brake.

Sporting success

The Ulster was by no means the first fast Rudge. The firm whose full name was Rudge-Whitworth had been created in 1894, when Whitworth Cycles acquired Rudge, another bicycle firm, and had built its first motorcycle in 1911. Sporting success came when Victor Surridge lapped Surrey's Brooklands track at 66.47mph (106.97km/h), a 500cc record. In 1914, Rudge's Cyril Pullin won the Isle of Man Senior TT at an impressive average speed of almost 50mph (80km/h).

Rudge's first landmark model was the Multi of 1912, which was named after its novel system of gears. The Multi used a pulley arrangement to maintain the tension of the final drive belt, allowing the rider to select from no fewer than 21 gear ratios using a long lever. In 1919 the firm introduced a 998cc V-twin, which was also available with the Multi gear system, and was then called the Multwin.

Unfortunately for Rudge, its racing success and the Ulster's roadgoing performance were not enough to make the firm profitable during the recession-hit 1930s. Rudge tried selling engines under the Python label, but in 1933 the receiver was called in and the racing department was closed. Production continued but Rudge's best days were over, and the firm would not survive the War.

Triumph Ricardo – Four-valve Pioneer

Rudge's four-valve engine layout owed much to the innovative Triumph Type R, designed by Harry Ricardo, which had been introduced in 1921. The 499cc single-cylinder engine featured four valves and a pentroof combustion chamber (the style still used by most modern bike motors), and produced an impressive 20hp. The Type R was good for over 80mph (129km/h), and set records including the world 500cc one-hour mark at 76.74mph (123.5km/h). But Triumph chose to concentrate production on a simpler two-valve single instead.

Specification	Rudge Ulster (1935)
Engine	Air-cooled ohv pushrod four-valve single
Capacity	499cc (85 x 88mm)
Maximum power	30bhp @ 5200rpm
Transmission	Four-speed, chain final drive
Frame	Steel twin downtube
Suspension	Girder front; rigid rear
Brakes	Drum front and rear
Weight	298lb (135kg)
Top speed	93mph (150km/h)

Left: The Ulster look had changed little when this bike was produced in 1938. Despite the four-valve single's excellent performance and Rudge's considerable racing success earlier in the decade, the firm was in financial trouble by then. This was one of the last Ulsters to be built before production ended with the Second World War.

Crocker V-Twin

**Top speed
110mph**
177km/h

*Below: The Crocker was a
neat looking bike,
especially when its
aluminium gas tank was
highlighted by a scalloped
paint finish, but most of all
the big V-twin was
outstanding for its speed,
light weight and high
quality engineering. It was
unfortunate for maker Al
Crocker that too few riders
could afford to pay for his
upmarket machine.*

 Albert Crocker was one of the outstanding
figures of American motorcycling in the
years before the Second World War. He
was a dealer and entrepreneur as well as a rider,
designer and engineer. And the big 1000cc V-twins
that bore his surname were some of the fastest and
most desirable machines on the road.

Crocker worked as a rider and engineer for
Thor before becoming an Indian agent in Denver,
Colorado, then Kansas City and finally Los
Angeles. In LA he developed a speedway racing
bike, in conjunction with a young engineer named
Paul Bigsby. Their first efforts were powered by the
750cc V-twin engine from an Indian Scout, but on
the tight speedway tracks this was at a disadvantage
against smaller single-cylinder rivals.

The duo's next move was to design a 500cc
single engine, with an overhead-valve, pushrod-
operated layout. This produced about 40bhp, good
for 65mph (105km/h) on short speedway gearing,
and weighed a competitive 240lb (109kg). Brothers
Jack and Cordy Milne, who would later win
speedway's world title aboard JAP-engined bikes,

helped develop the Crocker and had some good
results on it. But the American bike lacked power
compared to its British JAP rival, and Crocker
turned his sights to a roadgoing bike.

In 1936 he debuted a V-twin that owed much to
his single's design, and had its cylinders set at 45
degrees. As a competition enthusiast, Crocker had a
passion for light bikes with plenty of power. His
hemi-head, ohv pushrod V-twin had exposed valve
springs and produced an impressive 50bhp at
5800rpm. Its three-speed gearbox was of notably
heavy-duty construction, and was cast integral with
the frame, with steel plates on either side to allow it
to be aligned with the engine.

Weight-saving components

To reduce weight Crocker used aluminium for
numerous components including the fuel tank,
instrument panel, engine and generator cases,
footboards, and rear light. The result was that the
V-twin weighed a very competitive 480lb (218kg),
making it considerably lighter than Harley's new
Knucklehead, as well as 10bhp more powerful. It

was a handsome and well-engineered machine, with raised handlebars, girder front suspension and a rigid rear end with sprung saddle for the rider.

The Crocker roared to a top speed of about 110mph (177km/h), and had looks to match. It was a well-made machine in typical period style, with pulled-back handlebars, a large round headlamp, and a two-into-one exhaust system. The bikes were hand-built, some with engine specification modified at the request of customers. But sadly for Al Crocker, despite his bikes' quality his business found it hard to compete with the higher volumes and lower prices of rival firms.

It was Crocker's misfortune that his V-twin was released just as Harley came out with its overhead-valve Knucklehead. Although the Harley was heavier and less powerful, the much larger and better established Milwaukee marque's bike cost roughly $150 less than the Crocker, which sold for upwards of $500. While the Knucklehead was hugely successful and became the model on which so many later Harleys were based, fewer than 100 examples of the more exotic Californian machine were produced.

From 1939 onwards Crocker also built a scooter called the Scootabout, but this was also produced only in small numbers. He had been hoping that Indian, with which he still had links, would buy

rights to manufacture the V-twin. But his plans were dashed by the advent of the Second World War, and Crocker did not restart production of his excellent but unprofitable machine.

Above: Crocker's robust three-speed gearbox was operated by a hand change, complete in this bike's case with a dice-style customized shift-lever knob. Top speed exceeded 100mph (161km/h).

Left: The Crocker V-twin produced 50bhp and was very well engineered. This later model has enclosed pushrod tubes as well as dual oil pumps, a standard Crocker touch that contributed to the bike's high price.

Specification	Crocker V-Twin (1936)
Engine	Air-cooled ohv four-valve pushrod 45-degree V-twin
Capacity	998cc
Maximum power	50bhp @ 5800rpm
Transmission	Three-speed, chain final drive
Frame	Steel single downtube
Suspension	Springer forks; rigid rear
Brakes	Drum front and rear
Weight	480lb (218kg)
Top speed	110mph (177km/h)

Excelsior Manxman

**Top speed
80mph**
129km/h

*Below: A right side view
shows the Manxman 246cc
single-cylinder engine's
valve operation, which was
by bevel drive to a single
overhead camshaft. This
layout was much simpler
and cheaper to produce
than that of the radial four-
valve Mechanical Marvel,
yet gave excellent
performance plus good
reliability. Excelsior
promised its customers that
production competition
machines were genuine
hand-built racers, not
replicas.*

 The firm that is generally regarded as
Britain's first motorcycle manufacturer
produced mainly cheap, two-stroke
commuter machines throughout its long existence.
But Excelsior also earned a reputation for high
performance in the 1930s with some outstanding
sporting machines. The most successful of these
was the single-cylinder, overhead-cam Manxman,
whose speed and reliability made it popular for
racing and road use alike.

Excelsior did in fact build fast bikes almost
from its earliest days. After starting by making
penny-farthing bicycles in 1874, the company
began producing motorcycles in 1896 under its
original name of Bayliss, Thomas and Co. Track-
racing machines soon followed, powered by MMC
engines. The Coventry firm's works-supported rider
Sam Wright became one of the country's earliest
racing stars, and Harry Martin broke several records
at London's Canning Town cycle track in 1903.

After a short break, motorcycle production
resumed in 1910 under the name Excelsior,
following the demise of a German manufacturer of
that name. Large-capacity singles including an

850cc side-valve machine were introduced, and in
the 1920s, now under the direction of Birmingham-
based Eric Walker, Excelsior began to make a
reputation in racing with JAP-engined models.

The bike that really put Excelsior on the map
was the so-called Mechanical Marvel of 1933. This
was named after its innovative 250cc radial four-
valve single-cylinder engine, designed by Ike Hatch
of the Burney & Blackburne (B&B) engine firm in
conjunction with Walker. Unlike rival Rudge's
radial-valve motor, the Excelsior unit featured twin
inlet ports, each fed by a separate carburettor. Sid
Gleave rode the Mechanical Marvel to victory in
that year's Lightweight TT at a record average
speed of over 70mph (113km/h).

Powerful and robust

But the complex radial-valve single was difficult to
work on and to keep in tune, and Eric Walker
needed a bike that could not only be raced but
could form the basis of a production model. So he
and Hatch devised the Manxman, based on a much
simpler 250cc engine with shaft-and-bevel drive to
its single overhead camshaft. The powerful and

robust Manxman was a big success. Although it didn't win a TT, in the 1938 Lightweight race the Excelsiors took second to seventh places behind German firm DKW's supercharged two-stroke.

Excelsior had an impressive works team, led by H.G. Tyrell-Smith, who rode the Marvel to a total of two third places and a second in Lightweight (250cc) TTs in the 1930s. Equally importantly, the firm promised its customers that the production Manxman racebikes were 'genuine racing machines, not replicas'. Excelsior's publicity material claimed that all bikes were 'hand built and tested by our racing and experimental department', and that even the tyres were 'fitted by the Dunlop race mechanics'.

The Manxman was built in 350 and 500cc as well as its original 250cc capacity. It came not only in competition specification, either for road-racing or grass-track, but also as a high-performance roadster. For the street, it had a more conventional, upright riding position plus a full Miller Dynamag lighting system.

Blackburne closed its engine factory near the Brooklands racing circuit in 1937, but Manxman production continued. By this time Excelsior had begun producing some engine parts itself, with the rest being built by Beans Industries, a former car manufacturer. Manxman production ended in 1939

Specification	Excelsior Manxman 250 (1936)
Engine	Air-cooled sohc two-valve single
Capacity	246cc (63 x 79mm)
Maximum power	22bhp @ 6000rpm
Transmission	Four-speed, chain final drive
Frame	Steel single downtube
Suspension	Girder forks; rigid rear
Brakes	Drum front and rear
Weight	300lb (136kg)
Top speed	80mph (129km/h)

Left: The Manxman name and three-legged Isle of Man badge on the cam cover hinted at success in the TT, where the single failed to win but took second to seventh places in 1938.

Below: Low bars and lack of lights indicate that this Manxman is a racer, but the roadster was very similar. As well as this 250cc version, the Manxman was also available in 350 and 500cc capacities.

with the outbreak of the Second World War. Excelsior returned to its roots after the war, building Villiers-powered two-stroke lightweights including the 250cc Viking and Talisman. But sales fell in the 1950s, and production eventually ended in 1962.

Harley-Davidson Knucklehead

**Top speed
100mph**
161km/h

*Below: The basic shape of
the Model EL was very
similar to that of the
uprated, side-valve Model
VLH that was also
introduced in 1936, but
there was no doubt about
which bike was the faster
and more important. This
V-twin's shiny rocker-box
covers confirmed that this
was the firm's long-awaited
overhead-valve powerplant.*

Many Harley enthusiasts would argue that the Model 61E, nicknamed the Knucklehead, was the most important bike that the Motor Company has ever introduced. It was certainly one of the bravest. When the Knucklehead – so called after the shape of its rocker boxes – was being developed in the mid-1930s, America was struggling through the Depression. Businesses were closing, wages were being cut, bike sales were poor.

Yet after some debate, Harley – whose range had a reputation for reliability but not performance – went ahead with the new machine, which was introduced in 1936. The Model E's 45-degree V-twin engine had a capacity of 989cc (or 61 cubic inches, hence that part of its name), and was notable for two main reasons. The first was its lubrication system, which re-circulated the oil to a reservoir tank, instead of the relatively crude total-loss system used before.

Secondly, the Model E was Harley's first production bike with overhead valves, instead of the less efficient side-valves. This – at last! – meant extra power. A maximum of 37bhp for the basic Model 61E, with its 6.5:1 compression ratio, and an impressive 40bhp for the 61EL, which had 7:1 compression and was good for a genuine 100mph (161km/h) on the open road.

The twin-cradle steel frame was also new (it had also been designed to suit the large-capacity side-valve Model V), and held an improved version of Harley's springer front suspension system. Other features included a four-speed gearbox and a new fuel tank, which wore classical art-deco emblems as well as holding Harley's first standard-fitment speedometer in a console on its top.

The 61E was a very stylish motorcycle, with a purposeful, muscular look enhanced by the way the new oil tank filled the space between the V-twin engine and the rear fender. And although the bike

suffered from numerous teething problems – notably with oil leaks and the frame's inability to cope with the engine's power – the Knucklehead quickly captured American motorcyclists' imagination.

What made Milwaukee famous...

It was Harley's good luck – or, perhaps, a reward for earlier bravery – that the Depression was easing by the time the 61E reached the market in 1936. Almost 2000 units were built and sold in the first year, ahead of target. Even more importantly, the Knucklehead's design and performance gave Harley an edge over great rival Indian for the first time in years – an advantage that Milwaukee would never surrender.

Just to confirm the new model's performance potential, in March 1937 Harley sent racer Joe Petrali to Daytona Beach with a tuned Knucklehead modified for improved aerodynamics with a small fairing, disc front wheel and an all-enveloping tail section. Over a measured mile, Petrali roared to a two-way average speed of 136.183mph (219.2km/h), setting a new record and generating plenty of publicity in the process.

Back in 1937, not even Harley could have imagined that the Knucklehead's basic engine layout would serve the company into the 21st century. But after the first major overhaul, with the 1213cc Model 74F in 1941, the firm has repeatedly

Specification	Harley-Davidson Model 61EL (1936)
Engine	Air-cooled ohv four-valve pushrod 45-degree V-twin
Capacity	989cc (84 x 88.9mm)
Maximum power	40bhp @ 4800rpm
Transmission	Four-speed, chain final drive
Frame	Steel twin downtube
Suspension	Springer forks; rigid rear
Brakes	Drum front and rear
Weight	515lb (234kg)
Top speed	100mph (161km/h)

updated its big V-twin engine, without changing its essential design. And despite the recent arrival of more modern powerplants from Milwaukee, the faithful air-cooled, pushrod-operated, ohv 45-degree V-twin shows no sign of being abandoned just yet.

Left: Looking at those rocker-box covers, it's easy to understand why the Model E acquired the nickname Knucklehead. Harley's stylish fuel tank emblem was used between 1936 and 1939.

Below: The Model E had a new frame as well as its new engine, but there was still no sign of a rear suspension system. The four-speed gearbox was operated by a lever to the left of the fuel tank.

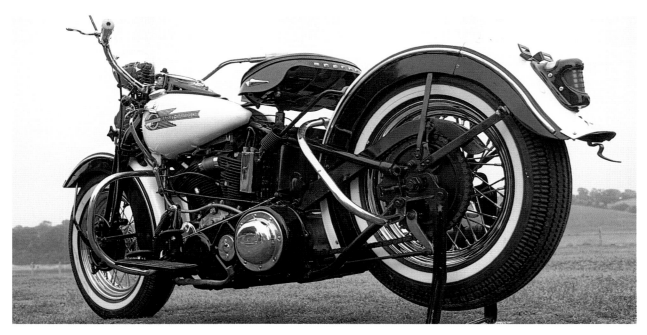

Triumph Speed Twin

**Top speed
93mph**
150km/h

*Below: Edward Turner was
a fine stylist as well as an
engineer, and the Speed
Twin had the looks to match
its parallel-twin engine's
performance. Early models
such as this had girder front
forks and rigid rear end;
later Twins combined
similar maroon and chrome
finish with telescopic forks
and plunger rear suspension.*

Motorcycling was changed for ever when
the Speed Twin burst onto the scene in
1937, dramatically proving that two
cylinders could be better than one, and triggering
an era of parallel twin dominance that would last
for more than three decades. It's doubtful whether
any British bike has had more influence on those
that followed.

The Speed Twin's appeal was easy to
understand. Triumph boss Edward Turner's 498cc
masterpiece was fast, stylish, practical and
reasonably priced, with a distinct performance
advantage over the majority of single-cylinder
machines that had dominated motorcycle
production until then. Turner himself, rarely
reluctant to express an opinion, was in no doubt
about a twin's attributes.

'A twin gives better torque,' he said. 'It will run
at higher revolutions than a single of similar
capacity without unduly stressing major
components. Because the firing intervals are equal,
which means even torque, the low-speed pulling is
better. The engine gives faster acceleration, is more
durable, is easier to silence and is better cooled. In
every way it is a more agreeable engine to handle.'

Effortless cruising

Most riders found it hard to disagree after riding
the Speed Twin, which was matched by some
singles in its top speed of just over 90mph
(145km/h), but not in the relatively smooth and
effortless way it would cruise at more than 70mph
(113km/h). The pushrod-operated engine, which
had a 360-degree firing arrangement (pistons rising
and falling together), was quite softly tuned, with a
7:1 compression ratio and a maximum output of
29bhp at 6000rpm. Although there was some
vibration, by single standards it was smooth.

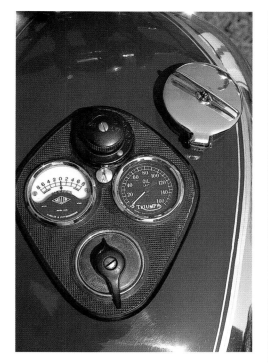

Turner had recently arrived from Ariel (where he had designed the Square Four), after that firm had taken over Triumph. He had announced himself by revamping Triumph's range of 500, 350 and 250cc singles, boosting sales with fresh styling and catchy new names: Tiger 90, 80 and 70. Turner's rare talent for both marketing and styling were again evident in the Speed Twin, with its evocative name and handsome lines.

Handling rated highly

The Twin's lean, simple look was not misleading. It used essentially the same frame and forks as the Tiger 90, was actually slightly lighter than the 500 single, and its engine was slightly narrower. The drum brakes were powerful and handling was rated highly, although the rigid rear end tended to hop over bumps.

It was the engine, though, that sent the testers of the day into rapture. 'On the open road the machine was utterly delightful,' reported *The Motor Cycle*. 'Ample power was always available at a turn of the twist-grip, and the lack of noise when the machine was cruising in the seventies was almost uncanny.' The magazine managed a two-way average of 93.7mph (151km/h) and a 'truly amazing' one-way best of 107mph (172km/h).

Predictably, given all this and the Triumph's competitive price of little more than the Tiger 90, the bike was a huge success. The outbreak of the Second World War put a halt to development, but by 1948, three year's after war's end, all the main manufacturers had parallel twins of their own. Meanwhile the Speed Twin had been tuned to create a sports model, the Tiger 100, and a 650cc derivative was also being developed. Triumph's parallel twin revolution was well under way.

Above left: A fuel tank insert containing dials was a typical Triumph feature of the 1930s.

Above: Triumph's powerful and relatively smooth 498cc engine triggered the British bike industry's adoption of the parallel twin layout.

Specification	Triumph Speed Twin (1938)
Engine	Air-cooled ohv four-valve pushrod parallel twin
Capacity	498cc (63 x 80mm)
Maximum power	29bhp @ 6000rpm
Transmission	Four-speed, chain final drive
Frame	Steel twin downtube
Suspension	Girder front; rigid rear
Brakes	Drum front and rear
Weight	365lb (166kg)
Top speed	93mph (150km/h)

Indian Four

**Top speed
90mph**
145km/h

*Below: This 1939 model
Four was one of the last
before the model was
redesigned with the large
'skirted' fenders that would
become an Indian
trademark. The 1939 bike
benefited from numerous
updates made over the
years, and incorporated
features including right-
hand gearchange (the lever
is visible alongside the
Indian's headdress logo on
the gas tank), and fringed
leather saddle.*

 Indian's Four was stylish, comfortable, fast and expensive. Rather too expensive ever to sell in large numbers, in fact, although it remained in production for more than 15 years. During that time the Springfield, Massachusetts-based giant made numerous updates to the Four, which it acquired in 1927 by purchasing the rights and tooling of the Philadelphia-based Ace firm, which had gone into liquidation three years earlier.

The Ace had been designed by William Henderson, co-founder of the Henderson marque, and had been updated following his death in a crash while testing one of his bikes in 1922. Ace had a fine reputation for speed and quality, and Indian's initial response after taking control was to restart production of the Four with virtually no changes. Under Indian production the bike was initially still called simply the Ace, although from June 1927 it was rebadged the Indian Ace, and offered in Indian's traditional dark red colour as well as the original blue.

By the standards of the day the Indian Ace was one fast and glamorous machine, with a smooth-running 1265cc, inlet-over-exhaust engine producing 35bhp, a top speed of 80mph (129km/h) and good handling too. In June 1927, *Motorcycling* magazine enthused that, 'just for fun we slipped the gears into second, slowed down to about 20mph [32km/h] and then opened the throttle wide. A twist of the wrist and we were nearly blown off the saddle... The new Indian Ace packs a wallop in all four barrels.'

In 1928, Indian decided that the Ace label was no longer needed, and introduced an updated Four that was badged simply as an Indian. Around this time the factory had a short-lived policy of introducing improvements as soon as they were ready, rather than waiting for specific model years. Over the next few years Indian modified the four with a stronger crankshaft (with five main bearings instead of the previous three), twin-downtube frame, leaf-spring front fork and a more efficient twin-shoe front brake.

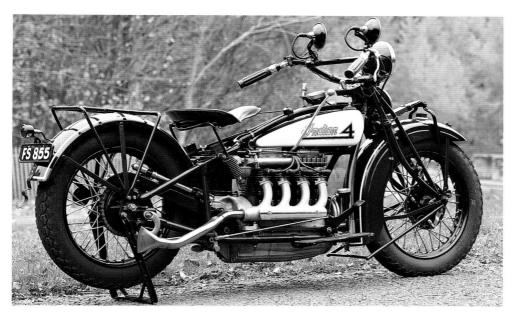

Left: By 1931 the Four had undergone improvements under Indian's policy of continual development, but still had the old-style fuel tank with a frame tube running above. Although less sophisticated than most later variants, the 1931 Four was also lighter. But sales in the early 1930s were very poor.

Below: Although its look is very similar, this is not an old Indian but a new four-cylinder machine called the Dakota 4, built in 2000. The Dakota 4 was designed in Sweden and produced in small numbers in Scotland by Alan Forbes, an Indian enthusiast and spares dealer who owned the Indian name in Britain and some other countries.

Weight gain

For the 1932 season the Four was restyled with a more streamlined tank, longer front forks and a stronger frame, gaining weight to a substantial 495lb (225kg) in the process. As before it came as standard with a left-hand throttle and right-hand shift for the three-speed gearbox, but from '32 could be ordered with the controls reversed for no extra cost. By this time Indian sales had slumped to a record low in the Depression, following the rest of the American auto industry.

In 1933 Indian built a lowest ever total of just 1667 bikes, of which only about 130 were the expensive Four. Many of those went to police forces, which rated the model highly. Three years later the economy had begun to recover, but Indian took a wrong turn with the Model 436 Four, which had its valve arrangement reversed in an 'exhaust over inlet' layout. Indian billed the bike as 'the world's finest, world's fastest stock motorcycle'. But its more cluttered engine look was unpopular, and the model gained the nickname 'upside-down Four' before the old-style valve layout was reinstated shortly afterwards.

The last Fours, built between 1940 and 1942, were redesigned with huge skirted fenders and rear suspension. They were stylish and comfortable, if heavy and slow-steering. Then came the Second World War, during which Indian produced large numbers of military V-twins, and developed prototype four-cylinder machines called the X44 and the Torque Four. But these came to nothing, and production of Indian's four-cylinder flagship did not restart after the war.

Specification	Indian Four (1939)
Engine	Air-cooled eight-valve inlet-over-exhaust in-line four
Capacity	1265cc (69.8 x 82.5mm)
Maximum power	40bhp @ 5000rpm
Transmission	Three-speed, chain final drive
Frame	Steel twin cradle
Suspension	Leaf spring front; none rear
Brakes	Drum front and rear
Weight	532lb (241kg)
Top speed	90mph (145km/h)

1941-1959
Twin's Peak

Triumph's 500cc Speed Twin had been introduced just before the Second World War, but its influence extended long afterwards. British manufacturers dominated the 1940s and 1950s, notably with variations on the parallel twin engine layout that was adopted, with varying degrees of success, by all the main firms.

Singles remained popular, with sporty models such as BSA's Gold Star and Gilera's Saturno adding style and performance to complement the more down-to-earth format of most other machines. Meanwhile firms such as Vincent, Harley-Davidson and Indian highlighted the exciting potential of a large-capacity V-twin.

Scott Flying Squirrel

**Top speed
90mph**
145km/h

*Right: A speeding Scott was
a fine sight, and also a treat
for the ears with its high-
pitched and very distinctive
two-stroke 'yowl'.*

*Below: Although more
conventional than the
earlier cylindrical-tanked
Scotts in its appearance,
the Flying Squirrel was still
an unusual looking bike,
and changed little over
the years.*

Few bikes have been produced for so long
with so few changes to either its
personality or technical specification as
the Scott Flying Squirrel. When introduced in 1926,
as an updated version of the Yorkshire firm's two-
stroke parallel twin, the Flying Squirrel was
available in either 498 or 596cc capacity, and it was
notable for its conventional frame and fuel tank,
instead of the open frame and cylindrical tank of
earlier Scotts.

When the last Flying Squirrel was built in 1978,
more than half a century later, it not only looked
very similar but still had a 596cc two-stroke engine
that had barely been updated since gaining
detachable cylinder heads in 1934. By the end of its
life the Scott was being built in tiny numbers, and
had long since lost any claim to competitive
performance. Even so, the model's long life gave
an indication of the advanced design of the
original, and the high regard in which Scotts were
held by a devoted band of owners.

Sounds distinctive

Sales and development work were very limited for
the last half of the Flying Squirrel's life. Founder
Alfred Scott had died of pneumonia in 1923, and
the firm had struggled financially since the early
1930s. But the two-stroke continued to offer lively
performance, as well as the distinctive feel and
sound that dated back to the advanced twins with
which Scott had entered production in 1904.

In 1939, just before the Second World War interrupted production, the firm's new Clubman's Special, also with 596cc capacity, was timed at over 90mph (145km/h) by *Motor Cycling* magazine. The Scott was described as 'a delightful machine capable of effortless high-speed cruising', although the tester noted that there was room for improvement in the way the bike handled over the bumps at Brooklands circuit.

The post-war Flying Squirrel brochure claimed that: 'Silence, performance, simplicity and smoothness give the Scott an individuality which cannot be rivalled by any other make of machine.' The brochure went on to praise 'the effortless power of the two-stroke twin; the smooth acceleration; its carefree stability; its insatiable thirst for hard work; its never tiring glide; no vibration; no clatter; no fuss; just the powerful yet pleasing musical purr of the exhaust.'

Some of that was typical advertising hype, but there was no doubt that the Flying Squirrel combined unusual style with a fair degree of performance. Its ability to sit smoothly at 70mph (113km/h) was impressive, as was the charismatic 'yowl' from the exhaust at high revs. For many riders the stroker's main drawback was not its performance but the regular maintenance required to keep it running well.

In 1947 Scott improved the chassis by replacing its girder forks with air forks, which worked quite well until the air seals wore. The rigid rear end was superseded in 1956 by a twin-shock frame introduced by new owner Matt Holder, a marque enthusiast who had taken over the bankrupt firm in 1950 and moved production to Birmingham. But Holder made few other attempts to improve the Scott after almost 30 years, and built fewer than 300 bikes in total.

Silk – a Scott for the 1970s

Although the Flying Squirrel changed little over the years, it inspired a new and more modern two-stroke parallel twin: the Silk 700S. George Silk was a Scott enthusiast who created a compact 653cc engine with electronic ignition, uprated lubrication and a peak output of 47bhp. Neatly styled and with a light, rigid frame from Spondon Engineering, the 700S handled superbly and was capable of 110mph (177km/h) when introduced in 1972. Despite the Silk's high price, more than 100 were sold, but production was not profitable and ended in 1979.

Specification	Scott Flying Squirrel (1947)
Engine	Liquid-cooled two-stroke parallel twin
Capacity	596cc (73 x 71.4mm)
Maximum power	30bhp @ 5000rpm
Transmission	Three-speed, chain final drive
Frame	Triangulated tubular steel
Suspension	Telescopic front; none rear
Brakes	Drum front and rear
Weight	407lb (185kg)
Top speed	90mph (145km/h)

Above left: This Flying Squirrel was built in 1947, so featured the air forks that were introduced in that year. Scott would not fit rear suspension for another nine years.

Left: Scott's liquid-cooled, 596cc two-stroke engine produced 30bhp and was pleasantly smooth. But it required regular maintenance to give of its best.

Ariel Square Four

**Top speed
100mph**
161km/h

*Below: The Square Four
4G MkI was a 997cc
machine that provided
plenty of smoothness and
comfort, if not outstanding
performance. This bike
dates from 1952, the year
before this model 'Squariel'
was replaced by the MkII
version, which featured
more power and improved
cooling, and was
distinguishable by its two
pairs of exhaust downpipes.*

'Ten to a hundred in top gear' was the proud boast that Ariel used in its advertising for the Square Four during the 1950s, emphasizing the machine's low-rev refinement as well as its top speed of over 100mph (161km/h). In fact, even the final version of the Square Four was not as fast as its impressive specification and high price suggested. It was more of a luxurious – if rather unreliable – grand tourer than a sports machine. But for many years Ariel's flagship was one of the most glamorous bikes on the road.

The Square Four went through numerous redesigns during its long life, which lasted from 1931 to 1958. During that 27-year period, the Ariel's engine capacity doubled, and its chassis and styling were transformed. Yet the air-cooled square four engine layout's advantages of power, smoothness and compact size remained throughout – as did its drawbacks of high production cost and the difficulty of providing sufficient cooling for the sheltered rear cylinders.

Cigarette packet sketch

Legend has it that this most exotic of motorcycles was born after a gifted young engineer, Edward Turner, had drawn up a novel square four engine layout on the back of a cigarette packet and tried unsuccessfully to sell the idea to a succession of bike manufacturers. Turner, later to find lasting fame at Triumph, eventually convinced Ariel chief Jack Sangster that the square four concept was sound, and was hired to put it into production.

Turner's design was basically a pair of parallel twins, sharing the same cylinder head, block and crankcase, with their crankshafts geared together. This gave a naturally smooth-running engine, and was so compact that the original 497cc unit could be fitted into a frame very similar to that of Ariel's current 500cc single. That first Square Four, introduced in 1931, featured a chain-driven overhead camshaft and exhaust manifolds integral with the cylinder head, so that only two exhaust pipes emerged from the engine. Turner's original design had used an integral three-speed gearbox,

but the production bike had chain primary drive to a separate four-speed Burman box.

After one year of production the engine was enlarged to 597cc, giving extra power that was particularly welcomed by sidecar owners. In this form the Square Four produced 24bhp at 6000rpm, and stayed smooth to its top speed of 85mph (137km/h). But the 'Squariel' suffered from cooling and other problems. In 1937, after Turner had left for Triumph, Ariel introduced revised 597cc and 997cc models, known as the 4F and 4G, designed by new chief engineer Val Page.

The new engines featured more cylinder head finning plus a tunnel between the cylinders to allow cooling air to the rear of the block. Other changes included pushrod valve operation and longer-stroke dimensions. The larger 4G produced 34bhp with plenty of low-down torque. But as well as some unreliability it also suffered from mediocre handling, being too heavy for the plunger rear suspension system that had been adopted along with telescopic forks.

In 1953 Ariel introduced an uprated version, the 4G MkII, incorporating a new cylinder head complete with four instead of two downpipes. Cooling was improved by the air that now ran over the exhaust ports. Reshaped pistons helped raise power to 40bhp at 5000rpm, increasing top speed to over 105mph (169km/h). But Ariel never got round to introducing the liquid-cooled engine that

might have solved the longstanding overheating problem for good.

The reason for lack of further development was simple: Ariel, by now part of the BSA group, had made its controversial decision to abandon four-stroke production in favour of the two-stroke Leader commuter bike. In 1958, the year the Leader was launched, the four-cylinder bike was dropped from the range, and an era that had lasted for almost 30 years came to an end. No rider who had experienced the Square Four's unique blend of performance, smoothness and sophistication would forget it.

Above: Handling of the plunger-framed Square Four 4G Mk1 was not a strong point, partly due to the bike's substantial weight, but the Ariel provided a comfortable ride.

Below left: Twin downpipes gave the square four engine a deceptively ordinary look. Despite heavy finning, cooling of the rear cylinders remained a problem throughout the model's life.

Left: The Square Four's good looks added to its glamour and appeal, and when the bike was running well there were few machines of the early 1950s that were more refined.

Specification	Ariel Square Four 4G MkI (1952)
Engine	Air-cooled ohv eight-valve pushrod square-four
Capacity	997cc (65 x 75mm)
Maximum power	34bhp @ 5400rpm
Transmission	Four-speed, chain final drive
Frame	Steel twin downtube
Suspension	Telescopic front; plunger rear
Brakes	Drum front and rear
Weight	433lb (196kg)
Top speed	100mph (161km/h)

Sunbeam S8

**Top speed
80mph**
129km/h

*Right: The S8's handling
was an improvement on that
of the S7, due to reduced
weight, new front forks plus
narrower wheels and tyres.*

*Below: Despite its unusual
tandem twin engine layout,
the S8's styling, black paint
finish and chassis design
were conventional, in
contrast to its heavier and
more eye-catching S7
predecessor.*

With its smooth and reliable 487cc twin-cylinder engine, good handling and a reasonable turn of speed, the S8 was the finest bike that the famous Sunbeam marque, whose history of motorcycle production stretched back to 1912, had ever built. The S8, introduced in 1949, was essentially a sportier and more reliable version of the S7, which had sold poorly following its release two years earlier.

The basic layout of the S8's engine was identical to that of the S7. Sunbeam's tandem twin unit had a 360-degree crankshaft and shaft final drive. It was also unusual in having a chain-driven single overhead camshaft, instead of the more common pushrods. Numerous changes, most of them made in a bid to cure the S7's unreliability, included extra oil capacity and redesigned pistons. The S8 was also more powerful than the original model. Its increased compression ratio and less restrictive exhaust pipe increased peak output slightly to a claimed 26bhp at 5800rpm.

Traditional black

Paint finish was black, Sunbeam's traditional choice in the days when the Wolverhampton marque was highly regarded for its top quality construction. The S8 retained the S7's twin-downtube steel frame and gained a significant

handling improvement with new front forks, as well as narrower wheels and tyres. The forks were conventional BSA telescopics, in place of the original twin's unsuccessful design, which had a single spring between the legs and no hydraulic damping at all. Rear suspension was by plunger, as before, backed up by a sprung single saddle.

The S8's top speed was just over 80mph (129km/h), about 5mph (8km/h) up on the S7, but it was on acceleration that the lighter bike had a bigger advantage. Its standing quarter-mile time of 18 seconds was several seconds quicker than the heavier S7 could manage, and the new bike generally had a much more lively feel. The S8's revised rubber-mounting system was very effective, almost completely isolating the traditional parallel-twin shakes. But the positive comments could not be extended to the S8's front brake, a single-leading-shoe drum that was rated as mediocre in contemporary tests.

Smooth and reliable

In most respects, though, the S8 was highly regarded, and it was certainly a more impressive machine than the S7. It was easy to start, smooth,

Specification	Sunbeam S8 (1949)
Engine	Air-cooled sohc four-valve tandem twin
Capacity	487cc (70 x 63.5mm)
Maximum power	26bhp @ 5800rpm
Transmission	Four-speed, shaft final drive
Frame	Steel twin downtube
Suspension	Telescopic front; plunger rear
Brakes	Drum front and rear
Weight	400lb (181kg)
Top speed	80mph (129km/h)

The S7 – Sunbeam's First Tandem Twin

Sunbeam's problems stemmed from the unsuccessful introduction, ten years earlier, of the S7 model on which the S8 was based. The distinctive S7, whose similar twin-cylinder engine was dwarfed by American-style parts including balloon tyres and big, skirted fenders, was intended as a luxurious and refined roadster. It was advertised as 'the world's most magnificent motor cycle', and was certainly one of the most expensive.

When running well, the S7 was a comfortable and agreeable tourer, but it suffered from a number of basic design flaws. For a 500cc twin it was rather heavy and not very fast. It handled poorly, due partly to its huge tyres, and had feeble brakes. Its shaft-drive motor was not particularly economical, and also developed a reputation for unreliability, with problems including overheating, cracked cylinder liners and main bearing failure. Inevitably, few were sold. And despite the arrival of the S8, Sunbeam's fortunes never recovered.

reliable and comfortable, once leaving *Motor Cycling* magazine's tester feeling reasonably fresh after covering over 500 miles (805km) in 24 hours – quite an achievement in the 1950s. The S8 was also more competitively priced than its predecessor, and accounted for the majority of the 10,000 Sunbeam twin sales during the four years to 1952. But from then on development of the S8 was minimal and, after BSA and Triumph had merged in late 1956, Sunbeam production was stopped.

Left: The S8's 487cc tandem twin engine was closely based on that of the S7, but incorporated modifications including new pistons and increased oil capacity, which made it more reliable. A new exhaust system helped increase output to 26bhp.

Vincent Black Shadow

**Top speed
125mph**
201km/h

*Below: The Black Shadow
Series C was the fastest
bike on the road in the late
1940s and early '50s, and
one of the most stylish.
Sadly for Philip Vincent and
his firm, the bike was so
expensive to produce that it
was not profitable, despite
its high price.*

Vincent was motorcycling's greatest name in the years after the Second World War, and the Black Shadow was the firm's brightest star. With its powerful 998cc V-twin engine and fine-handling chassis, the Shadow was an exotic, superbly crafted and very rapid machine. Its top speed of over 120mph (193km/h) fully justified the advertising line, 'The World's Fastest Standard Motorcycle'.

The Black Shadow was a tuned version of Vincent's Rapide V-twin, itself a magnificent machine. Both models were high-performance roadburners, assembled in small numbers at Vincent's workshop at Stevenage in Hertfordshire by a small team led by Philip Vincent, the firm's founder, and Phil Irving, his Australian chief engineer.

Starting in business

Philip Vincent had begun by designing a novel form of sprung motorcycle frame in 1927, while an engineering student at Cambridge University. He left Cambridge and, with backing from his father, set up in business. To give his venture credibility, Vincent bought the name of HRD Motors. The initials were those of Howard Davies, a racer and engineer who had won the 1925 Senior TT on a bike he had built himself, but whose firm had not survived the recession. Vincent kept little of HRD apart from its paint scheme of black with gold trim, but he too intended to produce high-quality, technically innovative bikes.

Early Vincents were powered by proprietary engines from firms including JAP and Rudge. But in 1934 Vincent and Irving were furious when the unreliability of JAP's 'special' racing engines wrecked the firm's first attempt at the TT. Following their return from the Isle of Man, Irving designed a 499cc single-cylinder engine with an innovative 'high-camshaft' layout.

The basic Meteor single and sportier Comet, which was capable of 90mph (145km/h), were a success. They led to the first Rapide V-twin, introduced in 1936, which produced 45bhp from an engine whose cylinders were set at 47 degrees apart. Nicknamed the 'Snarling Beast', or 'plumber's nightmare' due to its external oil lines, it was fast but suffered from transmission problems caused by its torque.

Vincent replaced it after the war with the improved Series B Rapide. Its new unit-construction V-twin motor had cylinders at 50 degrees, and formed a stressed member of the chassis, so no downtubes were needed. It combined 110mph (177km/h) top speed with abundant mid-range torque, cruised effortlessly at high speed, and handled well. Twin drums on each wheel gave plenty of stopping power.

The tuned Black Shadow, launched in 1948, was faster still. To emphasize its extra performance the Shadow had a large Smiths speedometer calibrated to 150mph (241km/h), and black-finished cylinders and crankcases. A year later Vincent introduced the Series C range, in touring Rapide, sports Black Shadow and racing Black Lightning forms.

Vincents proved their performance worldwide. In 1949 American ace Rollie Free, riding a tuned Black Lightning, famously stripped to his swimming trunks to set a world record for unsupercharged bikes at 150.313mph (241.89km/h) on the Bonneville salt flats in Utah. Another hero was George Brown, who set speed records and won many sprints on Gunga Din, Nero and the supercharged Super Nero.

Vincent's problem was that the exotic, hand-built V-twins could not be produced at a profit. The firm struggled during the mid 1950s, and was forced to assemble Firefly engines and NSU lightweight bikes under licence. In 1955 Vincent launched the fully-enclosed Series D models, the Black Knight and tuned Black Prince. But the public was not yet ready for their black fibreglass bodywork, and sales slumped. Revised Rapide and Black Shadow models were reintroduced, but in vain. By the end of the year, Vincent's mighty beast had snarled its last.

Above: Black finish confirms that this is a Black Shadow engine, in a higher state of tune than the grey unit of the Rapide tourer.

Left: The side view shows off the front girder suspension plus one of the pair of rear shock units, located diagonally beneath the seat.

Below left: The fortunate Black Shadow rider was treated to the sight of a big Smiths speedometer that was calibrated to 150mph (241km/h).

Specification	Vincent Black Shadow Series C (1949)
Engine	Air-cooled ohv four-valve pushrod 50-degree V-twin
Capacity	998cc (84 x 90mm)
Maximum power	55bhp @ 5700rpm
Transmission	Four-speed, chain final drive
Frame	Steel spine
Suspension	Girder front; twin shocks rear
Brakes	Twin drums front and rear
Weight	458lb (208kg)
Top speed	125mph (201km/h)

Gilera Saturno Sport

**Top speed
85mph**
137km/h

*Right: This 1950 model
Saturno Sport handled well,
thanks partly to its light
weight and rigid frame, but
shortly afterwards Gilera
uprated the model's chassis
with telescopic forks and
twin rear shocks.*

*Below: Simple styling and
Italian racing red
paintwork make the Sport a
very attractive roadster.
Removing lights and other
unnecessary accessories
converted it into a useful
racebike with minimal effort
and expense.*

 Lean, simple and finished in Italian Racing Red, the Saturno Sport was the high-performance model of the Milan-based firm's range of 500cc single-cylinder roadsters, which also included the softer Turismo model plus a police bike and a military machine.

Gilera's four-cylinder factory racers earned the company most of its fame by winning six world titles during the 1950s. But the Saturno was also an impressive performer on both road and track. Many owners simply removed the Sport's roadgoing parts such as lights and battery, then competed on Italian street circuits with considerable success.

For all its racy reputation, the Saturno was a simple machine. It was designed by Giuseppe Salmaggi, and was a development of the so-called 'eight-bolt' (*Otto Bulloni*) single that had been Gilera's main 500cc machine in the late 1930s. The first few Saturnos, introduced in 1940, were racing bikes. Gilera tester Massimo Masserini gave the model a good start when he won the prestigious Targa Florio road race, a test of endurance as well as speed, before production was interrupted by the outbreak of the Second World War.

Gilera began full-scale Saturno production in 1946. Its engine remained an air-cooled, vertical single, with long-stroke dimensions of 84 x 90mm – unchanged even on the racing versions – giving capacity of 499cc. It had pushrod-operated valves closed by hairpin springs, and a four-speed gearbox. The Sport had an aluminium cylinder head, 6:1 compression ratio, and produced 22bhp at 5000rpm. That gave it an advantage over the Touring model, with its iron head, lower compression and softer camshaft.

Gilera's Fabulous Fours

Gilera was founded in 1909 when Giuseppe Gellera, a young mechanic and hillclimber, produced a 317cc single-cylinder bike in his workshop near Milan. Gellera changed his name to Gilera, which he thought a better identity for his motorbike firm, and it quickly grew into one of Italy's most successful. Many Gileras were raced with good results in that period but the real glory came after Giuseppe Gilera bought the CNA Rondine (Swallow) bikes – supercharged 250cc fours that had won many races under previous ownership.

The marque's most glorious era was the 1950s, when its four-cylinder machines, designed by Piero Remor, dominated the 500cc world championship. Umberto Masetti won the title in 1950 and 1952, before Geoff Duke took over with a hat-trick for the Arcore factory. Libero Liberati added a sixth championship in 1957 before Gilera withdrew from racing, leaving the field open for MV Agusta to begin an even longer period of domination.

Top left: Gilera's powerful dohc four-cylinder grand prix bikes won six 500cc world titles, and led to many more because designer Piero Remor left to work for MV Agusta.

Far left: Saturno's crankcase is stamped with the name Arcore, the town near Milan where Gilera's factory was located before being closed in 1993.

Patented suspension system

Chassis layout of a 1950 Sport was mostly conventional, with a simple steel frame and girder forks, but rear suspension was by Gilera's unique patented system. An oval-section swingarm transmitted rear wheel movement, via two upright steel arms, to horizontal springs mounted in boxes above the swingarm. Each box contained a main spring to deal with bumps, plus a smaller rebound spring. Damping was provided by scissors-type friction units.

The Sport's performance did not approach that of Gilera's fiery, 110mph (177km/h) Sanremo competition single but, with plenty of low-rev torque and a top speed of about 85mph (137km/h), it was very lively. It also handled well in its original form, although by 1952 Gilera had updated the chassis with telescopic forks and twin rear shock absorbers.

Demand for the Saturno faded in the mid-

1950s, and production fell until it ended in 1959, when a total of almost 6500 had been built. By this time Gilera's management was more interested in the annual production of over 20,000 lightweight bikes with engines from 98 to 175cc. And crucially, the Sport's price of half a million lire would also buy a Fiat 500 car. That was one battle that even the Saturno Sport, with all its speed and spirit, could never win.

Above right: Gilera's patented rear suspension system used vertical steel arms to transfer wheel movement to springs that were mounted inside boxes above the swingarm. Damping was by scissors-type friction units to the rear.

Specification	Gilera Saturno Sport (1950)
Engine	Air-cooled ohv two-valve pushrod single
Capacity	499cc (84 x 90mm)
Maximum power	22bhp @ 5000rpm
Transmission	Four-speed, chain final drive
Frame	Steel single downtube
Suspension	Girder front; horizontal springs rear
Brakes	Drum front and rear
Weight	385lb (175kg)
Top speed	85mph (137km/h)

Indian Chief

**Top speed
90mph**
145km/h

*Below: The huge front
fender, complete with
Indian's head running light,
gives this late-model Chief
an unmistakable look. Even
enlarging the side-valve
V-twin to 80 cubic inches
(1311cc) did not give the
big, heavy Chief
outstanding performance,
but it was a comfortable,
reliable and stylish bike.
Sadly for Indian, that
wasn't enough to keep the
firm in business after 1953.*

 An Indian Chief of the 1940s or early '50s, with its big V-twin engine dwarfed by enormous and often brightly painted fenders over each wheel, is one of the most instantly recognizable motorcycles ever produced. Its story began long before those trademark fenders were introduced, however. The Chief was the heavyweight star of Indian's line-up for more than 30 years, following its introduction in 1922.

That first model, designed by Charles B. Franklin, combined elements of the 988cc Powerplus, which had been Indian's mainstay since its introduction in 1916, and the smaller-engined Scout, which had been launched in 1921. The original Chief's blend of 988cc, 42-degree, side-valve V-twin and Scout-style one-piece frame resulted in good handling and a top speed of 85mph (137km/h).

Even so, many riders believed the old adage that there was no substitute for cubes, so just a year later Indian enlarged the engine to 1213cc, or 74 cubic inches, to create the so-called 'Big Chief'.

Numerous updates were made in following years, most notably the addition of a front brake in 1928. Indian also equipped all its twins with a re-circulating oil system, in place of the original total loss arrangement, in 1933 – several years before rival Harley followed suit.

High-performance version

In 1935 the Chief could be ordered with the optional Y motor, whose aluminium heads and larger fins gave better cooling, plus other options including a four-speed gearbox instead of the standard three-speeder. Later in the decade Indian also offered a high-performance Bonneville motor whose hot cams, polished ports and precision ignition timing lifted top speed to an impressive 105mph (169km/h).

The mid-'30s Chief was also a good-looking bike, and could be ordered in a wide variety of colours because in 1930 Indian had been bought by Du Pont, the manufacturing giant that had connections in the paint industry. Around this time

Return of the Chief

Interest in Indian reawakened in the early 1990s when, with Harley sales booming, it became clear that there was room in the market for its old rival. The Indian name became a prized asset, fought over in law courts by a succession of firms, each of which claimed to have a new-generation Chief under development. When the dust settled in 1998, the winner emerged as the Indian Motorcycle Company, based at Gilroy in California. The following year, the firm began production of the Limited Edition 1999 Indian Chief, complete with trademark skirted fenders. Although the 'Harley clone' nature of its 1442cc V-twin engine displeased many traditionalists, the new Chief was well built and gave hope of a successful future for Indian.

Indian listed no fewer than 24 standard one- and two-colour schemes, plus the extra-cost option of any other colour from the Du Pont paint range.

But all was not well at the 'Wigwam', Indian's large Springfield factory, which by this time was running at only a fraction of its capacity. Indian struggled financially throughout the Depression-hit 1930s, and came close to bankruptcy in 1933. Although the company survived, it failed to compete with Harley by developing an overhead-valve V-twin to power the Chief, whose side-valve layout was becoming outdated.

The classical skirted-fender look was introduced in 1940. At the same time, Indian fitted the Chief with new cylinder heads and barrels whose larger cooling fins reduced running temperature. There was also a new frame, with plunger rear suspension. This resulted in an eye-catching, sweet-running and comfortable bike, but not a particularly quick one. The 558lb (253kg) Chief was fully 100lb (45kg) heavier than its 1935-model namesake. The days when an Indian rider

could 'dust' a Harley-mounted rival on the open road were over.

And although in 1950 Indian enlarged the V-twin engine to 1311cc (80ci), updated the chassis with telescopic forks in place of the previous girders, and fitted a conventional right-hand throttle as standard for the first time, it wasn't enough. Indian's financial problems, hastened by disastrous attempts to enter the small-capacity market, meant that relatively few Chiefs were built, and production ended in 1953.

Above left: The author takes a spin on a Chief owned by Californian-based Indian restorer and parts specialist Bob Stark.

Below left: Indian retained its traditional 42-degree cylinder angle from the days of its earliest V-twin engines.

Specification	Indian Chief (1953)
Engine	Air-cooled four-valve side-valve 42-degree V-twin
Capacity	1311cc (82.5 x 122mm)
Maximum power	50bhp @ 4800rpm
Transmission	Three-speed, chain final drive
Frame	Steel twin downtube
Suspension	Telescopic front; plunger rear
Brakes	Drum front and rear
Weight	570lb (259kg)
Top speed	90mph (145km/h)

Triumph Tiger 100

**Top speed
98mph**
158km/h

*Below: Edward Turner's
talent for styling at least
matched his engineering
ability, and the silver-
tanked Tiger 100 was one of
many good-looking
Triumphs of the period.
This bike dates from 1955,
and has the telescopic front
forks and twin rear shocks
that had by this time
replaced the original T100's
girder forks and sprung-hub
rear suspension system.*

The Tiger 100 was the bike on which Triumph's reputation for performance was built in the years following the Second World War. Powered by a 500cc parallel twin engine and named after its claimed top speed of 100mph (161km/h), the Triumph matched its speed with stylish looks and good handling to become one of the most desirable bikes of its day. It remained popular long after Triumph had introduced more powerful 650cc machines in the 1950s.

Like all British parallel twins, the T100 Tiger owed its inspiration to Edward Turner, as it was based on the Speed Twin with which the Triumph designer had revolutionized the industry in 1938. In fact the Tiger 100 was also introduced just before war broke out in the following year, only for production to be halted until Triumph restarted building motorcycles at Meriden in 1946. In that year, racer Ernie Lyons won the 500cc Manx Grand Prix on Triumph's GP racing version of the T100, which was fitted with a lightweight cylinder head and barrel for extra performance.

The standard Tiger 100 was essentially the sports version of the T5 Speed Twin, differing mainly in styling and engine tune, and for several years was the fastest and most popular 500cc twin on the roads. Its paintwork was silver instead of the 5T's red, its compression ratio was listed at 7.8:1 instead of 7:1, and its output was a claimed 30bhp at 6500rpm, compared to the Speed Twin's 27bhp at 6300rpm. Triumph's catalogue also boasted of polished engine internals, although by no means all production bikes were fitted with such parts.

Triumph did at least provide the Tiger with an alloy top end in 1951, by which time its chassis had also been uprated with telescopic forks in place of the original girders. By the mid-1950s Triumph had improved the chassis again, this time at the rear with a twin-shock swingarm suspension system in place of the original sprung hub design.

Those updates kept the T100 competitive in the bends as well as on the straights, even if Triumph's sportsters of the 1950s were generally not quite up to the standard of Norton's Featherbed-framed

rivals when it came to handling. Shutting the throttle in mid-corner could strain the single-downtube cradle frame enough to induce a wobble, but *Motor Cycling's* 1957 test reported that 'handling and steering, one or two-up, was as good as ever'.

Clubman's TT success

By this time further racing success had boosted the Triumph's appeal, both in America and also on the Isle of Man, where a T100 had won the Clubman's TT in 1952. The following year Triumph produced a race-ready replacement for the discontinued GP model. The T100C, complete with race-kit parts including hot cams, twin-carb conversion and megaphone pipes, put out a healthy 40bhp.

In standard form the twin did not initially quite live up to Triumph's 100mph (161km/h) claim without the help of hill or tail-wind, but it wasn't far off. *Motor Cycling* magazine timed a T100 roadster at 96mph (154km/h) in 1951, when a race-kitted version was good for almost 110mph (177km/h). And by 1957, when the basic Tiger had gained a twin-carb head and sportier cams, it managed a genuine 105mph (169km/h).

In 1960 the Tiger was replaced by an all-new model of the same name, complete with unit-construction engine and revised chassis with bathtub rear enclosure. By now the 500cc sportster had been put in the shade by the arrival of the 650cc Bonneville, but the smaller twin continued right through the 1960s, and formed the basis of the

Specification	Triumph Tiger 100 (1955)
Engine	Air-cooled ohv pushrod four-valve parallel twin
Capacity	499cc (63 x 80mm)
Maximum power	32bhp @ 6500rpm
Transmission	Four-speed, chain final drive
Frame	Steel cradle
Suspension	Telescopic front; twin shocks rear
Brakes	Drum front and rear
Weight	385lb (175kg)
Top speed	98mph (158km/h)

twin-carb T100T Daytona in 1967. Triumph's 500cc bikes had come a long way from the original Tiger 100 of almost 30 years before.

Above: A standard Tiger might have struggled to reach the 100mph (161km/h) speed suggested by its name, but it was one of the fastest bikes on the road in the mid-1950s. Hard-riding owners could expect to wait for their riding mates to catch up…

Left: Triumph's compact parallel twin engine contributed to the Tiger's lean good looks as well as to its impressive performance. In this original 499cc capacity the pushrod twin was also reasonably smooth, even at high revs. Combined with the T100's low, swept-back handlebars, this encouraged fast cruising.

Ariel Huntmaster

**Top speed
100mph**
161km/h

Right: Ariel's 646cc parallel twin engine was essentially the unit from BSA's Golden Flash, modified with a new gearbox, clutch and engine covers.

Below: The Huntmaster was a reasonably stylish machine that combined Ariel's traditional paint scheme with a high standard of finish. The marque was unique in producing models with one, two and four cylinders.

Ariel's variation on the familiar 650cc parallel twin theme was one of the more successful examples of the badge engineering common in the British motorcycle industry of the 1950s. The Huntmaster, produced when Ariel was a subsidiary of BSA, was a modified version of BSA's Golden Flash model. But there were sufficient differences between the two bikes to give them distinctly different appearances and personalities.

Most of Ariel's effort went into the Huntmaster's chassis. Its twin-downtube frame was widely regarded as stronger than that of the Golden Flash. Front forks were similar, as BSA had been using Ariel units for years, but the Huntmaster was fitted with rear shock units from Armstrong instead of Girling. The Ariel was finished to the firm's usual high standard and looked smart in its traditional deep red paintwork.

There were fewer differences in the two models' 646cc air-cooled, pushrod-operated, single-camshaft engines. Ariel fitted a new Burman four-speed gearbox and a dry clutch, and made some changes simply to disguise the unit's BSA origins. The right engine cover was reshaped into a triangular, rather than Y-shaped, form, and the rocker-box and its covers were redesigned. But peak output remained 35bhp at 5600rpm.

Cracking the ton

By the standards of 1954, when the Huntmaster was introduced, that gave good if not outstanding straight-line performance. Top speed was initially just under 100mph (161km/h), hindered slightly by tall gearing. Ariel lowered the final gear ratio slightly in 1956, after which the bike could just about 'crack the ton'. The Huntmaster also gave good acceleration through the range, though it was handicapped by typical parallel-twin vibration at high revs.

Handling was good, and combined with the new gearbox to give the Ariel a distinctly different feel to that of its BSA sibling. At 410lb (186kg) the Huntmaster was not particularly light, but it was stable, steered well and was comfortable, especially after Ariel redesigned the seat in 1956. Its drum brakes were reasonably powerful too, and owners soon grew to appreciate the bike's excellent fuel economy, even when fitted with a sidecar.

The Huntmaster was also impressively reliable. Later versions, especially, had numerous rider-friendly features such as an easily adjusted headlamp and brakes, enclosed final drive chain, plus a rear mudguard that hinged to facilitate rear wheel removal. The bike's practicality could also be increased by fitting factory-made accessories, which included a tall windscreen, crash-bars, luggage rack and panniers.

The Huntmaster's performance and versatility were enough to make it reasonably successful, and highly regarded by most who rode one. But those assets were not enough to save the model, or to keep Ariel from disaster once the firm undertook a controversial and ultimately suicidal decision to abandon four-stroke production completely.

The company had a proud if occasionally troubled history, having begun building motorbikes around the turn of the century. Ariel had been one of Britain's most important bike manufacturers in the 1930s, and had produced a succession of successful four-strokes, notably the Red Hunter range of singles. The Red Hunter name had also been used for a 500cc twin produced from 1948; and then there was the famous Square Four...

But in 1959, Ariel dropped the Huntmaster and all other four-stroke models to make way for the Leader, a 250cc two-stroke scooter with which the firm's bosses aimed to change the face of motorcycling. When the Leader failed to win sufficient converts, the firm had nothing to fall back on. In 1963 Ariel production was moved to BSA's factory, and a few years later ceased for good.

Above left: Although the Huntmaster had enough unique features to qualify as a new model, it was essentially an example of the 'badge engineering' that was popular with British manufacturers in the 1950s. Ariel had been part of the giant BSA group since 1944.

Above: The Huntmaster's new twin-downtube frame and Armstrong rear shocks gave handling that at least matched that of the BSA Gold Flash on which the Ariel was based. Braking power from the front and rear drums was good by mid-1950s standards, too.

Specification	Ariel FH Huntmaster 650 (1955)
Engine	Air-cooled ohv pushrod four-valve parallel twin
Capacity	646cc (70 x 84mm)
Maximum power	35bhp @ 5600rpm
Transmission	Four-speed, chain final drive
Frame	Steel twin downtube
Suspension	Telescopic front; twin shocks rear
Brakes	Drum front and rear
Weight	410lb (186kg)
Top speed	100mph (161km/h)

BSA Gold Star Clubman

**Top speed
110mph**
177km/h

For a competition-hungry motorcyclist in the 1950s, a Gold Star DBD34 Clubman was arguably the ultimate machine, whether for racing on the Isle of Man, on short circuits or on the street in unofficial burn-ups between coffee bars. Lean, purposeful and unmistakably aggressive, the DBD34 Clubman was the last, fastest and best known version of a series of Gold Star singles that included 350 and 500cc bikes in touring, trials and scrambles form.

Unmistakable appearance

Its look was unmistakable: chrome-panelled fuel tank with BSA's famous star-in-a-red-circle badge, headlight jutting up above a narrow pair of clip-ons, swept-back exhaust pipe leading from a heavily finned vertical cylinder. And the performance was unique, too. First gear was good for no less than 60mph (97km/h). With the rider's chin brushing the big steering damper knob, the 'Goldie' had a genuine top speed of over 110mph (177km/h).

The Gold Star story began in 1937, when racer Wal Handley earned a Brooklands Gold Star award for lapping the banked Surrey track at over 100mph (161km/h) on BSA's 500cc M23 Empire Star. In the following year BSA produced a replica marketed under the name M24 Gold Star, the name signifying that each machine had been built using selected components, tuned and dyno-tested, with polished ports, conrod and crankcases.

That first Gold Star also had magnesium gearbox casings and aluminium cylinder head and barrel. Power output was 28bhp when fuelled by petrol, or 33bhp when tuned to run on alcohol. Buyers received a certified dyno chart from their machine, a custom that was maintained with Gold Stars throughout. But BSA management decided

Above: There were few more exciting bikes in the 1950s than a well-set-up Gold Star Clubman, which combined engine power with light, agile handling and powerful braking.

Right: This 1956-model DBD34 Clubman has all its go-faster components present and correct, including low clip-on bars, rearset footrests, filterless Amal carburettor and free-breathing megaphone exhaust. Not to mention the free-revving engine whose 42bhp peak output gave a top speed of well over 100mph (161km/h).

that to reduce costs the sports Gold Star should resemble the standard single as much as possible, so its chassis was relatively standard.

After the Second World War, BSA produced a competition bike called the B32, based on its pushrod single the B31. This was initially made for use in trials, but when fitted with an aluminium cylinder head and barrel its racing potential was clear. For 1949 BSA introduced the 350cc ZB32 Gold Star, followed a year later by the 500cc ZB34. Both were rapid, competitively priced and came with various options – four camshafts, three different sets of gears (standard, scrambles and racing), four compression ratios (for use with different fuels), and choice of fuel tanks, exhaust systems and wheels.

Suddenly the clubman racer had a machine well suited to road and track. At the TT in 1949, Harold Clark averaged over 75mph (121km/h) on a ZB32 to win the Junior Clubman's race, and in following years the Gold Star dominated both the 350cc Junior and 500cc Senior. In the 1955 Junior, no fewer than 33 of the 37 riders were on Goldies. But BSA's supremacy led to the Clubman's TT being dropped after the following year.

Competition wins

In 1956 BSA introduced the DBD34, which benefited from a development programme that had seen factory aces including Bill Nicholson ride Goldies to many wins in scrambles and trials. Competition-proven modifications, including steeper steering geometry, swingarm rear suspension and a new front brake, had subsequently been fitted to the production machine. The DBD34 also incorporated engine updates introduced by

Specification	**BSA** DBD34 Gold Star Clubman (1956)
Engine	Air-cooled ohv two-valve pushrod single
Capacity	499cc (85 x 88mm)
Maximum power	42bhp @ 7000rpm
Transmission	Four-speed, chain final drive
Frame	Steel twin downtube
Suspension	Telescopic front; twin shocks rear
Brakes	Drum front and rear
Weight	384lb (174kg)
Top speed	110mph (177km/h)

BSA's chief designer Bert Hopwood. It featured a big Amal GP carburettor, ultra-close-ratio gearbox and peak output of 42bhp at 7000rpm.

Other changes for the DBD34 Clubman's included the provision, for the first time, of the lights required by that season's racing regulations. That gave the Gold Star a deceptively normal appearance, but there was no doubting its suitability for serious competition. This was a true racebike on the road: demanding, temperamental and – most of all – very fast indeed.

Below left: The Gold Star tank badge dated back to the Brooklands Gold Star award won by BSA rider Wal Handley.

Below: Slim, uncluttered lines not only helped the BSA's speed but made the bike look wonderfully purposeful too.

BSA Road Rocket 650

**Top speed
105mph**
169km/h

*Right: The Road Rocket's
handling might not have
been outstanding, but the
hard-accelerating twin went
round corners well enough
to be competitive with its
twin-cylinder rivals.*

*Below: Slim styling in the
BSA tradition gave the
Road Rocket good looks to
match its aggressive
performance. The 646cc
engine's tuning parts
included aluminium
cylinder head, hot cam and
high compression pistons.*

On its introduction in 1954, the 650cc
Road Rocket was the fastest and best bike
that BSA had ever built. More to the
point, it was quick and stylish enough not only to
become a hit in the big American market for which
it had essentially been developed, but also to boost
the image of the giant Birmingham factory, whose
existing twin-cylinder 650, the A10 Golden Flash,
was competent but not very exciting.

The Road Rocket was a distinctly sportier
machine than the Flash. As *Motor Cycling*
magazine commented when the model was
introduced to the home market in 1956, the Road
Rocket was a roadgoing solo 'with just that little bit
extra in the way of speed and specification luxury'.
It was well suited to an American market that
traditionally demanded style, capacity and
performance from its motorcycles.

In 1954, BSA was in the process of introducing
a new twin-shock frame for the Golden Flash, as a
replacement for the old design with plunger rear
suspension. The Road Rocket used the new chassis
to hold an engine based on that of the short-lived

A10 Super Flash, BSA's first sports 650cc model,
which had been sold almost exclusively in the
States the previous year.

The 646cc parallel twin unit was tuned with an
aluminium cylinder head, uprated exhaust valves,
Amal TT9 carburettor, hotter camshaft, toughened
heavy-duty crankshaft, and high-compression
pistons. It also had a manual advance-retard lever

The Road Rocket's speed and good looks, along with its dependable handling, earned it many admirers. Its motor proved impressively reliable, too. Its only mechanical weakness was in the area at the bottom of the cylinder block, which could give problems when the high-compression motor was revved hard.

The Road Rocket sold well in the States but, after being introduced to the home market midway through 1956, two years late, it lasted in production barely more than a year before being replaced by the Super Rocket, which was a very similar bike but which had slightly higher compression ratio, redesigned cylinder head, Amal Monobloc carburettor, and a headlamp nacelle. The Road Rocket was no more, but it had succeeded in proving that BSA was capable of producing a fast and exciting 650cc twin.

Left: The Road Rocket name and tank logo helped to emphasize the BSA's scorching performance. Not that this bike's rider needed much reminding, once the throttle was wound open…

Below: Chromed tank sides looked good when combined with the BSA's red paintwork. The Road Rocket model's mudguards were originally also chromed; this restored bike's red finish was introduced with the Super Rocket in 1958.

for adjusting the ignition, something that was not deemed necessary on the more softly tuned Golden Flash. Peak power rose to 40bhp at 6000rpm.

Home market Road Rockets were fitted with flatter handlebars and more efficient silencers than the original export machines. They were otherwise identical to the American market bikes, complete with red paintwork plus the partially chromed fuel tanks that had become a BSA trademark.

Brisk acceleration

Low-speed acceleration was very brisk, and despite its relatively high state of tune, the Road Rocket's twin-cylinder engine had plenty of low-down torque and a very docile nature. As *The Motor Cycle* magazine noted in its test of March 1957, the standard Golden Flash was well known for its wide spread of torque, but 'the trait seems to have been enhanced rather than impaired on the tuned engine. In practice this means that really lusty acceleration and power reserve for gradients, head winds and passenger carrying are available over a broad engine-speed range.'

More to the point, the Rocket was fast. BSA claimed a top speed of 105mph (169km/h), and the bike was timed at exactly that speed during one magazine's testing, despite a cross-wind. Triumph's rival hot 650, the Tiger 110, was arguably faster still, but only by the slimmest of margins. Equally importantly, the Road Rocket could be cruised 'without signs of fatigue' at between 95 and 100mph (153-161km/h), according to one contemporary test.

Specification	BSA Road Rocket (1956)
Engine	Air-cooled ohv pushrod four-valve parallel twin
Capacity	646cc (70 x 84mm)
Maximum power	40bhp @ 6000rpm
Transmission	Four-speed, chain final drive
Frame	Steel twin downtube
Suspension	Telescopic front; twin shocks rear
Brakes	Drum front and rear
Weight	418lb (190kg)
Top speed	105mph (169km/h)

Harley-Davidson Sportster

**Top speed
100mph**
161km/h

*Right: The Sportster's
883cc overhead-valve
V-twin engine produced
about 40bhp, giving 100mph
(161km/h) performance.
The so-called trumpet
jubilee horn was borrowed
from the big twin models.*

*Below: Early Sportsters are
hugely attractive bikes, with
a lean and simple profile
that is enhanced by two-
tone paint schemes and
chromed rear shocks.
Skyline blue and white was
an alternative to this bike's
Pepper red and black.*

 It's a long time now since the Harley Sportster lived up to its name. But there was a time, in the few years after the Sportster's release in 1957, when Milwaukee's lean and handsome charger could show a clean rear fender to just about any production bike on the road. On straight-line acceleration away from a stop-light, at any rate.

The feature that defined the XL was the overhead-valve engine layout that replaced the side-valve K series design. The new XL motor retained the KH's 883cc capacity although it had a wider bore and shorter stroke, which allowed bigger valves and higher revs. Other features of that first Sportster model were its cast iron cylinder heads, and the 'Sportster' logo cast into the engine's primary drive cover. The bike had two-tone paint, telescopic forks, twin shocks with chrome covers, and a single sprung saddle.

Cycle magazine found the XL capable of just over 100mph (161km/h), and reported that the XL had 'terrific acceleration all through the rev range', and that 'high cruising speeds can be sustained indefinitely without effort from the ruggedly

constructed engine.' Although such performance was not a huge improvement on that of the side-valve KHK model, the XL was an instant hit, selling almost twice the number that the K-series models had managed in 1956.

Growing reputation

A legend had been born, and in subsequent years it quickly grew, through a number of Sportster variants, many of which adopted the tiny factory-

option peanut gas tank that had originally been fitted to Harley's little two-stroke 125cc Model S or Hummer. There was the off-road XLC, stripped of lights and with open pipes; and the XLH with its tuned engine. Fastest of all was the XLCH – originally a California-only dirt-bike with no lights *and* hot motor, but in 1959 broadened to a full '50-state' road-legal model whose lean, basic, engine-dominated look and thunderous performance epitomized the Sportster's appeal.

From 1960 the hotter H engine was used for all Sportsters, and subsequent years saw other modifications including the adoption of bigger drum brakes, a headlamp nacelle, 12 volt electrics, a Tillotson instead of Linkert carburettor, and the aforementioned hot cams. Sportster buyers in 1968 could choose either the raw-and-simple XLCH or the XLH, which came with an electric starter for the first time.

The modified engine cases required for the electric foot resulted in the wheelbase lengthening, and new parts, including a bigger battery, increased the bike's dry weight to a substantial 519lb (235kg). But the XLH was still a very rapid motorbike. That V-twin punch and the deep soundtrack were totally addictive, and the Harley's ability to cruise at an indicated 70mph (113km/h), feeling relaxed and reasonably smooth, was undeniably impressive.

Harley continued to change the Sportster over the years, generally improving it slightly,

Specification	Harley-Davidson XL Sportster (1957)
Engine	Air-cooled ohv four-valve pushrod 45-degree V-twin
Capacity	883cc (76.2 x 96.8mm)
Maximum power	40bhp @ 5500rpm
Transmission	Four-speed, chain final drive
Frame	Steel twin downtube
Suspension	Telescopic front; twin shocks rear
Brakes	Drum front and rear
Weight	463lb (210kg)
Top speed	100mph (161km/h)

occasionally taking a step backwards (as with the ugly boat-tail seat, introduced in 1971 and quickly dropped). In 1974 the engine was bored out to 1000cc and a disc front brake was introduced. The 1978-model Anniversary Sportster featured cast wheels, twin discs and black paint. Other variants included the XLS Roadster of 1980, with its big tank and high bars; the rapid but unreliable XR-1000 special of 1983; and, most significantly, the 1986-model XLH 883, with its Evolution engine in the traditional 54 cubic inch (883cc) capacity.

The Sportster has remained successful into the 21st century, with innovations such as the 1200cc motor and the low-slung Hugger. Recent models have combined that unmistakable XLH look with belt final drive and Milwaukee's improved quality control. But for all the modern models' style and efficiency, there's one area where they are no match for the old Sportsters: they can't outrun the fastest opposition of the day.

Below left: This XL engine was uprated to XLH specification in 1958, when larger valves, lighter tappets and higher 9:1 compression ratio added 5bhp, giving a total of 45bhp. Later models gained style with a tiny peanut tank but lost this bike's Sportster chaincase logo.

Below: In recent years the Sportster has been hugely popular while not living up to its name, but the 1996 model XL1200S Sportster Sport gave a performance boost with its uprated suspension and brakes.

Triumph Thunderbird 650

**Top speed
103mph**
166km/h

*Right: This 1957-model
T-bird's handsome styling is
similar to that of Triumph's
499cc models, but the
649cc engine delivered
useful extra performance.*

*Below: Thunderbird
handling was improved with
the arrival of Triumph's
twin-shock chassis in the
mid-1950s, but it was for
straight-line speed that the
model remained best known.*

The world's most inviting motorcycle market in the 1950s was the USA, where Triumph boss Edward Turner, in particular, was eager to exploit the potential presented by hordes of performance-hungry motorcyclists and a struggling home industry. Turner's enthusiasm led directly to one of Triumph's most significant models, because it was largely American demand for more cubes and power that led to the Thunderbird, the British firm's fastest bike yet.

Essentially the T-bird, as it was commonly known, was a 650cc version of Triumph's existing 500cc Speed Twin. Enlarging the pushrod-operated parallel twin engine to 649cc gave a peak output of 34bhp at 6300rpm, a gain of 7bhp over the Speed Twin (4bhp over the sportier Tiger 100), plus a healthy increase in torque throughout the range. This resulted in a significant performance boost because at 385lb (175kg) the Thunderbird weighed barely more than the smaller models.

Triumph launched the Thunderbird in September 1949 at the banked circuit of Montlhéry, near Paris, where the first three bikes off the production line were ridden for 500 miles (805km) at an average speed of over 92mph (148km/h), with a last lap of over 100mph (161km/h). Apart from minor modifications including fitment of rearset footrests and racing tyres, they were standard, so it was an impressive introduction.

Predictably the T-bird was well received in Britain and abroad. More even than its top speed, it was the torquey 650's ability to maintain a high average that impressed testers. 'So fast is the Thunderbird that during the test the maximum speed at which the machine could be cruised, without engine fatigue becoming apparent, was never determined,' reported *The Motor Cycle*. 'When road conditions permitted, speeds of 80, 85, 90mph [129, 137, 145km/h] were often held for as long as the rider could withstand the buffeting force of wind pressure.'

High excitement

In America, *Cycle* magazine's test declared the T-bird almost faultless, though the original model's blue colour was unpopular. Triumph's American advertising emphasized the performance, screaming: 'See the most exciting motorcycle ever!' from the pages of the 1950 New York Show programme. 'Why be satisfied with second-rate performance, choose a Triumph and get ahead.'

Thousands did just that, and the Thunderbird became a huge success for Triumph, firmly establishing the marque on the American market. The model received a boost in 1953 from the movie *The Wild One*, in which Marlon Brando's lead character rode a 1950 model Thunderbird. Until this point, motorcycles had appeared in films with

Tiger 110 – Triumph's Hotter 650

The Thunderbird was a big hit but Triumph soon moved to upgrade it, and in 1954 launched a tuned 650cc model, the T110 Tiger. This had sportier cams, higher compression ratio, modified porting and a larger Amal carburettor, which increased peak output to 42bhp. The Tiger was Triumph's fastest model yet, and quickly became popular. Numerous updates included the fitment of a bathtub enclosure in 1960, by which time its status as Triumph's hot 650 had been taken by the twin-carb Bonneville.

Specification	Triumph Thunderbird (1957)
Engine	Air-cooled ohv pushrod four-valve parallel twin
Capacity	649cc (71 x 82mm)
Maximum power	34bhp @ 6300rpm
Transmission	Four-speed, chain final drive
Frame	Steel cradle
Suspension	Telescopic front; twin shocks rear
Brakes	Drum front and rear
Weight	385lb (175kg)
Top speed	103mph (166km/h)

their tank badges covered up. But the T-bird starred in all its glory, and plenty of extra sales resulted.

Handling was good without being outstanding, and was improved in the mid-1950s when Triumph introduced a new twin-shock frame, replacing the original model's option of hard-tail or sprung-hub rear suspension. A further chassis improvement came in 1960, when the Thunderbird was also one of numerous models to receive Triumph's controversial 'bathtub' enclosed rear end. By this time the T-bird had been relegated to a touring role by the faster Tiger 110, but its place in Triumph's history was assured.

Left: Triumph's pushrod twin had been hugely impressive in its original 499cc capacity, but gained valuable power and torque when enlarged to 649cc to power the Thunderbird. In this form it has a single Amal carburettor, separate four-speed gearbox, and maximum output of 34bhp. It vibrated at high revs, but was reliable as well as fast.

Royal Enfield Constellation

**Top speed
112mph**
180km/h

Right: Low handlebars and a big Smiths speedometer, calibrated to 150mph (241km/h), emphasized the Constellation's sporty nature.

Below: The Constellation's large chromed fuel tank and heavily finned engine gave a muscular look that was backed-up by the Enfield's storming straight-line performance.

If Royal Enfield could have endowed its Constellation with the reliability to match its performance, the result would have been a formidable machine. The 692cc parallel twin was one of the fastest bikes on the road following its launch in 1958. In that year one Constellation was clocked at 116mph (187km/h), giving it an edge over rival firms' twins, and a magazine tester recorded an equally impressive two-way average of 112mph (180km/h).

Very few bikes on the road could live with the Constellation on acceleration from a standing start either, and the big motor also had plenty of low-down torque. But Royal Enfield's hopes that the Constellation's straight-line speed would result in big sales came to nothing, largely because when ridden hard the big twin too often proved unreliable. Its list of problems included conrod failure at high revs, a slipping clutch and oil leaks.

The Constellation's problems were highlighted by Enfield's experiences in long-distance production racing. Factory ace Bob McIntyre led the prestigious Thruxton 500-mile (805km) race four years in a row but had trouble each time. He managed a third place in 1958, despite losing time

with a split fuel tank. But a year later the Scot crashed out of the race as he tried to make up ground after a clutch problem. And he crashed at high speed in each of the next two years' races, both times due to engine failure.

Biting the Bullet

Royal Enfield's big twins had always been distinctive, due to their styling and unusual engine size. That 692cc capacity, which made them the biggest British parallel twins, came about because Enfield had originally produced the engine for the 1953-model Meteor by combining two 346cc single-cylinder Bullet engines. The first Meteor produced only 36bhp, but this was increased to 40bhp in 1956 with the release of the Super Meteor.

Two years later the Constellation was launched with a comprehensively revised motor. Modifications included hotter camshafts positioned higher in the engine, lighter pushrods, reworked valves and cylinder heads, stronger crankshaft, higher compression ratio, new clutch and lower gearing. Peak output increased to 51bhp at 6250rpm. (The engines were manufactured not at Enfield's base at Redditch in Worcestershire, but underground in a bomb-proof former wartime factory near Bradford-on-Avon in Wiltshire.)

In Enfield tradition the motor formed a stressed member of the single-downtube frame, which was similar to that of the Super Meteor. Most cycle parts were also carried over but the Constellation had a new tank and siamesed exhaust system, plus a Smiths speedometer calibrated to 150mph (241km/h). The chassis worked reasonably well. Suspension and brakes were competent, and the Enfield could hold its own with most rivals in the bends.

The same was true on the straights, but making use of the Constellation's performance for extended periods was a risky business. The Enfield responded with a burst of speed when asked, but was happier cruising at 70mph (113km/h), at which pace it was smooth and reliable. The low handlebars gave a comfortable lean forward into the wind, and Enfield was also ahead of its time in offering an optional Airflow full fairing. But the bike's undoubted high-rev performance was compromised by its vibration and fragility.

By 1963, the Constellation's last year before its motor was enlarged to produce the Interceptor 750, Enfield had introduced numerous modifications that did much to improve it. Compression ratio was reduced, crankcase breathing improved in an

attempt to reduce oil leaks, the clutch redesigned and the crankshaft rebalanced to reduce vibration. But the Constellation's reputation ensured that its sales figures would never be as impressive as its performance statistics.

Above: The Constellation's siamesed exhaust system gave the bike an unusually clean look when viewed from the left. Its low bars dictated an aggressively forward-leaning riding position that was well suited to high speeds, especially when the bike was fitted with Enfield's optional Airflow full fairing.

Left: Straight-line performance was impressive all the way to a genuine top speed of well over 100mph (161km/h), provided the 692cc parallel twin motor remained reliable. At a more gentle pace, the Constellation was fairly smooth and undoubtedly pleasant to ride.

Specification	Royal Enfield Constellation (1958)
Engine	Air-cooled ohv pushrod four-valve parallel twin
Capacity	692cc (70 x 90mm)
Maximum power	51bhp @ 6250rpm
Transmission	Four-speed, chain final drive
Frame	Steel single downtube
Suspension	Telescopic front, twin shocks rear
Brakes	Drum front and rear
Weight	427lb (194kg)
Top speed	112mph (180km/h)

Moto Guzzi Falcone

**Top speed
75mph**
121km/h

*Right: The flat single
engine layout, with its big
'bacon slicer' flywheel, had
been a Moto Guzzi feature
for almost 30 years when
the Falcone was introduced
in 1950.*

*Below: Despite its racy red
paintwork, this 1964 model
Falcone's raised handlebars
signify that it's a Turismo
model, and not the slightly
more powerful Sport.*

The Falcone was the best known and
longest lived of the numerous 500cc flat
single models that Moto Guzzi produced
for more than half a century. Its distinctive engine
layout, incorporating the large 'bacon slicer'
external flywheel, dated all the way back to the
Normale model with which the firm's founders
Carlo Guzzi and Giorgio Parodi had begun
production in 1921.

Guzzi's singles had already established a strong
reputation when the Falcone was introduced in
1950. The new bike was a modified version of the
Astore, which had evolved from the similar GTV.
Those road bikes were closely related to an exotic
band of Guzzi customer road-racing singles – the
Condor, Albatros and Dondolino. The Condor had
been introduced in the mid-1930s. It was a street-
legal competition bike with lights and silencers,
and it won the Milano-Taranto race in 1940. After
the Second World War the single was reintroduced
with extra power and the rather unusual name of
Dondolino meaning rocking-chair.

The Falcone cost half as much as the exotic
Dondolino, but looked suitably sporty, with slim
lines, red paintwork and low handlebars. Its 498cc
pushrod-operated, alloy engine featured numerous
racing developments including a four-speed
gearbox from the Condor, though its crankcases
were cast from aluminium, rather than lightweight
electron, and its valves were enclosed rather than
exposed like those of the racing engines. Peak
output was 23bhp at 4500rpm.

Far left: Guzzi's unique chassis dated back to the 1920s and was very old-fashioned by 1964, but the Falcone handled acceptably nevertheless.

Left: The Falcone's curiously raised headlight allowed room for a siren, as the model was popular with the Carabinieri (police).

Its chassis was a uniquely Guzzi construction, based on a frame that combined steel plates with twin front downtubes. The rear suspension system was unusual, and dated back to Guzzis of the 1920s. The swingarm worked a pair of springs that sat in a box beneath the engine. Smaller rebound springs, between the engine and swingarm, worked in conjunction with adjustable friction dampers between the swingarm and rear subframe.

Most of the changes that Guzzi made to the Falcone over its long life were minor, the most significant coming in 1954 when the original model became the Falcone Sport and a new version, the Turismo, was introduced. This looked very similar and shared the same frame and suspension, but had higher handlebars, forward-set footrests and a detuned engine that produced 19bhp and reduced top speed slightly to 75mph (121km/h).

Limited production numbers

The Falcone was never produced in great numbers, with only a few hundred being built in most years. The model's fame spread, however, helped by the success of factory-entered Falcones in long-distance events such as the Milano-Taranto and Giro d'Italia during the early 1950s. That reputation was misleading, because those Falcones were far from standard, often using Dondolino engine parts that increased top speed to over 100mph (161km/h).

These race-winning machines were similar in looks but much faster than the dependable Falcone that finally reached the end of its production in 1968. Only a year later Guzzi introduced the Nuovo Falcone, combining an updated engine with a more modern twin-shock chassis. This sold quite well and remained in production for another seven years. But it lacked the style and sporty image of the original, much loved Falcone.

Specification	Moto Guzzi Falcone Turismo (1958)
Engine	Air-cooled ohv pushrod two-valve single
Capacity	498cc (88 x 82mm)
Maximum power	19bhp @ 4300rpm
Transmission	Four-speed, chain final drive
Frame	Steel twin downtube
Suspension	Telescopic front; horizontal springs & friction dampers rear
Brakes	Drum front and rear
Weight	368lb (167kg)
Top speed	75mph (121km/h)

Guzzi's Glamorous V8

Moto Guzzi had great racing success with its singles, notably in winning three 250cc world championships between 1949 and '52, and five consecutive 350cc titles from 1953. And racing inspired the most famous Guzzi of all: the 500cc V8 of 1956. Engineer Giulio Carcano's exotic liquid-cooled, quad-cam, 90-degree V8 revved to 12,000rpm, produced 72bhp and was timed at 178mph (286km/h) at the Belgian GP in 1957. But Guzzi pulled out of Grand Prix racing at the end of that season, before the V8 – pictured here with Bill Lomas, one of its original riders, at the Isle of Man TT in 1996 – had a chance to make its mark.

Norton Dominator 88

**Top speed
95mph**
153km/h

Right: This 1960 model
Dominator has the slimline
Featherbed frame and
narrower fuel tank that
were introduced in that
year, making the Norton
more manageable.

Below: The 1958 Dominator
88 combined the original
wideline Featherbed with
Norton's 497cc parallel
twin engine. The result was
superb handling plus lively
straight-line performance.

Norton took more than ten years to
compete with Triumph by producing a
parallel twin roadster of its own. But
eventually in 1949 the firm unleashed a rival to the
Speed Twin, in the form of the Model 7, known as
the Dominator. The new bike centred on a 497cc
ohv pushrod engine created by Norton's chief
designer Bert Hopwood, who had previously
worked with Speed Twin designer Edward Turner
at both Ariel and Triumph.

Hopwood's engine differed in numerous ways
from Triumph's twin, not least in having a single
camshaft in front of the engine, instead of two
separate cams at back and front. Although the
Dominator was not particularly powerful, with a
peak output of 29bhp, it was tractable, reliable and
reasonably smooth. The motor was also compact
because for cost-saving reasons it was designed to
fit in the frame from Norton's top-of-the-range
single, the ES2.

Featherbed frame

That was no handicap, because the Model 7's light weight and sound chassis combined to give good handling – at least until the plunger rear suspension system became worn, after which the bike would weave at speed. Norton's response came with the bike's replacement, the Dominator 88, which was launched on the export market in 1952 and in Britain in '53. This featured the 497cc engine in a roadgoing version of Norton's twin-shock Featherbed frame.

The Featherbed had become famous through its use on the single-cylinder racing Manx. But the McCandless brothers, its creators, had always intended it to be capable of housing various types of Norton engine and gearbox, and the distinctive twin-loop design proved ideally suited to the twin-cylinder powerplant. 'That this frame is race bred is universally known,' enthused *Motor Cycling* in a test of the Dominator. 'It deserves to be as widely known that the steering is a delight and the handling a bend-swinger's dream.'

Norton uprated the engine several times during the decade. In 1955 the 88 unit gained an alloy cylinder head, higher compression and Amal Monobloc carburettor. A year later came the Dominator 99, with its engine bored and stroked to increase capacity to 597cc, and output to 31bhp. The Dominator 99's race-developed Daytona camshaft, also adopted by the 88, helped lift the larger model's top speed to just over 100mph (161km/h).

In 1960 Norton made a further improvement by fitting both models with the firm's new slimline Featherbed frame – a narrower version of the original – along with a new rear sub-frame and narrower fuel tank. Some riders have argued that the wideline frame is more rigid and gives better handling under racing conditions. But for roadgoing use there was no difference, and the slimline Dominator was notably more manageable for the short of leg.

Either way, one of the Dominator's great strengths was that its chassis remained very much in control of its powerplant. Norton's engine was never the most powerful of contemporary twins. Although the Dominator 88 had reasonably brisk acceleration and a respectable top speed of about 95mph (153km/h), riders in search of straight-line thrills were better rewarded by rival twins from Triumph or BSA.

But if the 88's engine was unexceptional, its chassis made up for that. On a long, straight road

there were several bikes that would show the Norton Dominator a clean pair of silencers. But when there were plenty of bends on the route, the Dominator's flexible power delivery, superb handling and unbeatable roadholding made the Norton both very fast and wonderfully enjoyable to ride.

Above: The Dominator 88 engine of 1958 benefited from improvements, notably alloy cylinder head, higher compression ratio and Amal Monobloc carburettor.

Specification	Norton Dominator 88 (1958)
Engine	Air-cooled ohv pushrod four-valve parallel twin
Capacity	497cc (66 x 73mm)
Maximum power	30bhp @ 7000rpm
Transmission	Four-speed, chain final drive
Frame	Steel twin cradle Featherbed
Suspension	Roadholder telescopic front; twin shocks rear
Brakes	Drum front and rear
Weight	405lb (184kg)
Top speed	95mph (153km/h)

Matchless G12 de Luxe

**Top speed
100mph**
161km/h

*Below: This is a Matchless
G12 de Luxe from 1959,
when little more than fresh
paintwork and new badges
would have been enough to
turn it into an AJS Model
31. The motorcycling
public's loyalty to one or
other marque made such
'badge engineering'
worthwhile, although both
makes of bike were
produced at the Matchless
factory in south London.*

In many ways the story of the Matchless
parallel twin was typical of the British
industry: repeated increases in engine
capacity and power, though not always a better bike
as a result. After being introduced in 1949 with a
capacity of 498cc, the engine was enlarged over the
years, mainly to meet the demands of the American
export market. The original G9 became the 592cc
G11 in 1956, and three years later the G12 was
created when the motor was enlarged again, this
time to 646cc.

Plenty of riders were impressed with the result.
'Docility and high performance make a rare
combination,' said the tester from *The Motor
Cycle*. 'Top-gear tractability you can have, speed
you can have, but both? Yes both! In the latest
646cc Matchless G12 de Luxe you can. A bulldog
with all the get-up-and-go of a greyhound, this is
the twin to which everything comes alike, whether
it be a gentle potter about the lanes at 30mph
[48km/h] or a blast along the M1 at 80mph
[129km/h] on half throttle.'

Not every rider was as enthusiastic as that
tester, but the G12 was a competent and reasonably
popular machine, with lively acceleration, a top
speed of just over 100mph (161km/h), and
excellent handling. It was also acceptably reliable,
at least in Standard form or as the De Luxe, which
featured a quickly-detachable rear wheel and
uprated ignition system.

Over-developed engine

Fastest of the G12 family was the CSR, which had
a higher compression ratio, siamesed exhaust,
narrower seat and alloy mudguards. The G12 CSR
was good for a top speed of 108mph (174km/h) but
suffered from vibration and poor reliability, and
was regarded by many as an example of an engine
being developed too far.

There were significant differences between the
G12 family and rival parallel twins – though very
few between the G12 and the AJS Model 31, which
were essentially the same bike. Matchless was a
famous old south London-based marque whose co-
founder Charlie Collier had won the single-cylinder
race at the first ever Isle of Man TT back in 1907.
The firm had taken over its rival, AJS of
Wolverhampton, in 1931.

Left: The G12's sound handling combined with a broad spread of power and reasonable turn of speed to make the twin an enjoyable bike to ride, especially in this De Luxe version. The more powerful and sporty CSR model was faster, but vibrated more and was less reliable.

The combined firm took the name Associated Motor Cycles (AMC) and later acquired marques including Francis Barnett, James and, in 1952, once mighty Norton. AJS and Matchless were most closely linked because, in a blatant example of 'badge engineering', almost identical machines were built at the Matchless factory in Plumstead and marketed under both names. The Matchless 500cc G9 differed from the AJS Model 20 by little more than paint (typically red for Matchless, blue for AJS). The G11 was the Model 30, and the G12 the Model 31.

The main difference between the AMC engine and the other British twins of the period was its central crankshaft bearing. Designer Phil Walker's intention had been to stiffen the bottom end, to reduce high-rev vibration. In fact the Matchless/AJS motor shook to match the worst of them, and some experts considered its extra bearing a hindrance rather than a help.

Despite that the G9/Model 20 was a pleasant bike, with plenty of mid-range performance and a respectable top speed of 90mph (145km/h). That flexibility remained when the engine was bored-out to 592cc to create the G11/Model 30. As the engine could not be bored-out any further, a new long-stroke crankshaft was developed for the 646cc G12/Model 31. The larger engine's unreliability in tuned CSR form did not deter AMC, who in 1965

produced a Matchless G15/AJS Model 33 powered by the 750cc engine from the Norton Atlas. But by this time the firm was in financial trouble, and production ended in 1967.

Above: The Matchless 'winged M' badge was well known in the 1950s, when the firm had expanded under the AMC name to take over rivals including Norton, as well as AJS.

Left: The G12's engine differed from other British parallel twins mainly in having a central crankshaft bearing, which did little to reduce vibration. This 646cc motor was developed from the previous G11's 592cc unit, using a long-stroke crankshaft.

Specification	Matchless G12 de Luxe (1959)
Engine	Air-cooled ohv pushrod four-valve parallel twin
Capacity	646cc (72 x 79.3mm)
Maximum power	35bhp @ 6000rpm
Transmission	Four-speed, chain final drive
Frame	Steel twin cradle
Suspension	Telescopic front; twin shocks rear
Brakes	Drum front and rear
Weight	396lb (180kg)
Top speed	100mph (161km/h)

The 1960s
Britain's
Last Stand

In many respects the 1960s marked the high point of the British motorcycle industry. The bikes were faster and better than ever before. Rapid twins such as the Triumph Bonneville and Norton Commando traded blows with rivals as varied as Velocette's racy Venom Thruxton single and Triumph's three-cylinder Trident 750.

But the British firms' outstanding new machines could not hide the fact that problems were brewing with financial trouble ahead. Meanwhile the decade's most significant arrival was that of the Japanese. Models such as Honda's CB450 and Suzuki's T500 combined sophisticated engineering with increasingly impressive performance, and gave a hint of the exciting bikes soon to follow.

Triumph T120 Bonneville

**Top speed
110mph**
177km/h

*Right: Handling was less
of a Bonneville strong point
than engine performance,
but a 1961-model T120R
was well suited to rapid
cornering.*

*Below: Few Triumph
enthusiasts agree on which
Bonneville model is best or
most attractive, but this
1961 model would get
plenty of votes.*

The Bonneville remains Triumph's most
famous model of all, and for very good
reason. Launched in 1959 as a hotted-up,
twin-carb version of the Meriden firm's existing
650cc vertical twin, the T120 Bonneville was
advertised as offering 'the highest performance
available today from a standard production
motorcycle' – and the Bonnie lived up to its billing.

For much of the following decade the T120 was
as fast as any production bike on the road, and it
was a long-lasting hit for Triumph. Bonneville-
based bikes were also raced successfully all around
the world, from the Isle of Man TT to American
dirt tracks. The Bonnie was repeatedly updated,
enlarged to 750cc, and survived into the 1980s. No
wonder John Bloor's reborn Triumph concern
chose the famous name for its new generation
parallel twin, launched in 2001.

Back in 1959, the name Bonneville was
evocative of speed and excitement for a different
reason. Triumph's legendary boss Edward Turner
chose it in honour of the record-breaking run by
Johnny Allen, who in 1956 had taken a streamlined,
Triumph twin-engined machine to 214mph
(344km/h) at the Bonneville salt flats in Utah,
USA. The American market was Triumph's biggest,
and the name fitted the new bike perfectly.

The original T120 was relatively simple for Triumph to develop. Its format of 649cc parallel twin, with pushrod valve operation, four-speed gearbox and 360-degree crankshaft was that of the Tiger 110. In 1958 the Tiger had been available with an optional cylinder head with splayed inlet ports, for fitment of twin carburettors, plus a list of optional tuning parts including high-performance camshafts and Amal racing carbs.

Following demand from its US distributors for a high-performance model, Triumph incorporated hot cams and twin, filterless Amal Monobloc carbs in the new T120, increasing peak output by 4bhp to 46bhp. Initially the Bonneville, which was conceived in such a hurry that it wasn't even included in the firm's 1959 catalogue, retained the Tiger's headlamp nacelle and touring handlebars. For 1960 it gained a separate headlamp shell and sportier mudguards, plus a redesigned twin-cradle frame that gave steeper steering geometry and a shorter wheelbase.

The frame was strengthened for 1961, by which time the Bonneville had become firmly established as a stylish and fast road-burner. British magazine *Motor Cycling* wrote in June 1961 of the 'outstanding acceleration and high top speed – without temperament' of a bike that lapped a banked test-track at an impressive average of 108mph (174km/h). Three months later the magazine tripped the timing lights at 117mph (188km/h) on the same bike, now revving higher after being fitted with Triumph's high-performance option of 'chopped' Amal Monobloc carburettors sharing a single float bowl.

Easy handling and good looks

The Bonneville was regularly updated over the next decade, notably with the adoption of a unit-construction engine and gearbox in 1963. Chassis stability did not always match engine performance, but the Bonnie remained much loved for its light weight, easy handling and good looks. In 1971 the twin gained a new 'oil-in-frame' chassis, which was much criticized until lowered a year later. In 1973 Triumph increased capacity to 744cc to produce the T140 Bonneville, which was more flexible, if no faster and less smooth.

Bonnevilles were raced with great success, notably in the Isle of Man, where John Hartle won the production TT in 1967, and Malcolm Uphill set the first production 100mph (161km/h) lap on the way to victory in 1969. During the 1960s the T120 took four wins in the annual 500-mile (805km) production race at Thruxton and Brands Hatch, with riders including Triumph tester Percy Tait. The Bonnie was still competitive on the track in 1978, when Steve Trasler's T140 beat the Japanese fours to win the British production championship.

Above left: The Silver Jubilee Bonneville of 1977 was a special edition of the 750cc T140, built by Triumph to celebrate Queen Elizabeth II's 25 years on the British throne. The Bonnie was old-fashioned compared to Japanese rivals, though not without performance and charm.

Above right: The Bonneville made a return in 2001, when John Bloor's reborn Triumph firm introduced a roadster twin, styled after a 1968-model T120 but with a modern 790cc, dohc eight-valve engine. Ironically the new 61bhp Bonnie was no faster than many old models.

Specification	Triumph T120 Bonneville (1961)
Engine	Air-cooled four-valve ohv pushrod parallel twin
Capacity	649cc (71 x 82mm)
Maximum power	46bhp @ 6500rpm
Transmission	Four-speed, chain final drive
Frame	Steel twin downtube
Suspension	Telescopic front; twin shocks rear
Brakes	Drum front and rear
Weight	403lb (183kg) wet
Top speed	110mph (177km/h)

Norton 650SS

**Top speed
115mph**
185km/h

*Below: The 650SS was a
fine all-round sports
machine, with plenty of
straight-line speed plus
excellent handling from a
chassis combining
Featherbed frame and
Roadholder front forks. It
was very stylish too, with
paintwork in Norton's
traditional silver. This 1966
model is fitted with optional
rev-counter and chromed
mudguards.*

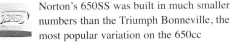 Norton's 650SS was built in much smaller
numbers than the Triumph Bonneville, the
most popular variation on the 650cc
vertical twin theme favoured by the British
manufacturers in the 1960s. But the disparity in
production levels was not a fair reflection on the
worth of the 650SS, whose speed, handling and
refinement made it one of the finest machines on
the road for much of the decade.

When the 650SS was launched in 1962, it was
the latest example of the Bert Hopwood-designed
Dominator twin line that had begun with the Model
7 in 1949. In 1956 the motor had been enlarged to
597cc to create the Dominator 99; and in 1961
Norton had produced a long-stroke 646cc engine to
power the Manxman 650 export model. By this
time there were also SS (Sports Special) versions of
the 500 and 600cc bikes, with twin carburettors and
higher compression.

Impressive powerplant

Combining the Sports Special specification with
the larger capacity gave an impressive new
powerplant, which also incorporated modifications
including larger big-end bearings and a heavier
flywheel. The 650SS also featured a new downdraft
cylinder head, developed from engineer Doug
Hele's Domiracer competition machine. Peak
output was 49bhp at 6800rpm.

The new engine was held in a familiar chassis
combining Norton's Featherbed twin-cradle frame
and Roadholder front forks. At 400lb (181kg) dry
the 650SS weighed barely more than the smaller
models, and had a racy look enhanced by
paintwork in Norton's traditional silver. Options
included chromed mudguards, and the addition of a
rev-counter alongside the Smiths speedometer. That
speedo was put to good use, because the 650SS
was capable of almost 120mph (193km/h). It was

also pleasantly flexible and impressively economical (though the downdraft carburettor arrangement caused a few flooding problems), as well as smooth by parallel twin standards.

Given Norton's reputation for handling, it was no surprise that the 650SS excelled in the bends. This was a real sports machine, with a firm ride and a thin seat. Its steering and stability were outstanding, as was the efficiency of its drum brakes. Like the other SS models, the 650 was fitted with an Avon Grand Prix rear tyre, which also helped justify Norton's advertising boast of it being 'the world's best road holder'.

Predictably the model was given enthusiastic reviews. *Motor Cycling* praised the 'sporting top end without the bad manners associated with such urge at low speeds'. Rival magazine *The Motor Cycle* speed-tested the 650SS at 118mph (190km/h), and applauded a bike whose 'quietness, smoothness and lack of fuss make speed deceptive; a machine with such superb handling and braking as to make nearly two miles a minute as safe as a stroll in the garden'.

The Norton impressed in production endurance races, taking Phil Read and Brian Setchell to wins in the Thruxton 500-mile (805km) and Silverstone 1000-mile (1609km) events within months of its launch. A 650SS also won the Thruxton race the following two years, and was voted *Motor Cycle News* machine of the year in 1962 and '63. Despite that, the 650SS never came close to matching the Bonneville in popularity, partly because it was more than 10 per cent more expensive, and partly because troubled Norton produced relatively few bikes at that time.

The final batch of machines built at Norton's famous factory in Bracebridge Street, Birmingham, were 650SS models in police specification, destined for Queensland in Australia. The model survived Norton's acquisition by Associated Motor Cycles in 1963, and the move to Woolwich in south London. It continued in production, with few changes, until 1968.

Above left: The SS initials stood for Sports Special, and the Norton lived up to its name. The silver machine was competitive whether roaring on the road, or in long-distance production races.

Above: Norton made few compromises to comfort with the 650SS, which had firm suspension, a fairly thin dual-seat and a sticky Avon Grand Prix rear tyre.

Left: The Norton's 646cc parallel twin engine was boosted with modifications including a downdraft cylinder head, and produced a healthy peak output of 49bhp plus plenty of low-rev torque.

Specification	Norton 650SS (1962)
Engine	Air-cooled ohv pushrod four-valve parallel twin
Capacity	646cc (68 x 89mm)
Maximum power	49bhp @ 6800rpm
Transmission	Four-speed, chain final drive
Frame	Steel twin-cradle Featherbed
Suspension	Roadholder telescopic front; twin shocks rear
Brakes	Drum front and rear
Weight	400lb (181kg)
Top speed	115mph (185km/h)

BSA Rocket Gold Star

**Top speed
115mph**
185km/h

*Right: Filterless carbs hint
at the tuned, 646cc twin-
cylinder engine, which
incorporated high-
compression pistons, hot
cams and racing style
magneto ignition.*

*Below: The Rocket Goldie's
resemblance to the famous
Gold Star single was clear
at a glance.*

 The final and most exciting of BSA's long
line of 'pre-unit' 646cc parallel twins,
which had started with the Golden Flash
back in 1949, came in 1962 with the launch of the
mighty Rocket Gold Star. In the same year that the
Birmingham firm introduced its new line of 'unit-
construction' motors, with combined engine and
gearbox, the Rocket Gold Star proved that there
was still plenty of life in the old format.

The Rocket Goldie was inspired by a one-off
special that Gold Star specialist Eddie Dow of
Banbury in Oxfordshire had built for a customer
several years earlier. That bike had simply been a
Gold Star single with a twin-cylinder engine fitted.
The production A10 RGS model incorporated a
number of modifications to this basic concept, but
was essentially a blend of BSA's Super Rocket
engine in a chassis based on that of the Gold Star.

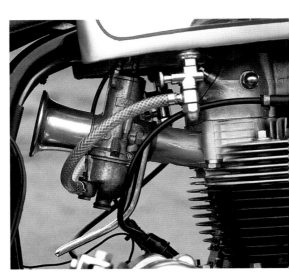

Specification	BSA Rocket Gold Star (1962)
Engine	Air-cooled ohv pushrod four-valve parallel twin
Capacity	646cc (70 x 84mm)
Maximum power	46bhp @ 6250rpm
Transmission	Four-speed, chain final drive
Frame	Steel twin downtube
Suspension	Telescopic front; twin shocks rear
Brakes	Drum front and rear
Weight	418lb (190kg)
Top speed	115mph (185km/h)

Twin-cradle frame

The frame was a twin-cradle design very similar to that of the single, but without the distinctive kink in its lower right loop that was needed to clear the Goldie's oil pump. The RGS look was very similar to that of the famed single, with chromed mudguards and a silver tank with chromed sides, plus the familiar Gold Star tank badge on a red circular background.

Cynics claimed the Rocket Gold Star had been created mainly to use up supplies of the pre-unit powerplant, which was uprated to power the new machine. The specification included an aluminium cylinder head with higher 9:1 compression ratio, hotter cams, plus a race-style magneto with manual advance-retard adjustment. This combined to increase peak output slightly to 46bhp at 6250rpm, or 50bhp if the optional Gold Star-type racing silencer was used.

The twin's chassis was every bit as purposeful as the engine. The RGS was available with a variety of options, and was typically fitted not only with low 'Ace' handlebars, but also Gold Star gaitered forks, large-capacity aluminium fuel tank, close-ratio gearbox, siamesed exhaust system, humped racing seat, alloy wheel rims, big front drum brake in a full-width hub, plus matching speedometer and rev-counter.

That added up to a strikingly stylish bike that was every bit as fast as it looked, and which became highly regarded by the cafe-racer crowd in particular. Top speed was a genuine 115mph (185km/h) in good conditions, with 90mph (145km/h) cruising a practical proposition thanks to the tucked-down riding position. Handling was also good, though not perfect; one contemporary test reported that the front wheel tended to wander at very high speed.

In 1963, *Motorcycle Mechanics* magazine tested a production-race specification Rocket Gold Star which, tuned further with higher-compression pistons and special valve springs, recorded a top speed of no less than 123mph (198km/h). But at the end of that year BSA abandoned production of the model to concentrate on the new generation of unit-construction motors. The Rocket Gold Star remains the most sought-after of the firm's pre-unit twins, and will long be remembered as a memorable way to end the line.

Above left: Typical view from the Rocket Gold Star's seat was of a pair of black Smiths clocks, a friction steering damper knob at the headstock, and a pair of low, clip-on handlebars that encouraged a suitably racy crouch.

Spitfire – Fast but Fragile

The Rocket Gold Star's successor as BSA's hot twin in 1966 was the A65 Spitfire MkII, which was powered by a tuned, 55bhp version of the firm's 654cc unit-construction engine. 'Here is a model that looks like 120mph [193km/h] and actually does it,' boasted BSA's publicity material of the racy Spitfire, with its red fibreglass fuel tank. But the Spitfire vibrated badly, ran poorly at low revs and was fragile if that performance was used to the full. The following year's Spitfire MkIII was detuned as a result.

Dresda Triton

**Top speed
120mph**
193km/h

*Right: Few bikes could live
with a good Triton's 650cc
Triumph performance in a
straight line, and the same
thing was true of its Norton
Featherbed chassis's
handling ability on a
twisty road.*

*Below: Classical Triton
features included low bars,
long alloy tank, humped
seat, big front drum,
lightweight alloy wheel rims
– plus, of course, the all-
important blend of Triumph
motor and Norton
Featherbed frame.*

 Of all the bikes built under the parallel
twin-cylinder format that dominated
motorcycling in the 1960s, the Triton
embodied the best of both worlds: the straight-line
performance of Triumph's powerful engine, and the
handling ability of the legendary Norton
Featherbed chassis. Tritons were built by numerous
firms and individuals, using a variety of engines
and chassis from those two major manufacturers.
The combination was so successful that the Triton
came to be regarded as a marque in its own right.

The Triton's precise origins are unclear, partly
because several enterprising individuals built
similar hybrids in the mid-1950s. As early as 1954,
London-based racer and engineer Doug Clark used
the chassis of a blown-up Manx Norton single to
house a 650cc Triumph engine. Clark rode the
resultant twin on both road and racetrack. But after
the bike had been noticed by a Triumph employee
while at Silverstone circuit, Clarke received a letter
from the factory threatening legal action if he
continued with the project. He also claimed that
Triumph told its London dealers to refuse to sell
him engine parts.

Appealing concept

The appeal of the Triton concept in the early 1960s
was easy to understand. Triumph's twin had held a
straight-line advantage ever since Norton's new
Model 7 had been outpaced by the Speed Twin in
1949. Ten years later, Triumph's 650cc Tiger 110
was a good 10mph (16km/h) faster than its 600cc
rival the Norton Dominator 99. By the time
Norton's more powerful 650SS arrived in 1962,
Triumph's reputation for speed was secure. But
handling was a different matter. Norton's

Left: These two Tritons were both built by Dresda Engineering, the famous London firm run by racer Dave Degens. The model on the left has a wideline Featherbed frame; the bike on the right is based on a frame from a genuine Manx Norton. One of the lasting attractions of the Triton is that no two bikes are identical.

Featherbed frame and Roadholder forks were notably stronger than their Triumph equivalents, and also came with an impressive racing pedigree.

Those contrasting reputations helped to establish the Triton as the 'dream ticket' for road and track. The bikes varied in their details, featuring different fuel tanks, instruments, seats, suspension parts, and exhaust systems. As well as Triumph's popular twin-carburettor 650cc Bonneville engine, Triton builders used 500cc motors (and later the 750cc unit too). The Featherbed frame could be used in its original Wideline or later Slimline form, as well as being sourced from the Manx single.

Specialist firms including Dresda Autos of west London began building complete Tritons and also conversion kits, some based around Featherbed replica frames of their own construction. The Triton received a boost in 1965 when Dresda boss Dave Degens, a top racer, rode one to victory in the 24-hour endurance event at Montjuic Park in Barcelona, with co-rider Rex Butcher. The winning machine was then ridden at high speed from London to Edinburgh and back by a journalist from *The Motor Cycle*, generating further interest.

Degens also won production races on Tritons, resulting in objections from riders of more standard machinery, but the controversy merely served to generate even more publicity for the hybrid machines. By the mid-1960s several firms were producing complete Tritons, and many others were offering engine plate kits plus parts including fuel tanks and seat units. Degens estimates that Dresda alone built more than 500 Tritons over the next few years, plus many replica frames.

A Triton was still a classy combination in 1969, when *Motorcycle Mechanics* tested a hotted-up Dresda special at 126mph (203km/h), but the boom was almost over. As well as the many high-quality hybrids, there had been more than a few Tritons built with limited expertise and a second-rate blend of Triumph and Norton components. But the legend of the Triton lived on, especially at Dresda, where Degens continued to build, sell and race Tritons into the 21st century.

Specification	Dresda Triton (1965)
Engine	Air-cooled ohv four-valve Triumph parallel twin
Capacity	649cc (71 x 82mm)
Maximum power	50bhp @ 6500rpm
Transmission	Four-speed, chain final drive
Frame	Steel twin-cradle Norton Featherbed
Suspension	Telescopic front; twin shocks rear
Brakes	Drum front and rear
Weight	350lb (159kg)
Top speed	120mph (193km/h)

Left: The very best of British: a tuned 650cc Triumph Bonneville engine in a Manx Featherbed frame. This motor benefits from internal modifications, filterless Amal carbs and a siamesed exhaust system, giving at least 50bhp. The Manx Featherbed frame is discernible by the gentle curve of the rear tube, at the top right of the photo.

Honda CB450

**Top speed
102mph**
164km/h

*Right: The unusual
instrument console included
both a speedometer and
rev-counter. Honda's
parallel twin engine
produced its maximum
power at 8500rpm and was
impressively reliable.*

*Below: The CB450's rather
heavy look was an accurate
reflection of its
performance, but there was
little doubt that this bike
represented the start of a
new era for Honda.*

 Honda made a vivid impact in road-racing
in the early 1960s, winning a string of
world championships with powerful,
high-revving, multi-cylinder machines. But the
Japanese firm's roadsters were limited to relatively
modest small-capacity models of 305cc and less,
which many people thought Honda would be
content to build for years to come. Then came the
CB450, Honda's first big bike – and suddenly the
motorcycle world seemed a very different place.

American magazine *Cycle World*, for one,
understood the significance of the biggest, most
powerful machine yet from Japan. 'Beyond any
doubt, the big news item of the preceding 12
months came when Honda finally announced
('admitted' would be a better word) that there was,
in fact, a new big-displacement addition to their
line of motorcycles,' the magazine commented
when testing the CB450 in 1965.

The 445cc parallel twin's look and layout were
in most respects similar to those of the smaller

twins with which Honda had been building a
reputation for performance and reliability. The
motor had oversquare dimensions of 70 x 57.8mm,
a four-speed gearbox and a 180-degree crankshaft.
It also incorporated several new features, notably
twin overhead camshafts, operated by a long
central chain. Valve springs were an unusual
torsion-bar arrangement, instead of conventional
coil springs.

Beefy Black Bomber

Chassis layout was conventional although the CB450 differed from Honda's smaller models in having a twin-cradle frame instead of the previous steel spine. Its humped fuel tank with chrome side-pieces also enhanced the family feel, while the black paint finish soon inspired the nickname 'Black Bomber'. This was encouraged by Honda's UK advertising line: 'Meet the big black bomber – the biggest beefiest touring twin from Japan!'

Ironically the CB450 did turn out to be more of a tourer than a sports machine. It was not outstandingly powerful or fast. Its maximum output of 43bhp at 8500rpm was 4bhp down on that of Triumph's Bonneville 650. And although Honda claimed a top speed of 112mph (180km/h), when tested by *Cycle World* the CB450 managed only 102mph (164km/h), due partly to over-tall gearing.

In the Honda's defence, it was torquey, smooth, comfortable, reliable, and handled well. But although that helped it become reasonably successful in the States, it was too heavy and softly tuned to make a big impression in Britain, where initial demands for the bike to be excluded from production racing due to its twin cams proved unnecessary. British twins were faster, and Honda never produced the sportier follow-up that was predicted by some observers.

Even so, the CB450 was a landmark model that proved Honda was no longer happy to stick to small-capacity bikes, but planned to challenge the British industry head-on. Before long, other Japanese manufacturers would produce large-capacity bikes to take on Triumph, BSA and Norton, using a variety of engine layouts that would end the long-standing dominance of the British twin. The Japanese were coming, and the CB450 had led the way.

Small Bike, Big Thrills – the CB92

Honda's attack on the world's motorcycle markets began with small-capacity twins, notably the sporty 125cc CB92 and its big brother, the 250cc CB72. The CB92 Benly Super Sport, to give the sohc twin its full name, appeared in export markets in 1961. It produced 15bhp at a heady 10,500rpm, and was good for an impressive 70mph (113km/h). Although the pressed-steel frame gave only average handling, the CB92 was stylish, well braked and neatly engineered. Boosted by Honda's grand prix triumphs, and joined in showrooms by the faster CB72 a year later, it did much to establish Honda as a manufacturer of high-performance bikes.

Above left: Honda's 445cc engine combined a British-style air-cooled parallel twin cylinder layout with twin overhead camshafts.

Left: Handling was quite responsive but the CB450 was not nearly as fast or as exciting as its specification suggested.

Specification	Honda CB450 (1965)
Engine	Air-cooled dohc four-valve parallel twin
Capacity	445cc (70 x 57.8mm)
Maximum power	43bhp @ 8500rpm
Transmission	Four-speed, chain final drive
Frame	Steel twin cradle
Suspension	Telescopic front; twin shocks rear
Brakes	Drum front and rear
Weight	411lb (186kg)
Top speed	102mph (164km/h)

Velocette Venom Thruxton

**Top speed
105mph**
169km/h

*Right: Thruxton's 499cc
motor used a big Amal
carburettor and new
cylinder head to increase
power output to 40bhp.*

*Below: Features including
low handlebars, sticking-up
twin instruments, big front
drum brake and humped
seat gave the Thruxton a
suitably racy appearance.*

The Velocette marque's speciality was
single-cylinder roadsters that were closely
related to racing machines, and the fastest
and most famous of them all was the Venom
Thruxton. Sleek, singleminded and ready to take to
the track with minimal modification, the 500cc
Thruxton was in many respects the ultimate street
racer of the 1960s.

Essentially a tuned and race-kitted version of
the Venom, Velocette's standard (though still
distinctly sporty and uncompromising) large-
capacity model, the Thruxton was named after the
Hampshire circuit where the marque had been
consistently successful in long-distance production
racing. Indeed, the model owed its existence
directly to the competition experience that the firm
from Hall Green in Birmingham had gained, most
notably at the gruelling and prestigious Thruxton
500-mile (805km) event.

Racy Clubman trim

Since 1956 the firm's main sports model had been
the Venom, powered by a 499cc pushrod single
engine with square dimensions of 86 x 86mm. Since
1960 it had been available in racier Clubman trim,
with low bars, high compression piston and other
mods. Then, in 1964, the factory offered a high-
performance kit. This comprised a new cylinder
head, with narrower valve angle, larger inlet valve
and revised porting; plus a big Amal Grand Prix
carburettor, which necessitated fuel and oil tanks
cut away to accommodate its gaping bell-mouth.

For the following year, Velocette incorporated
the kit into the new Venom Thruxton model, which
also featured a suitably shaped tank – finished in
striking silver – plus clip-on handlebars, humped
racing seat, rearset footrests, alloy wheel rims, and
a twin-leading-shoe front drum brake with a big
scoop for cooling air. At a few pence under £370
the Thruxton was expensive (Velo's hand-built
bikes were never cheap, anyway), but it promised a
seriously competitive level of performance.

The Venom Thruxton did not disappoint. Its
uprated engine produced a claimed 40bhp at
6200rpm, which was only a few horsepower up on
the Clubman but was enough to push the single's
top speed to 105mph (169km/h). Despite its high
state of tune the big thumper was tractable, too,

Left: The Thruxton's large-capacity fuel tank was initially finished in silver, and incorporated a cut-out in its base to allow room for the carburettor. The fishtail silencer is a Velocette trademark that dates back many decades.

Below: The idiosyncratic Thruxton is not one of the easiest of bikes to live with, but when running well it delivers a thrilling blend of long-legged cruising ability and stable high-speed handling.

pulling from 2000rpm in top gear and happily ambling along at 3000rpm with plenty of instant acceleration in hand. Inevitably there was some vibration, but this cleared at about 4500rpm, allowing reasonably comfortable 90mph (145km/h) cruising on the open road.

For such a race-bred machine the handling was not flawless, as the rear suspension generated some instability at racing speeds. At 390lb (177kg) the Thruxton was not especially light, either. Typically for such a sporty single, it was also hard to start and was prone to loose bolts due to vibration.

But this was exactly the sort of high-performance, race-derived and uncompromising machine that Velocette enthusiasts preferred. The Thruxton was a success, and more than 1100 were built over the next few years; some of them, by popular request, in Velocette's traditional black-and-gold colouring. The model finished first and second in its class at the Production TT too, both bikes lapping at almost 90mph (145km/h).

Sadly, the Thruxton was untypical of Velocette production, because for years the firm had been moving away from its traditional customer base, with disastrous result. During the 1950s, production of the four-stroke singles had almost been abandoned in favour of the lightweight, two-stroke, fully-enclosed LE, which had failed to sell. The Viceroy, a 250cc scooter, was even more of a flop. Even the plucky Venom Thruxton could not save Velocette, and in 1971 production ended for good.

Specification	Velocette Venom Thruxton (1965)
Engine	Air-cooled ohv two-valve pushrod single
Capacity	499cc (86 x 86mm)
Maximum power	40bhp @ 6200rpm
Transmission	Four-speed, chain final drive
Frame	Steel single downtube
Suspension	Telescopic front; twin shocks rear
Brakes	Drum front and rear
Weight	390lb (177kg)
Top speed	105mph (169km/h)

Suzuki T500

**Top speed
105mph**
169km/h

Right: Suzuki's 492cc two-stroke parallel twin engine lacked sophistication but produced 44bhp, was reliable and had plenty of tuning potential.

Below: The T500's styling was no more outstanding than its performance, but the Suzuki barely changed for almost a decade.

 Suzuki's T500 twin was by no means the most stylish or sophisticated bike of the late 1960s and early '70s, but in terms of providing speed at a cheap price it was outstanding. British twins were generally more expensive and less reliable; the Japanese multis that arrived in the 1970s cost far more. For two-wheeled thrills on a low budget, arguably the only bikes to touch the T500, which was known as the Titan in the States and the Cobra in the UK, were Yamaha's rival 350cc two-strokes.

On its introduction in 1967 the T500 was essentially a larger version of the T20 Super Six two-stroke twin that had shaken up the 250cc market a year earlier. The heavily finned, 492cc air-cooled motor was the centrepiece of a simply styled, reasonably good-looking roadster. The first models had twin 34mm carbs, but after 1969 the

Suzuki used 32mm Mikunis, producing a claimed maximum of 44bhp at 6000rpm. The motor's tuning potential was proved by Suzuki's TR500 twin racebikes, on which riders including Ron Grant and Art Baumann won many races and were timed at over 150mph (241km/h).

Suzuki's Three-cylinder Alternative

Suzuki had a rival two-stroke middleweight of its own in the 1970s, in the shape of the GT550 triple. Launched in 1972, the GT was similar in looks and layout to the GT380 model. Its 543cc air-cooled engine produced 53bhp, giving lively acceleration and a top speed of about 110mph (177km/h). The GT handled reasonably well and was a competent all-rounder, although it was heavier than the T500 as well as more expensive. Like Suzuki's other two-strokes, it fell victim to tightening emissions regulations towards the end of the 1970s.

For a two-stroke the T500 was reasonably torquey, the motor feeling flat at very low revs but pulling fairly crisply from 3000rpm. Above 4000rpm it took off, the note from the twin pipes rising to a high-pitched snarl as the tacho needle span faster towards the 7000rpm redline through the five-speed box. True top speed was between 100mph (161km/h) and a 110mph (177km/h). The earlier models were generally slightly faster due to less restrictive exhausts.

Specification	Suzuki T500 (1967)
Engine	Air-cooled two-stroke parallel twin
Capacity	492cc (70 x 64mm)
Maximum power	44bhp @ 6000rpm
Transmission	Five-speed, chain final drive
Frame	Steel twin cradle
Suspension	Telescopic front; twin shocks rear
Brakes	Drum front and rear
Weight	411lb (186kg)
Top speed	105mph (169km/h)

Not so classy chassis

The T500's chassis was less impressive. Its twin-downtube frame and swingarm were made from steel tubing of distinctly narrow diameter. Its 35mm diameter front forks had external springs under their gaiters. Like the twin rear shocks, they were ineffective devices that contemporary tests showed to be over-sprung and lacking in damping.

Much of the time the Suzuki nevertheless handled reasonably well, thanks to its combination of 19-inch front wheel, conservative steering geometry and a friction steering damper at the steering head. At a more aggressive pace, though, the twin could quickly get out of shape. Many owners replaced the original rear shocks with superior aftermarket units, such as Girlings, but even that modification could not make the T500 handle particularly well. Nor did its front and rear drum brakes provide much in the way of stopping power, though this could be improved with the use of aftermarket brake shoes.

Despite the T500's mediocre handling and braking, Suzuki introduced very few changes during the model's long life – partly because its competitive price ensured that it carried on selling quite well, particularly in America. But they did

eventually uprate the front brake. In 1976 the twin was given a single front disc, a bigger fuel tank, electronic ignition and a handful of other detail changes. It was also renamed the GT500A, in an attempt to bring it into the GT range of triples that Suzuki by then built in 380, 550 and 750cc sizes.

Below: Handling was not the T500's strong point but the Suzuki could corner reasonably hard, especially if its standard rear shocks were replaced.

Bridgestone 350 GTR

**Top speed
95mph**
153km/h

*Below: The 350 GTR's high
handlebarred styling was
aimed at riders in America,
where the bike was first
sold in 1966. The upright
riding position soon became
uncomfortable at speed, but
the powerful and light
Bridgestone's main asset
was its low-speed
acceleration, which was
aided by its six-speed
gearbox.*

 Bridgestone's quick and sophisticated 350 GTR two-stroke twin was produced only in small numbers for just a few years in the late 1960s, but it left a lasting impression on those who rode it. As well as arm-wrenching acceleration and agile handling, the GTR incorporated several advanced features that would later be adopted by other manufacturers.

The most notable aspect of the GTR's 345cc parallel twin engine was its rotary disc valve induction system, which allowed much more precise control of gases than the more simple piston-ported design then used by rival two-stroke roadsters. Ironically Bridgestone's rival Japanese company Suzuki had considerable experience of disc-valve racing two-strokes, but the firm's 250cc Super Six roadster, also a two-stroke twin, was piston ported. Suzuki's knowledge dated back to

1961, when noted MZ factory racer and engineer Ernst Degner had defected from East Germany, bringing his team's secrets with him.

Bridgestone's twin used a disc valve (one for each cylinder) on each end of its crankshaft, with a 26mm Mikuni carburettor bolted outside each valve. Another neat feature was the 'piggy-back' alternator, situated above the engine rather than at the end of the crankshaft, which allowed the GTR unit to be quite slim despite its side-mounted carbs. Peak output was normally claimed to be 37bhp at 7500rpm, although the figure of 40bhp was also quoted in places.

The GTR's advanced engine features did not end with its induction. Lubrication was by a Yamaha-style pump-operated system, to which the Bridgestone added the refinement of inspection windows for both engine and gearbox oil. Similarly

the GTR impressed with its six-speed gearbox, and with its facility to swap the gearlever and rear brake pedals to give a left- or right-foot gearchange, both of which were commonly (and confusingly!) used at the time.

But the Bridgestone also annoyed because its neutral was placed at the top of the six-speed gearbox, instead of between first and second as on most bikes. Similarly, although the GTR was unusual in allowing the rider to start the engine in any gear provided the clutch was pulled in, the kickstarter was rather inconveniently placed on the left side of the bike.

Such details were soon forgotten on the move, because the Bridgestone's exhilarating performance made the two-stroke a match for almost any bike away from the line. The high-revving power was allied to light weight of just 330lb (150kg), which added to the acceleration. Coupled with a slightly grabby clutch, this could occasionally result in that 1960s rarity of an unplanned wheelie.

But the GTR felt impressively composed and refined at higher speeds. Its slightly too tall sixth gear kept top speed down to about 95mph (153km/h). But the reasonably broad spread of torque, combined with the rubber-mounted motor's smoothness, allowed easy cruising, with speed limited mainly by wind pressure due to the upright riding position.

Specification	Bridgestone 350 GTR (1966)
Engine	Air-cooled two-stroke parallel twin
Capacity	345cc
Maximum power	37bhp @ 7500rpm
Transmission	Six-speed, chain final drive
Frame	Steel twin cradle
Suspension	Telescopic front; twin shocks rear
Brakes	Drum front and rear
Weight	330lb (150kg)
Top speed	95mph (153km/h)

High build quality

Handling was also very good by contemporary standards, thanks to a stiff twin-cradle steel frame, and suspension whose high quality typified the thorough way in which the whole bike was put together. Similarly, the GTR's drum brakes worked well, especially the twin-leading-shoe front unit.

Unfortunately for Bridgestone, the GTR's quality came at a high price, for the bike cost considerably more than rival Japanese two-strokes, and was competing directly with larger engined four-strokes. It also faced resistance from riders who doubted a high-performance two-stroke's reliability. Only small numbers were sold in America, following the model's introduction there in 1966. Two years later it went on sale in Britain but shortly afterwards Bridgestone, whose main business was making tyres rather than motorcycles, quit bike production altogether.

Above: Chassis design was conventional but of high quality, resulting in good handling and braking. Despite this and the GTR's speed, few riders were prepared to pay the resultant high price for a relatively little-known two-stroke.

Left: Unbolting an engine cover revealed the 345cc two-stroke twin's rotary disc valve intake system. One carburettor fed each cylinder via its own disc valve, which allowed more precise timing than the conventional piston-ported design.

Norton Commando

**Top speed
115mph**
185km/h

*Right: The stylish
Commando S, with its high-
level exhaust pipes on the
left, was introduced in 1969
mainly to gain sales in
America, where off-road
riding was popular.*

*Below: The classic
Commando look combines
the angled-forward parallel
twin engine with Norton's
so-called Fastback
tailpiece, designed more for
style than pillion comfort.*

For many riders, the Norton Commando
was the ultimate bike of the late 1960s
and early '70s. It combined a powerful,
torquey engine with a fine-handling chassis that
minimized the traditional British parallel twin
problem of vibration.

The original Commando, launched in 1968, was
powered by a 745cc pushrod-operated parallel twin
motor that was based on that of the previous Atlas,
but was angled forward in the chassis instead of
positioned vertically. Changes included higher
compression ratio and a single-plate diaphragm
clutch. Peak power was 58bhp at 6800rpm.

But it was the chassis that made the Commando
special; more specifically, the 'Isolastic' system of
rubber mounting that promised to get rid of the
vibration that had plagued the Atlas and other
larger-capacity British parallel twins. The system,
developed by a team headed by former Rolls-Royce
engineer Dr Stefan Bauer, attached the engine to
the frame by rubber mounts. The frame itself
comprised a large main spine plus twin downtubes.

Rear engine plates were also rubber-mounted,
isolating the motor while allowing the frame's
spine to counter torsional stresses.

The Commando, which combined this chassis
innovation with striking styling including a
streamlined 'Fastback' tailpiece, made an
immediate impact. The bike was fast, with a top
speed of 115mph (185km/h) and strong mid-range

Specification	Norton Commando (1968)
Engine	Air-cooled ohv four-valve pushrod parallel-twin
Capacity	745cc (73 x 89mm)
Maximum power	58bhp @ 6800rpm
Transmission	Four-speed, chain final drive
Frame	Steel spine with twin downtubes
Suspension	Telescopic front; twin shock rear
Brakes	Drum front and rear
Weight	420lb (191kg)
Top speed	115mph (185km/h)

acceleration. More to the point, the Isolastic frame really worked. Firstly, it succeeded in isolating the rider from vibration effectively, at least so long as the Isolastic bushes were well maintained. And in combination with Norton's Roadholder forks and Girling shocks, it gave handling that was well up to the old firm's traditional high standards.

Terrific power

Magazine tests were full of praise. *Motor Cycle*, reviewing the Commando's impact several months after its launch, summed-up: 'The terrific power of the modified 745cc Atlas twin was a new experience now it was rubber-mounted in an ingenious frame which did, in fact, virtually eliminate the effects of high-frequency vibration. The sceptics retired to swallow their doubts. Overnight the Commando became the most sought-after large-capacity roadster on the market.'

After a further 2000-mile (3200km) trip, the tester concluded that the Norton 'gave a new dimension to the sort of riding we have known on parallel twins in the past 20 years'. The Commando proceeded to win the *Motor Cycle News* Machine of the Year competition five years in a row. American riders also took to the Commando which, for that very important market, was fitted with high, wide handlebars.

Americans benefited from some of the special versions that Norton developed over the next few years, notably the 1971 model Commando SS, a street scrambler with a small gas tank and high-level pipes. The Commando Hi-Rider model added a chopper-style seat to its similar tank and high-level bars. Norton went the opposite way with the Combat Commando, which had flatter bars to suit its tuned, high-compression 65bhp motor. But the

Combat was an embarrassment. Its main bearings could not handle the extra power, and Norton's hurried attempts to fix the problem with a new head gasket backfired when these started leaking.

The factory had much more success in 1973, when the engine was bored-out to create the Commando 850, available in standard Roadster and large-tanked Interstate options. The bigger motor's extra torque gave a welcome performance boost to a parallel twin that by now was competing against Japanese multis. But the British bike's limitations were highlighted by Norton's difficulty in providing a reliable electric starter. By now parent company Norton Villiers Triumph was in financial trouble, and production finally ceased in 1977.

Above left: The Commando gave Norton fresh life, but even by enlarging the original 745cc engine to 828cc it could not keep the pushrod twin competitive in the 1970s.

Below: This 1972 specification machine was assembled in 1995 from new parts by British Norton parts specialist Fair Spares, one of several firms to offer freshly built Commandos.

Triumph Trident

**Top speed
125mph**
201km/h

*Right: The 1975-model
T160 Trident, with its
angled-forward engine and
stylish two-tone paint
scheme, was generally
regarded as a much more
handsome machine than the
original T150.*

*Below: Angular lines,
unusual paint scheme and
distinctive 'raygun' silencers
gave the T150 Trident an
old-fashioned look that was
unpopular with many
Triumph enthusiasts.*

When Triumph launched the T150 Trident in 1969, the 750cc triple's blend of smooth power and stable handling made it one of the fastest bikes on the road. In road-racing, too, Trident-based machines scored many notable victories, not least on the high-speed banking of Daytona. But the triple was never the success that Triumph had hoped, partly due to its angular styling, aquamarine paintwork and unusual 'ray-gun' silencers, all of which were especially unpopular in the States.

The Trident's design was also very much of the 1960s, in contrast to that of Honda's more refined CB750 four, which was launched a few months later. The 740cc triple had pushrod valve operation, and produced 58bhp at 7250rpm. The chassis was heavily based on that of Triumph's twins, including the frame which was a strengthened version of their single-downtube unit. Front forks, borrowed from the twins, had stiffer springs to cope with the triple's extra weight. The drum front brake also came from a 650cc twin.

High-speed cruising

The Trident was certainly fast. Its 125mph (201km/h) top speed and sub 14-second quarter-mile time were mighty impressive in 1969. So too was the smooth power delivery that allowed sustained high-speed cruising, and which made the Trident a much better long-distance bike than contemporary twins. The Trident could crack 100mph (161km/h) in third gear, and show its

fancy silencers to just about any vehicle on the road. For a big bike its handling was good, too.

Triumph attempted to uprate the Trident over the years, although the firm's financial problems ensured that many mods were merely cosmetic. The disappointing front brake was changed to a conical drum in 1971, then to a single disc. Styling changes included a smaller fuel tank that combined with the Trident's thirst to give very poor range. (Many American dealers threw away the standard tank and exhausts, fitting parts from the twin to make the Trident more appealing.)

Trident performance suffered when the 1973 model's revised carburation and silencers, introduced due to tightening emission laws, resulted in 10mph (16km/h) being lost from the top speed. Equally seriously, the Trident never really recovered from its early reputation for unreliability – much of which was caused by poor assembly rather than flawed design. Those problems and its high price meant that the Trident never had much chance of success.

In 1975, Triumph replaced the T150 with the redesigned T160 Trident. This was a handsome machine whose engine incorporated many new features including an electric starter and left-foot

Specification	Triumph T150 Trident (1969)
Engine	Air-cooled ohv six-valve pushrod triple
Capacity	740cc (67 x 70mm)
Maximum power	58bhp @ 7250rpm
Transmission	Four-speed, chain final drive
Frame	Steel single downtube
Suspension	Telescopic front; twin shocks rear
Brakes	Drum front and rear
Weight	468lb (212kg)
Top speed	125mph (201km/h)

gearchange. The new bike's frame angled the motor forward in the style of BSA's Rocket Three. Its layout was influenced by Triumph's works production race triples including the legendary Slippery Sam, which won five consecutive Isle of Man TT Production races from 1971 to '75.

Finally, the Trident was the bike it might have been all along, with good looks, excellent performance, fine handling and a smooth ride. Although it had some reliability problems, and a high price, the T160 was the fastest, most sophisticated British bike yet. But it did not last long. By the end of 1975, production had ended following the collapse of parent company Norton Villiers Triumph.

Below left: Triumph's three-cylinder engine was powerful and reasonably smooth, but was very much a design from the 1960s. The pushrod triple's lack of sophistication was further emphasized when compared with Honda's CB750 unit, with its overhead camshaft, additional cylinder, electric starter and superior reliability.

American Beauty: The Stunning X-75

The most stylish of Triumph's triples was the 1973 model X-75 Hurricane, created by young freelance American designer Craig Vetter. Commissioned by Triumph's American distributor, initially without the factory's knowledge, it was everything that the T150 wasn't: slim, curvy, and eye-catching. Geared for acceleration and with a tiny fuel tank, it was impractical – but unbeatable away from the lights. Fewer than 1200 were built, but decades later the Hurricane is remembered as an icon of two-wheeled style.

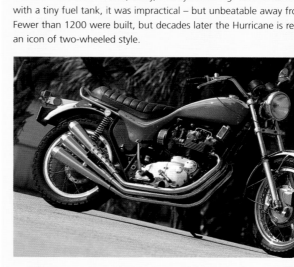

Yamaha XS-1

**Top speed
105mph**
169km/h

*Below: The XS-1's styling
and engine layout clearly
owed much to British
parallel twins. The
Yamaha's high bars, small
gas tank and torquey 654cc
engine made it a hit,
especially in America. This
model was quickly followed
by the XS-2 and then the
XS650. All were very
similar, and the Yamaha
twin changed little in more
than a decade.*

The look, the layout and the performance of the 650cc XS-1 that Yamaha launched on the American market in 1969 were all familiar to riders who had grown up with British parallel twins. But this bike had one big difference, as the name and the tuning fork logo on its fuel tank made clear. The XS-1 was built by Yamaha of Japan. The last area of Britain's two-wheeled domination was about to be lost.

By 1969, Yamaha was already establishing a reputation for high performance, through its smaller two-strokes, on road and track. Factory racing star Phil Read had won both 250 and 125cc world championships in the previous season. But until the XS-1, Yamaha had never built a four-stroke roadster – let alone a 650cc parallel twin that was so obviously aimed at the British opposition.

And which scored a direct hit, too. For although many riders questioned the wisdom of taking on the likes of Triumph's Bonneville and BSA's Lightning with such a similar bike, those doubts were rapidly

blown away. The XS-1 – and particularly its descendants the XS-2 and XS650, for the original model was promptly updated – soon became strong sellers in the important American market, firmly establishing Yamaha as a manufacturer of large-capacity bikes.

The 654cc XS-1 engine followed the British opposition in its use of a 360-degree crankshaft, and even its 75 x 74mm bore and stroke dimensions were identical to those of the Lightning. But the Japanese bike also had plenty of mechanical differences, notably its use of horizontally split crankcases. Instead of pushrods, its valves were operated by a single overhead camshaft, driven by a central chain. Peak output was a competitive 53bhp at 7000rpm.

The motor lived in a typical twin-downtube steel frame, which held front forks whose rubber gaiters concealed external springs. Brakes were drums at both ends, with a powerful twin-leading-shoe unit up front. Designed mainly for the

American market, the XS-1 looked lean and sporty despite high, wide bars – and despite the fact that it was heavier, at 429lb (195kg) with half a tank of fuel, than a genuine Bonneville.

Pulling power

That weight and the engine's fairly soft state of tune did not prevent the twin from having lively acceleration. It pulled cleanly from below 2000rpm in top gear, had plenty of mid-range punch, and was good for a top speed of 105mph (169km/h). Although the engine vibrated in typical parallel twin fashion at around 4000rpm, it smoothed as it approached the 7500rpm redline. And the twin was strong enough to be revved hard, even when tuned for flat-track racing.

The Yamaha's chassis was less impressive. The frame and swingarm lacked rigidity, and combined with the under-damped suspension to result in a frequent weave at high speed, and a choppy ride on bumpy roads. The Japanese bike was fine at a gentle pace, and had to be ridden really hard before it began to misbehave seriously. But its handling, unlike its engine, was no match for the better developed British opposition.

Cycle World was impressed, nevertheless, reporting that the XS-1 'supplied all the ingredients required to please the Big Twin fancier in an up-to-date, beautifully styled package. It looks good, rides good, stays clean and shows few of the faults one would expect in a first-year model.' Those assets plus the Yamaha's reliability and competitive price helped make it a hit in the States. Although it had its faults, the XS-1 was a fine first attempt that paved the way for its XS-2 and XS650 successors to establish themselves as some of the best-selling bikes of the 1970s.

Left: Yamaha's 654cc parallel twin owed much to British designs, but differed in its use of a chain-driven overhead camshaft and horizontally split crankcases.

Below: As well as becoming one of America's best-selling bikes of the 1970s, the XS650 continued into the following decade with models such as this Heritage Classic.

Below left: Among the XS-1's attractions were typically efficient Japanese instruments and electrics. The large steering damper knob hinted at the bike's tendency to weave at speed.

Specification	Yamaha XS-1 (1969)
Engine	Air-cooled sohc four-valve parallel twin
Capacity	654cc (75 x 74mm)
Maximum power	53bhp @ 7000rpm
Transmission	Five-speed, chain final drive
Frame	Steel twin cradle
Suspension	Telescopic front; twin shocks rear
Brakes	Drum front and rear
Weight	429lb (195kg)
Top speed	105mph (169km/h)

The 1970s
Superbikes
Roar In

In two-wheeled terms the decade of the 1970s really began in 1969, when Honda launched the CB750. Honda's 'first superbike' dazzled not simply with its four-cylinder engine layout, which would soon be adopted by the other Japanese marques, but also because it displayed a level of sophistication that was far above that of the British manufacturers, and which confirmed that a new era had begun.

By the end of the decade the Japanese firms had added a thrilling array of superbikes with two, three and even six cylinders, some with power outputs in excess of 100bhp. And European manufacturers, especially those from Italy, had added to the rich mixture with a variety of exotic machines.

Honda CB750

**Top speed
123mph**
198km/h

With a top speed of over 120mph (193km/h) and a standing quarter-mile time of under 13 seconds, Honda's original CB750 four was one of the fastest and hardest-accelerating bikes on the roads in the early 1970s. But it was not sheer speed alone that made the Honda such a huge success back then; nor that caused it to be widely regarded as the most important machine that the motorcycle industry has yet produced.

More than simply sheer performance, it was the CB750's unmatched sophistication that made it special. When it arrived in 1969, the Honda was the first mass-produced four, and it incorporated refinements including an electric starter, disc front brake and five-speed gearbox. As well as being competitively priced, it was also impressively well built. By this time, a generation of motorcyclists had grown up on smaller Hondas, and were confident that the Japanese firm's bikes would be mechanically reliable, and would have good electrics and no oil leaks. They would not be disappointed by the glamorous four.

Influenced by racebikes

Of all the Honda's attributes, that powerful, smooth-running engine was the most important. The 736cc unit's design was influenced by Honda's multi-cylinder racebikes of the 1960s, although the roadster relied on a single overhead camshaft and two valves per cylinder, in contrast to the racers with their twin cams and four valves per pot. The Honda's capacity of 736cc came from its relatively long-stroke dimensions of 61 x 63mm, which helped reduce width.

Above: The original CB750 had conventional styling and fairly high handlebars, but its disc front brake and especially its four-cylinder engine brought a new level of sophistication and performance to motorcycling. More than three decades later, its influence is still clear in the design of modern superbikes.

Right: Most of the first fours to be produced were sold in America, where the model went on sale in mid-1969. This bike, built in October of that year, was the first to be sold in Britain and was registered in January 1970.

Tuned For Speed – The CB750F2

Honda was slow to update the CB750 in the 1970s, despite the arrival of rivals including Kawasaki's more powerful 900cc Z1. In fact the CB was detuned over the years to reduce emissions. Even the 1976 model CB750F1, which looked sporty with flat handlebars and bright yellow paint, could manage only 115mph (185km/h). But a year later came the CB750F2. Its black-painted engine had bigger valves, high-lift camshaft, redesigned combustion chamber and produced 73bhp, an extra 6bhp. Chassis improvements included a strengthened frame, new suspension and triple disc brakes. With top speed of over 120mph (193km/h) and excellent handling, the F2 was the last and best of Honda's single-cam 750s.

The motor was angled slightly forward in a steel, twin cradle frame, which held gaitered front forks and twin rear shock absorbers. Honda created the initial CB750 as an all-rounder, aiming it primarily at the US market. It was a physically large machine with a wide seat. It also had fairly high handlebars, but the wind-blown riding position did not prevent it from being well suited to cruising at speed.

Chassis performance did not quite match that of the engine, with the flex-prone steel frame causing a few wobbles under very hard riding. But by early 1970s standards the Honda's handling was good. Although quite heavy, the four carried its weight well, thanks partly to firm suspension. Its disc front brake gave an edge in both image and performance over rival firms' drums, too.

Demand for the CB750 was huge, notably in America, where most of the early production was sold. Honda even got a barely necessary marketing boost from competition success, when veteran ace Dick Mann won the 1970 Daytona 200 on a modified CB750. *Cycle World* introduced the Honda as 'the ultimate weapon in one-upmanship – a magnificent, muscle-bound racer for the road', and concluded in its road test that the CB750 was 'the very best road bike in the world'.

Few who rode it at the time disagreed with that. And, as four-cylinder Japanese superbikes began to dominate the two-wheeled scene through the 1970s and '80s, the Honda's enormous influence became apparent. After the CB750, high-performance motorcycling would never be the same again.

Left: Honda's 736cc straight-four powerplant had a chain-driven single overhead camshaft and eight valves. Carburation and exhaust changes necessary to meet tightening emissions legislation meant that its 67bhp output was initially reduced, rather than increased, in subsequent years. Although the Honda had an electric starter, it was also fitted with a kick-starter as a back-up.

Specification	Honda CB750 (1969)
Engine	Air-cooled sohc eight-valve four
Capacity	736cc (61 x 63mm)
Maximum power	67bhp @ 8000rpm
Transmission	Five-speed, chain final drive
Frame	Steel twin downtube
Suspension	Telescopic front; twin shocks rear
Brakes	Single disc front; drum rear
Weight	506lb (230kg) wet
Top speed	123mph (198km/h)

Yamaha YR5

**Top speed
95mph**
153km/h

*Below: The YR5's styling
was simple and obviously
road-based, in contrast to
earlier dual-purpose
Yamaha twins. High
handlebars did little to
dilute the aggressive, rev-
happy image of a bike that
was closely related to
Yamaha's racers.*

Yamaha's two-stroke middleweight twins were among the outstanding bikes of the 1970s, providing a combination of performance and value that made them hugely popular. Best known were the RD350 and RD400 models but it was with the earlier YR5 that the legend of Yamaha's giant-killing 350cc two-stroke screamers began.

The initials RD stood for Race Developed, and that was very much true of the YR5 too. Yamaha had already begun to dominate 250cc grand prix racing when the YR5 was introduced in 1970. In that year Yamaha's TD2 air-cooled twin-cylinder production racer not only took British rider Ron Gould to the world championship, but it also occupied the first seven places. Much of the same

technology was used for the roadsters, which were also produced in 125, 200 and 250cc capacities.

Like its smaller siblings, as well as predecessors dating back to the YR1 of 1967, the 347cc YR5 was based around a piston-ported two-stroke twin with a 180-degree crankshaft arrangement. It breathed in through a pair of 28mm Mikuni carbs, and out through a pair of horizontal chromed pipes. The gearbox was a five-speeder, with a modern change pattern that put neutral between first and second, instead of at the bottom of the box like some rivals. Peak power was 36bhp at 7000rpm.

In contrast to the off-road-influenced styling of its predecessors, which had featured crossbar-style handlebars and high-level exhaust systems, the

Specification	Yamaha YR5 (1970)
Engine	Air-cooled two-stroke parallel twin
Capacity	347cc (64 x 54mm)
Maximum power	36bhp @ 7000rpm
Transmission	Five-speed, chain final drive
Frame	Steel twin downtube
Suspension	Telescopic front; twin shocks rear
Brakes	Drum front and rear
Weight	331lb (150kg)
Top speed	95mph (153km/h)

Far left: The 1973 RD350 boasted reed-valve induction, a six-speed gearbox and a disc front brake in place of the YR5's drum.

Left: Yamaha's screaming 347cc two-stroke twin revved to 8000rpm, produced 36bhp and brought a new dimension to middleweight performance.

YR5 was very much a roadster. Although its handlebars were still high, the bike had sleek and simple styling, and was shorter, lower and lighter at 331lb (150kg). Its frame was a twin-downtube steel structure, reinforced at the steering head and swingarm pivot with the benefit of Yamaha's grand prix racing experience.

Noise, smoke and acceleration

That racing heritage was clear on the road, where YR5 riders required little imagination to see themselves in the saddle of a high-revving grand prix racer. The Yamaha two-stroke burbled, rattled and smoked (when cold) like a true two-stroke, albeit a sophisticated and well-behaved one. More importantly it had thrilling acceleration, revved to 8000rpm through the gears, cruised smoothly at an indicated 80mph (129km/h) and reached a top speed of 95mph (153km/h).

Handling was pretty good, thanks to the rigid frame, light weight and simple but reasonably well-controlled suspension. *Cycle World* described the YR5 as a quick-handling machine, with 'little to inhibit the rider from pitching the machine aggressively through his favourite set of bends. Damping seems quite up to par, and the tyres deliver good tracking precision and traction.' The Yamaha's front and rear drum brakes were progressive, grab-free and with only a slight tendency to fade under repeated use.

The YR5's blend of good looks, reliability, lively performance and competitive price quickly made it popular on both sides of the Atlantic. For the next few years Yamaha's two-stroke twins would be hugely successful in the showrooms, just as they were on the racetrack. The old adage that 'racing improves the breed' was never more brilliantly proven.

Faster Still: the RD Series

Yamaha produced a string of outstanding sportsters as the two-stroke middleweight was updated throughout the 1970s. A notable jump came in 1973 with the first RD350 model, which featured a reed-valve induction system, six-speed gearbox, powerful disc front brake and, on a good day, a top speed of over 100mph (161km/h). The RD400C (below) arrived in 1976 with angular styling, improved handling and extra mid-range performance from its 398cc, 40bhp engine. Similar 250cc versions of both models provided almost as much speed for even less expense.

Rickman Interceptor

**Top speed
115mph**
185km/h

*Right: Wide handlebars
were a surprising feature of
the racy Rickman, as were
footrests on clamps around
the exhaust pipes.*

*Below: Handsome cafe-
racer styling gave the
Rickman a much more
aggressive image than the
standard Royal Enfield
Interceptor that supplied
its powerplant.*

 One of the most attractive and neatly engineered bikes of the early 1970s was the Rickman Interceptor, an improbable combination of 736cc Royal Enfield parallel twin engine and hand-built chassis from specialist firm Rickman. Although not particularly fast in a straight line, its light weight and agile handling confirmed that the old British parallel twin format still had plenty of potential.

The Rickman Interceptor owed its existence to the demise of Royal Enfield, the famous old marque that had gone out of business in 1969. One of the firm's last enterprises had been to sell a batch of twin-cylinder engines (originally designed for the Royal Enfield Interceptor) to America, where they were to have powered bikes marketed as Indian Enfields. The British firm's collapse meant that about 200 engines were left stranded at the docks.

Enter Rickman, the firm run by brothers Don and Derek Rickman, former motocross (scrambles) racers who had set up in business in Hampshire in the late 1950s. After starting by building off-road competition bikes using BSA frames, the Rickmans had begun constructing their own high-quality frames, and had then expanded to build roadgoing chassis too. In 1970 Rickman was commissioned by Royal Enfield's US export agency, which had been left with the engines, to build a bike to use them up.

In typical Rickman style the Interceptor was a lean, light and beautifully crafted machine based around a twin-downtube frame of Reynolds 531 chrome-molybdenum steel tubing. The frame, a wider version of Rickman's proven Métisse ('mongrel bitch' in French) design, was very rigid and finished in shiny nickel plate.

Cycle parts included Rickman's own motocross-derived telescopic forks, whose 41mm diameter was considerably wider than those commonly used at the time, plus Borrani wheel rims and single disc brakes at front and rear. The Rickman was a good-looking bike, with a racy fuel tank and seat unit made from high quality fibreglass. By contrast its handlebars were high and wide, and its fairly forward-set footrests were clamped to the exhaust pipes in unusual fashion.

Engine development

The 736cc engine was Royal Enfield's Series II Interceptor unit, the final development of a line of pushrod-operated parallel twins that dated back to the 692cc Meteor and Constellation of the 1950s. The Series II had been introduced in 1969, featuring wet- instead of dry-sump lubrication, and a more efficient oil pump. High-lift camshafts and a new ignition system helped give a peak output of either 52 or 56bhp (both figures were quoted) at 6750rpm.

That was enough to give both the standard Interceptor (which was produced mainly for export to America) and the Rickman a top speed of 115mph (185km/h). But it was the big twin's acceleration at lower speeds that was most impressive, especially in the case of the Rickman, which at just 353lb (160kg) was almost 100lb (45kg) lighter than the Enfield model. From as low as 2000rpm in top gear, the twin surged forward with almost enough force to bend those wide bars.

The Rickman was also smooth by parallel twin standards. It was reasonably reliable too, thanks to the Series II motor's improvements, although the four-speed gearbox was notably poor. Handling, roadholding and braking were excellent, though – good enough to give the lightweight Rickman the edge over most contemporary rivals when ridden hard on a twisty road.

That performance was not enough to keep the model in production after the initial batch of about 200 engines had been used up. But Rickman continued to thrive through the 1970s, building a series of fast and fine-handling CR ('Cafe Racer') specials around Japanese four-cylinder engines including Honda's CB750 and Kawasaki's Z900.

*Enfield's 736cc parallel twin engine (**above**) was ably supported by Rickman's nickel-plated frame. Fuel tank and seat (**left**) were in high quality fibreglass, a Rickman speciality. Light weight and taut chassis gave excellent handling (**far left**).*

Specification	Rickman Interceptor (1970)
Engine	Air-cooled ohv pushrod four-valve parallel twin
Capacity	736cc (71 x 93mm)
Maximum power	56bhp @ 6750rpm
Transmission	Four-speed, chain final drive
Frame	Steel twin cradle
Suspension	Telescopic front; twin shocks rear
Brakes	Disc front and rear
Weight	353lb (160kg)
Top speed	115mph (185km/h)

Kawasaki H2 750

**Top speed
120mph**
193km/h

*Right: Kawasaki's 748cc
two-stroke engine kicked
out 74bhp and had more
mid-range torque than its
500cc H1 predecessor.
Hydraulic steering damper
was a worthwhile addition.*

*Below: Lean, simple styling
gave little clue to the H2's
fearsome performance.
High handlebars were a
hindrance at high speed but
no handicap to the
Kawasaki's reputation as an
unbeatable sprinter away
from the traffic lights.*

For sheer excitement, there was nothing
on two wheels to match the 750 H2 two-
stroke triple that Kawasaki unleashed in
1972. Fast, loud, smoky, thirsty and ill-handling,
the bike that was also known as the Mach IV was a
wild ride that quickly earned a reputation for
unmatched speed and aggression. 'It's so quick it
demands the razor-sharp reactions of an
experienced rider,' bragged Kawasaki's publicity
material, and few who rode the triple disagreed.

The basis of the H2 was Kawasaki's first three-
cylinder two-stroke, the 500cc H1 (or Mach III),
which had been launched in 1969. This too was a
fast and fiery machine that became popular,
especially with American riders who valued
acceleration from a standing start above all else.
This group, labelled 'stoplight-to-stoplight freaks'
by one magazine, was even better served by the
larger model, whose 748cc air-cooled engine had a
peak output of 74bhp at 6800rpm.

That was not only 14bhp up on the smaller
triple, but also put rivals such as Suzuki's liquid-
cooled GT750 triple and Honda's CB750 four in
the shade. Physically the new model closely
resembled the Mach III, with fairly high and wide

handlebars and fuel tank that was narrow despite
the compact three-cylinder engine's thirst. The
chassis layout of twin-downtube frame, twin rear
shocks and slim forks holding a 19-inch front
wheel and single brake disc also matched that of
the smaller machine.

Searing acceleration

As well as its extra capacity the H2 had milder
porting and ignition timing, which helped give a
usefully broad spread of power. But although that
meant the triple could be ridden gently, with
minimal use of its five-speed gearbox, that was not
what this bike was built for. Sheer speed was its
forte, not so much the maximum of about 120mph
(193km/h) as the searing acceleration that enabled
it to reach over 100mph (161km/h) from a standing
start in less than 13 seconds, and to leave the line
in a cloud of smoke with its front wheel in the air.

Chassis performance was less impressive, as the
triple's blend of power, light weight and barely
adequate frame and suspension could provoke what
one report described as a 'deadly wobble'. Owners
were well advised to supplement the standard
friction steering damper with an optional hydraulic
damper, for which a frame lug was provided. At
least the single front disc brake was reasonably
powerful, although many riders boosted the system
by fitting an optional second disc.

Original Triple: the H1 500

Kawasaki's first mean and nasty two-stroke was the 500cc H1, also known as the Mach III, which was introduced in 1969 and did much to establish the firm's reputation for performance. The triple produced 60bhp at 7500rpm, was good for over 115mph (185km/h) and was a match for anything on wheels away from the line due to its spectacular power-to-weight ratio. It combined the H2's dubious handling and poor fuel economy with a narrow power band that made it even more demanding to ride. New Zealander Ginger Molloy rode the racing derivative, the H1R, to second place in the 500cc world championship in 1970.

Left: Conventional styling and a broad dual seat with grab-rail did not hide the fact that this was a scary bike by early 1970s standards. The single front brake disc gave reasonable stopping but twin-disc conversion was a popular modification. So was swapping the standard exhaust system for a set of expansion chambers, for extra power, noise and possibly holed pistons.

Plenty of riders were happy to accept the triple's handling and thirst because it was competitively priced and, most of all, so fast. 'The Mach IV rates as the ultimate stud bike now available in terms of raw power and sheer speed,' concluded American magazine *Cycle World*. 'If being the fastest on your block appeals to you, so will the Mach IV!' Although tightening emissions legislation meant that the triple was first detuned, then dropped, it would not be forgotten.

Specification	Kawasaki H2 (Mach IV) (1972)
Engine	Air-cooled two-stroke triple
Capacity	748cc (71 x 63mm)
Maximum power	74bhp @ 6800rpm
Transmission	Five-speed, chain final drive
Frame	Steel twin downtube
Suspension	Telescopic front; twin shocks rear
Brakes	Disc front; drum rear
Weight	454lb (206kg)
Top speed	120mph (193km/h)

Suzuki GT750

**Top speed
110mph**
177km/h

*Right: This front view
shows the big radiator and
broad engine of a bike
whose styling did not hide
its weight.*

*Below: Pink paintwork,
rounded styling and
reverse-cone silencers give
the GT750 an unmistakable
early 1970s appearance.
The front drum brake was
soon changed to twin discs.*

 With its bulbous styling, lurid paintwork
and distinctive liquid-cooled, two-stroke
triple engine, Suzuki's GT750 was one of
the most eye-catching of early superbikes. It was
also one of the most successful. Although built for
comfort, smoothness and low-rev torque more than
for pure performance, it was one of the fastest and
most glamorous bikes of its day.

Where the triple known as the 'Kettle' in
Britain and the 'Water Buffalo' in America excelled
was in keeping up a high cruising speed for long
distances. The GT was a Grand Tourer by name
and by nature, with plenty of mid-range torque, a
roomy and comfortable riding position and an
ability to sit at a steady 80mph (129km/h) or more
with a minimum of fuss and stress.

The GT's 738cc piston-ported two-stroke
engine was essentially one-and-a-half units from
the air-cooled T500 twin. Retaining the twin's 70 x

Specification	Suzuki GT750J (1972)
Engine	Liquid-cooled two-stroke triple
Capacity	738cc (70 x 64mm)
Maximum power	67bhp @ 6500rpm
Transmission	Five-speed, chain final drive
Frame	Steel twin downtube
Suspension	Telescopic front; twin shocks rear
Brakes	Drum front and rear
Weight	525lb (238kg)
Top speed	110mph (177km/h)

64mm cylinder dimensions, but adding an extra cylinder plus liquid cooling, resulted in much improved mid-range response plus a peak power output of 67bhp at 6500rpm.

Unmistakable styling

Its bold styling and unique engine layout ensured that the Suzuki looked like no other bike on the road. As well as the smooth, water-jacketed cylinders, it had a large radiator and black-tipped reverse-cone silencers. Its chassis was conventional, though, with a twin-downtube frame, gaitered front forks and twin shocks. The front brake was a double-sided, twin-leading-shoe drum.

Handling was never a GT750 forte. At 525lb (238kg) the triple was heavy. At modest cornering speeds it was stable, if rather ponderous, but at a more aggressive pace the overworked frame and suspension resulted in a few wobbles. But that didn't stop *Cycle World* from raving about the triple's 'effortless high-speed cruising, hairline steering and tremendous braking. It's a superbike in every sense of the word.'

The GT also formed the basis of a fearsome racing bike, the TR750, which was built for the 1972 Daytona 200 and earned the nickname 'flexy flyer' because of its poor high-speed handling. The TR produced 100bhp and was super-fast, with a top speed of over 175mph (282km/h). The TR had some successes although its power frequently caused problems for the clutch and tyres.

Suzuki made no attempt to produce a sporty roadgoing triple but did increase the GT's output slightly. The GT750L of 1974 produced 70bhp thanks to modifications including extra compression ratio, CV instead of slide carbs, revised cylinder porting and a new exhaust system. That made the liquid-cooled engine slightly more peaky, with a power step at about 4000rpm. At lower revs it lacked a little of the earlier triple's smoothness, but high-speed acceleration was better, and the GT's top speed increased slightly to about 115mph (185km/h).

Suzuki also uprated the chassis, replacing the front drum brake with a pair of discs in 1973. Later models had subtle modifications to frame and suspension, plus features such as a digital gear indicator and lockable fuel cap. Those details could not keep the two-stroke in production for long in a climate of rising oil prices and tightening emissions legislation, and in 1977 it was replaced by the GS750 four-cylinder four-stroke.

Left: The GT's 110mph (177km/h) top speed was nothing special even in 1972, but the big Suzuki triple's ability to cruise smoothly and in reasonable comfort for long distances at speed did much to make it popular. Straight line stability was very good.

Below: Later versions of the GT750 generated a little more power and featured an uprated chassis with twin front brake discs, but had lost the distinctive styling of the early models. This GT750B, which was produced in 1977, was one of the last of the line.

Laverda 750 SFC

**Top speed
125mph**
201km/h

One glance at the Laverda 750 SFC was enough to reveal why the Italian twin made an impact out of all proportion to the small number of machines that were produced. The SFC was hugely stylish and racy, with clip-on handlebars, rearset footrests, a half-fairing and single seat. Its bodywork was orange, because that colour made the model easier to spot at night during the 24-hour endurance races for which it was created.

Roadgoing racer

Unlike most so-called race replicas, the 750 SFC really was a racebike first and a roadster second. It was launched in 1971 as an endurance racing version of Laverda's SF series of 750cc parallel twins. Despite this, a large proportion of the 549 SFCs built in the following few years were ridden on the street, after fitment of such essentials as speedometer and number plate.

Laverda, the small firm from Breganze in north-eastern Italy, had first produced a 654cc parallel twin in 1967, before enlarging the motor to 744cc a year later. In 1969 the factory had introduced a sportier 750S model, which in turn had been followed by the 750 SF (F standing for freni, Italian for brakes, due to its uprated drums). These models had been campaigned on European endurance race circuits with some success. But the firm's boss, Massimo Laverda, decided that a purpose-built racer was needed so the SFC was born, the C of its name standing for Competizione.

Although it shared the SF's basic engine layout, which meant dimensions of 80 x 74mm, a 360-degree crankshaft and chain drive to the single overhead camshaft, the SFC shared few components. Special parts included high-

Above: The bright orange SFC, with its handlebar fairing and racy single seat, was one of the most handsome and purposeful of 1970s superbikes. This 1975 model bike has the disc brakes that replaced the original drums in the previous year.

Right: The Laverda had plenty of straight-line speed to complement its sublime handling ability. This bike is fitted with a reasonably quiet twin-silencer roadgoing exhaust system, and would also have come with a louder two-into-one system for racing use.

compression pistons, 36mm Amal carburettors and a close-ratio five-speed gearbox. Engine parts were selected by Laverda's race shop before being heat-treated to improve strength. Peak output was a claimed 70bhp at 7500rpm, enough for a top speed of 125mph (201km/h).

Similarly the SFC frame shared the original twin's layout of a spine made from four steel tubes above the engine, but was modified to take the fairing and rear-set footrests. Initial models featured Ceriani front and rear suspension plus Laverda's own drum brakes. The combination proved a success, as the SFC won its first race, the Barcelona 24 Hours at Montjuic Park in 1971.

For the next few years the SFC was one of the fastest bikes on the road, and one of the best handling too. But the high specification ensured that it was expensive, and fewer than 100 were built in each of the first three years. In 1974 Laverda subtly reshaped the bodywork and fitted uprated parts including thicker forks and triple disc

Specification	Laverda 750 SFC (1972)
Engine	Air-cooled sohc four-valve parallel twin
Capacity	744cc (80 x 74mm)
Maximum power	70bhp @ 7500rpm
Transmission	Five-speed, chain final drive
Frame	Tubular steel spine
Suspension	Telescopic front; twin shocks rear
Brakes	Drum front and rear
Weight	454lb (206kg)
Top speed	125mph (201km/h)

brakes. Production numbers increased slightly, and some bikes were built for road use with full instruments and even indicators.

Later SFCs featured electronic ignition and some had cast wheels too. The last models were the fastest, especially when fitted with the optional factory camshaft that gave extra power and a top speed of 135mph (217km/h). Fittingly, the SFC's racy look, paint scheme and personality remained very much intact until production ended in 1976.

Below: The SFC's 744c air-cooled sohc parallel twin engine looked similar to other Laverda units, but featured specially selected tuning parts. It was also fitted with bigger carbs, a close-ratio gearbox, uprated bearings and a larger capacity oil pump.

One-race Wonder: the Mighty V6

Laverda's fastest ever bike was another orange endurance racer: the 996cc V6 that was raced in the Bol d'Or 24 Hours in France in 1978. The 90-degree V6 unit featured 24 valves, liquid cooling and shaft final drive, and produced 139bhp at 10,500rpm. Although very heavy at 520lb (236kg), the V6 was stunningly fast, and was timed at 176mph (283km/h) before its drive shaft failed after eight hours. Laverda's financial problems meant that it did not race again, and a roadgoing version was never produced.

Moto Guzzi V7 Sport

**Top speed
125mph**
201km/h

*Below: This immaculate,
1973 model V7 Sport was
one of the last of fewer than
4000 that were built before
production was stopped
towards the end of that
year. All had the model's
distinctive lime green
paintwork and big twin-
leading-shoe front drum
brake. Neat details included
an inspection light, under
the seat, that came on when
the seat was raised.*

 The stylish, charismatic and impressively rapid V7 Sport was the bike with which Moto Guzzi established a reputation for performance that would last through the 1970s and beyond. The lime green Sport had a capacity of 748cc and was aptly named, as it was the first truly sporting model to be built using Guzzi's distinctive 90-degree transverse V-twin engine.

Guzzi's air-cooled, pushrod-operated V-twin motor had unlikely origins, as it had been developed for the Italian military in the late 1950s to power a tractor-like machine called the 3x3. The shaft-drive engine had then been adapted to power Guzzi's first V-twin bike, the 704cc V7 tourer, which had been launched in 1967. Two year later the engine had been enlarged to 757cc and used for the V7 Special, known as the Ambassador in America.

This model, too, was a softly tuned tourer but Guzzi's management could see its potential. In 1969, tuned and lightened V7s were ridden to a string of world speed records at Monza racetrack, including hour and 100km records at over 135mph (217km/h). Encouraged by this, the firm from Mandello del Lario began development of a purpose-built sportster.

Powerful engine

The V7's 757cc engine was reduced in capacity to 748cc, to allow entry in 750cc races, and tuned with a hotter camshaft, increased compression ratio, lighter valvegear and conrods, new ignition system and unfiltered 30mm Dell'Orto carburettors. With a peak output at the crankshaft of 70bhp at 7000rpm (52bhp at the rear wheel), the Sport motor was among motorcycling's most powerful, as well as considerably lighter than the old engine.

Another important change was the new engine's alternator on the front end of the crankshaft, replacing the old generator in the Vee. This enabled Guzzi engineer Lino Tonti to design a lower frame

Specification	Moto Guzzi V7 Sport (1972)
Engine	Air-cooled ohv pushrod four-valve 90-degree transverse V-twin
Capacity	748cc (82.5 x 70mm)
Maximum power	70bhp @ 7000rpm
Transmission	Five-speed, shaft final drive
Frame	Steel spine
Suspension	Telescopic front; twin shocks rear
Brakes	Drum front and rear
Weight	500lb (227kg)
Top speed	125mph (201km/h)

Updated Twin: the 750S3

Guzzi produced the V7 Sport until 1975, by which time it had been joined by alternative 750cc models. The 750S of 1974 was essentially a Sport with twin disc front brakes, plus black paintwork with diagonal stripes in red, orange or green. A year later came the 750S3, which combined similar styling with Guzzi's new brake system, which linked the two front and single rear discs. Although it looked superb and produced a claimed 72bhp, the S3 was slightly slower than the Sport, due to modifications including a milder camshaft and smaller carbs.

with a steel backbone between the cylinders. On the first batch of about 150 Sports, assembled in Guzzi's race department, the frame was painted red. Cycle parts were of high quality, including Guzzi forks with sealed damper units, Koni shocks plus a big twin-leading-shoe front drum brake.

The result was a stunning machine that combined aggressive looks with taut handling and a thrilling turn of speed – so much so that in the two years following its launch in 1971, the V7 Sport was arguably the world's fastest production motorcycle. In 1972 Italian magazine *Motociclismo* timed the Sport at 125mph (201km/h), faster than rivals including the Honda CB750, Kawasaki 750 H2, Laverda 750 SF and Ducati GT750. The magazine's testers also lapped Monza quickest on the Guzzi.

On the road the Sport cruised smoothly and effortlessly at 90mph (145km/h), and accelerated strongly from 4500rpm, although the motor lacked punch below that figure. High-speed stability was excellent, and cornering ability very good, with little adverse effect from the shaft final drive. The Sport was also raced successfully, finishing third in a 500km event at Monza on its debut in 1971, and also third at that year's Bol d'Or at Le Mans. Moto Guzzi had arrived as a superbike manufacturer.

Above left: Guzzi's transverse V-twin cylinders give a unique view from the front. 'Swan-neck' clip-on handlebars could be slid up the forks to give a more upright riding position.

Left: The Sport motor had reduced 748cc capacity, tuned internals and a new five-speed gearbox, plus a Bosch alternator at the front of the crankshaft.

MV Agusta 750 Sport

**Top speed
115mph**
185km/h

Right: MV's potent four-cylinder engine, with its gear-driven twin overhead cams, owed much to the firm's all-conquering grand prix racebikes.

Below: This Sport, built as Phil Read was winning MV's 16th consecutive 500cc world championship in 1973, has the disc front brake introduced that year.

The 750 Sport with which MV Agusta announced its arrival as a manufacturer of roadgoing superbikes was a long time coming, but it proved well worth the wait. The Sport, with its handsome lines, potent 743cc, dohc engine and impressive chassis specification, was stunning: a high performance roadster that was based on the Italian marque's all-conquering 500cc factory racebikes.

When the Sport reached production in the early 1970s, the small firm from Gallarate, near Milan, was nearing the end of a remarkable era of racetrack domination. MV's unbroken string of 500cc world titles stretched back to 1958, with riders including John Surtees, Mike Hailwood and Giacomo Agostini. For all this time the firm's autocratic boss, Count Domenico Agusta, had refused to produce a roadgoing version of the four-cylinder 'Gallarate fire engines'.

Instead, MV production had concentrated on the small-capacity singles with which Domenico had entered the motorcycle business in 1945, when the Agusta aircraft company was looking for a new direction at the end of the Second World War. Although a stylish 500cc four called the R19 Turismo had generated plenty of interest when

displayed at the Milan Show as early as 1950, it had not been produced. When MV did build a roadgoing four, it was an ugly 600cc, shaft-drive tourer that barely managed 100mph (161km/h) and sold in tiny numbers.

Designed for speed

The 750 Sport was dramatically different. This was an uncompromising sports machine. It had low handlebars, rearset footrests, bold red, white and blue paintwork, a humped race-style seat, a quartet of unfiltered Dell'Orto carburettors, and four shiny megaphone pipes. Its engine was based on that of the tourer, but bored out to 743cc, and tuned with higher compression plus larger exhaust valves.

It also produced considerably more power, its peak of 65bhp at 7900rpm being 13bhp up on that of the 600. Like that bike and MV's racers, the Sport used gear drive to its twin overhead cams. Its crankcases were sandcast, in aluminium rather than the racers' magnesium. The competition motor had no generator, so a combined starter/dynamo was added beneath the engine and connected by two belts.

Frame design owed more to the 600 than to the racebikes, as the Sport had one instead of two top tubes. The Sport also surprised many people by retaining the 600's shaft final drive system, reportedly because Count Domenico did not want the bike to be raced for fear that privateers would damage his factory team's reputation. But the Sport was equipped with top-quality cycle parts, including Ceriani forks and twin shocks, and Borrani alloy wheel rims. Early models had a big four-leading-shoe Grimeca front drum brake; later versions had twin discs.

For the few riders who could afford one, the Sport was a magnificent bike. Top speed was about 115mph (185km/h), rather than the factory's optimistic claim of 140mph (225km/h), but that was fast enough. And the MV's smooth acceleration, plus especially the aural treat of rustling motor and howling exhaust note, made every trip an event. Handling and braking were good, too, even if the heavy, shaft-drive Sport had nowhere near the agility or stability of MV's racers. Some owners later fitted chain-drive conversions from former MV race team boss Arturo Magni, who set up in business near Gallarate.

MV's dominance of the grand prix circuits was eventually halted by the Japanese two-strokes in 1975. The firm quit racing, and its roadsters did not last much longer. Despite their high prices, neither the Sport nor the later America and Monza fours were financially viable. Their intricate, hand-built engines were very costly to assemble, and production numbers were very low. By the end of the 1970s, MV had abandoned motorcycles to concentrate on helicopter production.

Left: The Sport's race-style full fairing was available as a factory option, as were a half fairing and a perspex flyscreen. The roadster's red, white and blue paint scheme did not match that of the scarlet 'Gallarate fire engine' grand prix bikes, but contributed to the MV's racy look.

Below: Despite its heavy drive-shaft assembly and a frame that was less rigid than that of the racers, the Sport handled reasonably well, especially when fitted with later Marzocchi shocks with remote damping fluid reservoirs, as is the case with this otherwise standard machine.

Specification	MV Agusta 750 Sport (1973)
Engine	Air-cooled dohc eight-valve four
Capacity	743cc (65 x 56mm)
Maximum power	65bhp @ 7900rpm
Transmission	Five-speed, shaft final drive
Frame	Steel twin downtube
Suspension	Telescopic front; twin shocks rear
Brakes	Twin discs front; drum rear
Weight	506lb (230kg)
Top speed	115mph (185km/h)

Kawasaki Z1

**Top speed
132mph**
212km/h

*Below: As well as being by
far the world's most
powerful production
motorcycle, the Z1 was a
handsome machine that
screamed power and speed
despite its high handlebars
and a thick dual seat. This
1974-model Z1-A differs
from the previous year's
original Z1 in its paint
scheme and alloy, instead
of black, engine finish.*

 They called it the King, and in the mid-1970s there was no disputing that Kawasaki's Z1 ruled the roads. When the 903cc four was launched in 1973, its top speed of over 130mph (210km/h) put the new bike 10mph (16km/h) ahead of Honda's CB750, its closest challenger. The Kawasaki was also more than a second quicker through the standing quarter mile, and just happened to be good-looking and very reliable too. No wonder it was an instant smash hit.

The Z1's early story is one of triumph over near disaster. Kawasaki originally intended to build a 750cc four, and was close to completing work on the project, codenamed New York Steak, when Honda unveiled the CB750. Once the initial disappointment had faded, Kawasaki's engineers realized that they now had the advantage of knowing what they had to beat. They enlarged their own engine to 903cc, and returned four years later to do just that.

Horsepower advantage

There was never any doubt that the Z1 engine, which featured twin overhead cams, working eight valves via bucket-and-shim adjustment, would have a substantial advantage over the smaller, sohc CB750 unit, which had changed little in the meantime. With a maximum output of 82bhp at 8500rpm, the Kawasaki motor was 15bhp more powerful, and produced considerably more low-rev torque too. It sat near vertically in a twin-downtube frame whose forks held a 19-inch wheel and single disc brake.

If the Z1's chassis specification was nothing out of the ordinary, its styling gained some extra advantage. Although the Kawasaki was undeniably big and heavy, weighing 542lb (246kg) with fuel, it was very well proportioned. Its curved fuel tank, small sidepanels and rear duck-tail behind the dual seat gave a stylish, vibrant look that was totally in keeping with its performance.

Not that the riders of any other bike got to see

A Faster Four – The Z1-R

Kawasaki's answer to increased challenges from rival Japanese fours in 1978 was the Z1-R, an uprated version of the current Z1000. The most obvious change was the bikini fairing, whose angular lines were echoed in the fuel tank and bodywork. The standard 1015cc engine remained, but bigger carbs and a four-into-one pipe increased output by 6bhp to 90bhp. Chassis updates included a braced frame, retuned suspension, cast wheels and revamped brakes. Top speed was increased to 130mph (209km/h), and the fairing boosted high-speed comfort, though not stability. Handling at lower speeds was marginally better, too. Overall this was the best big Kawasaki yet.

more than the back of the fast-disappearing Z1 on the road. Its acceleration was brutal by contemporary standards, with the big twin-cam motor churning out smooth, strong torque throughout its rev range. There was plenty of scope to make it faster still, too, as many tuners and racers soon confirmed.

Handling was a different matter. In normal use the Z1 gave no problem, and was even fairly comfortable despite its high handlebars. Pushed harder, the awesome motor was sometimes too much for the chassis, causing high-speed instability. Many owners fitted steering dampers and aftermarket rear shocks, which helped. Better still was a frame kit from a specialist such as Harris, Martin, Egli or Bakker.

Most owners found the Z1 plenty good enough as it was. Such was its performance lead that Kawasaki's only changes for the first two years were cosmetics and minor details. In 1976 a second front disc brake, previously an optional extra, became standard fitment, while smaller carbs and more restrictive pipes (to reduce emissions for the US market) reduced peak power slightly. The bike also gained a new name, becoming the Z900. One other thing didn't change: its status as the two-wheeled King of the road.

Above left: Kawasaki's dohc four-cylinder engine not only outclassed all opposition with its 82bhp power output, it also proved remarkably reliable.

Left: The Z1's high handlebars made life uncomfortable for its rider at high speed, and did nothing to aid stability.

Specification	Kawasaki Z1 (1973)
Engine	Air-cooled dohc eight-valve four
Capacity	903cc (66 x 66mm)
Maximum power	82bhp @ 8500rpm
Transmission	Five-speed, chain final drive
Frame	Steel twin downtube
Suspension	Telescopic front; twin shocks rear
Brakes	Single disc front; drum rear
Weight	542lb (246kg) wet
Top speed	132mph (212km/h)

BMW R90S

**Top speed
125mph**
201km/h

*Right: Dell'Orto pumper
carbs and high-compression
pistons raised the 898cc
boxer motor's output to
67bhp.*

*Below: The R90S's fairing
was as important as its
engine in increasing
practical performance.*

On pure performance, BMW's R90S was not the fastest superbike of the mid-1970s. Nor was it the quickest around a racetrack; at least, not often. But for a rider with a long distance to travel on straight roads and twisty ones, there was nothing on two wheels that would prove faster or more comfortable than the uniquely well-equipped flat twin.

The BMW's distinctive smoked paint scheme was perfectly in keeping with its image as a very refined and expensive sports-tourer. In many respects, the R90S was the best all-round superbike of its day. Certainly, no other production machine could match its combination of 125mph (201km/h) top speed, relaxed high-speed cruising ability, fine handling, reliability and impeccable finish.

BMW had plenty of practice in building horizontally opposed twins, and it showed. The R90S came from a line of flat twins stretching back to Max Fritz's original R32 of 1923. The German firm had been building competent, comfortable and conservative tourers for many years. But this bike, shaped by noted stylist Hans Muth, had a distinctly more aggressive personality.

The basics were typical BMW. Like the naked R90/6, which was launched at the same time in 1973, the R90S owed much to the previous year's R75. Enlarging the 745cc R75's bore from 82 to 90mm while retaining the 70.6mm stroke increased capacity to 898cc. BMW also made a few other updates, including a revised gearchange mechanism, more powerful 280W alternator and stronger bottom end.

There was more to the S-bike than just its fairing. The engine was given a higher compression ratio, 9.5:1 against the 9:1 of the R90/6, and breathed in through big 38mm Dell'Orto carbs with accelerator pumps. Maximum power was 67bhp at 7000rpm, an increase of 7bhp over the standard model. The R90S also had a steering damper in its cockpit, a larger fuel tank and a second front brake disc.

The extra power gave the S model a worthwhile boost at high revs, without hindering either its torquey mid-range response or its smoothness at most engine speeds. Better still, the fairing meant the engine's performance could be fully exploited by the rider, who was free of the wind-blast generated by every rival superbike. Other manufacturers would soon follow BMW's lead, but for the moment the fairing put the R90S in a class of its own.

Comfortable ride

Handling was good, too, despite suspension that was soft enough to give a comfortable ride. Notwithstanding its steering damper the S sometimes felt light at the front when approaching its top speed, but that was even more true of most naked rivals. The twin-disc front brake system was reliable but lacked feel until uprated in 1975. Neat touches included a dashboard clock, generous fuel range of 200 miles (322km) or more, and a seat that allowed the rider to cover that distance in comfort.

BMWs had never been cheap, and the R90S, with its all-inclusive specification, was no exception to this rule. In many markets it was more than twice the price of Honda's CB750. That ensured the R90S would be ridden only by a select band of riders. Although the bike was a success, it was outsold by the standard 90/5.

Those riders fortunate enough to cover serious distance on the R90S knew that it was a very special motorcycle. If what you needed was a speed, handling ability and comfort, the R90S delivered in style. Oh, and sometimes it was the

Specification	BMW R90S (1974)
Engine	Air-cooled ohv four-valve pushrod flat twin
Capacity	898cc (90 x 70.6mm)
Maximum power	67bhp @ 7000rpm
Transmission	Five-speed, shaft final drive
Frame	Steel twin downtube
Suspension	Telescopic front; twin shocks rear
Brakes	Twin discs front; single disc rear
Weight	474lb (215kg) wet
Top speed	125mph (201km/h)

quickest superbike round a racetrack, too. BMW ace Reg Pridmore's victory in the 1976 US Superbike championship was proof of that.

Above: At heart the R90S was a traditional BMW boxer, but its fairing and especially its bold smoked grey or orange paint schemes gave a much more modern and attractive look. The bike's performance was backed by typically practical features including gaitered forks, a generous dual seat and shaft final drive.

Left: Although the R90S chassis was built for comfort as much as speed, the bike's rigid frame and fairly well-controlled suspension gave reliable handling. On long journeys, especially, few contemporary superbikes could match the effortless performance of BMW's flagship, which unfortunately had a hefty price tag to match its impressive specification.

Benelli 750 Sei

**Top speed
115mph**
185km/h

*Right: Straight-line speed
was not the broad and
softly tuned Benelli's forte,
but it cruised smoothly and
effortlessly at speeds of
90mph (145km/h) and more.*

*Below: The Benelli's styling
was conventional, but its
engine width and number of
exhaust pipes were
certainly not. A luggage
rack was an optional extra.*

 Benelli's exotic six-cylinder superbike
deserves a place in any history of fast
motorcycles, despite one undeniable fact:
by the standards of mid-1970s superbikes, it wasn't
outstandingly fast. The Italian machine was
undeniably stylish, sophisticated and expensive but
lacked the outright speed of the best Japanese
superbikes and its Italian rivals alike.

Despite this the Sei was a fine all-round
performer, combining effortless acceleration,
remarkable smoothness and excellent handling in
an eye-catching package topped by six gleaming
chrome-plated exhaust mufflers. As well as being
the only six-cylinder bike on the market when it
was launched in 1974, the Sei also came with a
pedigree. Benelli, based at Pesaro on Italy's
Adriatic coast, had won the 250cc world
championship as recently as 1969, beating the two-
strokes with a four-cylinder four-stroke ridden by
Australian Kel Carruthers.

Inspired by Honda

Apart from its number of cylinders, the Sei's 748cc engine contained little innovative engineering, and was not outstandingly powerful despite a claimed peak output of 71bhp at 8500rpm. Cynics commented that the sohc unit was little more than one-and-a-half Honda CB500 motors. Like Honda's four it featured cylinder dimensions of 56 x 50.6mm, and a central camchain. Similar details such as the ribbed oil filter housing also revealed the main inspiration of the Italian firm's engineers.

But the Benelli motor also incorporated differences including its alternator, which sat not at the end of the crankshaft but behind the cylinders on the right, where it was driven by gears. That allowed the six-cylinder motor's crankcases to be narrow, as did the use of only three 24mm Dell'Orto carburettors, the outer two of which fed angled inlet manifolds that allowed the carbs to be close together beneath the fuel tank.

The motor was tuned for mid-range performance and was impressively tractable, producing useful torque everywhere above 2000rpm in top gear. Carburation was crisp, and there was barely a step in the power delivery as the revs rose through the range. This meant that although the Benelli's top speed of about 115mph (185km/h) was unexceptional, the bike impressed with its effortless high-speed cruising ability.

Rapid riding was also boosted by a chassis that was conventional in layout but which worked much better than most contemporary set-ups. The steel twin-cradle frame held Marzocchi forks, plus rear shocks either from the same firm or Sebac. Both ends were fairly firm in Italian sporting tradition. In combination with the reasonably rigid frame, that helped give good straight-line stability.

For a big bike the Benelli was also impressively agile, and could be cornered faster than many much smaller machines. It had fairly generous ground clearance, especially considering its engine layout. Powerful twin Brembo front disc brakes, backed up by a rear drum, added to the six-cylinder machine's impressive chassis performance.

Sadly for Benelli and particularly the firm's boss, Argentinean car baron Alejandro de Tomaso, the Sei was not a sales hit. Despite its array of cylinders the Benelli lacked the character and performance that made the best rival Italian superbikes popular. Potential owners were worried about reliability and high running costs as well as the bike's considerable purchase price.

The Sei nevertheless remained in production with few changes until the end of the decade, when its engine was enlarged to produce the 900 Sei. This had a little extra power and a neat headlamp fairing, but no more charisma. It sold in similarly small numbers and marked the end, at least for the next quarter century, of Benelli's attempt to become a major superbike manufacturer.

Left: Benelli emphasized the motor's layout with three shiny silencers on each side, leaving the owner plenty of polishing work. The bike sounded good although the pipes were too efficient to allow full benefit of the six-cylinder unit.

Below: The Sei's large frontal area and broad fuel tank gave a rather heavy look. Although the Benelli was not a sportster in the Italian tradition, it was reasonably light and handled well. Big Brembo front brake discs supplied plenty of stopping power.

Specification	Benelli 750 Sei (1975)
Engine	Air-cooled sohc 12-valve transverse six
Capacity	748cc (56 x 50.6mm)
Maximum power	71bhp @ 8500rpm
Transmission	Five-speed, chain final drive
Frame	Steel twin cradle
Suspension	Telescopic front; twin shocks rear
Brakes	Twin discs front; drum rear
Weight	485lb (220kg)
Top speed	115mph (185km/h)

Ducati 900SS

**Top speed
135mph**
217km/h

*Right: The Ducati's fairing
and slim build gave good
aerodynamics, which
combined with the twin's
light weight to make it
competitive against more
powerful rivals.*

*Below: Few bikes come
close to matching the
aggressive look of the
900SS, with its clip-on bars,
single seat and rearset
footrests, plus the desmo
V-twin engine's unfiltered
Dell'Orto carbs and free-
breathing Conti pipes.*

 Ducati's original 900 Super Sport was one
of the most singleminded sporting
superbikes that ever devoured an innocent
public road. It was essentially a street-legal
production racer: fast, raw and uncompromising. It
handled and stopped brilliantly, looked and
sounded gorgeous and was a match for anything on
road or track.

The 900SS owed its existence to Ducati's
victory in the Imola 200 race in 1972, when factory
pilots Paul Smart and Bruno Spaggiari had finished
first and second ahead of numerous factory
opponents. The factory celebrated by producing a
small batch of road-legal replicas of the racebike.
These were popular, so more were built, this time
called the 750 Super Sport instead of Imola Replica
as the model had initially been known.

The half-faired 750SS mimicked Smart's fully
faired racer with its silver finish. Its 748cc V-twin
engine came from the firm's 750 Sport, and was
tuned with desmodromic valve operation, high-
compression forged pistons, polished internals, big
Dell'Orto carbs and free-breathing Conti pipes.

Fabio Taglioni's engine format of 90-degree, inline
V-twin with bevel drive to single overhead
camshafts had already become a Ducati trademark,
but this was the first roadgoing twin to use his
desmodromic system of positive valve closure.

Racing success

Ducati built only about 200 bikes, but all were snapped up and some were raced with good results in 1974. The Bologna factory was encouraged, and the following year created the more widely available 900SS, by replacing the smaller engine with a V-twin unit based on that of the existing 860GT. This combined a bigger, 86mm bore with the original 74.4mm stroke, giving a capacity of 864cc. Like the smaller model, it featured desmo valvegear, polished conrods, unfiltered 40mm Dell'Ortos and barely silenced Contis.

Those mods lifted peak power to an impressive 79bhp at 7000rpm at the crankshaft, or 68bhp at the rear wheel, and the 900SS had the chassis to match. Like its 750SS predecessor it was starkly functional, with its half-fairing, clip-on handlebars, rearset footrests, twin drilled Brembo front discs, and racy single seat. There was no electric starter, nor anything else not required for the bike's sole purpose of providing high performance.

The 900SS roared to a top speed of 135mph (217km/h), and cruised at 100mph (161km/h) with a smooth, long-legged feel. That was seriously fast in 1975, and the Ducati's handling was even better. It was not the most agile of bikes, but no rival could match the cornering poise and high-speed

Just Like Mike's – The Hailwood Replica

Paul Smart's Imola 200 win of 1972 was one great moment in Ducati's history, and another came six years later when Mike Hailwood, returning to racing from retirement, won the Isle of Man Formula One TT on a Ducati V-twin prepared by Sports Motorcycles. The following year Ducati introduced a special 900SS Hailwood Replica in honour of the victory. As well as a full fairing in Hailwood's red and green paint scheme, it featured gold-anodized Brembo brake calipers, new cast wheels and longer rear shocks. The Replica immediately became a bestseller, and remained in Ducati's range, with various modifications along the way, right up until 1985.

stability provided by the lean V-twin's blend of rigid frame, long wheelbase and taut Marzocchi suspension. Roadholding, braking and ground clearance were all exemplary too.

The uncompromising 900SS demanded commitment from it rider, and was too extreme for some. But it made a superb production racer. And for road riders who were captivated by its beauty, speed and pure-bred character, there was no bike to touch it. To paraphrase a road test of the time, the 900SS was a distillation of all the thrills and sensations that made high-performance motorcycling worthwhile.

Left: Ducati's 864cc, 90-degree V-twin engine featured bevel-shaft drive to its sohc, desmodromic valvegear. Long-legged power delivery and unshakeable high-speed stability were the 900SS trademarks.

Specification	Ducati 900SS (1975)
Engine	Air-cooled sohc four-valve 90-degree V-twin
Capacity	864cc (86 x 74.4mm)
Maximum power	79bhp @ 7000rpm
Transmission	Five-speed, chain final drive
Frame	Steel ladder
Suspension	Telescopic front; twin shocks rear
Brakes	Twin discs front; single disc rear
Weight	414lb (188kg) wet
Top speed	135mph (217km/h)

Laverda Jota

**Top speed
140mph**
225km/h

*Below: The Jota's great
asset was engine
performance rather than
handling, but the big
Laverda cornered well
enough to keep it ahead of
its rivals on road and track.
Firm suspension helped
maintain stability in most
situations, despite the
combined effect of the
triple's size, weight and
sheer brute horsepower.*

There was no mistaking the appeal of the Laverda Jota. The Italian triple backed up its square-jawed naked style with massive, sometimes intimidating, performance. The Jota was big, brutal, loud and supremely powerful. In the right hands it was simply the fastest thing on two wheels in the late 1970s, as a string of production race victories confirmed.

This most famous of Laverda's 981cc air-cooled triples resulted from a collaboration between the firm from Breganze in northern Italy and Slater Brothers, its British importer. The basis of the Jota was the 3C, itself a potent and handsome machine, which Laverda had created in 1973, essentially by adding an extra cylinder to its existing 650cc parallel twin.

In 1975 brothers Roger and Richard Slater, intending to production race the triple, created a machine they called the 3CE – the 'E' standing for England – by fitting modifications including a free-breathing exhaust system, rearset footrests and

single seat. Meanwhile the factory was developing its own update, the 3CL, which featured cast wheels, triple disc brakes and a tail fairing, and was introduced as a 1976 model.

Combining the two bikes created the machine that the Slaters christened the Jota, after a Spanish dance in three-four time. This time they went further with the engine tuning, fitting the dohc triple with factory endurance race camshafts and high-compression pistons. The result was a substantially increased peak output of 90bhp at 8000rpm, with noise and performance to match.

This was an Italian bike that could live with Japan's finest for sheer horsepower and speed. The Jota felt rough below about 4000rpm due to its lumpy cams, but came alive above that figure with exhilarating acceleration, a soulful three-cylinder bellow and a top speed of 140mph (225km/h).

The triple was a demanding bike to ride, its power delivery and sheer speed combining with the unfaired riding position, engine vibration and a

Mirage – The Fast-Touring Triple

Laverda produced another fine superbike in 1978 by enlarging the 981cc engine to 1116cc, and fitting higher handlebars plus a larger dual seat to create a slightly softer, touring-oriented model called the 1200. Again, Slater Brothers uprated it with hot cams and a free-breathing exhaust system (compression ratio was left standard) to produce the Mirage. The result was a fast, yet very torquey and versatile, machine. The Laverda factory adopted the Mirage name, although for most markets the bike retained its standard cams and exhaust.

heavy clutch to make the rider work hard. In other respects the Laverda was well-equipped, with finish and electrics that were excellent by Italian standards. Handling was generally good, thanks to a strong frame and typically firm Ceriani suspension. But the triple was a tall, heavy machine that required plenty of muscle from its rider, and was prone to weave at high speed. The trio of big, cast iron Brembo discs gave plenty of stopping power, wet or dry.

Obvious appeal

Although the Jota was assembled in Breganze (apart from silencers and collector box), the tuned triple was officially a UK-only model. But limited numbers were sold in other markets including America. The price was high, but the appeal was obvious: this was arguably the world's fastest roadster in 1976. Slaters' racer Peter Davies supported that claim by dominating the British production race championship.

Laverda modified the triple in subsequent years, notably with a variety of half-fairings, and in 1982 produced a more refined version, the Jota 120. This had a 120-degree firing order, in place of the old 180-degree (one piston up, two down) arrangement. The Jota 120 was much smoother, yet retained the traditional triple character. Although short-lived, it was a fine way to end the famous line.

Below left: Laverda's 981cc dohc triple was a potent unit in standard form, and became even more impressive when tuned to Jota specification with factory endurance racing camshafts, plus pistons that raised compression ratio from 9:1 to 10:1. The result was a peak output of 90bhp.

Below: The Jota's raw, muscular styling was always a big part of its appeal. This bike has the classical early combination of low-set adjustable handlebars, humped seat and Laverda's traditional orange paintwork. In the 1980s the triple could be bought with an optional half-fairing that made high-speed cruising a more practical proposition.

Specification	Laverda Jota (1976)
Engine	Air-cooled dohc six-valve triple
Capacity	981cc (75 x 74mm)
Maximum power	90bhp @ 8000rpm
Transmission	Five-speed, chain final drive
Frame	Steel twin downtube
Suspension	Telescopic front; twin shocks rear
Brakes	Twin discs front; single disc rear
Weight	521lb (236kg) wet
Top speed	140mph (225km/h)

Moto Guzzi Le Mans

**Top speed
130mph**
209km/h

*Above right: The Le Mans'
top speed of about 130mph
(209km/h) made it one of
the fastest bikes on the road
in the mid-1970s, and that
performance was delivered
with a relaxed feel that
encouraged fast cruising.
So too did the Guzzi's
excellent high-speed
handling, aided by firm and
well-damped suspension.*

*Below: Essentially the Le
Mans look was similar to
that of previous sporting
Guzzis. But the addition of
a bikini fairing, plus a new
dual seat whose front
section covered the rear of
the fuel tank, combined with
the Italian firm's trademark
engine layout to produce
one of the most glamorous
and distinctive of superbikes.*

Long, lean and unmistakable, with its tiny
headlamp fairing and muscular transverse
V-twin engine, the Le Mans was arguably
the most stylish superbike of the mid-1970s. Much
more than that, it was fast, handled superbly and
had excellent brakes. Guzzi's flagship was a hard-
charging roadburner that could cruise effortlessly at
100mph (161km/h), carve through corners at a
rapid pace, and generally keep up with the best of
its rivals from Italy or Japan.

Moto Guzzi, based on the banks of Lake Como,
had a long history of racing success and innovative
bikes including the exotic 500cc V8 racer of the
1950s. Although still best known for its long-
running singles, Guzzi was having increasing
success with its distinctive transverse V-twins. But
it was the Le Mans, introduced in 1976, that put the
old firm back in the spotlight.

The Le Mans was based on the 750 S3, itself a
striking and deceptively rapid unfaired roadster that
had been developed from the earlier V7 Sport,
Guzzi's first high-performance V-twin. The new
bike's most obvious innovation was its striking
styling, which combined the headlamp fairing with
a curvaceous fuel tank and angular seat.

In search of more power, Guzzi enlarged the
S3's 748cc engine to 844cc, and increased
compression ratio from 9.8:1 to 10.2:1. They also
fitted unfiltered 36mm Dell'Orto carburettors plus a
new, free-breathing exhaust system. The shaft-drive
V-twin was still a fairly old-fashioned device with
pushrod valve operation and a slow-shifting five-
speed gearbox. But it now produced 80bhp at

7300rpm, an increase of 8bhp, and had plenty of
mid-range punch, which the smaller S3 motor had
rather disappointingly lacked.

That extra power was enough for a top speed of
130mph (209km/h), impressive at the time. The big
motor was lumpy at low speed, but smoothed out
as the revs rose, and pulled hard through the mid-
range. Where the Guzzi really scored was with its
uniquely long-legged feel which, in combination
with the leant-forward riding position and
protection from the flyscreen, enabled the Le
Mans' rider to keep up those speeds for long
periods without discomfort.

Fine handling

A rigid steel frame gave fine handling despite the
occasionally unsettling effect of the shaft final
drive. The Le Mans wasn't the lightest or most
manoeuvrable of bikes but its high-speed stability
was immense, thanks partly to typically stiff
suspension. At speeds that would have the riders of
rival Japanese superbikes weaving, the Guzzi
rumbled on without a twitch, its rider tucked down
at the clip-ons behind that neat flyscreen.

Guzzi's brake set-up of three linked, cast iron
Brembo discs was far superior to most rival
systems, too, especially in the wet. The handlebar
lever operated one front disc; the foot pedal the
other plus the rear. By Italian standards the Guzzi
was well built and reliable, too, although it suffered
from typically poor electrics.

The Le Mans' high price ensured that it was
never going to sell in huge numbers, but it gained a
cult following, opened many riders' eyes to Guzzi's
quirky V-twins, and remained in production for 19
years, through a series of updates. Unfortunately its
performance did not improve with age.

Left: Apart from its transverse V-twin motor's protruding cylinders, the Le Mans was a slim and compact bike. Its frame and front forks came from the earlier S3 model. Guzzi's linked braking system used the foot pedal to operate one front disc plus the rear disc, while the other front disc was worked by the handlebar lever.

On the contrary, the Le Mans Mk2 version of 1979 was slightly slower, though it at least gave its rider the benefit of an angular full fairing. The 1982 model Mk3 regained some power, but Guzzi made things worse in 1985 with the 949cc Le Mans Mk4, whose 16-inch front wheel gave unreliable handling. By this time, the stability and competitive speed of the 1976 model were just a fond memory. In the case of the Moto Guzzi Le Mans, original was definitely best.

Specification	Moto Guzzi Le Mans 850 (1976)
Engine	Air-cooled ohv four-valve pushrod 90-degree transverse V-twin
Capacity	844cc (83 x 78mm)
Maximum power	80bhp @ 7300rpm
Transmission	Five-speed, shaft final drive
Frame	Steel spine
Suspension	Telescopic front; twin shocks rear
Brakes	Twin discs front; single disc rear
Weight	476lb (216kg) wet
Top speed	130mph (209km/h)

Suzuki GS750

**Top speed
125mph**
201km/h

*Below: The Suzuki's styling
was smart without being
remotely imaginative. There
was also little that was
innovative in its dohc, four-
cylinder engine layout and
steel-framed, twin-shock
chassis. But the GS's speed
and generally high level of
performance, both in a
straight line and on a twisty
road, meant that Suzuki's
first big four-stroke provided
plenty of excitement.*

 Suzuki delayed for a long time before finally entering the market with a four-cylinder, four-stroke superbike in 1977, but the wait was worthwhile. The GS750 was a stunningly powerful and well-engineered bike that not only matched its rivals for speed and reliability, but surpassed them for handling. Coming from a company whose most notable previous model had been the GT750 two-stroke triple, the GS was a remarkable machine.

For all its merits the GS750 was far from the world's most imaginative motorcycle. In the finest tradition of Japanese motorcycle design it was closely based on the best existing machine of a few years earlier, in this case Kawasaki's Z900. The GS's dohc air-cooled engine shared the famously powerful and strong Kawasaki's 65mm piston diameter and even its valve sizes and timing, achieving its 748cc capacity with a shorter 56.4mm stroke. Peak output was 68bhp at 8500rpm, making the Suzuki the most powerful 750 on the market.

In contrast to the large and rather gaudy GT750 two-stroke that it was built to replace, the GS was conservatively styled, and disguised its substantial 505lb (229kg) fuelled-up weight well. There was a notable lack of fuss about the whole machine, which combined simple paintwork with black sidepanels, a slim front mudguard and a thick and effective dual-seat. The only remotely frivolous feature was a digital gear indicator in the instrument panel.

Superior chassis design

Chassis design was also conventional, based around a twin-downtube frame that outclassed several apparently similar rivals due partly to its heavily braced steering head area and needle-roller swingarm bearings. Similarly, although the front forks and twin rear shocks were of typical design, they proved to be above average in use. And the GS combined its 19-inch front and 18-inch rear wheels with a single disc brake at each end.

Smaller Four: the GS550

Suzuki moved rapidly to follow the GS750 with a middleweight four, the GS550, which appeared only a few months later in 1977. Although the similarly styled and inevitably slower 550 did not have the same impact as the bigger model, it too was an impressive machine, with a top speed of 110mph (177km/h), sound handling and superbly versatile performance. Like the GS750, it was impeccably reliable as well as competitively priced, and soon became popular.

Specification	Suzuki GS750 (1977)
Engine	Air-cooled dohc eight-valve four
Capacity	749cc (65 x 56.4mm)
Maximum power	68bhp @ 8500rpm
Transmission	Five-speed, chain final drive
Frame	Steel twin downtube
Suspension	Telescopic front; twin shocks rear
Brakes	Disc front and rear
Weight	505lb (229kg)
Top speed	125mph (201km/h)

The brakes combined to give reasonable stopping power and they were needed, too, because the GS750 was blindingly fast. At low revs it was docile in typical Japanese four fashion, pulling smoothly from as low as 2000rpm in the highest ratio of its smooth-shifting five-speed gearbox. Once the rev-counter needle reached 6000rpm, though, the Suzuki took off in fine style, storming smoothly towards the 9500rpm redline through the gears, as it headed for a top speed of over 120mph (193km/h).

Although the riding position was roomy and upright (especially on the American market model with its higher bars), the GS was fairly comfortable and easily powerful enough for sustained cruising at 80mph (129km/h) or more. And its handling was excellent, too, combining good stability with agility and steering precision that matched all of its mass-produced Japanese rivals, and surpassed quite a few by a distance.

Predictably the GS was a big success, instantly establishing Suzuki as a major superbike force. It also proved commendably reliable, so much so that when the model was revised in 1979, the only notable changes were new paint schemes, cast wheels and a second front brake disc. If the GS750 had been produced by any of the experienced superbike manufacturers it would have been a triumph. Coming as Suzuki's first ever big four-stroke, it was truly inspired.

Top left: The GS750's chassis was every bit as impressive as its smooth and powerful four-cylinder engine, and maintained stability even when the bike was being cornered at speed.

Above left: This US-market Suzuki's high handlebars did not add to high-speed comfort. But in this form or with flatter bars, the GS was one of the world's fastest superbikes.

Harley-Davidson Cafe Racer

**Top speed
115mph**
185km/h

*Right: The black-finished
engine was essentially the
same 998cc, 45-degree
pushrod V-twin that powered
the Sportster model,
complete with identical
61bhp peak output.*

*Below: With its handlebar
fairing, V-twin engine and
black paintwork, the XLCR
was one of the most stylish
bikes on the road, if not
the fastest.*

 The most improbable contender in the
superbike battle of 1977 was a racy-
looking 1000cc V-twin from Harley-
Davidson, complete with headlamp fairing, all
black paintwork and a serious dose of attitude. The
XLCR Cafe Racer was a bold move from the
Milwaukee firm, whose reputation for speed and
performance had been surrendered long before, and
whose range otherwise consisted only of cruisers
and tourers.

Harley was keen to promote the Cafe Racer as a
high-performance machine. The firm's
advertisements talked excitedly of 120mph
(193km/h) top speed, and about how this was the
most powerful production bike that Harley had ever
built. In reality the XLCR shared many components
with other models in the firm's range, and was
closer in performance and feel to Harley's own
laid-back Sportster than to rapid V-twins from the
likes of Ducati and Moto Guzzi.

Willie G.'s project

The Cafe Racer was a visually striking machine for all that. The model was created by Harley design chief Willie G. Davidson, whose Super Glide of six years earlier had put struggling Harley back on track. As well as the small fairing, the XLCR had a large (by Sportster standards) fuel tank, a single seat that blended neatly into the rear fender, a tiny front fender, and a siamesed exhaust system with twin silencers. All were finished in black.

So was the engine itself, although apart from its cosmetic update the 998cc pushrod-operated 45-degree V-twin was identical to that of the standard XL Sportster. Gearing was one tooth lower for improved acceleration, but carburation was still by a single 38mm Keihin. As the new exhaust system made no difference to performance, peak output remained the Sportster's 61bhp at 6200rpm.

Chassis changes centred on a new frame, which combined twin front downtubes from the Sportster with a new rear section based on that of the XR750 racebike. This was more rigid and provided a more suitable, rearward mounting point for the shocks, which bolted to a box-section swingarm that was stronger than the XL's tubular equivalent. Morris alloy wheels and a triple-disc brake system replaced the Sportster's wire spokes, single front disc and rear drum.

The Cafe Racer's riding position was sportier, too, thanks to near-flat handlebars and slightly rear-set footrests. This combined with the fairing's wind protection to make the XLCR a handy bike for highway cruising. It sat at 70mph (113km/h) feeling stable and relaxed. Vibration became a problem above that speed, though, and the Harley

Left: Handling was good by Harley standards, and the Cafe Racer was stable and fairly well controlled in slow speed bends, especially when its front forks were fitted with an aftermarket brace as with this example. But the combination of handlebar-mounted fairing and relatively thin steel frame tubes resulted in a tendency to weave at high speed.

lacked the power for truly competitive performance. Its top speed was not far off the claimed 120mph (193km/h), but acceleration was modest and the four-speed gearbox rather crude.

Handling was acceptable, despite a tendency to weave at high speed, and a ponderous feel in slower corners. The Cafe Racer's chassis was an improvement for Harley, who would later adopt its rear suspension arrangement on the Sportster too. But although the brakes were also praised, the XLCR's overall performance and image did not impress many performance-oriented motorcyclists.

More importantly for Harley, the Cafe Racer also held little appeal for the American riders who formed the majority of the firm's customers. This bike might have been Milwaukee's fastest ever production machine, but Harley fans preferred the laid-back Low Rider, which was introduced in the same year and was a huge success. By contrast only about 3200 Cafe Racers were built in 1977 and '78 before the model was dropped. The XLCR Cafe Racer was proof that, for Harley at least, faster did not necessarily mean better.

Below left: Some bikes look good from every angle, and the XLCR is one of them. The Harley's screen and flat handlebars combined to keep off the wind at speed. The twin disc front brake, backed up by another disc at the rear, gave much improved stopping power over the Sportster's set-up of single front disc and rear drum.

Specification	Harley-Davidson XLCR Cafe Racer (1977)
Engine	Air-cooled ohv pushrod four-valve 45-degree V-twin
Capacity	998cc (81 x 96.8mm)
Maximum power	61bhp @ 6200rpm
Transmission	Four-speed, chain final drive
Frame	Steel twin downtube
Suspension	Telescopic front; twin shocks rear
Brakes	Twin discs front; disc rear
Weight	515lb (234kg)
Top speed	115mph (185km/h)

Yamaha XS750

**Top speed
120mph**
193km/h

*Right: The Yamaha handled
well despite being a fairly
heavy bike with shaft final
drive.*

*Below: The original
XS750's rounded styling,
silver paintwork and black-
finished three-cylinder
engine gave a distinctive
look from the front.*

 Few bikes have arrived to such a warm
welcome as Yamaha's first big four-stroke
superbike, the XS750 triple, whose
performance, distinctive style and versatility made
it highly rated by press and public alike on its
launch in 1977. And fewer still have followed that
initial impact by fading from the scene quite so
quickly, having failed to make a mark on a
superbike market that was suddenly awash with
high-quality alternatives.

On paper, the Yamaha looked a winner to its
last, carefully considered detail. The basics were
very much in place. Its engine was a 747cc air-
cooled triple with twin overhead camshafts, a 120-
degree crankshaft (for smooth running) and shaft
final drive. Yamaha's designers had kept the engine

compact by using bevel gears to turn the
crankshaft's drive through 90 degrees for the drive
shaft. With a maximum output of 64bhp at
7200rpm and plenty of mid-range torque, the triple
came very close to matching its sportier chain-
driven four-cylinder rivals for pure power.

This unique engine was matched to rounded,
distinctive styling and a relatively conventional but
cleverly designed chassis. The twin-downtube steel
frame employed substantial bracing around the
steering head, in the fashion of the BMW's R75
twin. Forks and twin rear shocks were typical
Japanese items. The Yamaha was rather tall and it
was heavy at 514lb (233kg) dry. But it was also
well appointed, with a roomy riding position, clear
instruments and self-cancelling indicators.

Straight-line performance was undeniably
impressive. The Yamaha's motor was smooth,
tractable and powerful, sending the bike to a top
speed of 120mph (193km/h) and allowing effortless
high-speed cruising. Its three-cylinder layout gave a
pleasant character, with the bonus of a distinctive
exhaust note. And the XS had an efficient five-
speed gearbox as well as its shaft final drive
system, itself a real benefit in the days of fast-
wearing drive chains.

That drive shaft had almost no adverse effect on
the Yamaha's handling, which received much praise
although the bike was designed for comfort as
much as for agility. 'We failed to make it waggle,
weave or twitch and we tried our damnedest,'

enthused *Bike* magazine's experienced tester, who summed up the XS750 as the best Japanese bike and best all-round touring machine he'd ever ridden – including numerous more expensive BMWs.

Comfortable cruising

Long-distance comfort was good by the standards of unfaired bikes, thanks partly to the generously padded dual-seat. One criticism was that the fuel tank was too small for touring, but this and the poor headlamp were the only criticisms, apart from the mediocre wet-weather performance of both tyres and disc brakes, which was typical at the time. Given the Yamaha's very competitive price, it looked set to become a big hit.

But the motorcycling public decreed otherwise, partly because of the rival attraction of fours including Honda's proven CB750, Suzuki's new GS750 and Kawasaki's cheaper Z650; and partly because the Yamaha quickly earned a reputation for unreliability. Troubles included piston ring failure, seizure of the central cylinder, rapidly wearing primary drive chain and ignition points, plus the gearbox's occasional trick of jumping from fourth straight into first.

Word of the unreliability spread, and the XS750 never recovered. Yamaha made a series of updates to cure the problems, and in 1978 improved the triple with the XS750E model, which had an extra 4bhp, revised lubrication system and uprated front

Specification	Yamaha XS750 (1977)
Engine	Air-cooled dohc six-valve transverse triple
Capacity	747cc (68 x 68.6mm)
Maximum power	64bhp @ 7200rpm
Transmission	Five-speed, shaft final drive
Frame	Steel twin downtube
Suspension	Telescopic front; twin shocks rear
Brakes	Disc front and rear
Weight	514lb (233kg)
Top speed	120mph (193km/h)

suspension. But the damage had been done, and neither that model nor the revamped XS850 that followed two years later could bring Yamaha's triple the success that had once seemed so assured.

Above: Chassis layout was typical of the mid-1970s, with twin-downtube steel frame, non-adjustable telescopic forks and twin rear shocks. Compliant suspension and the broad dual seat helped make the Yamaha a useful long-distance machine, despite its small fuel tank.

Left: Yamaha's 747cc twin-cam triple initially impressed all who rode the bike with its 64bhp output, smoothness, abundance of mid-range torque, and unobtrusive shaft final drive system. But the Japanese firm's insufficient development testing of its first big four-stroke engine became clear from the XS750's inherent mechanical problems.

Bimota SB2

**Top speed
130mph**
210km/h

*Below: The SB2's stunning
styling and advanced
chassis technology resulted
in a bike that could almost
have been built more than
20 years after its actual
debut in 1977. The Bimota's
swooping one-piece tank
cover and seat unit was a
self-supporting structure
made from fibreglass and
aluminium. Other advanced
features included cast
wheels, drilled discs and
rising-rate monoshock
suspension.*

When Bimota, a small company from
Rimini in north-eastern Italy, released its
first streetbike in 1977, motorcycle design
took a sudden leap forward. The SB2, powered by
the 748cc four-cylinder engine from Suzuki's
recently released GS750 four, was visually striking,
brilliantly engineered and uniquely single-minded.
Its bold, fully-faired styling was matched by a
chassis that combined a technically advanced frame
with state-of-the-art cycle parts.

Bimota, whose co-founder and genius designer
Massimo Tamburini would later create such bikes
as the Ducati 916 and MV Agusta F4, had already
established an unmatched reputation in grand prix
racing, having produced the chassis that Johnny
Cecotto and Walter Villa had used to win 250 and
350cc world championships in 1975 and '76. With
the SB2, Tamburini brought to the street some of
that racing technology, including the first
monoshock rear suspension system seen on a
production motorcycle.

The SB2 frame was made from tubular steel,
but was a much more complex and advanced
structure than the twin-downtube affairs of most
mass-produced superbikes. Fabricated from
chrome-molybdenum tube of varying diameters, it
featured a heavily braced steering head area, used
the engine as a stressed member, and incorporated
conical couplings that enabled the front and rear
frame sections to be split, facilitating engine
removal. Steering geometry could be adjusted by
rotating eccentric bearings in the triple clamps.

The Bimota also held its fork legs at a different
angle to the steering head (28 degrees the forks, 24
the head), to reduce the change in trail under
braking. The vertically mounted rear De Carbon
unit was operated by a rising-rate rocker arm. The
box-section steel swingarm curved outwards to
pivot concentric with the final drive sprocket,
maintaining constant chain tension. Chassis details
such as triple clamps and foot controls were
machined from aircraft-grade aluminium alloy.

No expense spared

Tamburini also spared no expense in specifying the cycle parts, which included 35mm Ceriani forks with internals modified by Bimota, five-spoke alloy wheels in 18-inch diameters, and drilled Brembo discs gripped by twin-piston calipers. Even the dramatically shaped tank/seat unit was highly advanced. Made from fibreglass lined with aluminium, it was self-supporting, so required no rear subframe and was a predecessor of modern carbon-fibre structures of similar design. The SB2 weighed 440lb (200kg) without fuel – 60lb (27kg) less than the standard GS750.

The SB2 held Suzuki's dohc 16-valve air-cooled engine 25mm higher than in the standard bike for improved ground clearance. Bimota's basic SB2 model used a standard engine, but many owners opted for a tuning package. This typically combined Mikuni smoothbore carbs, 850cc big-bore kit, Yoshimura cams and high-compression pistons, plus a free-breathing four-into-one exhaust system. Peak output would typically be about 85bhp, up from the standard 68bhp.

That combined with the Bimota's sleek shape and light weight to give storming acceleration to a top speed of around 130mph (210km/h), but it was the bike's handling that really stood out. The SB2 was compact, firmly suspended and highly manoeuvrable. Yet it was also remarkably stable and controllable in tight turns and sweeping curves alike, thanks to its blend of race-developed geometry, chassis rigidity and suspension control. It also had powerful brakes, abundant ground clearance and excellent roadholding.

For all-round performance and cornering ability the SB2 was streets ahead of mass-produced superbikes in 1977. Inevitably it was hugely

expensive, and in many markets cost three times as much as the standard GS750. Only 70 units were built, and Bimota was forced to compromise slightly with subsequent machines. All of which merely adds to the reputation of the SB2; the finest, most advanced superbike of its era.

Above left: The rigid ladder frame featured adjustable geometry.

Above: The SB2's cornering performance was unrivalled.

Specification	Bimota SB2 (1977)
Engine	Air-cooled dohc eight-valve four (Suzuki GS750)
Capacity	749cc (65 x 56.4mm)
Maximum power	68bhp @ 8500rpm (standard engine)
Transmission	Five-speed, chain final drive
Frame	Tubular steel space-frame
Suspension	Telescopic front; monoshock rear
Brakes	Twin discs front; disc rear
Weight	440lb (200kg)
Top speed	130mph (210km/h)

MV Agusta Monza

**Top speed
145mph**
233km/h

*Right: MV's handsome
sand-cast dohc four was
enlarged to 837cc for the
Monza. High compression,
hot cams, big Dell'Orto
carbs and loud pipes
boosted claimed maximum
output to 85bhp.*

*Below: Red and silver
paintwork, low handlebars
and a suede-covered single
seat gave a racy look.
Owners faced a dilemma of
whether to cover the engine
with an optional fairing.*

 In 1977 the MV Agusta marque was nearing the end of its era of greatness on road and racetrack. Phil Read had won the factory's 17th consecutive 500cc world championship three years earlier, before the thundering Italian four-stroke had finally been outpaced by Japanese two-strokes. The Agusta firm's financial problems were not helped by sales of its unprofitable roadgoing fours.

But MV had one final throw of the dice in the Monza, the fastest and most exotic superbike that the original Agusta firm would ever build. Essentially a hotted-up version of the 750S America, which had been introduced to the US market two years earlier, the Monza combined breathtaking, racetrack-inspired styling with stunning performance from a biggest yet 837cc four-cylinder engine.

In both style and spirit the Monza was very close to the America, itself a direct descendent of the 750 Sport with which MV had belatedly arrived on the superbike scene at the start of the decade.

Like the Sport, the America was powered by a bellowing four-cylinder engine whose dohc layout, but not its shaft final drive, was inspired by MV's grand prix machines. The America was so named because it had been developed at the request of the firm's US agent, and had been intended for sale exclusively in the States.

As well as more angular styling plus a red and silver paint scheme inspired by the all-conquering racers, the America had a larger 790cc engine,

smaller 26mm carbuettors (they were easier to keep balanced), left-foot gearchange, improved output of 75bhp, and top speed of over 130mph (210km/h). The America was heavy, its high-speed handling was not perfect and it was expensive. (Its $6000 price explained why far fewer were sold than the US importer had predicted.) But it was a hugely desirable motorbike.

The Monza was even better. Its engine was enlarged by a 2mm increase in bore, giving dimensions of 69 x 56mm and capacity of 837cc. Compression ratio was increased, a new Marelli distributor was fitted, and the camshafts were new. Reverting to the Sport's larger 27mm Dell'Orto carburettors also helped increase claimed output to no less than 85bhp at 8750rpm.

Meticulous preparation

Monza performance was further boosted because the bikes were prepared by MV's former race team mechanics led by chief engineer Arturo Magni (who by this time, realizing that MV was nearing the end, had also set up his own firm nearby, selling cast wheels and tuning parts). This meticulous preparation meant that a new Monza roared to over 140mph (225km/h), especially when fitted with a Magni exhaust with its four elegantly curved black silencers.

Chassis changes were minimal, as the Monza combined MV's familiar frame with the cast wheels and triple-disc Brembo brake system that had been an option on later Americas. One thing that had changed was the bike's name, at least in Britain, where it had been called the Boxer until Ferrari (who had a car of that name) had objected. Whatever the name, few were built before MV ceased production in 1978. The Monza was a suitably glorious way to end the line.

Specification	MV Agusta Monza (1977)
Engine	Air-cooled dohc eight-valve four
Capacity	837cc (69 x 56mm)
Maximum power	85bhp @ 8750rpm
Transmission	Five-speed, shaft final drive
Frame	Steel twin downtube
Suspension	Telescopic front; twin shocks rear
Brakes	Twin discs front; disc rear
Weight	529lb (240kg)
Top speed	145mph (233km/h)

Left: MV's big roadsters differed from the grand prix bikes in their fitment of a heavy, power-sapping shaft final drive system.

Below left: The rear-threequarters view emphasizes the stylish curve of the free-breathing, black finished Magni exhaust system, essential for maximum power and noise.

MV Magni – Ultimate Agusta

In many enthusiasts' view the finest air-cooled MVs of all are those kitted out with parts from the firm run by former race team manager Arturo Magni and his son Giovanni. Magni's frame was a much more rigid twin-loop design, similar to those of MV's factory racers, and combined with a Magni chain drive conversion to give greatly improved handling. As well as the distinctive exhaust system, other Magni parts included a 862cc cylinder and piston kit, plus numerous chassis and bodywork components.

Honda CBX1000

**Top speed
135mph**
217km/h

*Below: The CBX1000 had
only two silencers, but even
so the six-cylinder engine
combined with neat styling
to give the Honda a
dramatic look from almost
every angle. Compared to
the large and muscular
motor, the bike's thin front
forks, narrow tyres and
small brake discs seem
insubstantial, although they
were top-class components
in 1978.*

Honda's mighty six-cylinder CBX1000 was the superbike that appeared to have it all. Its 24-valve engine produced a phenomenal 105bhp, making the CBX the most powerful production motorcycle on the road in 1978. Its searing speed was backed by remarkable smoothness and technical sophistication, even by Honda's high standards.

The Six was a handsome machine that had a pure-bred sporting image. It came with a sense of history, having been inspired by Honda's famous multi-cylinder racebikes of the mid-1960s. And its chassis was excellent, too, boosted by innovative use of weight-reducing materials.

Years after the bike's launch, it still inspires great loyalty from a devoted band of enthusiasts, and respect from most people who have ridden one. It remains a landmark machine, having combined style, technology and performance in a way arguably not seen before or since from Japan. Yet ironically the Six was a short-lived sales failure when new.

Multi-cylinder heritage

The CBX1000 was shaped by project leader Shoichiro Irimajiri, who as a young engineer in the 1960s had worked to create Honda's high-revving multi-cylinder grand prix bikes raced by Mike Hailwood, Luigi Taveri and others. The racers provided inspiration for the CBX's cylinder head, with its 24 tiny valves. The exhaust camshaft was hollow to save weight. The CBX trod new ground for a standard machine by using lightweight magnesium for several engine covers.

Irimajiri got round the potential width problem of a six-cylinder motor with a jackshaft, above the gearbox, which drove the alternator and ignition system. This allowed the 1047cc motor to be remarkably narrow at its base. Legroom was provided for the rider by tilting the cylinders forward by 33 degrees, and by angling the six carbs inwards in two pairs of three.

Honda created the CBX as a no-compromise sports bike. Its styling was dramatic, emphasized by the way in which the wide engine, which being

air-cooled required no radiator, was suspended by the tubular steel frame. The absence of downtubes added to the visual impact.

Straight-line performance was awesome, combining smoothness with the most ferocious acceleration yet seen from a production bike. Below 6000rpm the CBX responded crisply but without great force. Above that figure it came alive, surging towards its 135mph (217km/h) top-speed with a memorable, high-pitched howl from its exhaust. Most riders who rode the big six-cylinder machine were captivated by its unique blend of speed and charisma.

Its chassis worked, too. The CBX had good quality suspension, plus an efficient twin-disc front brake. Weight was kept to a minimum by use of aluminium handlebars, plastic mudguards and magnesium engine covers. Although the Honda still weighed a substantial 572lb (259kg), and could not match the composure of Suzuki's new GS1000 four, it handled well for such a big bike.

But for all its pace and panache, the CBX sold very poorly, especially in the vital (and touring oriented) American market. Part of the reason was simply that the Six cost far more than its less exotic rivals. In some markets it was 50 per cent more expensive than equivalent fours, yet offered no real advantage in terms of pure performance.

After a 1981 redesign that created the fully-faired CBX1000B, an attempt to add appeal for long-distance riders, the Six was dropped from the range. Honda's gamble had failed. But the CBX had given the firm's image a considerable boost. As one star-struck tester had put it in 1978, 'the Six is one of those rare machines that will never, ever be forgotten.' As long as fast bikes are ridden and admired, there is absolutely no danger of that.

Left: The CBX frame had no front downtubes to spoil the dramatic view of the six-cylinder powerplant, fitted here with Honda's crash-bars. The 24-valve unit's 105bhp output gave fierce acceleration and was very smooth and reliable.

Specification	Honda CBX1000 (1978)
Engine	Air-cooled dohc 24-valve six
Capacity	1047cc (64.5 x 53.4mm)
Maximum power	105bhp @ 9000rpm
Transmission	Five-speed, chain final drive
Frame	Tubular steel
Suspension	Telescopic front; twin shocks rear
Brakes	Twin discs front; disc rear
Weight	572lb (259kg) wet
Top speed	135mph (217km/h)

Left: Despite innovative use of lightweight materials such as aluminium, plastic and magnesium, the CBX was a heavy machine. But considering its size it handled well, partly because Honda had designed it very much as a sports bike, with reasonably firm suspension. The engine was even quite narrow at its base, giving good cornering clearance.

Suzuki GS1000

**Top speed
135mph**
217km/h

At first sight Suzuki's GS1000 was an unlikely bike to be regarded as outstanding; let alone as a machine that would be regarded as an all-time great even decades after its arrival in 1978. Although pleasantly styled, the GS was unexceptional to look at. Its air-cooled, dohc four-cylinder engine design was entirely conventional, as was its steel-framed, twin-shock chassis layout.

But the GS1000 *was* extra special, for two main reasons. Firstly, it was slightly better in just about every quantifiable way than its direct rival, Kawasaki's Z1000 – meaning that Suzuki's first ever open-class machine was the best big four on the road. More importantly, the GS could be ridden extremely hard without wobbles or weaves, which arguably made it the first Japanese superbike to match European levels of chassis performance.

Stability and cornering prowess

Coming as it did towards the end of a decade in which Japanese machines had gradually assumed dominance due to their powerful and reliable engines, without managing to shake off criticisms of second-rate chassis, the Suzuki's arrival was significant. Here at last was a bike that was not only faster than any other four in a straight line, but whose stability and cornering prowess allowed – no, positively encouraged – its rider to make the most of all that power.

Below: Suzuki's big four *was a good-looking machine whose style was very similar to that of the GS750 and 550 models, both of which had been launched one year earlier in 1977.*

Specification	Suzuki GS1000 (1978)
Engine	Air-cooled dohc eight-valve four
Capacity	997cc (70 x 64.8mm)
Maximum power	87bhp @ 8000rpm
Transmission	Five-speed, chain final drive
Frame	Steel twin downtube
Suspension	Telescopic front; twin shocks rear
Brakes	Twin discs front; disc rear
Weight	533lb (242kg) wet
Top speed	135mph (217km/h)

The achievement of Suzuki's engineers was all the greater given that the firm's first four-stroke multi, the excellent GS750, had itself been launched only one year earlier. The larger powerplant, which had a capacity of 997cc from dimensions of 70 x 64.8mm, followed the 750's dohc eight-valve layout and actually weighed slightly less, due to features including a lighter flywheel, thinner crankcases and lack of a kick-starter. But the bigger motor was considerably more powerful, producing a maximum of 87bhp at 8000rpm that was 19bhp up on the GS750, and gave a 4bhp advantage over the Z1000.

The GS1000 shared its overall look and steel, twin-downtube frame layout with the GS750. But the new bike's frame was thicker in places, and its tubular steel swingarm was stronger. The GS1000 also had wider tyres, plus an extra front brake disc. Its new forks were air-assisted, and its shocks could be adjusted through four rebound damping positions – giving the GS the most sophisticated suspension system yet seen on a mass-produced roadster. (So it did have some technical innovation, after all.)

This added-up to a stunning new superbike that seemingly had no real weakness, and which made the Z1000, until now the dominant big four, look slightly second rate. The GS stormed past the

100mph (161km/h) mark at a phenomenal rate, on the way to a top speed of 135mph (217km/h). Cruising speed was limited only by road conditions and the rider's ability to hang on. Even at high revs the motor felt unburstable and reasonably smooth, and it soon proved to be impressively reliable.

Better still, that chassis really was capable of keeping all that horsepower in check. One tester observed that the GS1000 felt safer at 110mph (177km/h) than most bikes did at less than half that speed. Although it was not a particularly light bike, its frame was rigid and its suspension was the best yet seen from Japan. Despite the bike's high-speed stability, it could be flicked into corners with the ease of a much smaller machine.

Considering that this was Suzuki's first attempt at a open-class superbike, the GS1000's overall performance was nothing short of sensational. Apart from a few minor criticisms such as the lack of a pillion grab-rail as standard fitment, the GS's only real failing was a slight lack of character. Given its speed, its reliability, and most of all its handling, very few riders complained about that.

Left: Round chromed caps at the ends of each camshaft distinguished the air-cooled, eight-valve GS1000 engine from the Kawasaki Z1000 unit that it closely resembled. Suzuki's engine was lighter as well as slightly more powerful, with a peak output of 87bhp.

Below: Handling was the most impressive yet from an open-class Japanese superbike, thanks mainly to the Suzuki's combination of rigid steel frame and superior suspension. The quality of the GS's air-assisted front forks and damping-adjustable rear shocks allowed the engine's power to be used to the full.

Yamaha XS1100

**Top speed
132mph**
212km/h

*Right: The Yamaha's
1101cc, dohc four-cylinder
engine developed maximum
torque at a low 6500rpm,
and had plenty of mid-
range muscle. Like the
XS750 triple unit, it
featured shaft final drive.*

*Below: High bars and short
pipes signify that this XS
was sold in America, where
the model was most
successful, and was often
fitted with a fairing for
touring use.*

There was not a great deal of subtlety
about the XS1100. Yamaha's first four-
cylinder superbike was huge, heavy and
rather basic. And the big bike's styling reflected its
personality, combining a bulbous fuel tank and
sidepanels with a large, rectangular headlamp that
merely emphasized the brute's enormous weight of
well over 600lb (272kg) when that tank was full.

Any such criticism was forgotten when its rider,
cruising at a gentle pace in top gear, saw a straight
piece of road stretching out ahead and wound back
the throttle. Even with as little as 50mph (80km/h)
showing on the square-shaped speedometer, the
Yamaha's massively torquey 1101cc powerplant
sent the bike storming forward with a breathtaking
surge of low-rev acceleration that no other
superbike could match.

Such arm-wrenching performance was fun, but
not really what the XS1100 was all about. Despite
the Yamaha's twin overhead camshafts, 95bhp peak
power output and top speed of over 130mph
(210km/h), it was designed less for violent

acceleration and flat-out blasts than for effortless
long-distance travel. For all its size and
intimidating look, the bike nicknamed the 'Excess
Eleven' was a bit of a softie.

Softly tuned powerplant

There was plenty of evidence to support that claim in the engine which, although it shared its basic air-cooled eight-valve transverse four-cylinder layout with the Suzuki GS1000 that was launched at the same time, was a less highly tuned unit. The Yamaha's impressive peak power figure was produced at 8000rpm, but a more relevant statistic was that much of its torque was developed much lower, between 2000 and 6500rpm. Not only that but, like Yamaha's XS750 triple, the big four had shaft final drive.

It also had a heavy-duty chassis, based around a twin-downtube steel frame that had ample bracing, plus fairing mounts as standard fitment. The swingarm was made from box-section steel on the right, and incorporated the driveshaft housing on the left. Like the rear shocks, the front fork legs were adjustable for spring preload but not damping. The specification sheet included cast wheels and a triple-disc brake system.

How efficiently the Yamaha worked depended largely on how fast its rider liked to travel, and on how straight the road was. On an empty American freeway it was happy to sit at whatever speed the pilot dialled in, remaining stable and always having a burst of acceleration ready at the end of the throttle wire. Even on twistier roads, its effortless torque made for pleasant riding and allowed its rider to make minimal use of the rather slow five-speed gearbox.

But if asked to deliver more sporting performance, the Yamaha struggled. Its power and weight overwhelmed the chassis when pushed hard, resulting in some nasty wobbles. Steering geometry that was designed for high speeds gave a rather awkward feel in slower turns, and the bike's bulk was inevitably a handicap in town. Although the XS found admirers among riders in the wide open spaces of America, it failed to catch on in Europe.

Yamaha did at least make efforts to improve the basic XS, firstly by creating an upmarket Martini touring version whose innovative full fairing incorporated a top section that turned with the handlebars. The mean and stylish XS1100 Sport, launched in 1981, featured black paintwork and a bikini fairing. It emphasized the Eleven's muscular nature and earned a cult following, but by this time the big shaft-drive four was even less of a genuine sport bike than ever.

Above left: The Yamaha XS1100's rounded styling did little to disguise its size and weight.

Above: Straight-line performance was excellent, as the big Yamaha's motor was smooth and flexible, as well as very powerful.

Specification	Yamaha XS1100 (1978)
Engine	Air-cooled dohc eight-valve four
Capacity	1101cc (71.5 x 68.6mm)
Maximum power	95bhp @ 8000rpm
Transmission	Five-speed, shaft final drive
Frame	Steel twin cradle
Suspension	Telescopic front; twin shocks rear
Brakes	Twin discs front; disc rear
Weight	600lb (272kg) wet
Top speed	132mph (212km/h)

Honda CB900F

**Top speed
135mph**
217km/h

*Right: Despite being
designed as a sports bike,
the CB900F's slightly
raised handlebars gave a
fairly upright riding
position that soon became
tiring at anything close to
the bike's top speed.*

*Below: The 900F's
'Eurostyle' shape was
attractive and quite sporty,
although it was reminiscent
of other Hondas. These
included not only the
CB750FZ that was
launched simultaneously,
but also small-capacity
Super Dream twins.*

 The arrival of the CB900F in 1979
marked an important upturn in Honda's
superbike fortunes. At that time, the
world's biggest bike firm badly needed a high-
performance machine to compete with Kawasaki's
ever-popular Z1000 and Suzuki's GS1000. Honda's
single-cam CB750 had long been outclassed by
bigger dohc fours, and the previous year's six-
cylinder CBX1000 had not been a success despite
its power and panache.

The more conventional 900F four pitched
Honda straight into the hard-fought superbike
battle, backed by a big promotional campaign
based on its race-developed technology. 'It's a
powerhouse that has evolved directly from our all-
conquering Endurance RCB machine,' ran the
advertising line. 'A thundering Super Sports bike
with devastating performance and unwavering
stamina that will be setting the pace for many years
to come.'

The hype and racing references were largely
justified. Honda's mighty 1000cc RCB fours had
dominated European endurance racing, notably in
the hands of French duo Christian Leon and Jean-

Claude Chemarin. (In 1978 RCBs took the first
three places in the prestigious Bol d'Or 24 hour
race and won a third consecutive Coupe
d'Endurance championship.) The CB900F was no
race-replica, but the roadster's development had
clearly been influenced by the RCB.

Styled for Europe

In contrast to most previous Japanese superbikes, which had been designed with the American market in mind, the 900F was aimed at Europe, and initially was not even sold in the States. Its angular Eurostyle shape, with fuel tank blending into sidepanels, was pleasant in an understated way. Indeed the 900F, with its twin silencers, looked very similar to Honda's humble CB400 Super Dream – a fact that did the bigger model no favours.

The 901cc engine was the bike's star attraction. Along with the CB750FZ that was launched at the same time, the 900F finally gave Honda a big twin-cam powerplant, six years after the arrival of Kawasaki's Z1. The 16-valve unit had fairly long-stroke dimensions of 64.5 x 69mm, and produced a claimed maximum of 95bhp at 9000rpm.

Despite its racing heritage and sporty image, the 900F was tuned for mid-range rather than ultimate power. It delivered arm-stretching acceleration from 4000rpm in top gear to the 9500rpm redline. At 90mph (145km/h) the motor's slight high-frequency vibration made it feel rather busy. But the leant-forward riding position and broad seat made the Honda comfortable at most speeds, if not at the bike's maximum of over 130mph (210km/h).

The 900F's chassis was arguably the best Honda had built for the street. There was nothing obviously special about the frame, with its top spine of three steel tubes. But it was very strong, and equipped with high quality suspension. The front forks were air-assisted, and the rear shocks were adjustable for compression and rebound damping, as well as spring preload.

Despite the Honda's 514lb (233kg) of weight, it handled well and had enough ground clearance to make fast cornering fun. Stopping power was less impressive, and braking was one of the things uprated in 1982, when a revised 900F appeared boasting twin-piston front calipers plus Honda's new TRAC anti-dive system. There was also the option of a full fairing, with which the bike was called the CB900 F2B (standing, some said, for 'Far 2 Big').

The unfaired CB900F remained in production for several more years, and also formed the basis of the exotic CB1100R production racer. Back in 1979 one tester had described the original twin-cam four as 'the nearest any manufacturer has come to producing the Perfect Motorcycle'. That might have been an exaggeration, but the CB900F had certainly put Honda's superbike range back on the right track.

Left: Honda's first dohc roadgoing four had long-stroke dimensions and a capacity of 901cc. The air-cooled unit held 16 valves and produced 95bhp with plenty of mid-range torque. It was conventional in design, apart from its two camchains: the first running from crankshaft to exhaust cam, the second from exhaust to inlet.

Below: The steel-framed, twin-shock chassis provided good handling, especially when fitted with aftermarket rear shock units, like this bike whose original FVQ units have been replaced by Konis. The wheels were Honda's composite Comstar design.

Specification	Honda CB900F (1979)
Engine	Air-cooled dohc 16-valve transverse four
Capacity	901cc (64.5 x 69mm)
Maximum power	95bhp @ 9000rpm
Transmission	Five-speed, chain final drive
Frame	Steel twin downtube
Suspension	Telescopic front; twin shocks rear
Brakes	Twin discs front; disc rear
Weight	514lb (233kg)
Top speed	135mph (217km/h)

Kawasaki Z1300

**Top speed
135mph**
217km/h

*Below: Kawasaki made no
attempt to disguise the size
of the Z1300, whose
oversized fuel tank and
bodywork dwarf even the
huge engine. There was
also little visual attempt to
highlight the six cylinder
layout. The exhaust
downpipes were partially
obscured by the radiator,
and there were only two
silencers.*

 The gigantic six-cylinder Z1300 arrived in 1979 to mark the end of a decade that had seen great change in superbikes' performance, size and technical specification. This 120bhp behemoth was not simply the world's most powerful production motorcycle, it was fully 15bhp more potent than its closest challenger, Honda's CBX1000, and also produced more power than many cars.

Ironically the Kawasaki was not the brutal performance machine that its vital statistics and enormous slab-sided bodywork suggested. The Z1300 was notable for its sophistication and smoothness, as much as for its horsepower. With its upright riding position, liquid cooling and shaft final drive, the big Six was less of an aggressive sports machine than a grand tourer, albeit one without the convenience of a fairing.

Fast and torquey

The Z1300 was mighty fast for all that, with a top speed of almost 140mph (225km/h) despite the aerodynamics of a small building. Although it weighed over 670lb (304kg) with fuel, it was awesomely quick off the line, matching even the best rival four-cylinder rivals. And the Kawasaki had superbly strong mid-range power delivery too, giving instant throttle response that made the big bike effortless to ride.

That performance came from a 1286cc motor that was conventional in its dohc, two-valves-per-cylinder top-end layout, if in nothing else. Liquid cooling allowed the cylinders to be spaced more closely together than with an air-cooled design. Long-stroke dimensions of 62 x 71mm also helped keep the motor reasonably narrow, despite its alternator's location on the end of the crankshaft.

Like the engine, the chassis owed much to Kawasaki's previous fours. The twin-cradle frame's steel tubes were thicker than normal, and held strong 41mm leading-axle forks. Simple twin shocks took care of suspension at the rear. Wheels and tyres were broad, in an attempt to control all that power and weight.

Considering the Kawasaki's size, it handled surprisingly well. The combination of strong frame and competent suspension made the Z1300 much less of a handful than it might have been, giving a reassuringly stable feel even at high speed. The big bike even felt respectably agile in tighter bends, and its triple-disc brake system worked well.

Even so, the Z1300 failed to sell in large numbers. That was partly because it was much more expensive than rival fours, but ultimately no faster, more practical or more exciting to ride. The bike was capable of cruising at 100mph (161km/h) indefinitely, but its high handlebars and forward-set footpegs meant its rider was not, at least not for long. Throttle response was slightly snatchy and, although the Six was smooth, it had a busy feel that did not make for relaxed cruising.

The Z1300's arrival highlighted Japanese manufacturers' fixation with ever greater power, weight and complexity, but Kawasaki's timing was not good. In the midst of an oil crisis, the West German government had recently introduced a 100bhp power limit. Thoughts were turning towards economy and efficiency. Words such as 'overkill' were commonly used in road tests, some of which claimed the Z1300 would lead to bikes being banned.

Specification	Kawasaki Z1300 (1979)
Engine	Liquid-cooled dohc 12-valve six
Capacity	1286cc (62 x 71mm)
Maximum power	120bhp @ 8000rpm
Transmission	Five-speed, shaft final drive
Frame	Steel twin cradle
Suspension	Telescopic front; twin shocks rear
Brakes	Twin discs front; disc rear
Weight	672lb (305kg) wet
Top speed	135mph (217km/h)

Left: Handling was good, given the limitations of the Kawasaki's size. Suspension was reasonably firm, the tubular steel frame was rigid, and the bike even had a respectable amount of ground clearance. At slower speeds, the Z1300's long wheelbase helped make for relatively easy manoeuvring, despite the bike's weight and tall seat.

That did not happen, but the Z1300 proved a turning point because, from then on, manufacturers aimed to improve performance through increased engine, aerodynamic and chassis efficiency, rather than simply raw power and size. The mighty Z1300 gained a certain cult status though, and remained in production, with very few changes, right up until 1989 – serving as a rolling reminder of 1970s' superbike excess.

Far left: The headlamp's angular shape was echoed in other features including indicators and instrument console. With so much power on tap, aerodynamics were not a consideration.

Left: At close to 300lb (136kg) even without its drive shaft, the Z1300's liquid-cooled engine alone weighed more than some complete bikes. The 1286cc six-cylinder 120bhp motor was motorcycling's most powerful by 15bhp.

The 1980s
Refining the Superbike

In contrast to the previous decade, which displayed a trend towards more power and size, the 1980s saw superbikes evolve in a variety of different ways. The era's first stars were a variation on the familiar theme: big, heavy beasts, most with air-cooled, multi-cylinder engines, tubular steel frames and twin rear shocks.

But subsequent bikes gained performance through refinement, as much as extra power. The new breed of superbike had a liquid-cooled engine, aluminium frame, monoshock rear suspension and aerodynamic fairing. Suzuki's GSX-R750, in particular, emphasized the value of light weight. By the end of the decade, the ultimate superbike was a smaller, lighter, more sophisticated machine.

Suzuki GSX1100

**Top speed
137mph**
220km/h

*Right: The GSX's styling
incorporated a rectangular
headlight and unique
instrument console.
Reception of the bike's look
was mixed but there was no
doubting the brilliance of
its all-round performance.*

*Below: Suzuki's first 16-
valve four was held in a
chassis of conventional
layout and superior quality.
Leading-axle front forks
and damping-adjustable
rear shocks coped well with
the bike's weight.*

 Suzuki's GSX1100 was far from the most
stylish machine on the roads when it was
launched in 1980, but it was arguably the
fastest and the best. Few people realized it at the
time, but the GSX, with its rather curious, unfaired
styling, its twin rear shock absorbers and its air-
cooled, four-cylinder engine, marked the end of an
era. With fairings, monoshock suspension systems
and liquid-cooled engines on the way, the GSX
would be the last of the old-style naked superbikes
to rule the roads.

For Suzuki the GSX also marked the start of a
new generation, because its engine was the first to
use the 16-valve layout that would become the
basis of the firm's four-cylinder range. To the twin-
cam format of the GS1000, the new engine added a
16-valve cylinder head that came with the acronym
TSCC. That stood for Twin Swirl Combustion
Chamber, after the way the combustion chamber
shape, with its central spark plug and sharp divides
between the valves, was designed to improve flame
spread and hence efficiency.

The engine's 1075cc capacity came from boring
and stroking the GS1000 unit to give dimensions of
72 x 66mm. The GSX's five-speed gearbox was
similar to that of the GS, but was made with
tougher alloy to cope with the added output.
Maximum power output was officially 99.6bhp at
8700rpm, and the big motor also produced
generous amounts of torque throughout the range.

Specification	Suzuki GSX1100 (1981)
Engine	Air-cooled dohc 16-valve four
Capacity	1075cc (72 x 66mm)
Maximum power	100bhp @ 8700rpm
Transmission	Five-speed, chain final drive
Frame	Steel twin downtube
Suspension	Telescopic front; twin shocks rear
Brakes	Twin discs front; disc rear
Weight	556lb (252kg) wet
Top speed	137mph (220km/h)

High quality chassis

At first glance the GSX was distinctive, due to its angular headlamp in a nacelle that held speedometer and rev-counter plus an innovative warning panel. Its twin-downtube steel frame and most other parts were of high quality, as was to be expected given the excellence of its GS predecessors. Forks and rear shocks were adjustable for preload and rebound damping. Although the big Suzuki couldn't match the agility of lighter Italian superbikes, it was stable, neutral, well braked, and cornered as well as could be expected of a bike weighing over 550lb (250kg) with fuel.

The GSX's key feature was that big, powerful and gloriously tractable motor. It started instantly, idled impeccably, and carburetted cleanly from next to nothing. A twist of the wrist sent the Suzuki hurtling forward from below 3000rpm, seamlessly switching to warp drive by 6000rpm, and storming to the redline as quickly as its rider could keep up using the five-speed gearbox.

The Suzuki's ability to cruise at 90mph (145km/h) or more was limited mainly by its rider's willingness to hold on, as the instrument nacelle with its centrally placed fuel gauge gave little wind protection, and the footrests were too far forward for high-speed riding. For those with the strength, the Suzuki was capable of over 135mph (217km/h), and was the world's hardest-accelerating superbike over the quarter-mile, too.

Bike magazine's tester summed-up the reaction of most who rode the Suzuki, concluding that 'the GSX1100 represents a quantum leap in motorcycle design when compared to the standard bike format that most of us cut our teeth on. It has a clean, quiet, economical motor of Herculean potential, a chassis of strength and rigidity with sophisticated tuneable suspension components, the entire mechanism served by low-maintenance auxiliaries. It goes like the clappers, stops like it was on a noose and looks as smart as a new pin.'

Even as those words were being written, Suzuki and other manufacturers were developing the fairings, fuel-injection systems, water jackets and monoshocks of a new generation of machines. But for now, the GSX1100 was king: newest and best of the naked, air-cooled, twin-shock superbikes.

Above left: Although the GSX was a naked bike with wide bars, its big fuel tank and broad dual seat made it reasonably comfortable.

Below: Straight line performance was stunning, and the Suzuki scored over most rivals by being equally at home on a twisty road.

Kawasaki GPz1100

**Top speed
140mph**
225km/h

*Right: The angular
instrument console included
a fuel gauge, but most GPz
riders were more interested
in the big numbers on its
speedometer.*

*Below: Bright red
paintwork plus black
finished engine and pipes
gave the big GPz a suitably
striking appearance.*

With its bright red paintwork, fancy new initials and high-tech fuel-injection system, the original GPz1100 was the biggest and fastest of a new three-bike range of high-performance fours that brought Kawasaki storming into the 1980s. But once glance confirmed that the big GPz was very much a superbike of the old school, with an air-cooled, two-valves-per-cylinder engine, twin-shock chassis and generous supplies of both power and weight.

Even at a standstill, the GPz was an imposing motorcycle. Its angular styling made no attempt to hide the fact that this bike was not built to be messed with. Its seat was high, its wheelbase was a long, and it weighed a substantial 562lb (255kg) with fuel. The engine's capacity of 1089cc was slightly smaller than that of Yamaha's rival XS1100, let alone Kawasaki's own Z1300 six. But

with a peak output of 108bhp at 8500rpm, the GPz was the world's most powerful four in 1981.

Kawasaki needed that credibility boost, because the Big K's reputation for all-conquering performance had slipped since the mid-1970s

heyday of the Z1 and Z900. Unlike its rival the 16-valve Suzuki GSX1100, the GPz relied on Kawasaki's age-old format of two valves per cylinder. But the new motor was substantially uprated from that of the Z1000H EFI, which had become the world's first fuel-injected roadster 12 months earlier.

Capacity was increased by boring out the cylinders to give dimensions of 72.5 x 66mm, and the larger pistons had higher domed crowns to increase compression ratio. The new motor had bigger valves and revised timing for its twin cams, the crankshaft was lightened, the five-speed gearbox strengthened and an oil-cooler added between the frame's twin downtubes.

Uprated chassis

The GPz's chassis was also based on that of the 1000H, with numerous modifications. Its main frame tubes were made from larger-diameter but thinner-walled steel. Rake and trail dimensions were increased. Front forks were 38mm in diameter and air-assisted. Rear shocks could be tuned for rebound damping as well as the normal preload. All this was state-of-the-art for a Japanese superbike. So too was the bike's large instrument console, with its voltmeter and fuel gauge set between the speedometer and rev-counter.

Those dials got to record plenty of action. With its big valves and hot cams the GPz liked to be revved, tugging hard on its rider's arms as it howled through the gears towards the 8500rpm redline and a top speed of around 140mph (225km/h). Acceleration away from the line was ferocious, making the GPz motorcycling's straight-line king in 1981. And its mid-range delivery was

excellent, too. The fuel-injection gave a crisp response, sending the bike surging forward even from below 3000rpm in top gear.

Stability at speed was good provided the GPz was pointed in a straight line and the throttle was held open. Competent suspension meant that the big bike could be good fun in corners, too. But braking and changing direction at the same time was more than the chassis could take without complaint. The GPz was slightly lighter than its Z1000H predecessor but there was still a lot of metal to throw around.

Kawasaki moved quickly to update the GPz, adding a handlebar fairing in 1982, and a year later revising it further with a larger, solid-mounted fairing plus single-shock rear suspension. In 1984 came a bigger step: the liquid-cooled, 16-valve GPZ900R. That was the bike with which Kawasaki entered the modern era, but its debt to its predecessor of 1981 should not be overlooked. For it was the first big red GPz1100 four that restored Kawasaki's justifiably proud reputation for full-blooded high performance.

Left: This 1981 model GPz was the last of Kawasaki's flagships to rely on the traditional naked layout. Just a year later the bike was given a handlebar fairing that made its mighty four-cylinder engine's performance more usable; and in 1983 the final air-cooled GPz had a more substantial fairing.

Below: Handling was fine at a reasonably rapid pace. But when pushed harder the GPz1100 was one of many big Japanese fours whose chassis sometimes struggled to control the bike's power and weight, resulting in high-speed instability.

Specification	Kawasaki GPz1100 (1981)
Engine	Air-cooled dohc eight-valve four
Capacity	1089cc (72.5 x 66mm)
Maximum power	108bhp @ 8500rpm
Transmission	Five-speed, chain final drive
Frame	Steel twin downtube
Suspension	Telescopic front; twin shocks rear
Brakes	Twin discs front; disc rear
Weight	562lb (255kg) wet
Top speed	140mph (225km/h)

Yamaha RD350LC

**Top speed
110mph**
177km/h

*Below: High handlebars
and neat, fairly rounded
styling barely hinted at the
high-revving excitement and
giant-humbling ability of
the bike that would soon
become a cult machine in
many countries. The
cantilever monoshock
suspension system, derived
like so much else from
Yamaha's racing
experience, contributed to
the LC's lean look as well
as to its excellent handling.*

 It might have produced less than 50bhp
and had a top speed of not much more
than 100mph (161km/h), but for many
riders Yamaha's brilliantly raw, racy RD350LC was
the high-performance bike of the 1980s – or any
other decade, come to that. Certainly, few machines
can have brought so much fast and furious
enjoyment to so many people, so cheaply, as the
liquid-cooled two-stroke twin that Yamaha
unleashed in 1981.

The LC's pedigree was impeccable, as it was a
descendant of the string of outstanding air-cooled
strokers with which Yamaha had established an
unmatched reputation for middleweight
performance. Models such as the YR5, RD350 and
RD400 had kept the tuning-fork logo to the fore
through the 1970s, while on the racetrack Yamaha's
all-conquering air-cooled twins had been
superseded by the liquid-cooled TZ250 and 350,
with equally spectacular results.

For all the Race Developed nature of this latest
in the RD series, the LC's 347cc engine owed more
to that of the RD400 roadster than to the TZ350
racer. The water jacket maintained a constant
temperature and allowed the engine to be in a
higher state of tune without loss of reliability.
Liquid cooling also helped make the 47bhp motor
cleaner and quieter than its air-cooled predecessor;
important for environmental reasons although not
enough to satisfy US emissions regulations.

Race-bred monoshock

The LC's other race-developed feature was its
cantilever rear suspension system, which featured a
single shock unit mounted diagonally under the
seat, instead of the RD400's twin shocks. Chassis
layout was otherwise conventional, with a twin-
downtube steel frame, non-adjustable front forks,
slightly raised handlebars, attractively rounded
styling and a twin-disc front brake.

Legalized Chaos: the Pro-Am Series

The LC's speed and fire were brought to a wider British audience by the spectacular RD350 Pro-Am series. The main attractions were that prize money was good; riders were aged under 25 (some professionals and some amateurs, hence the title); and the LCs were identical, prepared by Yamaha and allocated after keys were drawn out of a hat. The result was close, aggressive racing that saw the first year's title appropriately won by a rider named Wild, and which brought future grand prix stars including Niall Mackenzie annd Kenny Irons to prominence. The format spread, and led to an international 350LC series that was equally hotly contested.

One ride was enough to get most speed-happy motorcyclists addicted to the Yamaha's exuberant performance. Below 6000rpm it was ordinary; starting easily (with a kick), idling reliably and feeling docile. Then the motor came to life with a scream through its twin pipes, and a burst of acceleration that was as thrilling as it was sudden. With its rider's chin on the tank the LC was good for 110mph (177km/h), but it was the fierce way it got there that made this bike so special.

The Yamaha really handled, too. Its forks were slightly soft, particularly when the powerful front brake was used hard, and the front end could feel decidedly twitchy when the bike was accelerating out of a bend. But the frame was strong, the rear suspension worked well and the LC could be flicked around with the ease and precision of a race-bred machine weighing just 331lb (150kg) with fuel.

All in all the RD350LC was a magical motorbike: fast, reliable (at least when standard), agile, reasonably practical, tuneable, raceable, and most of all brilliant fun. Over the years it was updated several times, notably in 1983 to produce the RD350 YPVS, whose exhaust power valve added mid-range power; and three years later with a full fairing to create the RD350F2. All shared the same key assets: irresistible performance and unbeatable value for money.

Specification	Yamaha RD350LC (1981)
Engine	Liquid-cooled two-stroke parallel twin
Capacity	347cc (64 x 54mm)
Maximum power	47bhp @ 8500rpm
Transmission	Six-speed, chain final drive
Frame	Steel twin downtube
Suspension	Telescopic front; single shock rear
Brakes	Twin discs front; drum rear
Weight	311lb (141kg)
Top speed	110mph (177km/h)

Above left: Its twin disc front end was one way in which the RD350LC's chassis differed from that of the otherwise very similar 250cc model.

Left: Adding the liquid-cooling system to Yamaha's two-stroke parallel twin engine resulted in a brilliantly powerful unit that was also very reliable.

Honda CB1100R

**Top speed
142mph**
229km/h

*Below: The original 1981-
model CB1100R had a half-
fairing plus other features
designed for long-distance
production racing,
including a large-capacity
fuel tank and single seat.
Other key elements were its
twin-piston front brake
calipers, remote-reservoir
rear shocks, and the tuned
and strengthened 1062cc
four-cylinder engine with
its unmatched 115bhp
power output.*

The incomparable CB1100R provided proof that when mighty Honda set out to build the fastest production motorcycle in the world, the opposition didn't stand much chance. Especially when the bike in question was a purpose-built racer designed with little regard to cost, produced in very small numbers, and which competed against mass-produced machines that sold for half its price.

Honda's aim in creating the CB1100R was victory in high-profile long-distance production races in Australia (especially the prestigious Castrol Six Hour) and South Africa. Regulations for these races were strict, with very few modifications allowed. So Honda created its first 'homologation special' by treating its current top model, the naked CB900FZ, to a spectacular makeover.

The result was a stunning superbike that was head and shoulders above all opposition in 1981. Its racetrack dominance was predictable and sometimes dull. But for the fortunate few who got to ride an 1100R, there was nothing remotely boring about a bike that rocketed to over 140mph (225km/h), handled and braked better than any big four-cylinder rival, and was even refined and comfortable too.

Honda's first requirement was more power. The CB900's air-cooled, 16-valve four-cylinder motor was bored out to increase its capacity from 901 to 1062cc, and its compression ratio raised from 8.8 to 10:1. That lifted peak output by more than 20 per cent, to 115bhp at 9000rpm. Equally importantly, the motor was strengthened with modifications including new conrods, wider primary chain and redesigned crankcases.

Chassis layout remained conventional, but the 1100R benefited from a more rigid twin-downtube steel frame, plus the most sophisticated cycle parts yet seen on a production motorcycle. Front forks had thick 37mm legs and adjustable air pressure, while the shocks could be fine-tuned for compression and rebound damping, and had the novel feature of remote hydraulic reservoirs, to resist overheating. The front brake held another first, with its twin-piston calipers.

One thing that Honda didn't achieve was make the CB1100R particularly light: at 518lb (235kg) dry, it was slightly heavier the 900FZ despite much

use of plastic and aluminium. The production racer certainly looked the part, though, with its half-fairing, large fuel tank (for maximum racing range), and racy single seat. Nobody was in the slightest doubt about why the 1100R had been created, especially when Honda announced that only 1000 units would be built, and that in some markets the bike would cost almost twice as much as the CB900FZ.

Nothing this purposeful had been produced by a Japanese manufacturer before, and the 1100R duly trounced all opposition on the track. This was particularly true in the shorter races of the British Streetbike series, where the handful of Hondas were in a race of their own at the head of the field. The southern hemisphere long-distance events threw up more variables, but the CB1100R took plenty of wins.

Sensational road bike

Perhaps most impressively of all, the CB1100R made a sensational road bike. Its phenomenal top-end power was matched not only by storming mid-range acceleration, but also by impressive smoothness and low-rev refinement. The protective fairing allowed more of that performance to be used. And although the 1100R was prone to a slight weave at very high speed, its chassis gave superb suspension control, fierce braking and generous ground clearance.

Honda made the bike even better in the next couple of years. In 1982 came the CB1100R-C, with a full fairing (which cured the instability), dual seat, improved front forks and wider wheels.

Specification	Honda CB1100R (1981)
Engine	Air-cooled dohc 16-valve four
Capacity	1062cc (70 x 69mm)
Maximum power	115bhp @ 9000rpm
Transmission	Five-speed, chain final drive
Frame	Steel twin downtube
Suspension	Telescopic front; twin shocks rear
Brakes	Twin discs front; disc rear
Weight	518lb (235kg)
Top speed	142mph (229km/h)

A year later, the 1100R-D added damping-adjustable forks and an aluminium swingarm. The specification had changed, but one thing had not: the CB1100R was still the fastest production motorcycle in the world.

Above: As well as being an almost invincible production racer, the CB1100R made a superb roadster. This is the later fully-faired model, pictured on the Isle of Man during TT week. If there had been a Production TT race in the early 1980s, the CB1100R would doubtless have won that too.

Left: Joey Dunlop rode the CB1100R to some good results in the British production-based Streetbike championship in 1981. The Honda dominated and Ron Haslam won all but the final round, where he was beaten into second place by another future grand prix star, Wayne Gardner – also on a CB1100R.

Suzuki Katana 1100

**Top speed
140mph**
225km/h

The Katana 1100 that Suzuki unleashed on an unsuspecting motorcycle world in 1982 was a machine like nothing seen before from Japan. It was bold, stylish, imaginative, breathtaking; very different to the succession of fast but visually dull models that had preceded it. And underneath all the fancy bodywork, the Katana was an outstanding superbike too.

Katana was the Japanese word for a Samurai warrior's ceremonial sword, and it fitted Suzuki's sharp new silver blade perfectly. With its pointed nose, tiny flyscreen, low clip-on handlebars and swooping tank-seat section, the Katana was a unique machine with an infinitely more aggressive image than the GSX1100 roadster to which it was closely related.

This landmark in the history of Japanese superbike development had partly European parentage. The Katana had been shaped by the German group Target Design (which had also been responsible for BMW's striking R90S almost a decade earlier). Although some riders criticized the Suzuki for being more notable for style than practicality, most welcomed the alternative to the

formatted 'Universal Japanese Motorcycle' with its four-cylinder engine and unfaired, upright riding position that provided no wind protection.

Suzuki had the ideal basis for the Katana in the 1075cc air-cooled engine from the GSX1100, with its 16 valves, phenomenally broad spread of power, and reputation for reliability. To give the new bike extra teeth, the motor was tuned with a modified airbox, reworked carburettors, new exhaust camshaft and lightened alternator. It produced a maximum of 111bhp at 8500rpm, a useful 11bhp up on the standard unit.

Chassis layout remained conventional, and the twin-cradle steel frame was unchanged, but many parts were new. Suspension was stiffened at both ends, new triple clamps gave a shallower steering angle for added stability, and the front forks gained a hydraulic anti-dive system claimed to be similar to that of Suzuki's 500cc grand prix racers.

Breathtaking acceleration

The Katana looked lightning fast when standing still, and when moving it was much, much faster. The big GSX motor was already a superb

Below: The Katana's sleek and integrated style was a welcome departure following years of Japanese multis with conventional look and riding position. Although the nose fairing and tiny screen gave minimal wind protection, they combined with the fairly low handlebars to improve high-speed comfort. This bike's four-into-one exhaust and remote-reservoir shocks are later additions.

Left: Firm suspension and an anti-dive front suspension system, developed from the one fitted to Suzuki's grand prix racebikes, helped give the big Katana excellent handling by Japanese superbike standards. Sticky tyres and generous ground clearance encouraged enthusiastic cornering provided the road was dry.

powerplant, with huge reserves of instant mid-range torque. The Katana had breathtaking acceleration – and even more urge at the top end. Top speed was a genuine 140mph (225km/h). And the Katana's stretched-forward riding position, with its welcome bit of wind protection from the small screen, made that performance more usable than that of most rivals.

Handling was very good for such a big, heavy bike. The fairing and screen were solidly mounted, so contributing to the Katana's impressive high-speed stability. The firm suspension gave a level of control (and discomfort) that was almost Italian, marred only by the anti-dive's occasional tendency to make the forks lock up over a series of bumps. The triple-disc brake system worked well, even in the wet, though this could not be said of the standard fitment tyres.

Inevitably, the radical Katana did not suit every rider or every occasion. Its suspension was harsh and uncomfortable in town, its seat was hard, and its steering was quite heavy at slow speed. But this was not a bike to be ridden at slow speed. Its

purposeful nature was an integral part of its appeal. At last, this was a Japanese bike that provided both performance, handling and style, at a sensible price.

The Katana was a huge hit, and remained popular for years. Suzuki broadened the Katana range with a 1000cc version with slide carbs for production racing, watered-down middleweight models, and even pocket-sized 250 and 400cc replicas for the Japanese market. Years later they even restarted production of a 'special edition' Katana 1100 that was almost identical to the original. Fair reward for a brave and brilliant bike.

Above: Suzuki's 1075cc, air-cooled, 16-valve engine had been introduced with the conventionally styled GSX1100 in 1980, two years before the Katana's arrival. Its four-valves-per-cylinder layout, called TSCC (or Twin Swirl Combustion Chamber) by Suzuki, gave superbly strong mid-range output.

Specification	Suzuki GSX1100S Katana (1982)
Engine	Air-cooled dohc 16-valve four
Capacity	1075cc (72 x 66mm)
Maximum power	111bhp @ 8500rpm
Transmission	Five-speed, chain final drive
Frame	Steel twin downtube
Suspension	Telescopic front; twin shocks rear
Brakes	Twin discs front; disc rear
Weight	545lb (247kg) wet
Top speed	140mph (225km/h)

Bimota HB2

**Top speed
138mph**
222km/h

*Right: Thanks to a rigid
frame, top quality
suspension and light
weight, the HB2's handling
was in a different league to
that of most superbikes.*

*Below: The Bimota's full
fairing and one-piece tank-
seat unit were typically racy
touches from a firm with an
impressive history of grand
prix success.*

 Bimota's exotic HB2, with its rounded
half-fairing, one-piece tank-seat unit,
aluminium frame sections and rising-rate
rear suspension unit, seemed like a motorcycle
from a different planet when it was launched in
1982. The sleek Italian superbike's Japanese rivals
were mostly naked fours with steel frames and twin
shocks. Even Honda's mighty CB1100R was
almost old-fashioned by comparison.

The HB2's initials stood for Honda Bimota, and
its engine was the air-cooled, 901cc twin-cam
engine from the Japanese giant's CB900F. In
Bimota style the 16-valve motor was left standard,
complete with its bank of Keihin carbs and airbox,
although some owners fitted larger flat-slide
Mikunis. Bimota's twin-silencer exhaust system
saved some weight but barely increased the
standard 900F's output of 94bhp.

The big motor was partially covered by the
Bimota's half-fairing, which blended with the one-
piece tank-seat unit. (This could be removed after
undoing just four bolts plus an electrical
connector.) The screen was usefully tall and
protective; the view from the rider's thinly padded
single seat was of a top triple clamp machined from
a solid chunk of lightweight alloy.

Stiff and lightweight frame

When the tank-seat unit was removed, the quality of the HB2 became clear. The frame's visible steel tubes, which ran down to join the alloy plates at the swingarm pivot, were backed up by numerous smaller tubes around the steering head. The aluminium plates at the swingarm pivot provided strength and light weight in that crucial area. A De Carbon rear shock, vertically mounted and operated via a rising-rate linkage, replaced the 900F's twin shocks. Front suspension was exotic, too: a pair of Ceriani telescopic forks with gold-finished sliders and, at the top of the legs, adjusters that could be turned by hand.

In combination with the Bimota's reduced weight – at 441lb (200kg) it was over 70lb (32kg) lighter than the CB900F – that gave a substantial handling advantage. The suspension worked superbly well, giving a taut yet also very comfortable ride. Other high quality parts included five-spoke alloy wheels, produced in the 16-inch diameters that were popular in grand prix racing at the time. The front brake set-up of twin-piston Brembo calipers and drilled 280mm discs was state of the art, as was the fat Michelin rubber.

And the Italian bike was superb in a straight line, too. At low revs the Honda engine impressed with its smoothness and torque, especially with the original CV carbs in place. There were no glitches

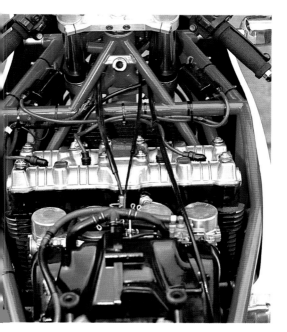

Original Bimota: the HB1

Bimota's first ever bike had also been powered by a four-cylinder Honda engine. The first HB1 was built from the wreck of the CB750 that Bimota design ace Massimo Tamburini had crashed at Misano. With its racetrack-derived styling and rigid tubular steel frame, the HB1 was a stunningly advanced machine when unveiled in 1972. Only ten examples were ever produced.

Specification	Bimota HB2 (1982)
Engine	Air-cooled dohc 16-valve four (Honda CB900F)
Capacity	901cc (64.5 x 69mm)
Maximum power	95bhp @ 9000rpm
Transmission	Five-speed, chain final drive
Frame	Tubular steel space-frame
Suspension	Telescopic front; monoshock rear
Brakes	Twin discs front; disc rear
Weight	441lb (200kg)
Top speed	138mph (222km/h)

or stumbles as the Bimota purred forward at a fearsome rate. Unlike the standard Honda, the HB2 had the fairing and the tucked-in riding position to make cruising speeds of 100mph (161km/h) or more hugely enjoyable for almost as long as its rider dared. And the HB2 remained impeccably stable as it headed towards a top speed that one magazine tested at 138mph (222km/h).

Fewer than 200 examples of the exotic HB2 were built, plus a further 100 units of its similarly styled successor the HB3, which was powered by the engine from Honda's CB1100R. The HB3 was produced until 1985, by which time the Japanese manufacturers, too, had introduced fairings, aluminium frames and monoshock suspension. In typical Bimota style, the HB2 had led the way.

Left: One secret of the HB2's handling prowess was the strength of its frame, which combined tubular steel with aluminium swingarm sections. The highly stressed steering head area was particularly well supported. High quality suspension components included a single rear shock, situated vertically behind the engine and operated by a linkage system.

Honda CX500 Turbo

**Top speed
125mph**
201km/h

*Right: The Turbo was a
big, heavy bike with shaft
drive, but it could be
cornered rapidly if its rider
was in the right mood.*

*Below: As well as its
turbocharged motor, the CX
was notable for chassis
features including twin-
piston front brake calipers,
anti-dive forks and
monoshock rear suspension.*

The CX500 Turbo with which Honda
stunned the motorcycle world in 1982 was
one of the least likely bikes ever to be put
into production. The turbocharged V-twin was
large, heavy, complex and expensive. From the
moment it was unveiled, many observers regarded
the Turbo as more of a corporate statement than a
serious superbike.

Honda's ostentatious V-twin was the first of the
string of turbocharged machines that would see all
of the big four Japanese manufacturers try their
luck with forced induction. The Honda was the
most curious in its choice of powerplant.
Turbochargers, which use exhaust gas to compress
the intake charge, are best suited to large engines
that operate at a steady load; the opposite of a
motorcycle's situation. In addition, multi-cylinder
motors help by smoothing the exhaust flow.

Despite this, Honda selected their middleweight
CX500, an 80-degree transverse V-twin with
pushrod valve operation. The CX's small cylinders
required the world's tiniest turbocharger, which was
built by IHI to Honda's specification. Its rotors
measured less than two inches (51mm) in diameter
and were designed to spin at 200,000rpm.

Strengthened engine

The CX's crankcases were strong enough to be retained, but much of liquid-cooled engine was uprated. A stronger crankshaft, clutch and conrods, plus Honda's first production-specification forged pistons, all helped to keep it together when the turbo increased peak power from the standard CX500's 50bhp to the Turbo's 82bhp at 8000rpm.

Honda's work by no means ended with the powerplant. The CX was a rolling showcase for other technical achievements, including its digital ignition and fuel-injection system, Pro-Link rear suspension, TRAC anti-dive, twin-piston brake calipers and redesigned Comstar wheels. In addition the fairing, with its lipped screen, enormous headlamp and integral indicators, was undeniably stylish. It held a sophisticated instrument console that contained a clock and fuel gauge, as well as the turbo boost gauge.

The fairing worked well, too, allowing high-speed cruising in comfort. The CX also handled very well considering its fuelled-up weight of over 550lb (250kg). But for such a big, expensive bike the Turbo was only moderately fast. It was good for 125mph (201km/h) but its acceleration was marred by all that weight. And the engine also suffered from turbo-lag, the intrusive delay between throttle opening and engine response which made precise throttle control difficult.

For long-distance riding at speed the Turbo was impressive even so, but it was not so outstanding that its weight, complexity and expense were overcome. A year later, in 1983, Honda followed it with the CX650 Turbo, which had less lag plus a substantial power increase that gave thrilling acceleration and a top speed of 135mph (217km/h). The bigger model was an even better grand tourer. But it was still not a sales success against simpler, cheaper rivals, and remained in production for only a year.

Specification	Honda CX500 Turbo (1982)
Engine	Liquid-cooled ohv pushrod four-valve 80-degree turbocharged transverse V-twin
Capacity	497cc (78 x 52mm)
Maximum power	82bhp @ 8000rpm
Transmission	Five-speed, shaft final drive
Frame	Steel spine
Suspension	Telescopic front; single shock rear
Brakes	Twin discs front; disc rear
Weight	529lb (240kg)
Top speed	125mph (201km/h)

Left: Among the Honda's sophisticated features was its efficient fairing, which combined with the broad dual seat to make the bike comfortable even at speed.

Below left: Honda's 497cc, pushrod-operated V-twin, surprisingly became the firm's first turbocharged motor, and had its output boosted by over 50 per cent.

Blown Four: the ZX750 Turbo

The last, fastest and best of the Japanese turbo-bikes was Kawasaki's ZX750 Turbo of 1984. Like Yamaha's XJ650 Turbo and Suzuki's XN85 (which also had a capacity of 650cc) the ZX was an in-line four. In style and chassis layout it resembled Kawasaki's GPz1100. Peak power was 112bhp, and the Kawasaki had very little turbo lag because its turbine was in front of the engine, so exhaust gas travelled a short distance before reaching it. With fine handling and a top speed of almost 140mph (225km/h), the ZX750 Turbo had comparable performance to the GPz1100. It sold in reasonable numbers before Kawasaki, too, finally abandoned turbo-bike production.

Kawasaki Z1100R

Top speed
145mph
233km/h

Below: With its high handlebars and bright green paintwork, the Z1100R captured the look of Eddie Lawson's US Superbike championship-winning racebike. That gave a high-performance image although the bike's air-cooled engine and twin-shock chassis layout had been made outdated by Kawasaki's own GPZ900R.

Big, green and brutal, Kawasaki's Z1100R was inspired by the factory Superbike on which Eddie Lawson had won the US championship in 1981 and '82. The brilliant Californian's high-handlebarred, production-based racebike had made headlines worldwide, and the Z1100R was a handsome roadgoing reproduction, even though its air-cooled, two-valves-per-cylinder format was outdated even when the model was launched in 1984.

In reality, the 1100R was more of a makeover of an ageing roadster than a close approximation of Lawson's Superbike. That championship-winning machine was essentially a Z1000 modified with parts including a green-painted GPz1100 tank and headlamp fairing, flat handlebars, highly tuned 150bhp engine plus race quality suspension, wheels and brakes.

For American riders, Kawasaki built a replica racebike that was sold to serious competitors only, then a 'Lawson Replica' roadster that combined green bodywork with modified steering geometry and a Kerker four-into-one exhaust. But the disappointing Z1000J that was sold outside the States in 1983 had no new frame or Kerker pipe, and in some countries including Britain it was white instead of green…

That was put right in 1984, when the Z1100R arrived with the correct paintwork plus a bigger, more powerful engine. Its 1089cc, air-cooled dohc eight-valve unit was essentially a GPz1100 powerplant with carburettors instead of fuel-injection. The new motor's peak output of 114bhp at 8500rpm matched that of the GPz, but the Z1100R lump had revised camshaft and ignition timing that put more of its power in the mid-range.

Looks like Lawson's

The motor was torquey and strong, and the rest of the Z1100R did not disappoint. There were still twin silencers instead of a four-into-one (though that was easily cured with an aftermarket exhaust), but the bike otherwise looked like Lawson's, with its contoured saddle, gold Kayaba remote-reservoir shocks, bikini fairing and high bars.

Its performance did not match that of the new-generation GPZ900R that Kawasaki introduced at the same time, but held plenty of appeal for riders brought up on big, torquey, air-cooled fours. The 1100R was tractable and generally smooth, cruised at a leisurely 80mph (129km/h), felt raw and exciting in typical big Kawasaki style, and wrenched its rider's arms to a top speed of over 140mph (225km/h).

The 1100R's brakes were excellent but the green machine's handling was less impressive, as the long, heavy, twin-shock chassis format was showing its age, and the handlebar-mounted fairing had a typically adverse effect on high-speed stability. As *SuperBike's* tester concluded, ultimately the Z1100R fell into a 'long line of Kawasaki big bikes where the sheer speed potential of their demon engines stretches the chassis and the rider long before it reaches max revs'.

Despite that, the tester enjoyed the big Kawasaki, and so did plenty of others. The Z1100R lacked sophistication but it had impeccable breeding, power to spare and plenty of old-fashioned charm. The old format had just about had its day, though. The Z1100R's blend of mighty engine and mediocre chassis brought Kawasaki's long and distinguished line of air-cooled high-performance fours to an end.

Eddie Lawson: Green King

Ironically Eddie Lawson won the 500cc world championship for Yamaha in 1984, the year the Z1100R was released, but his exploits aboard the high-barred Kawasaki Superbike remained a vivid memory. After finishing a close second in the US Superbike championship in 1980 Lawson won in style the following year, then retained the title in 1982 despite missing two races after breaking his neck at Laguna Seca. The Californian's smooth style transferred seamlessly to grands prix, where he followed three 500cc world titles for Yamaha by winning a fourth, for Honda, in 1989.

Specification	Kawasaki Z1100R (1984)
Engine	Air-cooled dohc eight-valve four
Capacity	1089cc (72.5 x 66mm)
Maximum power	114bhp @ 8500rpm
Transmission	Five-speed, chain final drive
Frame	Steel twin downtube
Suspension	Telescopic front; twin shocks rear
Brakes	Twin discs front; disc rear
Weight	525lb (238kg)
Top speed	145mph (233km/h)

Far left: The 1089cc, black-finished Z1100R unit ended an outstanding line of powerful and robust air-cooled, dohc eight-valve Kawasaki fours.

Left: *This bike's aftermarket four-into-one exhaust system enhances its Lawson-replica look. A stepped seat and gold-finished remote-reservoir shocks added to the racy look and gave a comfortable ride.*

Honda VF1000R

**Top speed
150mph**
241km/h

*Below: The lavishly
equipped, fully-faired
VF1000R had a very
advanced chassis
specification, incorporating
air-assisted front forks with
anti-dive, four-piston brake
calipers and adjustable
monoshock rear suspension.
But although it cornered
well on smooth surfaces
and made an excellent high-
speed roadster, the Honda
was too heavy and slow-
steering to be a success in
production racing.*

 Honda's enthusiasm for the V4 engine layout in the early 1980s was such that by 1984 the VF range comprised six models with capacities ranging from 400 to 1000cc. The fastest and most glamorous was the VF1000R: a limited-edition super-sports machine that was created, with little expense spared, to dominate production racing in the way that the straight-four CB1100R had done three years earlier.

With its full fairing and racy red, white and blue paintwork, the VF1000R looked every bit the street-legal competition machine. Its specification list was mouth-watering, based on a liquid-cooled, 90-degree V4 engine that incorporated gear-driven overhead camshafts and produced no less than 122bhp at 10,000rpm.

That peak power output was 6bhp up on that of the VF1000F, the standard 998cc, 16-valve V4 from which the R model was derived. The 1000F, also released in 1984, was an impressively fast and sophisticated bike. Its styling was similar to that of the original VF750F sportster, which had promised much before suffering widely publicized engine reliability problems. The VF1000F handled well and its engine was flexible, powerful and reliable.

The exotic VF1000R cost roughly 50 per cent more than the F, and oozed quality from every pore. Its fairing was reinforced with carbon-fibre, its adjustable handlebars were made from polished alloy, its streamlined seat hump fitted perfectly. Its engine's gear-driven cams allowed more precise valve timing at high revs, which accounted for some of the extra power.

Like the other VFs, the R had a frame of square-section steel tubes, but its chassis specification was decidedly upmarket. Big 41mm front forks incorporated air assistance, adjustable damping and TRAC anti-dive. Hinged fork bottoms allowed easy front wheel removal. The Pro-Link rear shock was easily adjustable; the impressive front brakes comprised sturdy four-piston calipers and large, floating discs.

Left: Despite the VF1000R's mixed reception and lack of racetrack success in its first year, only a few details including the paint scheme were changed for 1985. Although the V4 was not competitive, its stylish twin-headlamp fairing, made from plastic reinforced with carbon-fibre, gave excellent wind protection at high speed.

Below: Few bikes have looked as deceptively racy as the streamlined VF1000R, which was far more at home on a fast road than a production race grid. Ironically a Honda won the Isle of Man Production TT in 1985, but Geoff Johnson was riding the sports-touring VF1000 Bol d'Or model rather than the VF1000R.

Stability and power

For road riding the VF1000R was a seductively fast and comfortable companion. Its fairing combined with the racy riding position to give excellent wind protection. High-speed stability was absolute, and the engine was superbly powerful and torquey. The 1000R cruised effortlessly at well over 100mph (161km/h), and surged smoothly to a top speed of 150mph (241km/h).

The Honda's refined feel was marred by a snatchy transmission that became annoying in town, where the engine also had a tendency to heat up its carburettors, resulting in a misfire. But such problems were forgotten when the rider found the open road, and wound back the throttle to send the 1000R storming forward with a free-flowing feel from 5000rpm or below.

Handling was good at high speed, where the VF's stability counted for much. But at lower speeds the Honda suffered from a weight problem. At 524lb (238kg) dry it was more than 50lb (23kg) heavier than Kawasaki's GPz900R, and its handling was ponderous despite its 16-inch front wheel. That was a problem on the racetrack, in particular. Even Honda star Wayne Gardner just failed to take a bike that he described as a marshmallow to victory in the prestigious Castrol Six-Hour production race in his native Australia.

Unlike its all-conquering CB1100R predecessor, the VF1000R was rarely seen on a circuit, let alone in the winner's circle. That hit sales, especially as the V4's price put it on a level with race-bred exotica from firms such as Bimota and Harris. It was fortunate for Honda that they had intended to produce only a small number. The VF1000R was fast, sophisticated and easy on the eye, but underneath that sleek bodywork it hid too much weight to be a success.

Specification	Honda VF1000R (1984)
Engine	Liquid-cooled dohc 16-valve 90-degree V4
Capacity	998cc (77 x 53.6mm)
Maximum power	122bhp @ 10,000rpm
Transmission	Five-speed, chain final drive
Frame	Steel twin downtube
Suspension	Telescopic front; single shock rear
Brakes	Twin discs front; disc rear
Weight	524lb (238kg)
Top speed	150mph (241km/h)

Yamaha RD500LC

**Top speed
138mph**
222km/h

Few superbikes have been as eagerly anticipated as the RD500LC. In 1983 the long-standing success of Yamaha's middleweight two-stroke twins, combined with the factory's success in 500cc grand prix racing, made a 500cc four-cylinder race replica seem the logical next step. Such was the demand that some magazines went as far as publishing spoof road tests of a machine that did not exist.

When Yamaha finally put the real thing into production in the following year, few who rode one were disappointed. The RD500LC looked superb, with a racy full fairing in red and white colours similar to those of the factory OW76 that Eddie Lawson was riding to victory in that season's world championship. Like Lawson's racer, the 500LC was powered by a liquid-cooled V4 two-stroke engine. The roadster produced 90bhp, weighed an equally impressive 392lb (178kg) dry, and screamed to almost 140mph (225km/h).

Two-stroke heritage

Rather than being developed directly from the racebike engine, the LC's 499cc, 50-degree V4 powerplant was essentially two RD250LC units with bottom ends geared together, and with a gear-driven balancer shaft to reduce vibration. Induction system, engine porting and exhaust design were very different to the OW76 racer's, but bore and stroke dimensions of 56.4 x 50mm were almost identical, and the roadster also shared features including exhaust power valves.

Apart from the addition of lights and other roadgoing necessities, the main chassis difference between roadster and racer was that the RD500LC's frame was made from square-section steel tubing instead of aluminium. This was still one dramatically purposeful streetbike though, with high quality chassis parts including anti-dive equipped telescopic forks, plus a single rear shock unit positioned horizontally beneath the engine.

Below: The Yamaha engine felt flat below 6000rpm, but once the two-stroke V4 hit its power band in first gear, the lightweight LC liked nothing better than to scream off with its front wheel in the air. The race-replica four's need for high revs resulted in a thrilling ride on the road, and made obeying speed limits almost impossible.

Yamaha's V4 Revolution

Before building the RD500LC, Yamaha also led the move to V4 two-strokes in 500cc grands prix. Triple champion Kenny Roberts debuted the OW61 V4 in 1982, and is seen here leading fellow works rider Graeme Crosby, who is riding the previous OW60 square-four. The OW61, which had disc-valve induction, lacked mid-range power and also handled poorly but the 1984-model OW76, featuring reed-valve induction and a Deltabox aluminium frame, was infinitely better. Eddie Lawson's world championship victory that season was the first of six in nine years for Yamaha's 500cc V4.

The Yamaha's look and specification were mouth-watering, and its performance lived up to expectation. In typical two-stroke fashion the V4 felt flat at low revs, then came into its power band at 6000rpm with a crackle of its exhausts and a blast of acceleration that sent the lightweight machine shooting forward at breathtaking rate. That meant that in top gear it came alive only at about 100mph (161km/h). Fortunately, Yamaha had supplied a good pair of mirrors...

Even more importantly, the 500LC's handling was a match for its motor. As well as light and quick steering, aided by its 16-inch front wheel, it was stable in slower bends and high-speed curves alike. Sometimes the front end got slightly twitchy when the bike hit a bump under acceleration. But that was no real problem, and the Yamaha's powerful triple-disc brake system was among the best in motorcycling.

Yamaha had succeeded in creating a bike that felt like a racer on the road, and the RD500LC proved its ability on the track with victory, against many big four-strokes, in Australia's prestigious Castrol Six-Hour production race. In the showrooms it was less successful, despite all the pre-launch hysteria. Drawbacks included poor fuel consumption, vibration, mediocre finish and a high price. Perhaps the real problem was that the RD500LC was just a little too much like a real racebike for its own good.

Above left: In corners few bikes came close to matching the RD500LC, which combined light weight with a rigid steel frame, firm suspension and plenty of grip and ground clearance.

Left: With its full fairing, seat hump and two-stroke exhaust system, the RD500LC was the closest thing yet to a GP bike on the road.

Specification	Yamaha RD500LC (1984)
Engine	Liquid-cooled two-stroke 50-degree V4
Capacity	499cc (56.4 x 50mm)
Maximum power	90bhp @ 8500rpm
Transmission	Six-speed, chain final drive
Frame	Steel twin downtube
Suspension	Telescopic front; single shock rear
Brakes	Twin discs front; disc rear
Weight	392lb (178kg)
Top speed	138mph (222km/h)

Kawasaki GPZ900R

**Top speed
155mph**
249km/h

*Below: The Ninja's
aerodynamic full fairing
and compact dimensions
helped give the 908cc bike
a top speed of over 150mph
(241km/h). The original
bike's 16-inch front wheel
was changed to a wider 17-
inch unit on later models.*

The GPZ900R was the machine with which Kawasaki recaptured its reputation for unbeatable four-cylinder performance. When the firm's first liquid-cooled four stormed onto the streets in 1984, the manner in which it delivered 150mph (241km/h) top speed with smoothness and unprecedented refinement confirmed that a thrilling new era had begun.

And there was much more than sheer speed to the bike that in most markets was known as the Ninja. This was a 908cc machine that felt as compact as a 750 – and which outran its 1100cc rivals when you opened the throttle. Street riders took to it in droves, production racers adopted it as their own. Almost everyone who rode the Ninja was won over by a machine that combined speed with reliability, handling, comfort and its own unmistakable style.

Kawasaki had spent the previous decade earning a reputation for brilliant air-cooled eight-valve motors, but the GPZ unit was distinctly different. As well as liquid-cooling, it featured a 16-valve cylinder head plus developments including a balancer shaft, camchain at the end of the crankshaft, and alternator above the six-speed gearbox. It was small, light and powerful, though its peak output of 113bhp at 9500rpm was slightly below that of the old GPz1100.

The rest of the GPZ maintained the theme of high performance with minimum size and weight. Kawasaki called the bike's frame layout a 'diamond' but essentially it was a steel spine design

that used the engine as a stressed member, and which dispensed with the conventional downtubes. Aluminium was used for the square-section rear subframe, the box-section swingarm, and the large alloy footrest hangers on which it pivoted.

Front forks were 38mm units incorporating an anti-dive system that increased compression damping with suspension travel. Rear suspension was by Kawasaki's Uni-Trak monoshock layout, with an air-assisted shock unit that could be adjusted for rebound damping. The front wheel was 16 inches in diameter, following the fashion of the day.

Searing speed

The sharply styled full fairing did a reasonable job of shielding the rider, who leant forward to fairly flat handlebars. The Ninja was low, sleek – and most of all it was fast. Due to its superior aerodynamics it had a top-speed edge over its GPz1100 predecessor, with dramatic acceleration above 6000rpm and searing speed from 8000rpm to the 10,500rpm redline.

And the rest of the bike did not let it down. High-speed stability was exemplary, partly due to suspension that gave a superbly taut feel at the expense of some harshness at slower speeds. At over 500lb (227kg) the 900 was no lightweight, but by superbike standards it was very manageable, and its twin front disc brakes were hugely powerful. The Kawasaki was also practical, combining a generous fuel range with reasonable comfort plus neat details including luggage hooks and a strong pillion grab-rail.

The Ninja's success when launched was predictable, but even Kawasaki must have been pleasantly surprised by its long life. The 900 outlasted its intended replacements, the GPZ1000RX and the ZX-10, and even in 1990 was

not replaced but merely updated. The front wheel grew from 16 to 17 inches in diameter; both wheels were widened to allow fitment of fatter tyres; forks were thickened to 41mm; and front brake discs were enlarged to 300mm and treated to new four-piston calipers.

As it remained in Kawasaki's range during the 1990s, the once mighty Ninja came to be regarded as a budget-priced sports-tourer rather than a serious high-performance machine. But that should not diminish its reputation. What should be remembered is that in 1984 the GPZ900R was the undisputed king of the road. And that it started the dynasty of liquid-cooled, 16-valve Kawasaki fours that continues to this day.

Far left: Handling was superb by 1984 standards, thanks to a rigid steel frame, plus firm, anti-dive-equipped front forks and an efficient rising-rate monoshock rear suspension system.

Left: Kawasaki's first four-valves-per-cylinder engine was a suitably impressive successor to the firm's mighty two-valve fours. The initial 'GPz' logo was later amended to 'GPZ' to distinguish the liquid-cooled range.

Below: The GPZ 900R was the world's top superbike in 1984. Its roadgoing prowess was confirmed by victories in numerous production races, including the revived Production TT.

Specification	Kawasaki GPZ900R (1984)
Engine	Liquid-cooled dohc 16-valve four
Capacity	908cc (72.5 x 55mm)
Maximum power	113bhp @ 9500rpm
Transmission	Six-speed, chain final drive
Frame	Steel spine
Suspension	Telescopic front; single shock rear
Brakes	Twin discs front; disc rear
Weight	502lb (228kg)
Top speed	155mph (249km/h)

Laverda SFC 1000

**Top speed
140mph**
225km/h

*Below: The SFC's rather
tall look hinted at its 1970s
origins, but the half-fairing,
generous screen and roomy
riding position also made
the bike comfortable for
high-speed cruising. Having
lost some of the original
triples' raw character with
preceding models in the
1980s, Laverda was careful
to keep the handsome air-
cooled engine visible.*

Laverda's powerful air-cooled triples had
been some of the fastest and most
glamorous superbikes of the 1970s, but
during the following decade the Italian firm lacked
the financial resources to develop an equally
competitive successor. Instead, the triple was
restyled and refined to produce a more modern and
sophisticated series of machines, the last and best
of which was the SFC 1000.

With its tall half-fairing blending smoothly into
the fuel tank, below which sat a familiar 981cc
three-cylinder engine, the SFC was a direct
development of the RGS 1000 model with which
Laverda had begun its new generation of triples in
1982. In contrast to the loud, raw earlier triples
such as the Jota, the RGS had a slightly softer,
more flexible engine whose more restrictive
exhaust system enabled the bike to pass stricter
noise regulations.

Updated image

The RGS had succeeded in giving Laverda a more
modern image for the 1980s, but had lacked both
the all-conquering speed and the raw character that
had traditionally attracted the marque's enthusiasts.
In 1984 Laverda had added some performance with
the RGS 1000 Corsa whose engine, tuned with
high-compression pistons, new valves, modified
airbox and revised exhaust system, increased peak
output to about 90bhp.

For 1985 Laverda used the Corsa engine as the
basis of a new model, the SFC 1000. Its name was
designed to bring to mind the thunderous 750 SFC
production racer of the 1970s, although in reality
the new triple was a modified Corsa with red
instead of black paintwork, subtly reshaped fairing
and tank, and some new cycle parts. Its twin-
downtube steel frame was identical except for its
gold finish, and held a new box-section aluminium

swingarm. Other new parts included the rearset footrests, cast alloy wheels, plus Marzocchi forks and remote-reservoir rear shocks.

With its high tinted screen the SFC was tall by 1985 standards, its air-cooled engine was undeniably outdated, and it was heavy at 538lb (244kg). Inevitably the stirring three-cylinder bellow of old was stifled by emissions regulations. But despite that the big Laverda was a good-looking and distinctive machine that had enough pace and character to get its rider's adrenaline flowing.

The engine sometimes felt rough at very low revs, but once into its stride the SFC was tractable as well as powerful, pulling smoothly all the way from 3000rpm to a top speed of 140mph (225km/h). In corners the big Laverda could not match the best Japanese bikes in terms of agility or grip from its unfashionably narrow 18-inch tyres, but it was still very enjoyable. Its Marzocchi suspension was firm and well damped; the Brembo Gold Line brakes gave superbly powerful stopping.

Although the SFC was far from being a competitive super-sports machine, it combined its performance with enough comfort to make it an excellent sports-tourer. There was potential for more speed, too, as the factory offered a sports kit of three-into-one exhaust system and larger main jets for the Dell'Orto carburettors. Really serious owners could opt for the racetrack kit comprising hot cams, valve springs, bigger 36mm carburettors and close-ratio gearbox.

Specification	Laverda SFC 1000 (1985)
Engine	Air-cooled dohc six-valve triple
Capacity	981cc (75 x 74mm)
Maximum power	90bhp @ 7000rpm
Transmission	Five-speed, chain final drive
Frame	Steel twin downtube
Suspension	Telescopic front; twin shocks rear
Brakes	Twin discs front; disc rear
Weight	538lb (244kg) wet
Top speed	140mph (225km/h)

Left: This Laverda might have been expensive, and uncompetitive with the latest Japanese superbikes, but this was still a very stylish machine that turned heads, had heaps of character and generated adrenaline by the bucketful.

Laverda had been planning to build only 200 units of the SFC 1000 before moving on to produce a more modern range of three-cylinder middleweights. But the firm's financial problems meant that the new bikes never appeared, and the final batch of SFC 1000s left the factory at Breganze in 1987. Laverda would be revived in the 1990s under new ownership – with a range of parallel twins. The story of the famous air-cooled triples had come to an end.

Above: The 981cc air-cooled dohc three-cylinder engine incorporated a few refining touches that had been introduced over the years, but it was still closely related to the unit from the Jota of the mid-1970s.

Left: Twin rear shock absorbers and 18-inch wheels were old-fashioned by the time the SFC appeared in 1985. But with its reasonably rigid frame and high-quality suspension, the big Laverda could hold its own with many more modern machines in the corners.

Yamaha FZ750

**Top speed
145mph**
233km/h

Right: Yamaha's liquid-cooled, 749cc four-cylinder engine may not have gained an edge with its 20-valve layout, but was certainly an outstanding powerplant.

Below: The original, half-faired FZ750 could not quite match the racy image of Suzuki's rival GSX-R750, but it backed-up its straight-line speed with excellent handling.

Yamaha's modern generation of superbikes began in 1985 with the FZ750. Much more than just a superb machine with a level of all-round performance unmatched in the 750cc class, the FZ introduced the engine layout of four angled-forward, liquid-cooled cylinders, each with five valves, on which Yamaha's big bike range would be based for many years to come.

The FZ's 749cc motor was a revelation. Tilting its cylinders forward at 45 degrees moved the centre of gravity forwards and downwards, and also made room for an innovative breathing arrangement. The bank of Mikuni downdraft carburettors sat where the cylinder head would normally have been. The airbox was shifted forwards to a new position just behind the steering head, and the fuel tank extended down into the space normally occupied by the carbs.

Unique inlet layout

This gave a large volume of cool air with a straight run down to the engine – where it met the unique sight of three tiny inlet valves to each cylinder. Yamaha claimed the five-valve layout gave significant benefits over four-valve designs, mainly because although the total valve area was slightly smaller than with two larger inlet valves, the trio's total circumference – more important, because the valves were almost always only partially open – was larger. The figures were promising, with a peak output of 105bhp at 10,500rpm.

The FZ750's chassis was designed to complement the engine layout but was conventional, based around a frame of square-section steel tubes, rather than the aluminium of Suzuki's rival GSX-R750. Front forks were air-assisted and, like most sporty set-ups at the time, held a 16-inch front wheel. Rear suspension was by vertical monoshock. Styling was smart but conservative, with an angular half-fairing that left the black-finished motor on display.

And what a motor it was. When Yamaha had announced the 20-valve layout the previous year, cynics had commented that it was a complex gimmick that gave no benefit over the normal 16-valve design. Some had second thoughts after riding the FZ750, whose combination of engine power and flexibility would have been impressive for a large-capacity bike, let alone a compact and easy-handling 750.

No matter what engine speed was being indicated by its tachometer, the FZ surged smoothly forward when its throttle was wound open. Even from below 2000rpm it responded cleanly, when most larger-engined bikes would have hesitated. By 7000rpm in the highest of its six gears the Yamaha was already close to 100mph (161km/h) and pulling hard. Then it kicked again, moving into warp speed and pushing its rider back as it headed for a top speed of over 140mph (225km/h).

Chassis performance was less spectacular but still very good. Handling was stable and precise. The fairly upright riding position combined with the excellent suspension to give comfortable high-speed cruising, although the screen was quite low. Other practical features included a generous fuel range, and the fact that the valve train not only proved very reliable, but required adjustment only every 28,000 miles (45,000km).

Apart from a twin-disc front brake that lacked power compared to its rivals, the FZ was an outstanding machine: fine-handling yet reasonably comfortable; rapid but remarkably tractable; aggressive in looks and feel, yet well-equipped and as suited to everyday riding as almost every other Japanese four. Unfortunately for Yamaha, it did not achieve the sales success it deserved, even when uprated a year later with a full fairing. But as the first of many great 20-valve fours the FZ750 was one of the most influential bikes of its generation, as well as one of the best.

Specification	Yamaha FZ750 (1985)
Engine	Liquid-cooled dohc 20-valve four
Capacity	749cc (68 x 51.6mm)
Maximum power	105bhp @ 10,500rpm
Transmission	Six-speed, chain final drive
Frame	Steel twin downtube
Suspension	Telescopic front; monoshock rear
Brakes	Twin discs front; disc rear
Weight	460lb (209kg)
Top speed	145mph (233km/h)

Above: Yamaha updated the FZ with a full fairing only a year after its launch, and also gave its initially rather disappointing front brake some extra bite. The result was a less distinctive but an even more competent machine.

Left: With its broad spread of power, reasonable comfort and excellent handling, the FZ impressed both as a sports bike and an all-rounder. Handling was slightly less agile than that of some rivals, but the Yamaha was stable even at serious cornering speeds.

Suzuki GSX-R750

**Top speed
145mph**
233km/h

*Below: One glance
confirmed that the GSX-R
was the spitting image of
Suzuki's endurance race
bike, and the roadster's
power, light weight and
handling ability soon made
it a hit on road and track.
This is a 1986-model
GSX-R, featuring the longer
swingarm introduced to
improve high-speed stability.*

 The original GSX-R750 was the bike with
which modern Japanese super-sports
motorcycles were invented. True, there
had been plenty of fast and fiery superbikes before
the oil-cooled four was unleashed in 1985. But the
GSX-R750 was the first modern race replica; a
uniquely single-minded machine built for
performance above all else.

Its layout matched that of Suzuki's endurance
racers of the previous year, from the shape of the
twin-headlamp fairing to the use of 18-inch wheels
(favoured by endurance race teams because the
larger diameter facilitated brake pad changes)
instead of the then fashionable 16-inchers. Its frame
was made from aluminium, instead of the steel
used by rival superbikes. And its 749cc, dohc 16-
valve engine was powerful, with a peak output of
100bhp at 10,500rpm.

Oil cooling system

That output came from a motor that used the novel
(for bikes) system of oil-cooling to reduce cylinder
temperatures without the added bulk and weight of
a water jacket. The Suzuki Advanced Cooling
System, SACS for short, allowed the engineers to
redesign the previous air-cooled GSX750 unit on a
smaller, higher-revving scale. Almost every
component lost weight by being smaller or, in the
case of the cam cover, made from exotic
magnesium instead of aluminium.

The GSX-R motor's output and lightness were
impressive, but it was the chassis that did most to
give this bike its unmatched power-to-weight ratio.
At 388lb (176kg) the GSX-R was far lighter than
any rival 750. According to Suzuki, the new
aluminium frame, constructed from a combination
of cast sections and extruded tubes, weighed just

18lb (8kg), half as much as the GSX750's less rigid steel item. Front forks were stout 41mm units, their rigidity boosted by an aluminium brace.

A racy instrument console, with dials mounted in foam, hinted at the motor's liking for revs. Despite its row of Mikuni flat-slide carburettors the Suzuki was quite rideable even at low engine speed, feeling slightly buzzy without ever producing serious vibration. But its delivery was flat until 7000rpm, when the bike suddenly came alive, howling forward as the revs headed towards the 11,000rpm limit.

High-revving performance

That high-revving performance, allied to a slick six-speed gearbox and a top speed of 145mph (233km/h), made the GSX-R a straight-line match for all its 750cc rivals. And in the bends the Suzuki pressed home its advantage. Despite its 18-inch front wheel the bike could be flicked into a turn with little effort, and was stable once leant over. The GSX-R's lack of weight was a benefit in corners and under braking, where it allowed the front brake – a combination of 300mm discs and four-piston calipers – to deliver unprecedented stopping power and feel.

But the GSX-R was one of the first road bikes to require careful setting-up, and preferably a steering damper, to handle well. The original model's occasional high-speed wobble prompted Suzuki to introduce a slightly longer swingarm in 1986. Practicality had barely been a consideration for the Suzuki's designers, but the GSX-R750 did have a protective fairing and a strong pillion grab-rail, to offset against its aggressive riding position, poor fuel range and narrow mirrors.

Specification	Suzuki GSX-R750 (1985)
Engine	Oil-cooled dohc 16-valve four
Capacity	749cc (70 x 48.7mm)
Maximum power	100bhp @ 10,500rpm
Transmission	Six-speed, chain final drive
Frame	Aluminium twin downtube
Suspension	Telescopic front; single shock rear
Brakes	Twin discs front; disc rear
Weight	388lb (176kg)
Top speed	145mph (233km/h)

Not that many riders who bought GSX-R750s for use on road or track were concerned about such details. The GSX-R was built for speed, and it delivered. It became hugely popular, was repeatedly updated in subsequent years (not always successfully), and established a race replica format that would be followed by Suzuki and its rival firms into the 21st century.

Below: Whether carving through turns or flat-out on a straight, the GSX-R was a fast and exciting ride. Its light yet rigid aluminium frame (bottom left) heralded a new era in sports bike chassis design.

Yamaha V-Max

**Top speed
140mph**
225km/h

*Right: High speed on the
V-Max was great fun,
provided you were travelling
in a straight line. Corners
were a different matter.*

*Below: In a contest to find
the ultimate production
musclebike, there would be
only one contender. The
aggressive, engine-
dominated styling would
barely change in almost two
decades of production.*

There has never been a production
motorcycle like the V-Max. Nor has there
been a modern high-performance bike that
has remained successful with so few changes as
Yamaha's intimidating and brutally powerful V4,
which was unleashed on an unsuspecting public
back in 1985.

On its introduction, the V-Max's muscular
styling and its 1198cc engine's 143bhp output put it
in a different league to every other bike on the
road. It was designed by Americans and resembled
a two-wheeled muscle car, with big alloy air-scoops
jutting out from the side of its dummy fuel tank.
The scoops and tank were fake but the V-Max's
performance was certainly not. Nothing wrenched
your arms like the Max. The fact that its chassis
was barely able to cope simply added to the impact.

The undoubted centrepiece of the V-Max was
its engine, a 72-degree, shaft-drive V4 borrowed
from the Venture tourer. Yamaha's engineers tuned
the Venture's 95bhp, 16-valve engine with

conventional hot-rodding components including
high-lift cams, big valves, lightened pistons and a
toughened crankshaft. They also added V-boost, a
system that linked the carburettors to provide extra
mixture – and instant extra power – at high revs.

Storming acceleration

The effect of snapping open the throttle was breathtaking. When the needle of the Yamaha's tiny tachometer hit 6000rpm, the V-boost cut in to send the bike hurtling in a barely controlled frenzy towards the horizon. Other bikes were ultimately faster than the Yamaha, whose aerodynamics limited top speed to 140mph (225km/h). But nothing could live with the V-Max away from the line. It stormed off, painting a black stripe on the ground with its wildly spinning rear tyre, which at 150 x 15in was motorcycling's widest.

Cornering was often equally exciting, and not always for the right reasons. The Yamaha carried its weight low (fuel lived under the seat, which helped), but there was no disguising the fact that this was one heavy, fairly crudely suspended motorbike that didn't much like changing direction. At moderate cornering speeds it was stable, but more aggressive riding resulted in the big Yamaha shaking its head in annoyance.

Not that most owners seemed to mind, for part of the V-Max's uniquely macho appeal was that it had too much motor for its chassis. In an era of increasingly sweet-handling superbikes it stood out

Egli's Madder Max

The V-Max's power and aggressive image made it an ideal base for tuners and specials builders, who have used it as the basis of many outstanding creations over the years. Among the most outrageous was the supercharged monster built by veteran Swiss engineer Fritz Egli in 1995. Egli bolted on a Roots supercharger, driven by toothed belt from the crankshaft, and fed by a gaping twin-choke Weber carburettor in the dummy fuel tank. The result was over 200bhp, ear-splitting noise, and performance that was terrifying despite the mildly uprated chassis. Despite requests, Egli refused to build more bikes for sale.

as a mean, nasty machine that was unbeatable in a straight line but hard work through the bends. Yet it was also easy to live with, when required. That big V4 was docile at low revs, and also commendably reliable.

The V-Max's unique style and performance earned it a cult following back in 1985 (although, ironically, it was initially detuned in some markets including Britain), and it remained in Yamaha's range for many years with few changes. In 1993 it gained thicker front forks and an uprated front brake. But the mighty Max entered its third decade with its essential look and personality barely changed at all. And with its reputation for raw, brutal power very much in place.

Left: The air-scoops sticking out above each side of the engine were fake, and the fuel tank was a dummy because fuel lived under the seat. But the big V4's engine performance, at least in unrestricted form, was the real thing. Front forks and brakes were uprated on later models, but there was no need to tune the 143bhp motor.

Specification	Yamaha V-Max (1985)
Engine	Liquid-cooled dohc 16-valve 72-degree V4
Capacity	1198cc (76 x 66mm)
Maximum power	143bhp @ 8000rpm
Transmission	Five-speed, shaft final drive
Frame	Steel twin downtube
Suspension	Telescopic front; twin shocks rear
Brakes	Twin discs front; disc rear
Weight	560lb (254kg)
Top speed	140mph (225km/h)

Honda VFR750F

**Top speed
145mph**
233km/h

*Right: This 1989-model
VFR incorporates the 17-
inch front wheel that was
introduced in the previous
year. The full fairing gave
excellent wind protection
at speed.*

*Below: VFR logos were
changed to Interceptor for
the American market.
Whatever its name, the V4
Honda was a brilliantly
fast, capable and well
balanced superbike.*

During the late 1980s and throughout the following decade, the unique and sophisticated VFR750F came to epitomize all that was best about Honda. The VFR, known as the Interceptor in the States, was fast and handled well. Equally importantly it was comfortable, good looking, well equipped and built to a standard that was arguably not matched by any other mass-produced superbike.

Yet ironically the VFR's launch in 1986 had come at a very difficult time for Honda. The firm's reputation had been hit hard by the unreliability of several models, notably the VF750F whose engine, also a liquid-cooled V4, had proved disastrously unreliable following the bike's introduction three years earlier. The VFR was launched to an unprecedented level of scrutiny. It had to be good, and even more importantly it had to be reliable.

The VFR, created using all Honda's V4 experience, was both of those things and more. Its 748cc engine retained not only the VF's 90-degree,

16-valve V4 format but also its dimensions of 70 x 48.6mm and even its compression ratio. Like the VF1000R, it turned its camshafts with gears instead of chains, making a positive feature of an area that had been a Honda weakness.

Lighter valves, pistons and conrods helped boost power, as did Keihin CV carburettors that were larger than their VF equivalents, and re-angled to provide a straighter intake path. The crankshaft gave a 180- instead of 360-degree firing order, and the lubrication was uprated to cope with a maximum output of 105bhp at 10,500rpm, a gain of 15bhp over the VF750F.

Lightweight frame

The key chassis feature was the new aluminium frame which, in typical Japanese style, combined cast sections at steering head and swingarm pivot with extruded main rails. The frame was stiff and light, helping the VFR weigh a competitive 436lb (198kg). Suspension and the triple-disc brake system were of excellent quality, too. The forks used air assistance; the rear monoshock could be adjusted for spring preload using a remote knob behind a sidepanel.

As well as impressive top-end power, the engine had plenty of mid-range torque and an engaging V4 character. A twist of the throttle was enough to send the Honda surging smoothly towards a top speed of over 140mph (225km/h). Crucially, the V4 engine also proved superbly reliable, and the VFR was finished to a notably high level. The bike's handling was excellent, too, combining light, precise steering with flawless stability and excellent suspension control.

It added up to a brilliantly balanced superbike that almost single-handedly restored Honda's reputation for engineering quality. The VFR750 won praise from just about everyone who rode it for its performance and practicality. It was comfortable enough for commuting or touring, yet also fast enough to keep up with its 750cc rivals anywhere other than on a racetrack – and it could be competitive even there, as Honda star Ron Haslam showed with an heroic ride on a near standard VFR in the 1986 Transatlantic Challenge.

When the pressure had been on, Honda had produced one of its finest superbikes. And the VFR was successfully updated in subsequent years, starting in 1988 when it gained a modified fairing and screen, plus a 17- instead of 16-inch front wheel. The VFR750F gradually became slightly sportier without losing its famed all-round ability. Only a few years after the bike's launch, Honda's V4 problems were a distant memory, and the initials VFR had come to stand for unmatched versatility and refinement.

Left: Honda's reliability problems with previous models meant the VFR's 748cc, liquid-cooled V4 engine was closely scrutinized. A new valve train used gear-driven double overhead camshafts to operate the 16 valves, and helped produce 105bhp with flawless reliability.

Below: Although the VFR could not quite match the agility of more aggressive race-replicas, it was a respectably light bike with a rigid aluminium frame, and handled very well despite suspension that was designed for comfort as much as cornering speed.

Specification	Honda VFR750F (1986)
Engine	Liquid-cooled dohc 16-valve 90-degree V4
Capacity	748cc (70 x 48.6mm)
Maximum power	105bhp @ 10,500rpm
Transmission	Six-speed, chain final drive
Frame	Aluminium twin spar
Suspension	Telescopic front; single shock rear
Brakes	Twin discs front; disc rear
Weight	436lb (198kg)
Top speed	145mph (233km/h)

Suzuki GSX-R1100

**Top speed
155mph**
249km/h

*Right: The lightweight
Suzuki's remarkable
cornering ability combined
with its straight-line speed
to give performance that no
bike could match.*

*Below: The GSX-R1100's
look was almost identical to
that of the 750cc model that
had been launched a year
earlier.*

In look and in layout, the machine with
which Suzuki rocked the superbike world
in 1986 was almost identical to the GSX-
R750 that had made such a huge impact the
previous year. To that first GSX-R's format of 16-
valve, oil-cooled four-cylinder engine and
aluminium frame, the open-class machine added
not only more top-end power but also a storming
supply of mid-range performance. The result was
an unbeatable superbike.

At a glance the GSX-R1100 was almost
indistinguishable from its smaller sibling. The two
models shared Suzuki's endurance racer styling,
with round twin headlamps in a tall full fairing and
a four-into-one exhaust. The aluminium frame's
design was very similar, too: a collection of
rectangular-section extrusions in a twin-downtube
arrangement, with cast sections at the steering head

and around the pivot of a box-section swingarm
that was made from the same lightweight alloy.

But if the engine's basic layout was unchanged,
its larger 1052cc capacity gave dramatically
different power characteristics. Where the 750cc

RG500 Gamma: Grand Prix Replica

Suzuki brought an even more extreme level of performance to the street in 1985 with the RG500 Gamma which, with its square-four two-stroke engine, was a street-legal replica of the bike on which Barry Sheene, Marco Lucchinelli and Franco Uncini had recently won world championships. The Gamma's disc-valve induction engine produced 95bhp but was flat until 8000rpm, at which point it took off to send the bike screaming towards a top speed of over 140mph (225km/h). The aluminium-framed, fully-faired RG500 weighed just 342lb (155kg), and had wonderfully agile handling plus superb braking. But the two-stroke was too expensive and impractical to sell in large numbers.

Below: Tucked behind the GSX-R's aerodynamic, endurance racer-style full fairing, its 1052cc, oil-cooled 16-valve engine was notable for its 125bhp peak output, storming mid-range performance and impressive reliability. The aluminium frame combined extruded main rails with cast sections in areas including the swingarm pivot.

bike was highly strung and demanding, the GSX-R1100, which also differed in having a lower, 10:1 compression ratio, and CV instead of slide carburettors, was much more flexible. Its power curve impressed not just with its peak of 125bhp at 8500rpm, but also with its enormously broad spread of torque.

Muscular mid-range

The big Suzuki's white-faced tachometer did not register below 3000rpm, by which time the bike was already accelerating with considerable enthusiasm. By 5000rpm it was ripping forward violently enough to lift its front wheel in first gear; or, more usefully, to surge past a line of traffic in the highest ratio of its new five-speed gearbox. At 7000rpm, where the smaller GSX-R engine came alive, the 1100 was breathing even deeper as it headed for the 10,500rpm redline and a top speed of 155mph (249km/h).

Straight-line acceleration was also aided by the GSX-R1100's light weight. At 434lb (197kg) dry it was 44lb (20kg) heavier than the 750, due to many of its apparently identical parts being slightly larger and stronger. But that figure still made the Suzuki by far the lightest open-class machine, and its standing quarter-mile time of less than 11 seconds put the GSX-R far ahead of the opposition.

An excellent chassis added further to the Suzuki's all-conquering performance. That rigid aluminium frame was backed-up by anti-dive equipped front forks borrowed from the 750, plus a new rear shock, larger front brake discs, and wider 18-inch wheels and tyres. Its steering was precise

and its stability impeccable, aided by the addition of a steering damper in front of the steering head.

In the fashion of the smaller GSX-R, the 1100 was an uncompromisingly aggressive machine with a stretched-out riding position and high footrests that made it uncomfortable in town. But its fairing gave enough protection to allow effortless high-speed cruising. Besides, many riders would have been happy to accept a far lower level of practicality because, for pure performance, nothing on two wheels came close to the GSX-R1100.

Left: The GSX-R's twin-headlamp fairing, humped fuel tank, aluminium frame design and 18-inch wheel sizes were inspired by Suzuki's 1000cc endurance racer of a few years earlier. Unlike the peaky GSX-R750, the GSX-R1100 was a flexible roadster that was easy to ride as well as fast.

Specification	Suzuki GSX-R1100 (1986)
Engine	Oil-cooled dohc 16-valve four
Capacity	1052cc (76 x 58mm)
Maximum power	125bhp @ 8500rpm
Transmission	Five-speed, chain final drive
Frame	Aluminium twin downtube
Suspension	Telescopic front; single shock rear
Brakes	Twin discs front; disc rear
Weight	434lb (197kg)
Top speed	155mph (249km/h)

Yamaha FJ1200

**Top speed
150mph**
241km/h

Right: Despite its origins as a sports bike, the FJ excelled in a sports-touring role and was often fitted with panniers.

Below: The FJ's distinctive look, with fairing cut away to reveal the big air-cooled four-cylinder engine beneath, changed very little in a decade of production.

Yamaha took a long time to build a big four-stroke that matched the popularity of the firm's smaller two-stroke models. Success finally came with the FJ1200 sports-tourer, which changed little during a decade in production. Yet ironically the Yamaha found its niche almost by accident, as its predecessor the FJ1100, released two years earlier in 1984, had been created as an 'out-and-out high performance sports machine', in Yamaha's words – only to be outgunned by Kawasaki's more aggressive GPZ900R.

The FJ1100 itself was a fast and fine bike that finally proved the ability of Yamaha's four-stroke engineers, and in any previous year would have taken the honours for pure performance. Instead, the sportier Kawasaki's arrival meant that the FJ became known as a long-distance roadburner – a role for which it was superbly well equipped due to its torquey engine, stable handling and comfort.

Sporting pretensions

That Yamaha was capable of producing a powerful and reliable four-cylinder engine came as no surprise, for the firm's experience stretched back to the XS1100 of 1978. The FJ format incorporated a 16-valve cylinder head for the first time, although ironically the bike's sporting pretensions ensured that final drive was by chain instead of a more practical shaft. Yamaha moved fast to improve the original FJ, enlarging its 1097cc air-cooled, 16-valve four-cylinder engine to 1188cc to produce the FJ1200. At the same time some details were refined while the basic layout was retained.

If the FJ's engine owed much to previous Yamahas, its chassis was much more innovative. The frame was a rectangular-section steel unit that appeared to have been influenced by Bimota. Main rails ran from the swingarm pivot area, around the cylinder head, then around the forks and steering head before joining at the front of the bike. Yamaha called the design 'Lateral' or 'Perimeter' Frame Concept, depending on the market.

Even when the FJ1200 was released, its air-cooled engine was described by one magazine tester as an anachronism. But neither that rider, nor many others, complained about the bike's performance. The bigger motor had the same peak power output of 125bhp, and produced even more of the strong, seamless low-rev torque for which the original FJ had become renowned.

Whether it had one person to carry or two, the Yamaha surged smoothly forward from walking pace in third gear. And once out of town, the rider's left boot was barely required as the FJ delivered

Specification	Yamaha FJ1200 (1986)
Engine	Air-cooled dohc 16-valve four
Capacity	1188cc (77 x 63.8mm)
Maximum power	125bhp @ 8500rpm
Transmission	Five-speed, chain final drive
Frame	Steel perimeter
Suspension	Telescopic front; monoshock rear
Brakes	Twin discs front; disc rear
Weight	576lb (261kg)
Top speed	150mph (241km/h)

scorching performance without leaving the tallest ratio of its five-speed gearbox. Given enough room the Yamaha was good for 150mph (241km/h), but more important was its effortless feel and the smoothness with which it sat at high speed.

At 576lb (261kg) the FJ1200 was not the lightest of superbikes, but it handled well. Its frame was strong, its suspension well-damped if slightly soft for hard riding, and for such a big, roomy bike it was easy to manoeuvre. And the Yamaha was practical too. Its half-fairing and reasonably tall screen combined with features including a large fuel tank, thick dual-seat and roomy riding position to make for relaxed long-distance travel.

In 1988, two years after its introduction, the FJ1200 was updated with a 17-inch front wheel, in place of the original 16-incher, plus revised suspension, brakes and screen. By this time the FJ had become the yardstick against which other sports-tourers were judged. It remained popular well into the following decade, gaining features including optional anti-lock brakes, but retaining its look and personality to the end.

Below left: Enlarging the FJ1100's engine to 1188cc did not alter its 125bhp peak output, but added to the low-rev and mid-range response for which the air-cooled unit was famous. Had Yamaha's designers known the FJ's eventual role, they might have chosen final drive by shaft.

Below: Although the FJ was too heavy and softly sprung to compete with sportier superbikes on a racetrack, it matched most bikes on the road. Ground clearance was lacking at severe lean angles, but for most riders the Yamaha's roomy riding position was adequate compensation.

Honda RC30

**Top speed
155mph**
249km/h

*Below: Behind the RC30's
compact twin-headlamp
fairing, which was closely
based on that of the RVF
racebike, were the two
elaborately constructed
curved radiators necessary
to cool the powerful V4
engine. The Honda's front
brake and multi-adjustable
front forks were the best yet
seen on a streetbike.*

 The concept of the race replica was firmly
established when Honda launched its
RC30 in 1988, but there had never been a
superbike remotely like this. With its exotic
specification, its race-bred V4 engine and its high
price, the bike officially known as the VFR750R
was a direct descendant of Honda's mighty
RVF750 works machines, which had dominated
world championship Formula One and endurance
racing in the mid-1980s.

Like Honda's CB1100R and VF1000R before
it, the RC30 was a homologation special; created as
a limited-edition, money-no-object basis for
competition success. But the gorgeous V4 was
more purposeful even than its predecessors. Its
style and format followed the RVF to an
unprecedented degree, from its compact twin-

headlamp fairing and single seat unit to a
lightweight twin-spar aluminium frame that was
rumoured to be cast from the same dies as the
racer's. It had a single-sided swingarm, as
employed on Honda's endurance racers to speed
wheel changes.

The RC30's liquid-cooled, dohc 90-degree V4
was a tuned and lightened version of the unit from
Honda's VFR750F roadster. It used a 360-degree
crankshaft, like the RVF racers but unlike the 180-
degree 750F, as this gave better drive out of
corners. Conrods were forged from lightweight
titanium. The 16 valves were operated by buckets
and shims instead of tappets.

Larger carburettors, twin curved radiators and a
complex single-muffler exhaust system were
further RFV style features. Maximum output was
112bhp at 11,000rpm, an increase of 7bhp over the
750F. Equally importantly, the RC30 churned out
generous helpings of smooth, free-revving power
from low revs, which combined with the close-ratio
gearbox to make the bike wonderfully easy to ride
very fast indeed.

Droning exhaust note

The Honda's top speed of 155mph (249km/h) was
impressive; equally so was the rapid but
deceptively lazy feeling way in which it
accelerated, with a trademark flat drone from the
360-degree V4's exhaust. Inevitably the engine was
far less happy in town, where its ultra-tall first gear,
good for more than 80mph (129km/h), strained the
clutch and was as impractical as the stretched-out
riding position (not to mention other features
including the small fuel tank, inaccessible tap and
narrow mirrors).

Chassis layout and ergonomics were designed
solely for the track. The screen and handlebars
were low, the footrests high. The all-important
tachometer and temperature gauge were foam-
mounted, while unnecessary parts including the
speedometer were separate for easy removal. The
compact wheelbase and steering geometry matched
the RVF's, and at 407lb (185kg) the RC30 was
light even with all its roadgoing parts fitted.

Cycle parts were of very high quality, with
43mm forks and 310mm diameter front brake discs,
just like the RVF. Front and rear suspension were

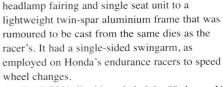

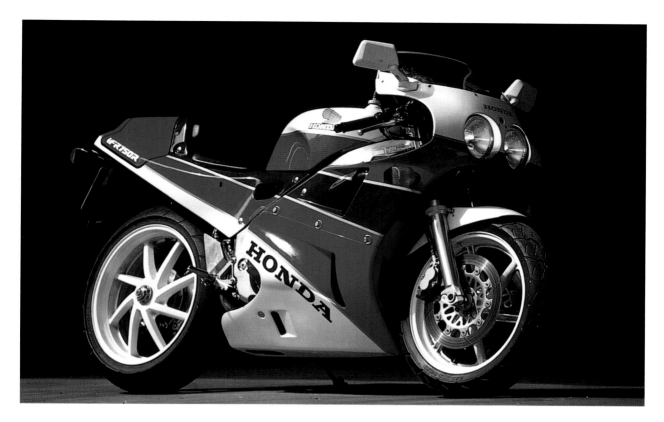

adjustable for compression and rebound damping. Although the single-sided swingarm was slightly heavier than a twin-sider of equal strength (despite Honda's claims to the contrary), it looked sensational and emphasized the RVF heritage.

The RC30 had been built to win races, and it duly delivered. America's Fred Merkel (Superbike) and Britain's Carl Fogarty (Formula One) rode race-kitted RC30s to consecutive world titles in 1988 and '89, against works opposition. Less desirably, in National level production-based racing, there was little chance of winning unless you rode a Honda, which cost almost twice as much as rival 750s.

That soured the RC30's impact for some riders, but those lucky enough to ride one were soon won over. On the right road, just as on a racetrack, the RC30 was supremely rapid and rewarding. Its power and throttle response were magnificent; its agility, suspension control and braking power without equal. The RC30 remained a fine roadster and an outstanding example of Honda's engineering ability, long after its impact on the world's racetracks had faded.

Above: Half-close your eyes and the RC30 could be a factory RVF endurance racer, complete with single-sided swingarm for rapid rear wheel changes.

Left: At its best the RC30's handling was unbeatable but, like the racebike that in many ways it was, the Honda required careful setting-up.

Specification	**Honda** RC30 (1988)
Engine	Liquid-cooled dohc 16-valve 90-degree V4
Capacity	748cc (70 x 48.6mm)
Maximum power	112bhp @ 11,000rpm
Transmission	Six-speed, chain final drive
Frame	Aluminium twin spar
Suspension	Telescopic front; single shock rear
Brakes	Twin discs front; disc rear
Weight	407lb (185kg)
Top speed	155mph (249km/h)

Ducati 900SS

**Top speed
135mph**
217km/h

*Right: A traditional tubular
steel ladder frame used the
V-twin engine as a stressed
member of the chassis, and
gave excellent rigidity.*

*Below: The original 900SS
handled well despite its
simple cantilever rear
suspension system and
rather basic, non-adjustable
front forks, which were
uprated when the model
was restyled in 1991.*

Ducati sprung a surprise in 1989 when the firm reintroduced the 900 Super Sport name, made famous in the 1970s, with a totally new V-twin. The revival of the name was no coincidence, for this Ducati was a relatively lean and simple sportster, designed along much the same lines as the thundering air-cooled 900SS model of the previous decade. It was intended as a relatively simple and inexpensive bike for riders who liked their Bolognese dish red and raw.

The new Super Sport's 904cc, two-valves-per-cylinder motor was cooled by a combination of air and oil, rather than by water like the 851 flagship. The cooling system was one that Ducati had used on its Paris-Dakar racing bikes, and had the advantage of reducing noise without adding much to either weight or expense. Valve operation was by Ducati's traditional desmodromic (positive closure) system. But soft tuning and a low compression ratio combined to keep maximum power to a relatively modest 83bhp at 8400rpm.

Tucked away behind the red-and-white full fairing, the engine was barely visible. The 900's steel ladder frame was red, too. It used the engine as a stressed member and held its rear shock unit diagonally, attaching it directly to the swingarm instead of via a rising-rate system. Low clip-on handlebars gave a fairly sporty riding position in combination with the tall seat.

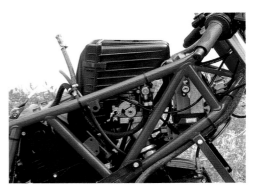

Evolution of the Super Sport

The 1989 model 900SS was a fitting bike with which to revive the famous old name, and Ducati moved quickly to improve it. Two years later the SS was comprehensively revamped, gaining superior Showa front forks and Mikuni carburettors, as well as new styling and all-red paintwork. By now the air/oil-cooled V-twin was very popular. Subsequent redesigns, notably in 1998, kept it that way into the new millennium – still delivering the traditional Super Sport blend of raw V-twin performance.

Great fun to ride

Although the 900SS was not the most powerful machine Ducati had ever produced, it was certainly one of the most fun to ride. The motor made plenty of mechanical noise, and the throaty exhaust bark left the rider in no doubt about the bike's character. Low rev response was rather rough, mainly due to the Weber twin-choke carburettor. But the 900 came alive in the mid-range, before smoothing out and pulling harder still at 5000rpm.

By 6000rpm the Super Sport was accelerating hard past 100mph (161km/h). Shortly after that point it began to vibrate slightly through handlebars and footpegs. But there was still more to come before the top speed of about 135mph (217km/h). The 900 lacked a little straight-line performance compared to many rival superbikes, but had the advantage of feeling faster than it really was.

Handling was basically good, thanks mainly to the Ducati's light weight and rigid frame. Its non-adjustable front forks were rather basic, but the Marzocchi shock gave good control. The front brake consisted of big twin discs gripped by four-piston Brembo calipers and was normally very powerful, although the system was prone to a soft feel at the lever.

In some respects the 900 felt crude alongside the sleek sophistication of Ducati's 851 flagship and most Japanese superbikes. It was an impressive machine, even so, and equally importantly it was very much a Ducati. Other bikes might have been faster and more sophisticated. But when it came to the feeling of excitement generated by cracking open the throttle, banking into a curve or even just blipping the throttle at a standstill, there were few bikes that could live with the 900SS.

Above left: Despite the Super Sport's full fairing, its air/oil-cooled V-twin engine was partially visible, adding to the bike's character along with the rumbling sound from its twin silencers.

Left: The Ducati's slim lines and racy riding position gave good aerodynamics, helping the bike to make the most of its relatively modest 83bhp power output.

Specification	Ducati 900SS (1989)
Engine	Air/oil-cooled sohc four-valve 90-degree V-twin
Capacity	904cc (92 x 68mm)
Maximum power	83bhp @ 8400rpm
Transmission	Six-speed, chain final drive
Frame	Tubular steel ladder
Suspension	Telescopic front; single shock rear
Brakes	Twin discs front; disc rear
Weight	396lb (180kg)
Top speed	135mph (217km/h)

Buell RS1200

**Top speed
120mph**
193km/h

*Below: Buell's RS1200, also
known as the Westwind,
featured streamlined
bodywork but left its
Harley-Davidson V-twin
engine visible beneath the
flowing fibreglass fairing/
tank/seat unit. Particularly
distinctive features included
the hinged pillion-seat
backrest and the rear shock,
which was located
horizontally beneath the
engine and worked in
tension rather than the
normal compression.*

In recent years, motorcyclists worldwide
have become familiar with Buell's
growing range of sport bikes, powered by
V-twin engines from the marque's parent company
Harley-Davidson. Buell's status was very different
back in 1989, when founder Erik Buell and his
small team from Mukwonago in Wisconsin – close
to Harley's Milwaukee base – began production of
the RS1200.

Just like modern Buells, the RS1200 was a
sporty, American-built machine, powered by a
Harley-Davidson engine. It combined innovative
chassis engineering with distinctive styling that left
the big V-twin in full view. And it fully lived up to
Buell's slogan: 'America's Faaast Motorcycle'.

The RS1200 was not Buell's first Harley-
powered model. Erik, a former National level road-
racer and Harley engineer, had begun in 1987 by
creating the RR1000 Battletwin, which held a
Harley XR1000 engine in a chassis of his own
construction. The RR1000, and also the 1200cc

Sportster-engined RR1200 that followed when
stocks of the XR unit ran out, featured wind-
cheating bodywork, incorporating a huge front
mudguard plus integrated fairing and single seat.

Its aerodynamics boosted the Battletwin's
performance but detracted from the impact of the
Harley powerplant, even when the bodywork was
painted in Milwaukee's traditional orange, black
and white. So Erik Buell went back to the drawing
board for his next model, the RS1200, which
retained the RR's mechanical format but put the
engine on show.

Rubber-mounted engine

In standard form the RS1200 left the Sportster
motor untouched, although it was boosted slightly
by a SuperTrapp exhaust system that increased
output to about 60bhp. But it was for its chassis
that the RS1200 was special. Erik Buell's frame
was a tubular steel ladder that held the motor via
his Uniplanar system, which used rods and joints to

Specification	Buell RS1200 (1989)
Engine	Air-cooled ohv pushrod four-valve 45-degree V-twin
Capacity	1200cc (88.8 x 98.8mm)
Maximum power	60bhp @ 5000rpm
Transmission	Four-speed, chain final drive
Frame	Tubular steel ladder
Suspension	Telescopic front; single shock rear
Brakes	Twin discs front; disc rear
Weight	450lb (204kg)
Top speed	120mph (193km/h)

Far left: The softly tuned 1200cc pushrod V-twin from Harley's Sportster was left internally standard, but a new SuperTrapp exhaust system increased peak output slightly to 60bhp.

Left: Buell's innovative chassis worked well, giving the RS1200 a smooth ride plus handling that enabled it to compete with more powerful bikes in corners.

restrict engine vibration to the vertical plane. This allowed the engine to be rubber-mounted, while also adding rigidity as a stressed member of the chassis. The Works Performance rear shock sat horizontally beneath the engine, working in tension rather than compression.

Front forks were Marzocchi units modified with Buell's own anti-dive system. Even the 17-inch wheels and four-piston front brake calipers were his own work, as was the fibreglass bodywork. The neat fairing/tank/tailpiece unit featured a seat hump which hinged to become a backrest for the pillion.

The RS1200 was a light and torquey bike which, although not hugely powerful, was very quick on the right road. Acceleration from low engine speeds was addictively strong, and the Uniplanar system was effective in isolating the Harley motor's normal vibration. Even when revved hard, the Buell remained very smooth to its top speed of 120mph (193km/h).

More to the point, the RS1200's compact, rigid chassis provided very good handling. The RS1200's racy steering geometry and firm forks gave quick steering plus excellent stability, marred slightly by the rather vague rear suspension set-up. Although the hand-built Buell was expensive, costing more than twice as much as a Sportster, its style, innovative engineering and V-twin punch made an appealing combination.

Faaaster Still: the S2 Thunderbolt

Erik Buell's big break came in 1993, when his former employer Harley-Davidson, looking to get into the sport bike market, bought a 49 per cent stake in his firm. The following year, the renamed Buell Motorcycle Company launched the S2 Thunderbolt, based on the RS1200 but with fresh styling, numerous detail improvements and a 20 per cent power increase due to improved breathing. With top speed up to 130mph (209km/h), and a lower price due to increased production, the Thunderbolt was the fastest and most competitive Buell yet.

BMW K1

**Top speed
145mph**
233km/h

*Right: For such a long,
heavy bike the K1 went
round corners well, and it
remained stable in a
straight line to its top speed
of over 140mph (225km/h).*

*Below: The K1's radical
look, thanks mainly to its
streamlined, all-enveloping
bodywork, would have been
a big surprise coming from
any manufacturer, let alone
traditionally conservative
BMW.*

 Few such striking bikes have ever come
from such an unlikely source as the big,
bold and colourful K1 with which BMW
stunned the motorcycling world in 1989. In recent
years the German firm has introduced many
innovative and eye-catching machines. But until the
K1 appeared, the BMW's name was synonymous
with efficient but unexciting tourers.

The K1 had been given its big, aerodynamic
coat for two main reasons: firstly as a radical two-
wheeled statement, and secondly because BMW
had decided to restrict its power output to 100bhp,
the voluntary German limit, so the bike needed all
the help it could get to boost performance. The big
front mudguard, all-covering fairing, swoopy seat
and built-in panniers helped the K1 to a top speed
of 145mph (233km/h), faster than most bikes
managed from 100bhp.

Those 100 horses were produced by a 16-valve
version of the liquid-cooled 987cc four-cylinder
motor from the K100RS sports-tourer. Unlike
Japanese fours, the German firm's K-series engines

had cylinders lying horizontally and arranged along
the line of the bike. The K1 motor gained 10bhp
through its more sophisticated fuel-injection
system, new exhaust and a few other tuning tricks.

Beneath the bold bodywork, the K1's chassis
was conservative. It was based around a steel
space-frame that used the powerplant as a stressed
member. Suspension was a combination of

Marzocchi front forks and BMW's well-proven arrangement of a single rear shock acting on the swingarm/shaft-drive housing. Brakes were from Brembo; cast wheels carried wide, low-profile radial rubber.

High speed cruising

Despite being BMW's most powerful ever roadster, the K1 was in a modest state of tune. Its engine was docile at low speeds, pulling cleanly from tickover right to the 8500rpm redline with no real step in its power delivery. The bike cruised effortlessly at high speed, with a burst of acceleration in hand when required. But acceleration was good rather than exceptional, due partly to the bike's 570lb (259kg) of weight, and the motor vibrated noticeably above 5000rpm.

Handling showed much the same characteristics: it was not racer-sharp but fairly laid-back, requiring a reasonable amount of effort at the handlebars. One advantage of that was that the K1 remained reassuringly stable all the way to its top speed, swallowing high-speed curves without a twitch. The forks were excellent, and although the rear suspension was a little harsh the K1 tracked well over bumps.

Specification	BMW K1 (1989)
Engine	Liquid-cooled dohc 16-valve inline four
Capacity	987cc (67 x 70mm)
Maximum power	100bhp @ 8000rpm
Transmission	Five-speed, shaft final drive
Frame	Tubular steel spaceframe
Suspension	Telescopic front; monoshock rear
Brakes	Twin discs front; disc rear
Weight	570lb (259kg)
Top speed	145mph (233km/h)

Blown BMW: the Luftmeister K1

The ultimate fast BMW was a turbocharged K1 special from Luftmeister, the California-based tuning company. Fitting an IHI turbocharger beneath the K1's bulky bodywork doubled peak output to approximately 160bhp at the rear wheel, with minimal engine strengthening work required. The BMW's shaft final drive made altering its gearing difficult, but with a suitably tall ratio the Luftmeister K1 was good for over 185mph (298km/h).

It was when there were serious distances to be covered that the K1 came into its own. Its big fairing not only boosted performance but diverted wind from everywhere but the rider's helmet, allowing high cruising speeds. Fuel economy and range were excellent, too, and the broad seat added to the comfort. Annoyingly for such a good long-distance machine, the bike's wind-smoothing rear pockets, barely big enough to carry a toothbrush and credit card, made panniers impossible to fit.

The K1 was a success, for all that. It was a fine sports-tourer. And more importantly, it was a unique and striking machine that began BMW's move from one of the most conservative of bike manufacturers to one of the most bold and imaginative.

Left: The front wheel's huge, wheel-hugging mudguard was an important part of the K1's style, as well as combining with the fairing to give the smooth air flow that increased top speed. Although the BMW was too heavy to be a sports bike, its Marzocchi front forks helped give good handling. Brembo, another Italian firm, supplied the front brake system.

Kawasaki ZXR750

**Top speed
150mph**
241km/h

Right: The ZXR's most eye-catching feature were the twin air scoops that curved dramatically from fairing to airbox.

Below: Kawasaki's new race-replica looked good in red, but it was the lime green option that resembled the factory racer.

 Kawasaki's ZXR750 looked every bit a street-legal racebike, with its sleek bodywork, race-team inspired paint scheme and a big pair of air ducts leading back from its nose towards the uprated four-cylinder engine. The reality was rather more down-to-earth, but an exciting bike for all that. Despite being a much more straightforward machine than purpose-built exotica such as Honda's RC30, the ZXR matched its good looks with speed, handling and a competitive price that made it an instant hit.

In developing the ZXR, Kawasaki resisted the temptation to produce a high-priced special intended purely as a basis for a World Superbike challenger. Instead, the firm's engineers combined a reworked engine from the GPX750 roadster with a new chassis based on that of the aluminium-framed

ZXR-7 factory racebike. Although the power and weight figures were not spectacular, the result was a rapid and reasonably practical machine.

The 748cc engine was surprisingly unchanged from the GPX unit, considering that it was powering an all-new model with such obvious racing heritage and intent. The GPX format of a liquid-cooled 16-valve four with twin camshafts driven by a central chain remained. Main changes were bigger valves, higher compression ratio and a lightened crankshaft. The peak output of 105bhp at 10,500rpm was only slightly up on that of the GPX.

Most of Kawasaki's development effort went into the ZXR's new chassis, especially the aluminium twin-beam frame that appeared to be stiff enough to justify weighing 8lb (3.6kg) more than the GPX's steel equivalent. Other new features included a bolt-on rear subframe, braced swingarm, multi-adjustable suspension, plus wheels that were wide enough to take racing tyres.

Racy performance

The ZXR's stretched-out riding position and harsh, solid feel at low speed gave a racy feel, and the Kawasaki had plenty of performance to back it up. Its engine's response below 2000rpm was poor. But above that figure the Kawasaki carburetted crisply through its bank of 36mm Keihins, storming towards its 12,000rpm redline and its top speed of 150mph (241km/h).

Handling was solid, stable and confidence-inspiring, without approaching the quick steering of its more exotic race-replica rivals. Although the rear shock was firm, both that and the front forks were well damped, and the big front brake discs gave plenty of bite. Essentially the ZXR was a road bike that worked best on fast, smooth surfaces, rather than a racebike adapted for the street. It was

Russell's World-beating ZXR

Kawasaki's efforts with the ZXR750 in World Superbike racing were rewarded in 1993, when American ace Scott Russell won the championship after a close fight against Ducati's Carl Fogarty. Russell's 750cc bike often lacked speed against the 926cc V-twin, and the Georgian won only five races to Fogarty's 11. But both the green Kawasaki and its rider proved very reliable throughout the season, and Russell held on to take what would prove to be a rare championship win for an in-line four-cylinder machine.

Specification	Kawasaki ZXR750 (1989)
Engine	Liquid-cooled dohc 16-valve four
Capacity	748cc (68 x 51.5mm)
Maximum power	105bhp @ 10,500rpm
Transmission	Six-speed, chain final drive
Frame	Aluminium twin beam
Suspension	Telescopic front; monoshock rear
Brakes	Twin discs front; disc rear
Weight	452lb (205kg)
Top speed	150mph (241km/h)

not the most comfortable of bikes but it had character in abundance, and most owners were very content with that.

Kawasaki acted quickly to fine-tune the ZXR, adding power and reducing weight slightly just a year after its launch. For 1991 it was more comprehensively redesigned with a shorter-stroke engine, lighter frame, steeper steering geometry and upside-down forks. And the same year also saw the release of the limited-edition ZXR750R, with 118bhp engine, less weight and improved suspension. The R model was the street-legal racebike that the ZXR750 had always threatened to be.

Left: Early ZXRs had firm suspension that worked well on smooth surfaces but gave a harsh ride on bumpy roads. The twin-spar frame was rigid and the Kawasaki was superbly stable at speed, but lacked the agility of some super-sports bikes. Few owners were too worried about that, and the ZXR's performance and image made it a big hit.

Bimota YB6 EXUP

**Top speed
170mph**
274km/h

*Below: The YB6 EXUP's
format of twin-headlamp
fairing and aluminium
beam frame was identical to
that of the Yamaha
FZR1000 that provided its
1002cc engine. But the
Bimota, developed from the
750cc YB4 EI that formed
the basis of Bimota's world
Formula One championship
winning racebike, was a
singleminded race-replica.*

Bimota's YB series machines were among the finest sports bikes of the late 1980s, combining powerful four-cylinder Yamaha motors with the twin-spar aluminium frame layout that would be adopted by major manufacturers in subsequent years. To that basic format the small Rimini firm added sharp styling, high-quality cycle parts and top-level racetrack development, plus the exclusivity that came with a bike that was hand-built in very small numbers.

The story of Bimota's Yamaha-engined four began in 1987, when factory rider Virginio Ferrari won the Formula One world championship, then the leading four-stroke race series. Ferrari's YB4 was powered by Yamaha's liquid-cooled 20-valve FZ750 engine. Bimota's subsequent YB4 EI roadster was a replica of Ferrari's machine, and was quickly followed by a similar YB6 model

using the larger engine from the FZR1000. Unlike the YB4, whose EI initials signified that it was fuel-injected, the YB6 used carburettors.

The YB6 was a big success and was followed a year later by the YB6 EXUP model, also known as the YB8, following Yamaha's release of the FZR1000 EXUP. This combined an uprated engine plus the new EXUP exhaust valve that increased mid-range power delivery. As usual, Bimota retained the Yamaha engine in standard form, but added a less restrictive silencer that added a claimed 4bhp to the power output, giving a maximum of 147bhp at 10,000rpm.

Like the standard YB6, the EXUP version used a YB4 style frame with rectangular-section aluminium spars. Front forks and the rear shock, complete with remove reservoir, were from Italian specialist Marzocchi. Four-piston Brembo front

Specification	Bimota YB6 EXUP (1989)
Engine	Liquid-cooled dohc 20-valve four
Capacity	1002cc (75.5 x 56mm)
Maximum power	147bhp @ 10,000rpm
Transmission	Six-speed, chain final drive
Frame	Aluminium twin spar
Suspension	Telescopic front; monoshock rear
Brakes	Twin discs front; disc rear
Weight	407lb (185kg) wet
Top speed	170mph (274km/h)

Tuatara – World's Fastest Lizard

Bimota produced an even more exotic variation on the YB6 theme in 1989, with the Tuatara model of which only 60 units were built. This bike, named after a lizard that was one of the world's slowest animals, was powered by the previous 989cc Yamaha FZR1000 engine, fitted with a Weber-Marelli fuel-injection system in place of carburettors. The result was a claimed peak output of 152bhp at 9500rpm. Other changes included upside-down Marzocchi forks, ultra-light magnesium wheels, and a futuristic digital instrument console. Bimota claimed a top speed of 180mph (290km/h), which proved highly optimistic. But very few things, on two wheels or four legs, were faster.

brake calipers gripped huge fully floating discs. The riding position was racy, with low clip-on handlebars, high footrests and a thinly padded single seat.

Compact and aerodynamic

Along with its slightly increased power, the YB6 EXUP was more compact and aerodynamic than the standard FZR1000, as well as 50lb (23kg) lighter. That meant that it was probably the fastest and hardest-accelerating production motorcycle in the world. Its smooth, high-revving power sent the Bimota storming to a top speed of 170mph (274km/h). Equally impressive was the big 20-valve Yamaha motor's smooth, torquey feel throughout the rev range.

Given the Bimota's race-developed background and its close links to the factory YB4, it was no surprise that the YB6 EXUP was very stable even when approaching its maximum velocity. And it also handled superbly at all speeds. Steering was light and neutral, grip from the fat Michelin radial tyres immense, ground clearance absolute. The brakes were excellent, too, with a combination of bite and feel to rival the very best.

The extra torque and refinement of Yamaha's new motor had added the finishing touch to make a magnificent sports bike. Inevitably the YB6 models were also hugely expensive. Despite that they were a success for Bimota, which built a total of more than 650 over the next few years – a large number by the standards of the tiny Rimini firm.

Top left: Light weight, a rigid frame and top-class parts gave the YB6 superb handling and braking power.

Left: Bimota team-mates Davide Tardozzi and 1987 world Formula One champion Virginio Ferrari line up with their YB4 EI factory racebikes.

Ducati 851

**Top speed
145mph**
233km/h

The 851, with its powerful liquid-cooled eight-valve V-twin engine, heralded the start of the modern era for Ducati. Previous superbikes from Bologna had been powered by air-cooled V-twin engines. Many had used the marque's unique desmodromic system, which closes the valves with cams instead of the conventional springs. But the 851, with its four-valve heads and fuel-injection, was a considerably more modern and powerful unit.

Chief engineer Massimo Bordi had been determined to create an eight-valve desmo twin, something his famous predecessor Fabio Taglioni had always resisted. Bordi's 851cc engine retained Ducati's traditional 90-degree V-twin layout. Liquid cooling, Weber-Marelli injection and the improved breathing of the new cylinder heads gave plenty of mid-range torque and a maximum output of 100bhp, making this the most powerful Ducati roadster yet.

Smooth and refined engine

The eight-valve motor was an immediate success. Smooth and refined, it was particularly notable for its exhilarating top-end rush. But the chassis was a different story. Problems of supply meant the original 1988-model 851, which was finished in patriotic red, white and green, was fitted with 16-inch wheels, instead of the 17-inchers it should have worn. The result was unpredictable handling despite the steel ladder frame's rigidity.

Above: The original 'tricolore' 851, introduced in 1988, was a landmark machine for Ducati due to its liquid-cooled eight-valve desmo V-twin engine. But the first 851 suffered from mis-matched chassis parts that adversely affected its handling.

Right: Just a year after its launch the 851 was tuned, painted red and fitted with a modified frame and 17-inch wheels, resulting in a bike with looks, speed and superbly agile handling. The revitalized 851 made a brilliant roadster and formed the basis of Ducati's World Superbike racer.

The fastest Ducati roadsters of all during the late 1980s and early '90s were the limited-edition Sport Production or SP models created mainly for Italian racing. By 1992 the SP series had reached the SP4, and in that year came the most exotic version of all: the 888SPS, or Sport Production Special, of which only 100 were built. The SPS featured an enlarged 888cc engine with big valves, racing camshafts, higher compression, revised fuel-injection and loud exhaust system. Peak output was 120bhp at the rear wheel, 25bhp up on standard. Kevlar and carbon-fibre fuel tank and bodywork, Öhlins suspension and other chassis modifications resulted in a roadgoing racebike with superb handling, a top speed of over 160mph (257km/h), and a fearsome price tag to match.

A year later the 851 was revamped with all-red paint and so many changes that it was almost a completely new bike. Although the frame had a minor modification at the steering head, the key chassis features were the new 17-inch wheels. The Marzocchi suspension was of the highest quality, especially the longer rear shock, which had a compression-damping adjuster knob in the seat hump allowing easy fine-tuning.

The engine was also improved. Higher compression ratio, reshaped camshafts, modified fuel-injection and new exhaust mufflers combined to increase peak output to 104bhp, and the peaks of both power and torque were moved down the rev range. That meant that the 851 now had generous reserves of torque from 3000rpm to 10,000rpm. The Ducati simply stretched its legs as the throttle was opened, and charged forward towards its top speed of almost 150mph (241km/h).

The original 851 had been a disappointment but its successor was the opposite. Its engine was stronger still, its detailing slicker, and most of all its handling had been transformed from disappointing to outstanding. As well as being a great roadster, the revised 851 formed the basis of a hugely successful racebike that took riders Raymond Roche and Doug Polen to three consecutive World Superbike championships.

Not only that, but the 851's liquid-cooled eight-valve V-twin engine was repeatedly enlarged and refined over the following decade and more, powering the string of stunning road bikes and World Superbike racing machines that made Ducati one of motorcycling's biggest success stories. Few false starts can ever have been put right so promptly and to such brilliant effect.

Above left: Slots to either side of the rectangular headlamp ducted air to the fuel-injected 851's airbox.

Left: The liquid-cooled, eight-valve, 851cc V-twin engine formed a stressed member of a typical Ducati-style tubular steel ladder frame.

Specification	Ducati 851 (1989)
Engine	Liquid-cooled dohc eight-valve 90-degree V-twin
Capacity	851cc (92 x 64mm)
Maximum power	104bhp @ 9000rpm
Transmission	Six-speed, chain final drive
Frame	Tubular steel ladder
Suspension	Telescopic front; single shock rear
Brakes	Twin discs front; disc rear
Weight	396lb (180kg)
Top speed	145mph (233km/h)

The 1990s
Pushing the
Envelope

Superbikes got faster and better in several ways during the 1990s. Top speeds of over 150mph (241km/h) became commonplace. The handling of standard, mass-produced machines was equal to that of factory racebikes of a few years earlier. Advanced technology was there for those who wanted and could afford it, with oval pistons from Honda and forkless front suspension from Yamaha and Bimota.

But most riders preferred more conventional machines. Many of the best superbikes were improved versions of established formats: sleek Ducati V-twins led by the 916, or fast, light Japanese fours, such as Honda's FireBlade and Yamaha's YZF-R1. For pure speed, there was nothing to touch Suzuki's streamlined Hayabusa.

Kawasaki ZZ-R1100

**Top speed
175mph**
282km/h

*Right: Sheer power and
speed were the original
ZZ-R's main claims to fame,
but for a big machine the
Kawasaki went round
corners in style.*

*Below: In 1993 the ZZ-R
was revised with a taller
screen, larger fuel tank and
new frame. Its high-speed
ability remained – following
the press launch in Arizona,
three journalists were jailed
for speeding.*

When Kawasaki's engineers set out to
create the world's fastest bike in the late
1980s, they had the advantage of many
years' experience in designing powerful four-
cylinder engines – plus one very significant
technical innovation. The result was a new
superbike, the ZZ-R1100, whose liquid-cooled,
four-cylinder engine, boosted by a novel 'ram-air'
system, produced 145bhp and sent the bike hurtling
to 175mph (282km/h).

That level of performance put the Kawasaki far
ahead of all opposition when it was launched in
1990, and it remained the world's fastest bike for
the next five years. There was much more to the
ZZ-R (known as the ZX-11 in the States) than its
engine, for it was a refined and efficient sports-
tourer. But there was no escaping the fact that the
Kawasaki's trump card was its phenomenal
straight-line speed.

Forced induction, to give the ram-air system its
conventional name, was derived from Formula One
racecar technology. It was a sealed system that
ducted air from a slot in the fairing's nose, directly

to the unusually large airbox. The faster the
Kawasaki went, the more cool air was forced
through its carburettors and into the engine.

Intake system apart, the ZZ-R had much in
common with the ZX-10, its predecessor as
Kawasaki's flagship. Bulbous bodywork held
faired-in indicators; the chassis was based on a
rigid twin-spar aluminium frame. The new engine
shared the ZX-10's liquid-cooled, 16-valve layout
but had a 2mm larger bore, increasing capacity to
1052cc. Other changes included larger valves, new

camshafts, lightened pistons, a new curved radiator and a more efficient twin-silencer exhaust system.

When the throttle was wound open above 5000rpm, smooth power sent the bike rocketing forward. It kicked into hyperdrive at around 7000rpm and kept the rider's arms and reflexes stretched as it snarled to the 11,000rpm redline through the efficient six-speed gearbox. In contrast the response below 4000rpm was weak, though an improvement over that of the ZX-10.

High speed composure and stability were remarkable. Even with the scenery and road flashing past at over 150mph (241km/h), the protection of its fairing and the quality of its chassis give the impression of travelling much less rapidly. American magazine *Cycle* managed a genuine 175mph (282km/h) from their full-power ZZ-R1100. Bikes in many European countries left the dealerships slightly slower due to politically enforced power limits. In most cases these were implemented by carburettor restrictors that were easy to remove.

Although the ZZ-R's frame resembled that of the ZX-10 it was slightly thicker and stiffer, as well as 10mm (0.4in) shorter in the wheelbase. Steering geometry was steeper and the cycle parts were also new. Fork legs were enlarged to 43mm in diameter and, like the single rear shock, were adjustable for rebound damping as well as spring preload.

Well-balanced feel

The ZZ-R was a long, roomy bike that was far too heavy to be mistaken for a sports bike, but it handled well. Much of the mass seemed to drop away on the move, and the stiff chassis and firm suspension gave the Kawasaki a well-balanced feel. It was stable even at high speed, and its triple disc brake system was powerful.

This was just as well, because if any bike needed good brakes it was the ZZ-R. The bike's comfort and practicality contributed to its reputation as a fine all-rounder. Numerous neat details included a comfortable seat, clear mirrors, bungee hooks and a much-needed grab-rail. But all those things were insignificant when compared with the ZZ-R1100's greatest asset: the magnificent, ram-air assisted motor that generated its all-conquering speed.

Above: The distinctive ZZ-R shape would remain essentially unchanged through several revisions and more than a decade of development. Key to the 16-valve motor's performance was its ram-air induction system, fed via a slot in the fairing nose. But despite its deserved reputation for speed, the ZZ-R was always more of an all-rounder than a pure performance machine.

Specification	Kawasaki ZZ-R1100 (ZX-11) (1990)
Engine	Liquid-cooled dohc 16-valve four
Capacity	1052cc (76 x 58mm)
Maximum power	145bhp @ 9500rpm
Transmission	Six-speed, chain final drive
Frame	Aluminium twin spar
Suspension	Telescopic front; single shock rear
Brakes	Twin discs front; disc rear
Weight	502lb (228kg)
Top speed	175mph (282km/h)

Yamaha FZR1000

**Top speed
165mph**
266km/h

*Below: The FZR1000 was
updated over the years while
keeping its angled-forward
20-valve engine and twin-
spar aluminium frame. This
1994 FZR1000 has twin
'fox-eye' headlamps and
six-piston front brake
calipers from the YZF750
race-replica, plus front
forks from Yamaha-owned
Swedish specialist Öhlins.*

At the start of the 1990s, Yamaha's
FZR1000R EXUP was in most respects
the world's finest production super-sports
bike. It had a 1002cc, 20-valve, liquid-cooled
engine that produced over 140bhp with heaps of
mid-range, housed in a light, taut and superbly
neutral-steering chassis. The Yamaha was lightning
fast, handled superbly, looked good and was
impeccably reliable.

Perhaps the only thing that the 1991-model
FZR1000 lacked was the mean and nasty image
that made its main rival, Suzuki's GSX-R1100, so
popular despite inferior power delivery and
handling. For despite its top speed of more than
160mph (257km/h) and the ability to cover a
quarter mile from a standing start in less than 11
seconds, the FZR was so flexible, easy to ride and

generally well behaved that some riders found it
lacking in character.

That was hard on the FZR1000, which had been
updated to good effect since the model's debut in
1987. The first FZR was developed from the
FZ750, which two years earlier had introduced
Yamaha's 20-valve engine layout with its angled-
forward cylinder block. The original FZR1000
featured a 989cc engine that produced 125bhp, and
a rigid twin-spar aluminium 'Deltabox' frame,
based on that of Yamaha's Genesis factory racer.

Storming acceleration

The FZR1000 was instantly competitive with the
fastest and best sports bikes, and got better still in
1989, with a larger 1002cc engine that made
140bhp, and also benefited from an electronically

Faster Still: the Thunderace

When Yamaha uprated the FZR yet again in 1996, the new model incorporated so many changes that it was renamed the YZF1000R Thunderace. Its 1002cc engine produced 145bhp and was stronger than ever in the mid-range. A lighter, more rigid frame from the YZF750, plus new suspension and brakes, gave even better handling and stopping. And bodywork was more streamlined, taking top speed to 170mph (274km/h). The Ace was a wonderfully fast and capable bike, but it was less racy than Honda's FireBlade – and Yamaha knew it. Even as the Thunderace was being launched, development of the more radical YZF-R1 had begun.

operated exhaust valve whose acronym led to the FZR often being known as the 'EXUP'. It was partly this valve that gave the Yamaha such storming mid-range acceleration.

That 1989-model EXUP, with its round twin headlamps, was a fine machine that was described by one tester as the closest thing yet to a perfect sportster. Yet Yamaha improved on it in 1991 with the FZR1000RU, which featured a new single-lens headlamp plus upside-down forks for the first time. Not everyone was convinced of the need to alter either the old FZR's look or its suspension, but one ride on the new bike was normally enough to change their mind.

There was no change to the breathtaking power delivery of the 140bhp motor, whose top-end rush of power was matched by smooth mid-range delivery of the kind for which the FZR had become known. But the new model, which was respectably light at 461lb (209kg), steered with even more precision and could be cornered even faster due to the extra control of its high quality chassis.

The FZR was the fastest, most agile super-sports machine of its day, though its reign was short-lived, because Honda's ultra light and compact FireBlade followed in 1992. Not that development of the FZR1000 stood still. In 1994 it was uprated again, with twin 'fox-eye' lights in a new fairing, plus six-piston front brake calipers. The result was even more of the style, speed and all-round high performance for which the FZR1000 was rightly famous.

Specification	Yamaha FZR1000RU (1991)
Engine	Liquid-cooled dohc 20-valve four
Capacity	1002cc (75.5 x 56mm)
Maximum power	140bhp @ 10,000rpm
Transmission	Five-speed, chain final drive
Frame	Aluminium twin spar
Suspension	Telescopic front; single shock rear
Brakes	Twin discs front; disc rear
Weight	461lb (209kg)
Top speed	165mph (266km/h)

Above left: The original FZR1000, introduced in 1987, had two round headlights in its fairing, and a 989cc four-cylinder motor producing 125bhp.

Left: By 1991 the Yamaha featured a single headlight, and a 1002cc engine boosted by an EXUP exhaust valve.

Triumph Trophy 1200

**Top speed
153mph**
246km/h

*Right: Previous Triumphs
might not have encouraged
a knee-down cornering
style, but the Trophy was
from a new generation.*

*Below: The Trophy's styling
was neat and efficient
rather then spectacular, and
the same could be said of
its engineering.*

When Britain's reborn Triumph began
production in 1991, few people expected
the first model to be a powerful superbike
with a liquid-cooled engine and monoshock
suspension – let alone a fully-faired, 1180cc, 16-
valve four that produced 125bhp and purred
smoothly to a top speed of over 150mph
(241km/h). From a manufacturer whose name had
most recently been associated with old-fashioned
air-cooled twins, the Trophy 1200 was a sensation.

Perhaps the greatest compliment that was paid
to the new British sports-tourer was that it could
have been built by one of the big four Japanese
firms. In fact the Trophy, like the naked Trident and
sportier Daytona models that followed shortly
afterwards, had been created by a team led by John
Bloor, a multi-millionaire builder. Bloor had bought
bankrupt Triumph in 1983 and spent the

intervening period creating a state-of-the-art factory at Hinckley, near the former Triumph base at Meriden in the English Midlands.

Range of models

The Trophy 1200 sports-tourer was the largest of an initial range of six bikes that were built using a unique modular concept. All six used an identical steel spine frame. Triumph's three- and four-cylinder engines with choice of short- or long-stroke crankshafts gave four engine capacities from 750cc triple to 1200cc four. In other respects the Trophy's dohc, liquid-cooled 16-valve engine layout was conventional.

That large-diameter steel spine frame used the engine as a stressed member. The frame held 43mm forks and a vertical rear monoshock, both from Japanese specialists Kayaba. Brakes were also made in Japan, by Nissin. Some British bike enthusiasts were critical of this, but Britain's motorcycle parts industry was a shadow of its former self, and Bloor had no time for sentiment.

Nor did most superbike-buying enthusiasts, but Triumph did not need to rely on nostalgia to make the Trophy a success. Its big motor was superbly strong, with a broad power band that delivered crisp acceleration everywhere between 2000rpm and the 9500rpm redline. The Trophy cruised effortlessly at 100mph (161km/h) with plenty of speed in hand. It was smooth, thanks to twin balancer shafts, and its six-speed gearbox was slick. Crucially this Triumph, unlike numerous predecessors, was also reliable and oil-tight.

Triumph's steel spine frame was slightly dated when compared to twin-spar aluminium layouts, and the Trophy was quite a tall bike with a high centre of gravity. At 529lb (240kg) it was fairly heavy, too. But it handled well, combining flawless

Specification	Triumph Trophy 1200 (1991)
Engine	Liquid-cooled dohc 16-valve four
Capacity	1180cc (76 x 65mm)
Maximum power	125bhp @ 9000rpm
Transmission	Six-speed, chain final drive
Frame	Steel spine
Suspension	Telescopic front; single shock rear
Brakes	Twin disc front; disc rear
Weight	529lb (240kg)
Top speed	153mph (246km/h)

Modular Sport: the Daytona 1200

Triumph's reputation for performance leapt in 1993 when the British firm released the Daytona 1200, powered by a tuned, 145bhp version of the Trophy's four-cylinder engine. Although named after the Daytona speedway in Florida, scene of famous Triumph wins in the 1960s, the 1200 was not a race-replica but a muscular roadburner with a top speed of 160mph (257km/h). Its modular steel frame held high-quality cycle parts that helped give good handling despite over 500lb (227kg) of weight. The Daytona wasn't the world's sharpest sports bike, but it generated plenty of speed and excitement.

straight-line stability with neutral steering and good quality suspension that gave plenty of control along with a high level of comfort.

Other impressive features included an efficient full fairing, large fuel tank and comfortable dual-seat with pillion grab-rail. Some other details such as the small mirrors and mediocre headlamp were less impressive, but most people who rode the Trophy were surprised to find it competitive with the best Japanese sports-tourers. That would have been impressive for any new bike, let alone a new manufacturer's debut model. The Trophy 1200 was a Triumph not only in name.

Left: Triumph's modular format used an identical tubular steel spine frame for six models. Most engine components were also shared, but using either three or four cylinders, plus alternative crankshafts, gave a line-up of 1000 or 1200cc fours, and 750 or 900cc triples. The Trophy 900 triple produced 99bhp.

Honda CBR900RR

**Top speed
160mph**
257km/h

*Right: The fairing's holes
were designed to 'enhance
airflow to improve
cornering performance',
according to Honda. The
feature was quietly dropped
on later models.*

*Below: Apart from using a
16-inch front wheel instead
of the normal 17-incher, the
original Blade's layout was
ordinary. Its combination of
power and light weight was
anything but.*

In retrospect, it all seemed so simple. The key to Honda's stunning CBR900RR was that it packed a powerful, open-class four-cylinder engine in a chassis small and light enough to belong to a 600cc middleweight. The result was dynamite. When the bike they named the FireBlade was launched in 1992, it was the hardest-charging, sharpest-handling, shortest-stopping big-bore sports machine ever seen.

Of course, Honda's task had in reality been far from easy. To create such a powerful yet compact and reliable engine was very difficult; to package it in an ultra-light chassis that was both agile and stable even harder. Yet the team led by Tadao Baba succeeded, and in the process created the legend of the FireBlade and began a new era of two-wheeled high performance.

The CBR relied on the conventional technology of a twin-cam, liquid-cooled, 16-valve straight four. The 893cc motor was physically barely larger than Honda's CBR600F engine. It was very light, too,

despite the absence of expensive titanium. There was nothing radical about the design, it was just that nobody before had put together such a refined and compact package that approached the Blade's peak output of 124bhp at 10,500rpm.

The same was true of the chassis, which added a few twists to the familiar twin-spar alloy design to produce a bike whose 407lb (185kg) weight

Erion's Racing RR

The CBR900RR's capacity made it ineligible for World Superbike and many other four-stroke race series, but the Honda was very successful in America. Erion Racing's highly tuned, 170bhp, 180mph (290km/h) RRs won the 1993 AMA endurance title and the following season's Unlimited Team Challenge. In late 1994, team boss Kevin Erion launched a roadgoing replica, incorporating ram air, 918cc capacity, polished engine internals, new cams, Keihin flat-slide carbs, race pipe and 144 rear-wheel horsepower. Numerous chassis modifications reduced weight to 378lb (172kg) and improved handling too. At $35,000, the Erion 900RR Replica was expensive, but very few bikes provided comparable roadgoing performance.

figure belonged in the middleweight class. The thick conventional forks held a 16-inch front wheel; four-piston front brake calipers bit on drilled discs. Steering geometry was remarkable at the time; closer to grand prix racebike figures than to those of the Honda's roadster rivals.

More to the point, the RR performed like a purpose-built racebike too. Engine performance combined instant throttle response, minimal vibration and adequate low-rev power, before the serious urge arrived at 6000rpm. At 9000rpm the RR shifted into hyperdrive, screaming to the 11,000rpm redline with renewed thrust. Top speed was around 160mph (257km/h), slightly down on larger-engined rivals from Suzuki and Yamaha. The smaller engine also lacked a little mid-range by comparison, encouraging frequent use of its six-speed gearbox. But the lightweight Honda was a match for anything on acceleration.

Stunningly light steering

It was in corners that the FireBlade's lack of size and weight made most difference, for no other open-class Japanese sportster provided agility in the same league. Steering was stunningly light and quick, bordering on the nervous yet responding to every command with pinpoint accuracy. The CBR's cornering ability was also partly due to its firm and well-damped suspension.

A combination of efficient fairing, wide seat and generous leg-room made the FireBlade reasonably comfortable. This was no sports-tourer, however, but a brilliant, purpose-built sportster; the

quickest, nimblest superbike ever to come out of Japan. Honda claimed that in developing the FireBlade, they had set out to rewrite the rules of motorcycle design. For once, what sounded like a typical piece of advertising hype rang true.

Below: Compact dimensions, light weight and a taut chassis gave handling that was agile to the point of occasional instability.

Specification	Honda CBR900RR (1992)
Engine	Liquid-cooled dohc 16-valve four
Capacity	893cc (70 x 58mm)
Maximum power	124bhp @ 10,500rpm
Transmission	Six-speed, chain final drive
Frame	Aluminium twin spar
Suspension	Telescopic front; single shock rear
Brakes	Twin discs front; disc rear
Weight	407lb (185kg)
Top speed	160mph (257km/h)

Ducati 900 Superlight

**Top speed
138mph**
222km/h

*Below: Visually the
Superlight was almost
identical to the standard
900SS, but its carbon-fibre
front mudguard, single seat
and raised silencers gave a
sportier look. Red paintwork
echoed that of Ducati's
racers; the Superlight was
also available in yellow for
the US market only.*

In launching the 900 Superlight in 1992,
Ducati revealed a new-found ability to
broaden its range with a new bike that
was closely related to an existing model. The
Superlight was a sportier version of the 900SS, the
air/oil-cooled, two-valves-per-cylinder V-twin that
offered a simpler and less expensive alternative to
the Bologna firm's more powerful and exotic eight-
valve superbikes.

Ducati hardly needed to produce another new
model, because the 900SS itself had been
successfully restyled and updated only the year
before. But the Bologna firm saw the opportunity
to create a significantly more sporty bike with little
extra effort. Hence the arrival of the Superlight,
complete with more aggressive image, reduced
weight and no room for a pillion.

With the exception of a ventilated cover for its
dry clutch the engine was unchanged. That meant a
904cc, 90-degree, sohc desmodromic V-twin,
cooled by oil and air, and putting out a 73bhp at
7000rpm. (Ducati by now measured power in a
more conservative way than in previous years.)
Much of the chassis was also borrowed from the
900SS, including the steel ladder frame, Showa
upside-down forks, and rear shock unit from the
same Japanese firm.

The Superlight got its name from its weight-
reducing chassis modifications. These included 17-
inch Marvic wheels that combined aluminium rims
with magnesium spokes and hubs. The front
mudguard was made from carbon-fibre instead of
plastic. The rest of the bodywork was shared with
the 900SS, apart from the single-seat which, in
conjunction with the removal of pillion footrests,
allowed the twin tailpipes to be raised slightly.

Raw and racy feel

For many riders, one of the most appealing things
about the oil/air-cooled Ducatis was the way in
which they managed to retain so much of the older
bevel-drive V-twins' raw feel despite ever-
tightening regulations. When the Superlight's
throttle was blipped at a standstill, the noise and
feel left no doubt that this bike was a big V-twin.

The view was suitably simple too: foam-
mounted clocks, and multi-adjustable forks poking
through an alloy top yoke. The single-seat's
padding was thinner than that of the standard SS,
but those bars were high enough to make the
Superlight reasonably comfortable. Its dry weight
was just 388lb (176kg), a reduction of 15lb (7kg)
on the SS, which helped make the bike manageable
at slow speed despite its limited steering lock.

That light weight was partly due to the lean,
basic nature of the engine, whose relatively modest
peak output meant that the Superlight had a top
speed of just under 140mph (225km/h), at least
10mph (16km/h) down on rival Japanese 750s. But
the 900's combination of lightness and the way that
power was produced allowed it to stay with all but
the fastest opposition on the road. The motor was
rough below 4000rpm but from then on produced
storming mid-range torque that made the bike very
easy to ride.

Handling was as good as might have been expected of a light, moderately powerful bike with a rigid frame and high-quality suspension. Steering was effortless and neutral, giving the Ducati the feel of a middleweight. Its upside-down forks were well-sprung without being harsh, and gave a finely controlled ride. Despite its relative simplicity, the cantilever rear-end also worked well. And the Superlight's front brake was powerful and progressive thanks to big twin discs and new Brembo Gold Line calipers.

The advantage of the Superlight's reduced weight was not dramatic, and in purely functional terms the bike offered only a slight edge over the 900SS. It was also considerably more expensive. But the Superlight was a worthy addition to Ducati's range, providing even more of the raw, characterful performance and fine handling that had made the 900SS so popular.

Above: The Superlight's reduced weight, partly due to its Marvic wheels, gave a slight handling advantage over the standard 900SS, which itself went round corners very well.

Left: Essential ingredients included a racy look and tubular steel ladder frame, which used the desmo V-twin engine as a stressed member of the chassis.

Below left: The name was inspired by a traditional Italian auto industry 'Superleggera' label. Lack of pillion footpegs allowed the silencers to be raised.

Specification	Ducati 900 Superlight (1992)
Engine	Air/oil-cooled sohc four-valve 90-degree V-twin
Capacity	904cc (92 x 68mm)
Maximum power	73bhp @ 7000rpm
Transmission	Six-speed, chain final drive
Frame	Tubular steel ladder
Suspension	Telescopic front; monoshock rear
Brakes	Twin disc front; single disc rear
Weight	388lb (176kg)
Top speed	138mph (222km/h)

Moto Guzzi Daytona

**Top speed
145mph**
233km/h

*Right: The Daytona's 992cc
engine produced 95bhp and
brought a new level of
refinement to Guzzi's
traditional transverse
V-twin layout.*

*Below: Guzzi's flagship was
a sportster in the finest
Italian tradition, with sleek
scarlet bodywork, a big air-
cooled V-twin engine and a
high quality chassis.*

 With its big pair of air-cooled transverse
V-twin cylinders jutting up and out from
beneath a bright red fuel tank, the
Daytona 1000 was unmistakably a Moto Guzzi. But
this was a Guzzi with a difference: a faster, sharper-
handling, more sophisticated sportster that arrived
in 1992 to re-establish the famous old firm from
Mandello del Lario in northern Italy as a serious
superbike manufacturer.

Guzzi had been in the doldrums for years, its
air-cooled, pushrod-operated V-twins becoming
increasingly uncompetitive. Then Guzzi boss
Alejandro de Tomaso hired Dr John Wittner to
develop a roadgoing version of the Guzzi-powered
racebike with which the American engineer and
former dentist had been having spectacular success
in twin-cylinder racing. After three years' work at
the Mandello del Lario factory, Wittner had the
Daytona 1000 ready for production.

New generation V-twin

Its 992cc 'high-cam' powerplant was Guzzi's most
advanced roadgoing V-twin yet. Each cylinder's
belt-driven camshaft was located on the inside of
the 90-degree Vee, from where it worked the valves
via a pair of rocker-arms. The bottom-end was a
revised version of the old Le Mans unit, with
lightened flywheel and straight-cut gears. A Weber-

Essential Guzzi: the 1100 Sport

In 1994, two years after launching the Daytona, Guzzi added to the range with simpler new model along similar lines. The 1100 Sport combined a Daytona-based chassis with an old-style 1064cc pushrod V-twin engine that used carburettors instead of fuel-injection. The result was a bike that produced 90bhp, 5bhp down on the Daytona, and was a fair bit cheaper and almost as fast.

Two years later Guzzi created the 1100 Sport Injection (pictured) by giving the Sport a Daytona-style fuel-injection system. Peak power was unchanged, but the low-rev response was much improved. At the same time the eight-valve model was uprated with the new Daytona RS. Its 992cc engine featured higher compression ratio, hotter camshaft, forged pistons, Carrillo conrods and a lightened crankshaft. The RS produced 102bhp and was good for 150mph (241km/h).

Marelli fuel-injection system contributed to a peak output of 95bhp at 8000rpm.

Guzzi's traditional transverse V-twin layout was well suited to a spine frame. The Daytona used a rectangular steel tube running through the middle of the Vee, from the steering-head to aluminium sections that held the swingarm and footrests. The rear end comprised a steel cantilever swingarm acting directly on a diagonally-placed shock unit. A parallelogram linkage, developed by Wittner, combated shaft-drive reaction.

The Daytona was notably revvier, more responsive and faster than its predecessors, with the trade-off that it lacked a little of their trademark bottom-end torque. Even so the Daytona pulled cleanly from as low as 2000rpm – below 40mph (64km/h) – in top gear. At around 4000rpm it breathed more deeply, giving strong acceleration towards a top speed of 145mph (233km/h).

Handling combined old-style Guzzi stability with a more modern feel. Thanks to the parallelogram swingarm linkage there was little of the traditional shaft-drive reaction when the throttle was open or closed in mid-turn. At 452lb (205kg) the Daytona was respectably light and manoeuvrable. Its suspension consisted of 41mm Marzocchi forks and a Koni rear unit. Brembo's brake system dispensed with the linked discs of previous Guzzis, and gave efficient, if not outstanding, stopping power.

Specification	Moto Guzzi Daytona 1000 (1992)
Engine	Air-cooled high-cam eight-valve 90-degree transverse V-twin
Capacity	992cc (90 x 78mm)
Maximum power	95bhp @ 8000rpm
Transmission	Five-speed, shaft final drive
Frame	Steel spine with aluminium plates
Suspension	Telescopic front; monoshock rear
Brakes	Twin discs front; disc rear
Weight	452lb (205kg)
Top speed	145mph (233km/h)

For all its advances over the Le Mans, the days when Guzzi's finest could show a pack of production racers the way around a circuit were gone. Despite its racy name and competition background, the Daytona excelled in traditional fashion: as a sporty, long-legged roadster that provided performance in its own unique way. It was modern, but not that modern. Above all, the Daytona 1000 was still every bit a Moto Guzzi.

Left: The Daytona was impressive in corners despite being slightly heavy. Its rigid steel frame and firm suspension worked well, and the swingarm's race-developed parallelogram linkage minimized the effect of the drive shaft.

Honda NR750

**Top speed
160mph**
257km/h

*Right: A stripped-down
NR750 revealed the highest
level of streetbike technology
yet seen. Its exhaust system
was a hugely complex 8-4-
2-1-2 arrangement with
twin high-level silencers in
the tailpiece.*

*Below: A rigid twin-spar
aluminium frame and top
quality cycle parts gave the
NR excellent handling,
despite its weight. But on a
racetrack it was no more
competitive than its NR500
grand prix predecessor.*

The unique NR750 was a bike that only
Honda, the world's largest, boldest and
arguably also most stubborn motorcycle
firm, could have built. Gloriously stylish and
technically advanced but complex, heavy and
hugely expensive, it was inspired by the NR500
grand prix racer of the late 1970s and early '80s.
Like the racebike, the roadgoing NR was most
notable for its 'oval' pistons, each with two
conrods, two spark plugs and no fewer than eight
tiny valves.

There was much more to the NR750 than its
piston shape. The bike was visually stunning, with
a futuristic twin-headlamp full fairing and matching
tank-seat unit that was made from a blend of
carbon-fibre and fibreglass, and was rumoured to
cost more than any other complete mass-produced
superbike. The paint finish was outstanding; the
titanium-coated screen alone was hugely expensive.

The chassis was of similarly high quality,
although its design was relatively conventional. A
rigid twin-spar frame of polished aluminium held a
Pro-Arm single-sided swingarm, similar to that of
the RC30. The front end specification included
45mm diameter Showa upside-down front forks, a
16-inch front wheel, and large twin brake discs
gripped by four-piston calipers.

But it was the 748cc V4 engine that was in
every way the NR750's main attraction. The liquid-
cooled, 32-valve motor's cylinders were set at 90
degrees, with gear drive to the twin overhead
camshafts. The eight conrods were made of
lightweight titanium. Fuel was delivered by a

sophisticated injection system. The complex exhaust system ended in twin high-level silencers in the tailpiece.

The reason for the NR750's existence was that Honda was keen to utilize some of the technology that had been developed more than a decade earlier for the NR500 racer. Back then, there had been a valid technical reason for using oval pistons (in fact they were shaped like a running track, with straight sides and semi-circular ends), following Honda's decision to take on Suzuki's and Yamaha's two-strokes with a four-stroke.

Characteristics of a V8

Honda's successful grand prix bikes of the 1960s had been high-revving four-strokes, many of them small-capacity multis with four valves per cylinder. By 1979, 500cc GP bikes were limited to four cylinders, so Honda developed the NR as the nearest they could get to a V8. Despite costing billions of yen the 'Nearly Ready' was never competitive, and it was abandoned in 1981.

There was no comparable incentive to use oval pistons on a roadster, but the high-revving NR was the world's most powerful 750, with a peak output of 125bhp at 14,000rpm. Top speed was 160mph (257km/h), and the V4 also had an outstandingly broad spread of torque. But despite extensive use of lightweight materials the NR was heavy, at 489lb (222kg), and accelerated no harder than much cheaper 750cc rivals.

Despite its weight the Honda handled superbly, its brakes were powerful and its combination of style and sheer quality of finish made the NR a very special machine for the small number riders who could afford one. But ultimately it is for its looks, technology and price, rather than its performance, that the NR750 will be remembered.

Specification	Honda NR750 (1992)
Engine	Liquid-cooled dohc 32-valve 90-degree V4
Capacity	748cc (101.2 x 50.6mm)
Maximum power	125bhp @ 14,000rpm
Transmission	Six-speed, chain final drive
Frame	Aluminium twin spar
Suspension	Telescopic front; single shock rear
Brakes	Twin discs front; disc rear
Weight	489lb (222kg)
Top speed	160mph (257km/h)

Left: The NR's magnificent styling and quality of finish were worthy of Honda's exotic and hugely expensive technical tour-de-force.

Below left: The 748cc V4 engine featured 'oval' pistons, eight fuel injectors, eight titanium conrods, and 32 valves operated by four gear-driven camshafts.

Race-bred V4: the RC45

Two years after the NR750, Honda produced another exotic 750cc V4 in the RC45, which had a more conventional 16-valve engine and was essentially a follow-up to the all-conquering RC30. Designed mainly as a basis for a World Superbike racer, the RC45 (officially known as the RVF750F) produced 118bhp and was fast, flexible and agile. Although it initially struggled in Superbike racing, and never matched the impact of the RC30, the RC45 earned its share of glory when American ace John Kocinski won the world title in 1997.

Yamaha GTS1000

**Top speed
140mph**
225km/h

*Right: Yamaha hoped this
was the shape of future
sports-tourers but, like
Bimota's forkless Tesi, the
GTS failed to sell.*

*Below: Handling was stable
even under hard braking
into a turn, but ironically
the Yamaha's lack of fork
dive under braking gave
slow steering.*

As the first mass-produced bike of the
modern era with non-telescopic front
suspension, the GTS1000 was an
innovative machine that Yamaha hoped would
trigger a brave new world of chassis design. Like
the Tesi 1D that had been built in tiny numbers by
Bimota, the GTS featured a forkless front end
whose theoretical advantage was that it separated
the distinct elements of suspension and steering.

Suspension was handled by a horizontal alloy
beam leading from the front wheel hub to a pivot
on the C-shaped aluminium frame. A diagonal
shock linked the two. Steering was accomplished
using the vertical strut that led up from the hub to a
telescoping steering box which took up suspension
movement, and was linked to the handlebars. There
was no room for a brake disc on the left, so the
GTS was fitted with a single, central front disc and
six-piston caliper with ABS.

Power came from a modified version of
Yamaha's FZR1000 unit, and had four liquid-
cooled and angled-forward cylinders, 20 valves
worked by twin overhead camshafts, and capacity
of 1002cc. Fuel injection, softer cams, narrower

intake ports and reduced compression ratio combined to reduce peak output from 140bhp to 100bhp at 9000rpm.

The rest of the bike represented Yamaha's attempt to bridge the gap between adrenaline-pumping sportster and long-distance tourer. Its styling was streamlined, although this was a physically big and heavy machine. Its riding position was more sports than touring, giving a slight lean forward to near-flat handlebars, plus plenty of legroom.

Effortless cruising

Straight-line performance was reasonable, although in comparison with the FRZ, the four-cylinder engine seemed to have lost more top-end power than it had gained lower down. The GTS pulled reasonably well from below 3000rpm, and kicked again at 6000rpm, cruising lazily at 100mph (161km/h) with power in hand for a top speed of around 140mph (225km/h). But the GTS was uninspiring at high revs, and faded well before the 10,500rpm redline.

Its suspension system impressed with its ability to absorb bumps without the steering being affected. Handling was biased towards stability rather than agility, partly because there was no fork dive to quicken the steering entering a turn. Its stability was often welcome, but during slower-speed manoeuvres the GTS seemed tall and unwieldy. The Yamaha's most impressive braking was done with the bike banked over into a turn,

Forkless Pioneer – the RADD MC²

Yamaha's GTS front suspension layout had been designed ten years earlier by James Parker, an American bike enthusiast and engineer whose firm RADD was based in Santa Fe, New Mexico. Parker developed his idea with a Honda XL600-based prototype that was tested by future 500cc world champion Wayne Rainey. This led to a striking Yamaha FZ750-powered prototype, the RADD MC², built in 1987 in conjunction with *Motorcyclist* magazine and Los Angeles studio GK Design. Yamaha then bought rights to Parker's design, and contracted the American to help develop the GTS1000.

Specification	Yamaha GTS1000 (1993)
Engine	Liquid-cooled dohc 20-valve four
Capacity	1002cc (75.5 x 56mm)
Maximum power	100bhp @ 9000rpm
Transmission	Six-speed, chain final drive
Frame	Aluminium U-section
Suspension	Monoshock front and rear
Brakes	Single disc front and rear
Weight	553lb (251kg)
Top speed	140mph (225km/h)

when its front suspension kept working in a way that a telescopic system could not approach. There was plenty of outright stopping power, too, although the ABS system was too sensitive.

Unfortunately several failings, unrelated to suspension design, limited the GTS1000's appeal as a sports-tourer. Fuel consumption was poor and the tank range small. The fairing was narrow, and its screen generated turbulence. Worst of all the GTS was extremely expensive. Those factors, and the absence of any major advantage in most situations, resulted in poor sales. The Yamaha's failure ensured that telescopic forks would dominate motorcycle front suspension for years to come.

Left: From the right the view of the GTS's apparently unsuspended 17-inch front wheel was striking. Yamaha's 'Omega' chassis linked the handlebars to a steering box in the fairing nose, from which a strut on the wheel's left led to the hub-centre steering mechanism. The single 320mm brake disc was gripped by a six-piston caliper with an anti-lock system.

Boss Hoss V8

**Top speed
165mph**
266km/h

*Below: The Boss Hoss was
about as streamlined as a
garage door, but with
almost six litres of V8
muscle producing well over
300bhp, it did not need
efficient aerodynamics to go
fast. Such was the bike's
sheer size that its Chevy V8
powerplant, partially
hidden behind a vast
radiator, did not look out
of place.*

 The enormous and hugely powerful Boss
Hoss was one of motorcycling's most
outrageous machines, and one of its least
likely success stories. Tennessee-based Monty
Warne built his first bike around a Chevrolet V8
car engine in 1991, mainly for his own amusement.
He had no idea that the bike would become popular
with other riders; let alone that, ten years later, he
would have a thriving business having sold more
than 1000 of these crazy machines.

Big numbers were at the heart of the Boss
Hoss's appeal. An early Hoss's typical capacity was
5735cc; its maximum power output no less than
345bhp. The bike's dry weight was 1028lb (466kg)
and its wheelbase 76in (1930mm), both figures far
exceeding those of Honda's GL1500 Gold Wing.
Claimed top speed was 'over 160mph' (257km/h) –
and few people argued with that.

The Hoss (called Boss Hog until Harley-
Davidson's trademark lawyers objected) was

gigantic, with a big square radiator, frame tubes
like scaffold poles and a square-section rear tyre
that made the sidestand seem barely necessary.
Several dials were lost in the expanse of the fuel
tank, which managed to overhang the engine itself.
Long kicked-out forks led to a front wheel that held
twin brake discs.

Muscular monster

The motor was the ubiquitous small-block Chevy,
produced by General Motors since the 1950s. This
was horsepower by the old-fashioned American
route: nearly six litres of liquid-cooled, 90-degree
V8 muscle. It was big, thirsty and crude, with
monster low-rev torque to match its guttural growl
and gas-gulping greed.

For four-wheeled use the motor came with
automatic or manual gearbox but the Hoss,
weighing far less than any car for all its bulk, had
no such luxury. The Chevy produced more power at

Ladies' Bike – the Hoss V6

The success of the V8 allowed Warne to introduce numerous modifications over the years, and in 1998 to add a second model: the Boss Hoss V6. Powered by a 4.3 litre Chevy motor, this 200bhp brute was laughingly referred to by Warne as his 'ladies' model'. Like the latest V8, it incorporated improvements including custom-designed front suspension, new brakes and tyres, plus an automatic transmission system. The $25,000 V6 was slightly smaller, lighter and less powerful than the V8 – which made it the second largest, second heaviest and second most powerful production bike in the world.

1000rpm than most bikes did at full throttle. So there was just one gear, 'fast forward'. The V8's single-plate clutch led to a custom-made angle drive that took motion to a sprocket on the left.

With so much torque, the Hoss rider could simply let the clutch lever right out almost immediately, and accelerate away on the throttle. At 60mph (97km/h), when it was turning at just 2500rpm, the V8 cruised with a smooth, relaxed feel, and answered a crack of the throttle with fearsome acceleration that made Warne's top speed claim totally believable.

Although crude, the heavy-duty chassis was strong enough to cope. Corners were not a Boss

Specification	Boss Hoss V8 (1993)
Engine	Liquid-cooled ohv pushrod 16-valve 90-degree V8
Capacity	5735cc (101.6 x 88.4mm)
Maximum power	345bhp @ 5000rpm
Transmission	Single-speed, chain final drive
Frame	Tubular steel
Suspension	Telescopic front; twin shocks rear
Brakes	Twin discs front; single disc rear
Weight	1028lb (466kg)
Top speed	165mph (266km/h)

Hoss forte though, due mainly to the square-section rear tyre that preferred going straight to lifting onto its edge for a bend. The big bike didn't stop as hard as it accelerated, but it pulled up tolerably well when required.

Fast riding on the Boss Hoss was distinctly scary at times, but this bike was fun even if its rider used only a fraction of the V8's awesome potential. The attraction of the Boss Hoss was that it was one seriously excessive piece of machinery. Motorcycles simply didn't come bigger or more powerful than this.

Above left: Riding in a straight line on the Boss Hoss was fun, thanks to acceleration that was almost capable of bending those high handlebars.

Left: Single-speed transmission and chain drive took power to a 15-inch tyre whose huge width did not help cornering.

Ducati 916

**Top speed
160mph**
257km/h

*Below: Stunning on the
916's launch in 1994, and
still being produced with a
barely changed look well
into the 21st century,
Ducati's eight-valve flagship
proved that high style need
not go out of fashion. The
Italian firm had considered
using an aluminium beam
frame, before opting to
combine a traditional
tubular steel ladder frame
with an eye-catching single-
sided swingarm.*

Rarely has a motorcycle combined style and speed to such devastating effect as Ducati's 916. The Italian V-twin's blend of breathtaking beauty, thunderous engine performance and sublime handling made it an instant hit on the bike's launch in 1994. By the end of the decade, 916-based machines had won a string of World Superbike titles. Meanwhile the roadster went from strength to strength, its engine enlarged but its look proudly intact.

The 916 was a development of the liquid-cooled, eight-valve desmodromic V-twin line that stretched back to the 851 of 1988. More than simply aerodynamic, designer Massimo Tamburini's creation was inspired. The fairing's sharp nose held aggressive twin headlights. Elegant scarlet shapes were everywhere in the fuel tank and fairing. The rear end, with its diminutive tailpiece, high-level silencers and single-sided swingarm, was equally dramatic.

Ducati's 916cc motor was a bored-out version of the unit from the previous 888 model. Other changes included a revised Weber fuel-injection system plus the addition of a larger, curved radiator. Breathing was uprated with a large airbox fed by intakes running back from the fairing nose. In combination with a new exhaust system, this raised the eight-valve motor's peak output by a few horsepower to 114bhp at 9000rpm.

Chassis design combined Ducati's traditional steel ladder frame with a tubular aluminium rear subframe. The 916 differed from the 888 by using a second rear engine mount for extra rigidity. There was nothing traditional about the aluminium swingarm that curved round the huge 190-section rear tyre before swooping back to anchor the three-spoke wheel. Tamburini admitted that this was not the purest engineering solution, but considered the compromise worthwhile for the boost it brought to the bike's high-tech image.

Neat engineering

There was more neat engineering at the steering head, which featured adjustable geometry plus a horizontally mounted steering damper. More conventionally, the swingarm worked a vertical, multi-adjustable Showa shock. The Japanese firm also provided the 43mm upside-down forks, which held a 17-inch front wheel. Braking was by Brembo.

Ducati's eight-valve engine had long been a torquey, charismatic powerplant, and the 916 unit was the best yet. Its mid-range response was majestic, sending the bike rocketing out of corners from as low as 5000rpm to the accompaniment of a spine-tingling exhaust growl. High-rev acceleration was smooth and strong, too, sending the 916 to a top speed of 160mph (257km/h).

Handling was superb, justifying Ducati's decision to stick with a steel frame, after considering a switch to aluminium. At 429lb (195kg) the 916 was light, its frame was rigid, and its suspension of high quality. Although the Ducati was not the quickest-steering of superbikes, it had a confidence-inspiring blend of stability and neutral cornering feel.

This most purposeful of Italian sportsters was not always an easy companion, especially in town, where its racy riding position, firm suspension and snatchy power delivery made life unpleasant. On the right road, though, the 916 was simply magical; one of those rare machines that left all those who rode it stunned by its unmatched combination of beauty, character and performance.

Ducati's Superbike Dominance

The roadgoing 916 was a hit in the showrooms, and Ducati's factory racebike of the same name was even more successful in the World Superbike championship. The red V-twins were the dominant force in the most prestigious four-stroke racing series, notably with Carl Fogarty. The British rider won in 1994 and again a year later. Australian ace Troy Corser retained the crown for Ducati in 1996 before Fogarty, who had left for Honda, returned to regain the title in 1998. His fourth championship, in 1999, made it five in six years for the Italian V-twin.

Left: The 916cc capacity came from enlarging the previous 888cc V-twin engine. Other revisions included the fuel-injection system, a bigger airbox and a new exhaust system.

Below left: Superb handling was a key factor in the 916's success on road and track. Although not the quickest-steering of bikes, the Ducati was beautifully balanced and immensely stable.

Specification	Ducati 916 (1994)
Engine	Liquid-cooled dohc eight-valve 90-degree V-twin
Capacity	916cc (94 x 66mm)
Maximum power	114bhp @ 9000rpm
Transmission	Six-speed, chain final drive
Frame	Tubular steel ladder
Suspension	Telescopic front; single shock rear
Brakes	Twin discs front; disc rear
Weight	429lb (195kg)
Top speed	160mph (257km/h)

Triumph Speed Triple

**Top speed
130mph**
209km/h

The bold and charismatic Speed Triple summed-up all that was best about the new Triumph firm from Hinckley. With its sleek styling, racy riding position, high-quality cycle parts and exposed three-cylinder engine, the original Speed Triple, launched in 1994, was a spiritual descendant of the cafe racers of the 1960s – the days when British bikes, including old-style Triumphs, ruled the roads.

Aggressive and sleek

If there was one thing above all that the Triple shared with those old cafe racers it was attitude. Lean, simple, unfaired but at the same time aggressive and sleek, the Triple was from the same naked musclebike school as Ducati's Monster. With a torquey three-cylinder motor, high quality cycle parts and no unnecessary frills, it was built for coffee-bar cowboys who took their bikes expresso style: simple, black and strong.

Depending on how it was viewed, the Speed Triple – whose name recalled one of the great early Triumphs, the 500cc Speed Twin of 1938 – was either a sporty version of Triumph's naked Trident 900 or a naked version of the Daytona 900 sportster. While sharing the basic liquid-cooled, 885cc three-cylinder engine layout and steel spine frame of both bikes, the Triple differed enough from either to be very much a distinct model.

Its engine was the same 97bhp unit that powered several other bikes in the range, but the Speed Triple alone had five gears instead of six. To match its lean look and all-black engine and bodywork (yellow paint was an option), the Triple was also fitted with aluminium silencers whose dark finish resembled carbon-fibre.

Above: Triumph's modular construction meant that the original 1994-model Speed Triple used the same frame and 885cc three-cylinder engine as the Trident roadster and Daytona sports bike. Low bars, black engine finish and upmarket cycle parts gave the new bike a distinct personality.

Right: Although engine performance was not increased from the Trident's 97bhp, the Speed Triple had a more aggressive look and became popular. Early models had a five-speed gearbox, but the sixth ratio was later reintroduced.

Tweaking the Triple

In many ways the Speed Triple came of age in 1997, when Triumph introduced the T509 version, complete with not only a revamped, 885cc three-cylinder engine but also distinctive twin headlamps and tubular aluminium frame. The T509 Speed Triple was just like the original model, but more so: faster, torquier and more charismatic. Triumph continued to upgrade the naked bruiser, until the 2002 model Triple (below) had a 955cc engine producing 118bhp, superbly agile handling, and more entertainment value than just about anything on wheels.

There was no pretence with the cycle-parts. Forks were 43mm, multi-adjustable Kayaba units; the same Japanese firm's shock could be set for preload and rebound damping. Front brakes were a high-quality blend of 310mm discs and four-piston calipers from Nissin, also of Japan. And the three-spoke wheels held sticky Michelins, the rear a massive 180-section radial.

The Speed Triple certainly lived up to its name, thanks mainly to its supremely responsive motor. By superbike standards the British machine's top speed of about 130mph (209km/h) was unremarkable, but the Triumph scored with outstanding smoothness and flexibility. Almost regardless of revs, it stormed forward in thrilling fashion in response to a twist of the rider's wrist.

Handling was very good, although like other Triumphs the Triple was tall and, at 460lb (209kg), rather heavy. Its rigid frame combined with the sophisticated suspension to give agile cornering without compromising stability. This was the lightest and lowest Triumph model yet, as well as one of the best equipped for hard and fast riding.

For day-to-day use the Triple was also reasonably practical, its lack of luxuries offset by a generous fuel range, comfortable seat and good standard of finish. Despite its similarity to other Triumph models, the Triple managed to project a strong and entertaining character all of its own. In many countries the naked bike became Triumph's best-selling model, and it was easy to see why. The spirit of the pure, simple British cafe-racer lived on in the Speed Triple.

Above left: The original Speed Triple's single round headlamp was not the dominant styling feature that twin lights would become in later years.

Left: The T509 Speed Triple, initially known by its factory code number but later renamed, used the same tubular aluminium frame as the 1997 Daytona sportster.

Specification	Triumph Speed Triple (1994)
Engine	Liquid-cooled dohc 12-valve triple
Capacity	885cc (76 x 65mm)
Maximum power	97bhp @ 9000rpm
Transmission	Five-speed, chain final drive
Frame	Steel spine
Suspension	Telescopic front; single shock rear
Brakes	Twin discs front; disc rear
Weight	460lb (209kg)
Top speed	130mph (209km/h)

Kawasaki ZX-9R

**Top speed
165mph**
266km/h

*Below: The ZX-9R looked
just like what it was: a
sporty but practical model
that sat midway between
Kawasaki's racy ZXR750
and the bigger ZZ-R1100.
That meant the 9R couldn't
match lighter, more focused
rivals on a racetrack, but
for riders looking for an
efficient, comfortable bike
with shoulder-splitting
straight-line performance,
the Kawasaki had much
to offer.*

 Kawasaki's tradition of building
outstanding 900cc superbikes suggested
that a hot new contender would appear in
the mid-1990s. The Z1 of 1973 and the GPZ900R
Ninja of 1984 had firmly established the Big K's
reputation for powerful, rapid and bullet-proof
900cc fours. And in 1994 came the model that was
intended to maintain that reputation for another
decade: the ZX-9R.

The superbike world had become increasingly
specialized since the days of the Z1 and Ninja,
when a single brilliant new machine could
outperform all opposition and be a top all-rounder
at the same time. Nevertheless, Kawasaki designed
the ZX-9R to fit between the firm's race-replica
ZXR750 and sports-touring ZZ-R1100. Its style and
emphasis were on performance, but the 9R was less
extreme than some super-sports rivals.

It was certainly one very rapid motorcycle, for
all that. The Kawasaki's engine was an enlarged,
899cc version of the 749cc, liquid-cooled
powerplant from the ZXR750. It had a ZZ-R1100
type ram-air system, big 40mm carburettors plus
detailed smoothing of the induction and exhaust
systems. The result was a peak output of 137bhp at
10,500rpm, and thrillingly strong power right
through the rev range.

Strong but heavy chassis

The motor was held by a large, aluminium twin-
beam frame similar to that of the ZZ-R1100,
backed-up by an equally sturdy box-section alloy
swingarm, with multi-adjustable suspension at each
end. Chassis geometry was sporty, with forks set at
24 degrees. But the Kawasaki weighed 474lb
(215kg), considerably more than several of its rivals,
and 66lb (30kg) more than Honda's FireBlade.

Styling was very sharp and aggressive, owing
much to Kawasaki's World Superbike racer. But by
sports bike standards the ZX-9R was a fairly big

ZX-9R Gets Faster Still

Kawasaki revised the ZX-9R over the next few years, and for 2000 introduced a new version that incorporated many changes but still had the look and feel of the original. Producing 142bhp from its 16-valve engine, now fed via one big slot in the nose of its twin-headlamp fairing, the 9R was faster and torquier than ever. Weight was down to 403lb (183kg); agility was increased. But the Kawasaki was still a super-sports bike that was roomy and comfortable enough for touring – and which took no prisoners on the way.

Specification	Kawasaki ZX-9R (1994)
Engine	Liquid-cooled dohc 16-valve four
Capacity	899cc (73 x 53.7mm)
Maximum power	137bhp @ 10,500rpm
Transmission	Six-speed, chain final drive
Frame	Aluminium twin beam
Suspension	Telescopic front; monoshock rear
Brakes	Twin discs front; disc rear
Weight	474lb (215kg)
Top speed	165mph (266km/h)

machine, with a broad fuel tank and a long stretch forward to the handlebars. The roomy riding position and wide seat helped make the Kawasaki comfortable while emphasizing that it was no ultra-light race replica.

The ZX-9R was at its best on a fast, open road where its motor's phenomenal power never failed to impress. At low revs the 16-valve four growled impatiently; straining at the leash. By 7000rpm the Kawasaki was storming forward with real conviction, and around 10,000rpm it kicked again, howling towards the 12,500rpm rev-limiter with a gloriously smooth, free-revving feel that took the 9R to a top speed of 165mph (266km/h).

Handling was superb on sweeping main roads where the Kawasaki's stability and neutral steering allowed its rider to exploit the engine's power to the full. On twistier roads the bike was less

impressive, as its weight and relatively slow steering made it cumbersome in comparison with racier rivals.

There was no doubt that the ZX-9R failed to raise the superbike stakes in the way that its Z1 and GPZ900R predecessors had done. By race-replica standards it was too big and heavy; and as a long-distance bike its lack of features such as centre-stand and grabrail told against it. But for riders looking for a genuine super-sports bike with a fair degree of practicality, the ZX-9R was arguably the pick of the bunch.

Above left: There was plenty of power available for wheelies. Hard acceleration from a standstill was almost impossible without the front wheel lifting off. Large slots beneath the headlight are air intakes leading to the ram-air system, which gave a major boost to the 137bhp unit's high-speed performance.

Ducati 748SP

**Top speed
150mph**
241km/h

*Right: Handling and
general cornering
performance were sublime,
thanks largely to the
Ducati's rigid ladder frame
and classy Showa
suspension parts. Abundant
ground clearance and fat,
sticky radials helped too.*

*Below: Having created one
of the world's most beautiful
motorcycles in 1994 with
the 916, Ducati sensibly
built another that looked
identical, apart from yellow
paintwork, just a year later.*

 Few bikes have assaulted the rider's
senses quite like Ducati's 748SP. The
Italian V-twin's bright yellow bodywork
caught the eye; its booming exhaust note battered
the ears; its fierce combination of acceleration,
braking power and cornering ability took the breath
away. A day at speed on the SP left reflexes
sharpened, riding skills honed and body
pummelled. Relaxing, the 748SP wasn't. Exciting it
certainly was.

Building a smaller version of the previous
year's 916 flagship was a logical move for Ducati
in 1995. The race-ready 748SP, which was
launched along with a cheaper, dual-seat 748
Biposto model, was designed to compete against
the Japanese fours in the increasingly important
600 Supersport class. The new 748cc capacity
came from a reduction in the 916's bore and stroke,
while the bottom-end contained a lightened
flywheel and close-ratio gearbox. With a revised
Weber-Marelli injection system and a pair of
carbon-fibre Termignoni cans, the 748SP produced

a maximum of 100bhp at 11,000rpm, 9bhp less
than the standard 916.

Both 748 models shared their basic chassis
layout with the 916, including an identical blend of
tubular steel frame and single-sided aluminium
swingarm. Both used 43mm Showa upside-down
forks, but the upmarket SP wore a rear shock from
Öhlins rather than Showa. There was a change in
braking, too, where the SP's Brembo discs were
made from cast iron rather than steel.

The racy 748SP was uncomfortable and demanding in town, and low-rev response was poor, but on the open road it came thrillingly to life. Provided its rider kept the revs above 7000rpm, the Ducati was addictively fast. At 10,000rpm, where the 916 would have been getting distinctly breathless, the 748 was still roaring towards the 11,000rpm redline through its sweet-shifting six-speed gearbox, heading for a top speed of 150mph (241km/h).

Concentration required

The 748's peakier nature made it more demanding than the 916 to ride. Approaching a slight bend with a gentle dab of brakes, the 748 needed a down-change where the bigger bike would have stormed forward again without. That was sometimes frustrating, but the greater effort and concentration required to get the best out of the 748SP often made for even more enjoyment, especially on a twisty road.

That was also partly due to the brilliance of its chassis. Suspension at both ends was firm, which made for a harsh ride on a bumpy road, but on smoother surfaces the Ducati was superb. Its steering was not outstandingly quick but stability in mid-corner was sublime, and the Öhlins shock supplied an awe-inspiring level of feedback and control. Braking power from the big iron Brembos was excellent, too.

The fast, loud, demanding 748SP was certainly not a bike for every rider or every trip, but on the right day and the right road there was arguably not another machine that was faster or more fun. Ducati's new star became a hit in Supersport racing, too, where the V-twin successfully challenged the Japanese fours to bring the Italian firm a string of world titles.

Next Generation – the 748R

Ducati dramatically updated its 748 line in 2000 with the 748R, which the Bologna firm described as the 'most advanced bike it had ever produced'. A comprehensively revised fuel-injection system combined with larger airbox, bigger valves, new cams and pistons, CNC-machined cylinder heads and titanium conrods to give 106bhp, or 112bhp with race exhaust. A revised frame and new Showa forks also contributed to a bike of stunning roadgoing performance and unprecedented racetrack ability. But in its initial seasons the 748R failed to win back the World Superbike championship for Ducati.

Above left: A single seat, free-breathing Termignoni exhaust mufflers and a fat, soft-compound rear radial gave the 748SP's rear end a suitably racy appearance.

Left: Even banked over at 45 degrees, the supremely capable Ducati had ground clearance and grip to spare. Few bikes have ever been easier or more enjoyable to ride fast.

Specification	Ducati 748SP (1995)
Engine	Liquid-cooled dohc eight-valve 90-degree V-twin
Capacity	748cc (88 x 61.5mm)
Maximum power	100bhp @ 11,000rpm
Transmission	Six-speed, chain final drive
Frame	Tubular steel ladder
Suspension	Telescopic front; monoshock rear
Brakes	Twin discs front; disc rear
Weight	441lb (200kg)
Top speed	150mph (241km/h)

Honda Super Blackbird

**Top speed
180mph**
290km/h

*Below: Aerodynamics
played a key part in the
Blackbird's design, as the
bike's bodywork was shaped
to give minimum frontal
area and a drag coefficient
lower even than that of
Honda's tiny NSR250
sportster. The fairing's
narrow width was achieved
partly thanks to the
innovative 'piggy-back'
headlight with its main
beam unit set above and
behind the dip beam.*

 There was little doubt about Honda's prime motivation in designing the CBR1100XX. The bike that was named the Super Blackbird, after the high-speed American spy-plane, was built to recapture the unofficial title of World's Fastest Motorcycle from Kawasaki's ZZ-R1100. The bid was successful, as the Super Blackbird's blend of powerful straight-four engine and aerodynamic bodywork sent it flying to 180mph (290km/h). Better still, in the process, Honda created a fine sports-touring superbike.

If the Blackbird's main aim was outrageous speed, the way it went about it was anything but. Its 1137cc powerplant was a conventional liquid-cooled, dohc 16-valve transverse four. Its only unusual feature – apart from its huge peak output of 162bhp at 10,000rpm – was the use of twin balancer shafts, which made the engine so smooth that it was able to aid chassis rigidity by being solidly mounted in the aluminium twin-spar frame.

Shark-like nose

Aerodynamics was a major part of the CBR's design. The bike's disappointingly ordinary looking bodywork was shaped to give minimum frontal area and an ultra-low drag coefficient. Much of the benefit came from the fairing's shark-like pointed nose, whose narrow width was aided by a piggy-back headlight, with twin lenses set one above the other instead of side-by-side as normal.

If the Blackbird's look was dull, its performance certainly was not. The mighty motor was a real star, generating violent acceleration with a deceptively refined feel. The serious power arrived at about 5000rpm, sending the rev-counter needle flashing round the dial to the 10,800rpm redline. The CBR could not manage the 190mph (306km/h) that Honda implied it could, but it was close – and fast enough for most.

At low revs the Honda was typically docile, too, but the emphasis on top-end performance had resulted in mid-range torque being compromised slightly. Cracking open the throttle at 4000rpm in top gear revealed a rather lazy response, which momentarily hindered overtaking. Shifting down through the reasonably smooth six-speed gearbox was rarely necessary, even so.

Straight-line stability

Predictably the Blackbird was very much at home on fast, open main roads. Its straight-line stability was flawless, steering reasonably light, the overall feel sophisticated and very, very fast. The non-adjustable, 43mm front forks worked well, as did the single rear shock unit. Inevitably the 491lb (223kg) Blackbird was rather heavy and softly sprung for racetrack use, but even on a circuit it acquitted itself well.

Braking incorporated a revised version of Honda's Dual-CBS system, which linked front and rear discs, operating both when either the hand lever or foot pedal was used. The CBR stopped rapidly, and some riders were particularly glad of the linked system in the wet or when carrying a pillion. Others were less convinced. Lever feel was slightly vague, and braking power seemed to fade fractionally after strong initial bite.

Neat details included a clock and fuel gauge on the dashboard (there was no reserve tap), luggage

hooks and a strong grab-rail, plus wide, clear mirrors that neatly incorporated the indicators. Less impressive was the low screen, which directed wind at a tall rider's head, generating some turbulence at normal cruising speeds.

Those criticisms did not prevent the Super Blackbird from being a success, boosted considerably by its status as the fastest thing on two wheels. Honda updated the bike in subsequent years, notably improving low-rev response with fuel-injection, and adding some bolder paint schemes. The arrival of Suzuki's Hayabusa meant that the XX was no longer the world's fastest. But for riders looking for mindblowing speed matched with refinement, stable handling and all-round ability, the Blackbird still had plenty to offer.

Above: A top speed of about 180mph (290km/h) was enough to make the Super Blackbird the world's fastest production motorcycle, but mid-range response was relatively flat until Honda introduced fuel-injection instead of carbs.

Left: Conventional styling contained some clever features. Air intakes high in the side of the fairing fed the carburettors; the holes below the headlight were to cool the engine.

Below left: The Blackbird was by no means ugly, but its rather dull styling was not helped by its paintwork. Alternatives to this grey were black and dark red.

Specification	Honda CBR1100XX (1996)
Engine	Liquid-cooled dohc 16-valve four
Capacity	1137cc (79 x 58mm)
Maximum power	162bhp @ 10,000rpm
Transmission	Six-speed, chain final drive
Frame	Aluminium twin spar
Suspension	Telescopic front; single shock rear
Brakes	Twin discs front; disc rear
Weight	491lb (223kg)
Top speed	180mph (290km/h)

Suzuki GSX-R750T

**Top speed
160mph**
257km/h

Suzuki's fast and light original GSX-R750 had become the first modern race replica on its release in 1985. But although the 16-valve machine had been updated several times in following years, by the middle of the following decade it had become heavier and less competitive, and the GSX-R initials had lost their sparkle. Then, in 1996, Suzuki struck back in fine style with an all-new GSX-R that was lean, mean and shared the original model's no-compromise approach.

Light and powerful

Simple statistics gave an indication of the new bike's fearsome performance. The GSX-R750T's peak power output of 126bhp matched that of Honda's CBR900RR and far exceeded all other 750s. The Suzuki weighed just 395lb (179kg), making it lighter than every 600cc four, let alone machines of similar capacity. It had the same steering geometry and wheelbase as Suzuki's RGV500 grand prix bike.

This motor's dramatically increased power output and reduced size and weight required some major modifications, notably the adoption of a ram-air intake system. Internal changes to the 749cc, 16-valve, liquid-cooled engine (Suzuki had dropped the original oil-cooled engine design four years earlier) included more oversquare cylinder dimensions, the camchain moved to the end of the crankshaft, cylinders set closer together, and numerous parts shrunk, lightened or both.

The frame was all new: a conventional twin-beam aluminium construction instead of the traditional, but taller and less rigid, GSX-R design. Despite its neat styling and distinctively swoopy tail-section, this made the Suzuki look rather ordinary – but riding it soon dispelled that idea. Even at a standstill the bike felt outrageously light

Above: The all-conquering 1996 GSX-R750 had none of the distinctive appearance or radical chassis design of the original twin-headlamp GSX-R of 11 years earlier.

Right: Race-derived features included a sleek fairing and large tailpiece to aid aerodynamics; a wheelbase identical to that of Suzuki's RGV500 grand prix missile; and a dry weight of 395lb (179kg) that made this bike only 7lb (3kg) heavier than the famously featherweight 1985 GSX-R750.

Far left: Straight-line performance was superb due to the GSX-R's light weight and revamped 126bhp engine, boosted by a ram-air system fed via slots in the fairing nose.

Left: Suzuki's long-awaited twin-spar aluminium frame used extruded spars and cast swingarm pivot sections, had very steep geometry, and was stiff enough to give brilliant handling.

and manoeuvrable. Once under way, the ultra-responsive GSX-R could be flicked into corners with astonishing speed and precision.

Almost inevitably the ultra-short, light Suzuki could feel twitchy when accelerating hard over bumps. But its high-speed stability was generally very good, thanks to the frame's rigidity and the control provided by sophisticated, multi-adjustable upside-down forks and monoshock. Fat radial rubber gave massive grip. The front brake combination of big twin discs and six-piston calipers, although rather wooden in town, was phenomenally powerful at speed.

And the GSX-R750's rider certainly got to see plenty of speed. The engine thrived on revs, requiring frequent use of the six-speed gearbox to give of its best. Provided the rev-counter needle was kept close to the 13,500rpm red-line, the Suzuki provided searing acceleration towards a top speed of about 160mph (257km/h). Although there was nothing like as much performance available at lower revs, for such a single-minded machine the GSX-R was reasonably tractable.

Not everyone was initially pleased to see the new bike. Some hardcore GSX-R750 enthusiasts felt that it was not a true GSX-R; that by abandoning the original format of oil-cooled motor and cradle frame Suzuki had lost too many essential ingredients. Such doubts were normally very quickly forgotten once the new bike was ridden. Even the shortest of journeys was enough to confirm that this was every bit a true GSX-R750: super-fast, supremely agile and absolutely crazy.

Specification	Suzuki GSX-R750T (1996)
Engine	Liquid-cooled dohc 16-valve four
Capacity	749cc (72 x 46mm)
Maximum power	126bhp @ 11,600rpm
Transmission	Six-speed, chain final drive
Frame	Aluminium twin spar
Suspension	Telescopic front; monoshock rear
Brakes	Twin discs front; disc rear
Weight	395lb (179kg)
Top speed	160mph (257km/h)

Revvier Still: the GSX-R600

Even the GSX-R750 seemed almost laid-back and sensible compared to the GSX-R600 that Suzuki released in 1997. Closely based on its big brother, the 599cc four produced 104bhp at a sky-high 12,000rpm, was even lighter at 384lb (174kg) and kept almost all its performance between 10,000rpm and the 13,500rpm redline. In typical GSX-R style it was the sportiest and most focused middleweight on the market, with a top speed of 155mph (249km/h), brilliant handling and very little in the way of comfort or compromise.

Harris Magnum 5

**Top speed
165mph**
266km/h

*Below: The Magnum's
shape was similar to that of
many four-cylinder sports
bikes, but its 35mm
diameter steel frame tubes
gave a very different look to
the typical twin aluminium
beams. The Harris bike's
fuel tank was made from
aluminium and was wide
because it enclosed the
large airbox. The self-
supporting carbon-fibre
seat unit held the twin
exhaust silencers.*

 The lean and powerful Magnum 5 that
brothers Steve and Lester Harris
constructed around Honda's CBR900RR
engine in 1996 was the latest of a line of Harris
Magnums that stretched back almost 20 years.
Distinguished by four-cylinder powerplants, race-
bred chassis and top-quality craftsmanship, the
Magnums were outstanding cafe racers that helped
make Harris one of the world's best-known
specialist manufacturers.

Inspiration for the original Magnum had come
from the Harris Kawasaki Z1000 endurance racer
of the late 1970s. In those days the Harris brothers
ran a team that competed in events including the Le
Mans 24 hour race. Adapting their racebike with a
new fairing, tank cover and other modifications
resulted in a fine-handling roadster, the Magnum 1.
In 1981 a restyle by Target Design, creators of
Suzuki's Katana, resulted in the Magnum 2, of
which more than 800 were sold.

Most Magnum 2s held the 16-valve engine
from Suzuki's GSX1100, and the later Magnum 4
would also be Suzuki-powered. Harris returned to
Kawasaki power with the Magnum 3 in the mid-
1980s. A decade later, inspired by the popularity of
the CBR900RR FireBlade, the firm from
Hertfordshire created the Magnum 5 around
Honda's liquid-cooled, 16-valve powerplant. (The
Magnum 4 is described in the sidebar.)

This was the most stylish Magnum so far, with
a neat twin-headlamp fairing, numerous carbon-
fibre details and a high-level exhaust system.
Ironically, unlike previous models, the Magnum 5
was less of a radical super-sports machine than the
Japanese bike whose engine it used. The early
FireBlade was notoriously twitchy and
uncompromising, so Harris designed the Magnum's
rigid tubular steel frame to give slightly less steep
steering geometry, a longer wheelbase and a less
extreme riding position.

Specification	**Harris** Magnum 5 (1996)
Engine	Liquid-cooled dohc 16-valve four (Honda FireBlade)
Capacity	893cc (70 x 58mm)
Maximum power	135bhp @ 10,500rpm
Transmission	Six-speed, chain final drive
Frame	Tubular steel ladder
Suspension	Telescopic front; monoshock rear
Brakes	Twin discs front; disc rear
Weight	407lb (185kg) wet
Top speed	165mph (266km/h)

Magnum 4 – the Harris GSX-R

The Magnum 5's predecessor in the line was produced in 1991 around the four-cylinder, 16-valve oil-cooled engine of Suzuki's GSX-R1100. This was an ideal powerplant for Harris because Suzuki's standard GSX-R of this era, although popular, handled poorly. The Magnum 4 remedied that with its rigid ladder-style steel frame, huge aluminium swingarm and top-quality cycle parts. The bike was often assembled with no fairing to give an aggressive, streetfighter look.

Poise and stability

This meant that the Magnum required slightly more rider input than the standard CBR, but it still had superbly light, neutral steering. More to the point, the Harris was more stable than the standard Honda, especially under hard acceleration. One reason for that was the superb control of the Öhlins rear shock. To reduce cost, parts including front forks and yokes, wheels and brakes were standard 900RR items. All were of high quality and contributed the Magnum's cornering poise.

Straight-line performance was boosted by a Harris four-into-one exhaust system plus carburettor changes, and many owners also took the opportunity to tune the four-cylinder Honda motor. The standard RR's 124bhp output was typically raised to 135bhp at 10,500rpm, and its top speed to around 165mph (266km/h).

Ironically, another attraction of the Magnum 5 was its price, which had been the biggest drawback of its predecessors in the 1980s. In most cases the Harris was sold in kit form, at a price that allowed the owner of a crashed standard 900RR, for example, to build a Magnum 5 for no more than the cost of returning the bike to standard.

The increase in performance was nowhere near as great as with the old Magnum models, due to advances in Japanese superbike chassis design. In fact some CBR900RR riders considered the

Magnum's gain in stability at the expense of agility a retrograde step. But there was no doubting that the Magnum 5 was a fine-handling and very fast motorbike, as well as a handsome and exotic one.

Above left: A neat twin-headlamp fairing provided good aerodynamics. Harris retained many standard Honda components, including front forks and triple clamps, brakes, instruments and switchgear.

Left: Unlike previous Magnums, the Mk5 had slightly less racy steering geometry and a longer wheelbase than the CBR900RR that provided its engine.

Bimota YB11

**Top speed
170mph**
274km/h

Bimota's reputation as a manufacturer of top class super-sports bikes had been based on its advanced and lightweight chassis. This left the tiny Italian firm vulnerable during the mid-1990s, when mass-produced Japanese superbike chassis had become so good

that many were difficult to equal, let alone better. But Bimota continued to produce super-sports machines offering outstanding performance, notably the YB11 Superleggera of 1996.

Ironically, the YB11's twin-spar aluminium frame, far from being futuristic in Bimota tradition, was closely based on that of the YB6 of several years earlier. But that took nothing away from the YB11, which was beautifully styled, fitted with top quality cycle parts, and had an uncompromisingly aggressive personality.

The YB11 justified its Superleggera, or 'superlight', name by scaling just 403lb (183kg), a substantial 33lb (15kg) lighter than the Yamaha YZF1000R Thunderace that supplied its 1002cc four-cylinder engine. Although the frame's main beams were unchanged from the YB6, the top cross-member was located nearer the steering head, adding rigidity. A sophisticated Paioli rear shock operated a new aluminium swingarm; Paioli also supplied the large-diameter front forks.

Bimota made no internal changes to the 20-valve, liquid-cooled Thunderace motor, which in standard form produced 145bhp. But the Rimini firm fitted a larger airbox, fed via ducts in the

Above: Bimota claimed the YB11 produced slightly more power than the standard Yamaha Thunderace whose engine it used. Combined with the Italian bike's light weight, this resulted in devastating straight-line performance.

Right: Although the YB11 held its 20-valve Yamaha engine in a chassis whose layout was very similar to that of the standard YZR1000 Thunderace, the Italian bike had a distinctly sportier personality. Its slim fairing, firm suspension, single seat and racy geometry gave a typically aggressive Bimota feel.

fairing nose. According to Bimota, this added a few horsepower in conjunction with a new four-into-one pipe and reworked carburettors.

Although the YB11 shared its engine and chassis type with the YZF1000R, the two bikes felt distinctly different. The Bimota was more racy, with firmer suspension, thinner seat and stretched-out riding position. The Italian bike's reduced weight gave a slight edge to straight-line performance, as the Superleggera had a power-to-weight ratio that no mass-produced rival could match.

Vicious acceleration

A crack of the throttle sent the Bimota hurtling forward towards a top speed of 170mph (274km/h). Peak power was produced at 10,000rpm, and the acceleration at high revs was vicious. But its Yamaha engine's greatest strength was mid-range response, and that remained true of the YB11. It pulled with stunning urgency when the throttle was wound open even from below 4000rpm in top gear.

Like most Bimotas, this was not a practical motorbike. Its suspension was too firm to work properly at low speed on bumpy roads, but on smooth surfaces the bike handled superbly. Its Brembo brakes were wrist-punishingly powerful, and its levels of steering agility, roadholding and ground clearance immense.

Inevitably the YB11 could not match the performance advantage that some of its predecessors had enjoyed over their mass-produced contemporaries. Equally inevitably, the hand-built Italian bike was hugely expensive as well as impractical. But it was beautiful and rare as well as seriously fast, and enough people were prepared to pay the premium to make the Superleggera a success.

Tesi: the Forkless Failure

Bimota's Tesi, with its futuristic hub-centre front suspension system in place of telescopic forks, was intended to lead the motorcycle world into a new era of advanced chassis design. Chief engineer Pierluigi Marconi's creation, begun when he was a student (Tesi means 'thesis' in Italian), featured a twin-sided swingarm supporting the front wheel, which steered by pivoting on a bearing inside its hub. A series of rods linked handlebars to front wheel.

Powered by the liquid-cooled, eight-valve V-twin engine from Ducati's 851, the Tesi 1D was fast and glamorous when it appeared in 1991. But although its unique chassis gave an advantage when braking into a turn, the Tesi's handling was inconsistent, partly due to the complex steering system being prone to wear. These problems combined with the bike's high price to make the Tesi a failure that Bimota's reputation and finances could ill afford.

Left: Lean styling, broad frame spars and four-into-one silencer gave the Bimota a racy appearance.

Below left: The YB11's frame was a development of the twin-spar aluminium structure introduced on the YB4ie racebike in 1987.

Specification	Bimota YB11 (1996)
Engine	Liquid-cooled dohc 20-valve four (Yamaha Thunderace)
Capacity	1002cc (75.5 x 56mm)
Maximum power	148bhp @ 10,000rpm
Transmission	Five-speed, chain final drive
Frame	Aluminium twin beam
Suspension	Telescopic front; monoshock rear
Brakes	Twin discs front; disc rear
Weight	403lb (183kg)
Top speed	170mph (274km/h)

Honda Valkyrie

**Top speed
130mph**
210km/h

*Right: The Valkyrie's shape
was unmistakably that of a
cruiser, but its huge six-
cylinder engine hinted at its
brutal performance.*

*Below: Perhaps the
Honda's most surprising
feature was the ability of its
chassis, notably its forks
and powerful front brake.*

Honda's gigantic six-cylinder Valkyrie
was far from most people's idea of a
superbike. It had high handlebars, twin
rear shocks, cruiser-based styling and a 1520cc flat
six engine based on that of the Gold Wing tourer.
Yet the bike that was also known (outside America)
as the F6C soon proved that, despite its sheer size
and laid-back look, it had the performance to make
for a memorable ride.

The concept of a Wing-based naked bike was
logical, given the US market's enthusiasm for
cruisers and the GL1500's huge popularity over the
years. The Valkyrie embraced the American style of
high bars, big fenders and long wheelbase. But that
flat six engine gave the bike a unique character. It
dominated the bike's look, its copious chrome
backed-up by more on the headlamp and pair of
stylishly flattened silencers.

The six's unchanged 1520cc capacity made the
Valkyrie the largest-engined cruiser on the market.
The sohc motor gained hotter camshafts and
revised valvegear. As well as the new exhaust
system, designed to boost mid-range output, this

bike had six 28mm Keihin carbs in place of the Gold Wing's pair of 33mm units. The result was a maximum power output of 100bhp at 6000rpm – hot stuff by cruiser standards – plus huge reserves of low-rev torque.

Chassis layout was conventional in all but size, with a tubular steel frame, and fuel tank in the normal place (instead of under the seat, like the Wing). Front forks were thick upside-down units. A pair of chrome-covered shocks held up the back end of a bike that weighed a substantial 683lb (310kg). But the Honda's low centre of gravity, conservative steering geometry and long wheelbase combined to make it very stable and easy to ride at low speed.

Ride of the Valkyries

Much of the big bike's user-friendly feel was due to its engine. The Valkyrie had so much low-down torque that it barely needed its five-speed gearbox. The big six pulled without complaint with just 20mph (32km/h) and 800rpm showing on its pair of white-faced dials. Acceleration at such speeds was inevitably gentle, but the F6C didn't have to be revved much harder to show a strong, seamless, almost totally smooth build-up of momentum. At an indicated 100mph (161km/h) the bike was still pulling hard and in thrilling fashion towards a top speed of over 125mph (201km/h).

If the engine's performance was impressive, so too was the Valkyrie's chassis. The frame was strong enough to cope with all the weight, and suspension was firm and well damped enough to make quick cornering not only possible but

Specification	Honda Valkyrie (1996)
Engine	Liquid-cooled sohc 12-valve flat six
Capacity	1520cc (71 x 64mm)
Maximum power	100bhp @ 6000rpm
Transmission	Five-speed, shaft final drive
Frame	Tubular steel
Suspension	Telescopic front; twin shocks rear
Brakes	Twin discs front; disc rear
Weight	683lb (310kg) wet
Top speed	130mph (210km/h)

Erion's Ultimate Valkyrie

Numerous riders and custom builders created distinctive bikes based on the Valkyrie, but for power, looks and noise none approached the bike named Odin – 'King of the Valkyries'. Craig Erion, boss of Californian firm Two Brothers Racing, created it by bolting two superchargers to the six-cylinder motor, giving a power output that could be set between 140bhp and over 200bhp. Even at the lower limit, Odin was outrageous, combining brutal acceleration with a deafening noise through its six-pipe exhaust system.

enjoyable. Ground clearance was generous by cruiser standards, and the Valkyrie's braking was good too, thanks to a pair of front discs gripped by twin-piston calipers, plus a larger rear disc.

Many motorcyclists dismissed Honda's 'performance cruiser' tag and refused to take the bike seriously, but most who rode the Valkyrie were won over. It combined distinctive looks with a smooth, powerful, supremely flexible engine and a remarkably competent chassis. Honda had set out to build a giant cruiser with the performance to match its size, and had achieved exactly that.

Left: The 1520cc flat six was heavily based on the Gold Wing unit, but had hotter camshafts plus screw-and-locknut valvegear, instead of the Wing's hydraulic valve lifters. As well as a new exhaust system, the Valkyrie had six 28mm Keihin carbs instead of two 33mm units.

BMW K1200RS

**Top speed
150mph**
241km/h

*Below: The RS's bodywork
hid not only the 1171cc
inline four-cylinder engine
but also most of the frame,
which broke with BMW
tradition both by being
made from aluminium, and
because it did not employ
the engine as a stressed
member. This allowed the
motor to be rubber-
mounted, which combined
with the adjustable
ergonomics to give a
comfortable ride.*

 BMW had already gone a long way towards shedding its reputation for building competent but rather dull bikes when the K1200RS was launched in 1997, but even so the big four-cylinder sports-tourer was a revelation. With its swoopy styling, aluminium frame, Telelever front suspension system and potent liquid-cooled, four-cylinder powerplant, the RS was every bit a modern superbike. And with a claimed 130bhp on tap, it blew wide open the self-imposed 100bhp limit that had handicapped the German marque for years.

The K1200RS was still very much a BMW, for all that. Unlike the majority of sports-tourers, it placed as much emphasis on the touring side of the equation as the sports. Typical BMW touches included handlebars, seat and footrests that could all be adjusted. The screen could also be set in one of two positions, which further added to the rider's comfort at speed.

Tuned 16-valve engine

But it was for the stunning performance of its engine, a revamped version of the longitudinally mounted 16-valve four from the K1100RS, that the RS was most memorable. Capacity was increased from 1092 to 1171cc by use of a new, longer stroke crankshaft. Lightweight pistons and valvegear, higher compression ratio and a ram-air intake system all contributed to its peak output of 130bhp at 8750rpm.

That made the K12 by far BMW's most powerful bike ever, and the German firm's engineers had managed to combine its new-found high-rev power with the K-series motors' traditionally strong mid-range torque. The revised Motronic injection system provided instant, snatch-free response from below 3000rpm even in top gear, from which point the RS just kept pulling harder until its power started to drop off towards the 9000rpm redline.

Such was the motor's mid-range punch that there was little reason to rev it above 8000rpm, but it was tempting to do so just because the newly rubber-mounted powerplant felt so smooth at almost all speeds. A slight tingle intruded at 4500rpm, ironically a useful 85mph (137km/h) cruising speed in top gear. But the traditional K-series buzz was gone, and the RS felt very refined. It was fast, too: good for a genuine 150mph (241km/h) without luggage. And its new six-speed gearbox was not just the best ever fitted to a BMW, but the first to match Japanese standards.

The K12's chassis was also impressive. The frame was an aluminium spine design, much more substantial than previous steel structures because the rubber-mounted K12 motor was not a stressed member of the chassis. Weighing 573lb (260kg) dry, and with a long wheelbase, the K1200RS was a big and heavy bike, but was well-suited to maintaining a fast pace on curving main roads. Its steering was quite slow but neutral and precise, and high-speed stability was good even when loaded with luggage.

Front suspension was by a revised, frame-mounted version of the Telelever system fitted to the R1100RS flat twin, and worked well. Twin-piston Brembo front calipers and large floating discs combined with an ABS system to give powerful and reliable braking. The single-sided Paralever rear swingarm pivoted on the frame and worked a single shock, placed diagonally on the right of the bike. The RS was too soft and heavy to

be much fun in tight turns, but it could corner respectably rapidly when requested.

Ironically, arguably the RS's only real weakness, apart perhaps from a high price and its sheer size and weight, was the mediocre fuel range provided by its combination of high-speed thirst and too-small tank. That untypical BMW fault did little to lessen the appeal of a very fast and refined long-distance machine.

Above left: BMW's Telelever front suspension system looked like conventional front forks at first glance, but featured a single shock unit in the fairing nose.

Above: The K1200RS was very fast but too heavy for aggressive riding, and was at its best when laden with tank bag and panniers.

Left: The two-way adjustable screen was less efficient than fully adjustable predecessors, but better than most rivals. BMW's quirky switchgear took some getting used to.

Specification	BMW K1200RS (1997)
Engine	Liquid-cooled dohc 16-valve inline four
Capacity	1171cc (70.5 x 75mm)
Maximum power	130bhp @ 8750rpm
Transmission	Six-speed, shaft final drive
Frame	Aluminium twin spar
Suspension	Telelever monoshock front; monoshock rear
Brakes	Twin discs front; disc rear
Weight	573lb (260kg)
Top speed	150mph (241km/h)

Triumph T595 Daytona

**Top speed
165mph**
266km/h

*Below: The Daytona's
aggressive styling,
dominated by its sleek twin-
headlamp fairing, hinted at
the 955cc triple's
performance. Although the
Triumph was not quite as
racy as the most
singleminded of its rivals,
the British firm had finally
produced a purpose-built
sports machine that could
trade punches with the best
in the world.*

The T595 Daytona was the bike with
which Triumph came of age as a
superbike manufacturer. Fast and fine-
handling, the Daytona was the first sports bike
from the reborn British firm that was designed to
compete head-on with the best from Italy and
Japan. And although the Triumph was slightly less
racy than some super-sports rivals, its unique blend
of style, performance and three-cylinder character
made it a big success.

A crucial factor in the Daytona's development
was Triumph boss John Bloor's decision to
abandon the modular format with which his firm
had entered the market in 1991. Modular design
involved several different models sharing many
components, and had proved a cost-effective way
of developing a range of bikes rapidly. But it
involved too many compromises for a competitive
super-sports machine.

The Daytona changed all that. This time,
Triumph's designers had no such handicap in
developing a purpose-built triple. The T595 title
came from Triumph's factory codename, a factory
tradition dating back to the T120 Bonneville and
beyond, but the bike was later renamed the
Daytona 955i because many people thought the 595
referred to capacity. This was in fact 955cc, as the
motor was a bored-out version of the previous
Daytona's 885cc liquid-cooled, dohc 12-valve unit.

Inside the motor, new semi-forged pistons held
thinner, low-friction rings and moved in new
aluminium liners. Lotus Engineering helped tune
the motor by improving its breathing with larger
valves, new cams and lightened crankshaft.
Magnesium engine covers, modified crankcases
and a redesigned gearbox and clutch further
reduced weight. Other engine-related changes
included a new airbox, three-into-one exhaust
system and Sagem fuel-injection system.

If the motor was a development of its
predecessor, then the chassis of which it formed a
stressed member was totally new. In place of the
old steel spine was a perimeter frame of twin oval-
section aluminium tubes. Styling was a key factor
in the chassis design, hence the frame's polished
tubes and the single-sided swingarm that enhanced
the Daytona's sleek and distinctive look.
Suspension was by Showa of Japan, with 45mm
forks and a similarly multi-adjustable shock.

Compact and eager to rev

From the rider's seat the Daytona felt notably more
compact than previous Triumphs, and it was
certainly much faster too. The new motor was
smooth and eager to rev. It kicked hard anywhere
above 6000rpm to send the triple surging forward
and its rev-counter needle flicking towards the
10,500rpm redline. Peak output was 128bhp at
10,200rpm, giving a 15bhp advantage over the
previous Daytona Super III. With its rider tucked
down behind the fairly low screen the triple was
good for over 160mph (257km/h). Only the slightly
notchy six-speed gearbox and a noticeable power
dip at about 5500rpm marred the impression of a
superbly fast and sophisticated sportster.

There were no such complaints about the
handling, particularly on the road where the

Triumph's combination of light, neutral steering and confidence-inspiring stability was very impressive. The top-heaviness of previous Triumphs was gone, replaced by a pleasantly manageable feel, and backed-up by excellent control from the firm yet compliant suspension. Although the Daytona could not quite match the agility of its raciest rivals, it was not far behind, and its Nissin brake system gave outstanding stopping power.

The T595 Daytona was more than an excellent sports bike, it was proof that Triumph was truly back in the big time. Almost 30 years after Honda's CB750 had arrived to outclass the previous Meriden-based factory's T150 Trident triple and

hasten the demise of the once dominant British motorcycle industry, Triumph once again had a sporting superbike that stood comparison with the very best in the world.

Above: The Daytona's look was enhanced by its frame, made from oval-section aluminium tubes.

Specification	Triumph T595 Daytona (1997)
Engine	Liquid-cooled dohc 12-valve triple
Capacity	955cc (79 x 65mm)
Maximum power	128bhp @ 10,200rpm
Transmission	Six-speed, chain final drive
Frame	Tubular aluminium perimeter
Suspension	Telescopic front; single shock rear
Brakes	Twin discs front; disc rear
Weight	436lb (198kg)
Top speed	165mph (266km/h)

Suzuki TL1000S

**Top speed
160mph**
257km/h

Suzuki's launch of the TL1000S seemed to herald a new era of V-twin Japanese super-sports bikes. The TL's powerful 996cc, eight-valve engine was held in a light and technically innovative chassis; and the half-faired Suzuki was stylish, aggressive and competitively priced. This was the bike that proved the Japanese could build exciting V-twins, and which promised to give Ducati some serious competition.

Unfortunately for Suzuki, that was not how things worked out. The TL1000S was introduced to near universal praise, for its stunningly powerful and torquey engine and also for its handling and high level of technology. But that agility occasionally turned into instability. Rumours of severe wobbles ('tank-slappers') caused the TL to be recalled for fitment of a steering damper. Its sales never recovered.

Powerful and charismatic

In reality the scare stories (which appeared in only a few countries) were often exaggerated, and the TL1000S was in almost every respect an outstanding superbike. Its engine was a liquid-cooled, dohc 90-degree V-twin. A ram-air system fed a Mikuni-Denso fuel-injection set-up, giving a maximum output of 123bhp at 8500rpm – more than both Ducati's 916 and also Honda's VTR1000F, the less charismatic rival Japanese V-twin that was launched at the same time.

Above: When flat-out with its rider's head on the tank, the TL1000S was normally a thrillingly fast bike. But it was when under hard acceleration, with little weight over the front wheel and especially with a light rider on board, that the Suzuki was prone to shake its head.

Right: One of the TL's attractions was the aggressive image provided by its sleek half-fairing and its engine on display. The Japanese manufacturers had taken a long time to follow Ducati in producing a big V-twin, and when Suzuki finally did so it was clear that a new era of competition had begun.

Racy Relation: the TL1000R

Suzuki waited only a year before following-up the TL1000S with a fully-faired, beam-framed derivative, the TL1000R. This was designed as the basis of the firm's challenge in World Superbikes, where the rules traditionally favoured twins over fours. The 134bhp TL1000R was more powerful, smoother and more controllable than the S model. But it lacked some of the storming mid-range power that made the half-faired bike so much fun, and was also bulkier and heavier. That would not have mattered if the TL-R had been a winner on the track, but it was uncompetitive in US racing and did not displace the GSX-R750 four as Suzuki's choice in World Superbikes.

The frame was a tubular aluminium construction that incorporated a unique rear suspension system consisting of a single spring (placed near-horizontally on the right) and separate rotary damper. This compact arrangement allowed the engine to be placed further back, giving a short wheelbase for extra manoeuvrability. Other cycle parts were conventional and of high quality, notably the multi-adjustable, upside-down Kayaba forks, and the front brake combination of 320mm discs and four-piston Nissin calipers.

The motor was a real star, with all the performance and character of a good V-twin. The TL pulled crisply at low revs and was wonderfully strong through the mid-range, giving enough instant acceleration to lift the front wheel with a gentle twist of the throttle. And the free-revving engine really took off at 6500rpm, sending the tacho needle shooting round to the 10,500rpm redline, and hurling the Suzuki forward towards a top speed of 160mph (257km/h).

Handling was good in most situations, though the TL was rather fussy about suspension set-up, and few experts were convinced about the benefits of the rotary shock damper. The Suzuki was light at 412lb (187kg), and its steering angle was steep. This contributed to effortless steering response and rapid direction changes, as well as the twitchiness that earned the TL its bad reputation.

With its handling calmed by a steering damper (preferably of higher quality than the cheap item that was belatedly specified by Suzuki) there was very little wrong with the bad-boy V-twin, and a great deal that was right. It was fast, light, flexible, reasonably comfortable, and bursting with V-twin character. Perhaps more than anything, the TL1000S got its rider's adrenaline flowing like few other bikes on the road.

Above left: When parked it looked innocent, but the TL's bad-boy reputation hit sales and ultimately ended its production in 2001.

Left: As well as Suzuki's first super-sports V-twin engine, the TL featured a tubular aluminium frame whose rear shock had an innovative rotary damping unit.

Specification	Suzuki TL1000S (1997)
Engine	Liquid-cooled dohc eight-valve 90-degree V-twin
Capacity	996cc (98 x 66mm)
Maximum power	123bhp @ 8500rpm
Transmission	Six-speed, chain final drive
Frame	Tubular aluminium
Suspension	Telescopic front; monoshock rear
Brakes	Twin discs front; disc rear
Weight	412lb (187kg)
Top speed	160mph (257km/h)

Yamaha YZF-R1

**Top speed
170mph**
274km/h

*Right: The view from the
front was dominated by the
R1's aggressively angled
headlights, which perfectly
matched the bike's take-no-
prisoners personality.*

*Below: The Yamaha's
chassis, based on a twin-
spar aluminium frame, set
new handling standards.
The main innovation was
the blend of ultra-short
wheelbase and long
swingarm.*

Three numbers said it all about the YZF-
R1 with which Yamaha stunned the
superbike world in 1998. The four-
cylinder charger produced 150bhp, weighed just
389lb (176kg) and had an ultra-short wheelbase of
55in (1395mm). That made it the most powerful,
lightest and most compact large-capacity sports
bike ever built. And with its aggressive styling, the
R1 had the looks to match.

Beneath the sharp twin-headlamp fairing, the
R1 incorporated some clever engineering. Its basic
layout was Yamaha's familiar blend of 20-valve,
four-cylinder engine and aluminium twin-beam
frame. But the R1 design team, led by Kunihiko
Miwa, put the six-speed gearbox higher than
normal behind the liquid-cooled cylinders, making
the 998cc engine very compact. This in turn
allowed the bike to be very short while having a
long rear swingarm, as used by grand prix bikes for
added stability.

Innovative crankcase design

The R1's new engine also contributed with its
innovative one-piece cylinder and crankcase
assembly, which was stiffer than the conventional
design and allowed the powerplant to be used as a
stressed member of the chassis. This meant that the

R1's Deltabox II frame needed to be less strong, which helped explain how the bike could weigh less than most 600cc sportsters.

The R1 engine was a spectacular performer in its own right, never mind its contribution to the handling. The bike felt light, racy and purposeful, with low, narrow handlebars, high footpegs, a firm seat and the smallest of windscreens. And such was the motor's gloriously broad spread of power that the moment its throttle was wound open, the R1 hurtled forward as though fired from a canon.

It was not so much the fearsome acceleration when revved towards its 11,750rpm limit that made the Yamaha so special, nor even its 170mph (274km/h) top speed. Where the R1 engine really scored was in its flexibility, which ensured that smooth, addictively strong acceleration was always available, making it a supremely easy bike to ride very rapidly indeed.

And the R1's handling was equally impressive. The bike's combination of light weight, rigidity, racy dimensions and excellent suspension gave it the feel of a much smaller machine. This was an open-class bike that handled better than any 600cc sportster. The R1 was not infallible, and like many short, light, powerful bikes it shook its head under hard acceleration over a series of bumps. But most of the time the R1 just felt so responsive and controllable that its rider could seemingly do no wrong, despite the bike's sheer speed.

Specification	Yamaha YZF-R1 (1998)
Engine	Liquid-cooled dohc 20-valve four
Capacity	998cc (74 x 58mm)
Maximum power	150bhp @ 10,000rpm
Transmission	Six-speed, chain final drive
Frame	Aluminium twin spar
Suspension	Telescopic front; single shock rear
Brakes	Twin discs front; disc rear
Weight	389lb (176kg)
Top speed	170mph (274km/h)

Its front brake was a match for that of any rival, combining fierce power with plenty of feel. Detailing was generally good, notably the instrument console, which combined a digital speedometer and traditional analogue rev-counter with the welcome addition of a clock. Despite that useful touch the R1 was not a bike for everyday use. It was uncomfortable for its rider at slow speed, and hopeless for a pillion at any speed. It was so fast and furious that even some experienced riders found their needs better met by a slightly less focused alternative.

But for those who valued pure performance above all else, the YZF-R1 was simply sensational. Even before it had turned a wheel in anger, those figures for power, weight and wheelbase had made Yamaha's new star the world's best superbike on paper. On road and racetrack alike, it fully lived up to that promise.

BMW R1100S

**Top speed
140mph**
225km/h

*Right: High-compression
pistons and improved
breathing helped make the
1085cc engine BMW's most
powerful boxer motor ever.
Cylinder head covers were
magnesium to save weight.*

*Below: Swoopy styling, low
handlebars, bright yellow
paintwork, a high-level
exhaust system with under-
seat silencers, and a single-
sided swingarm all
combined to give the
R1100S a truly sporty look.*

The stylish and rapid R1100S arrived in
1998 to prove that BMW's traditional flat-
twin format was still very viable for high-
performance motorcycling. This was the most
aggressive roadgoing boxer that BMW had ever
built. The German firm referred to it as a 'sports-
tourer with the emphasis on sport', and the 1100S
was quick, agile and well-braked enough to hold its
own in serious company.

With its two sticking-out cylinder heads, there
was no mistaking that this bike was a BMW. But
the S had a very distinct style of its own, notably at
the front end with its big ellipsoidal headlamp lens.
The asymmetrical theme was echoed in the fuel cap
and instruments; further back, the rear end was
notably lean and sporty.

The new bike's 1085cc air-cooled engine, based
on the eight-valve, high-cam unit from the touring-
oriented R1100RS, made this BMW's most
powerful flat twin yet. It was tuned with new
pistons that gave increased compression ratio.

Breathing was also improved by a new air filter
design, plus a revised Motronic engine-
management system.

A new exhaust system, complete with twin
silencers in the tailpiece, also helped increase peak
output by 8bhp to 98bhp at 7500rpm. Forged
conrods helped keep the engine together at its
higher 8500rpm rev limit, and crankcase oil
circulation was improved. Although it retained

shaft final drive, the 1100S also had a new six-speed gearbox.

Much of BMW's effort in the R1100S's chassis design went in ensuring that this was not just the best-handling boxer yet, but also reasonably light. At 461lb (209kg) dry it was still heavier than its closest rivals – but not by much. Some of the weight-saving came from a new and lighter version of BMW's Telelever monoshock front suspension system, which featured a remote rebound damping adjustment knob in the steering head area.

Aluminium main frame

As with other four-valve boxers, the engine and gearbox housing were also stressed members of the chassis, but the 1100S differed in having an aluminium main frame. A tubular steel rear subframe supported the Paralever rear suspension system, which gave a clean and racy look from the left. Wheels were new, lighter 17-inchers wearing sticky radial rubber.

The mildly tuned boxer engine pulled well from low down, and revved with more enthusiasm than previous boxers. The S was very happy to sit at an indicated 85mph (137km/h), just under 5000rpm in top gear, feeling smooth, stable and unstressed. Above that figure the engine felt a bit harsh, but the BMW had plenty of acceleration in hand to a top speed of 140mph (225km/h).

It was the new bike's chassis that made the biggest impression, because this R1100S handled like no other BMW roadster. Its chassis geometry was close to the race-replica norm, and the bike impressed with the ease and precision with which it went round corners given a light flick of the sportily low-set handlebars.

The Telelever front end gave a great combination of quick steering and stability, particularly when braking hard into a turn. Suspension at both ends delivered plenty of

feedback, and was well-damped enough that the bike remained composed even when accelerating hard out of bumpy bends. The front-brake combination of four-piston Brembo calipers and 305mm discs was excellent, too.

The R1100S was a bike that stood out not for traditional BMW attributes such as long-distance comfort or refinement, but for light steering, powerful brakes and a liking for speed. It was an enjoyably fast, fine-handling machine that put BMW firmly in the sports bike market for the first time since the R90S of the mid-1970s.

Above left: Handling was excellent, with a light and neutral steering feel, reasonably firm and well-damped suspension, and impressive stability.

Above: Not everyone liked the asymmetrical headlight design, but this was one BMW that nobody could accuse of looking ordinary.

Specification	BMW R1100S (1998)
Engine	Air-cooled high cam eight-valve flat twin
Capacity	1085cc (99 x 70.5mm)
Maximum power	98bhp @ 7500rpm
Transmission	Six-speed, shaft final drive
Frame	Cast aluminium and tubular steel
Suspension	Telelever monoshock front; monoshock rear
Brakes	Twin discs front; single disc rear
Weight	461lb (209kg)
Top speed	140mph (225km/h)

Aprilia RSV Mille

**Top speed
170mph**
274km/h

*Right: The RSV's distinctive
and aerodynamic shape
owed much to Aprilia's
grand prix racebikes, and
incorporated a unique
triple-lens headlamp design.*

*Below: The view from the
left reveals the large and
highly rigid aluminium
swingarm which, like the
twin-spar frame, was
designed with the benefit of
Aprilia's long experience in
top-level racing.*

Aprilia's credentials for building a top-
class superbike were impeccable. The
firm from Noale in northern Italy had
risen rapidly from being a small producer of
lightweight bikes to become Europe's second
largest motorcycle manufacturer. Along the way,
Ivano Beggio's firm had taken on and beaten the
Japanese to win a string of world titles in the ultra-
competitive 250 and 125cc grand prix classes. So
nobody should have been surprised by the speed
and all-round ability of the RSV Mille, Aprilia's
first big four-stroke.

This was one very purposeful motorcycle. The
Mille was intended as the basis for a World
Superbike racer, plus a range of V-twin roadsters,
and its conservative styling had its origins in
Aprilia's wind tunnel. Similarly, the alloy twin-
beam frame and twin-sided swingarm were
designed by race department engineers not for
style, but to give maximum strength for minimum
weight. The exhaust system ended in a large

silencer on the right side, rather than twin pipes
under the seat, because that was the lightest way of
achieving the necessary volume.

There was much innovative engineering in the
Mille, notably in its 998cc, dohc V-twin
powerplant. After considering a Ducati-style 90-
degree V-twin, Aprilia decided instead to position
their engine's liquid-cooled cylinders at 60 degrees

apart, as this gave a more compact unit. A 60-degree V-twin also produces more vibration, which was cancelled by twin balancer shafts, one in front of the crankshaft plus a smaller shaft inside the rear cylinder head.

Competitive power output

Other notable engine features were the dry sump – more compact than the normal wet sump – and the 'power clutch', designed to prevent the rear wheel lifting under hard braking. In other respects the fuel-injected, eight-valve V-twin engine was unexceptional. Its internal dimensions were almost identical to those of the 90-degree motors from Ducati, Honda and Suzuki. Peak power was a competitive 128bhp at 9250rpm.

The rest of the Mille was conventional but very much state-of-the-art. Suspension comprised 43mm upside-down forks from Showa of Japan, and a rear shock from Sachs. At 416lb (189kg), the Mille was slightly lighter than its Ducati rival but weighed more than the lightest of the Japanese opposition. Neat details included a high-tech instrument panel which, as well as housing a big digital speedometer, could record up to 40 lap times.

The motor was superb: strong at the top end, torquey in the mid-range and with plenty of V-twin character. Revved hard, it zipped towards the 10,000rpm limit through the excellent six-speed gearbox, a racer-style red light flickering on the dashboard to let its rider know when to change up. That top-end rush had not been achieved at the expense of power lower down the scale, either. The Mille responded crisply from low engine speeds

and simply got stronger as the revs rose, heading towards its 170mph (274km/h) top speed.

If the motor was brilliant, the RSV's chassis was just as impressive, combining high speed stability (aided by a steering damper inside the fairing nose) with light, responsive steering. Its typical super-sports geometry, rigid frame and excellent suspension resulted in a bike that could corner with the best. The only slight disappointment was a Brembo front brake that required a firm squeeze of the lever for maximum stopping power.

Some critics complained that the Aprilia lacked a little Italian glamour, but its high-quality engineering and all-round performance more than made up for that. The RSV Mille was a brilliant first effort that fully succeeded in establishing Aprilia as a major league superbike manufacturer. And which, before long, also led to a competitive World Superbike racer and a range of fast and stylish V-twins.

Left: Aprilia surprised many people by setting its 998cc V-twin engine's cylinders at 60 degrees apart. The main advantage of the narrower angle was reduced length. The chief drawback, increased vibration, was addressed by twin balancer shafts.

Below: As well as allowing the engine to be shorter, the Mille unit's dry sump layout ensured that prolonged wheelies did not starve the motor of oil. Given the RSV's tempting blend of instant throttle response and light weight, this was probably just as well.

Specification	Aprilia RSV Mille (1998)
Engine	Liquid-cooled dohc eight-valve 60-degree V-twin
Capacity	998cc (97 x 67.5mm)
Maximum power	128bhp @ 9250rpm
Transmission	Six-speed, chain final drive
Frame	Aluminium twin spar
Suspension	Telescopic front; single shock rear
Brakes	Twin discs front; disc rear
Weight	416lb (189kg)
Top speed	170mph (274km/h)

Yamaha YZF-R7

**Top speed
180mph**
290km/h

*Right: Few production
bikes have looked better
with fairing removed. This
R7's top radiator is a
thicker race-kit component.*

*Below: In look and layout
the R7 echoed the R1, but
its engine and chassis were
considerably more exotic.*

Yamaha did not pull any punches in developing the YZF-R7, codenamed the OW02. The 749cc four was created as the basis for a challenger in the World Superbike championship, and was the most sophisticated and purposeful production motorcycle that Yamaha had ever built. With only 500 units being produced, it was also one of the rarest. And at almost three times the price of the firm's open-class flagship the YZF-R1, it was one of the most expensive.

More than any streetbike before it, the R7 was not simply a roadgoing machine that could be raced, but a competition motorcycle with lights and a starter-motor. The Yamaha's roots were clear from the layout of its engine, which shared the R1's five-valves-per-cylinder arrangement, one-piece cylinder-and-crankcase design, and vertically stacked gearbox.

Fuel-injected powerplant

Engine dimensions were identical to those of the YZF750SP, Yamaha's previous Superbike challenger. Unlike that bike the R7 was fuel-injected. Cylinder head parts were CNC (computer numeric control) machined, in Formula One racecar

Specification	Yamaha YZF-R7 (1999)
Engine	Liquid-cooled dohc 20-valve four
Capacity	749cc (72 x 46mm)
Maximum power	160bhp @ 13,700rpm (with race kit)
Transmission	Six-speed, chain final drive
Frame	Aluminium twin spar
Suspension	Telescopic front; single shock rear
Brakes	Twin discs front; disc rear
Weight	387lb (176kg) wet
Top speed	180mph (290km/h)

Nori's Narrow Miss

The YZF-R7 was designed for just one thing, and ultimately it failed to achieve it. After a disappointing learning year with the new bike in 1999, factory star Noriyuki Haga came close to lifting the World Superbike crown in 2000. But by the end of a season that was marred by a positive drug test following his use of a slimming aid during pre-season training, the Japanese ace finished second in the title race behind Honda's Colin Edwards. Yamaha then disbanded its World Superbike team. The R7's challenge was over.

style, to ensure precise dimensions and perfect balance between cylinders. The lightweight internals included titanium valves and conrods, plus forged pistons with nickel-plated tops for high-revving durability.

The chassis was equally exotic. The frame's black finish hinted that its design owed more to Yamaha's 500cc GP racers than to previous streetbikes. Those main frame spars incorporated an additional layer of aluminium, which helped give torsional stiffness twice that of the R1. Front forks were sophisticated 43mm upside-down units from Öhlins, who also supplied the rear shock. Steering geometry and swingarm pivot location were adjustable.

The R7 was designed to be fitted with a race-kit, although this was small because the bike required a minimum of modification to be competitive on the track. (Peak output without the kit was just 100bhp, to simplify worldwide homologation.) The most important component was the large carbon-fibre airbox, which transformed the intake set-up to provide a ram-air system. Other kit parts included a competition carbon-fibre exhaust muffler.

Low clip-on handlebars, rearset footrests and a single seat confirmed the R7's racy intent. The engine's reasonable flexibility made the bike easy to ride at modest speeds, but it was at high revs that those lightweight internals came into their own, sending the Yamaha howling forward with breathtaking force. In race-kitted form, the R7 produced roughly 160bhp at 13,700rpm; enough for a top speed of 180mph (290km/h).

The R7's rigid, ultra-adjustable chassis combined razor-sharp steering with amazing stability and precision. Every detail about road or track surface and traction was transmitted straight to the rider, allowing cornering control far in excess of a normal sports bike. Much credit went to the sublime Öhlins suspension. Large twin front disc brakes gave fierce stopping power, too.

Riding the R7 was a uniquely thrilling experience, but this bike was not built for ordinary roads or riders. Like its predecessor the OW01, a similarly exotic 750cc four of ten years earlier, the YZF-R7 was designed to bring World Superbike glory. The OW01 had won races but never the title. For the YZF-R7, only the delivery of Yamaha's first World Superbike championship would suffice.

Above left: Ironically the YZF-R7 was rarely seen in standard form with headlamps and mirrors, because the majority of the 500 built were used on the racetrack. Such was the demand that in many countries the R7 was initially sold only to riders with a suitably impressive racing CV. On road or track, the race-kit was an absolute necessity.

MV Agusta 750 F4

**Top speed
165mph**
266km/h

*Right: The F4's quartet of
high-level silencers gave a
unique rear view. Exhaust
and intake notes were tuned
for rider enjoyment as well
as performance.*

*Below: Indisputably one of
the world's most stylish
superbikes, the F4 echoed
the mighty MVs of the past
with its red and silver paint
scheme and four-cylinder
engine layout.*

If ever there was a bike that epitomized
the Italian love of glamour, speed and all
things mechanical it was the 750 F4 with
which MV Agusta was reborn in 1999. The F4 was
gorgeous and brilliantly engineered, from the tiny
twin headlights in its fairing's nose all the way to
the four cigar-shaped tailpipes that emerged from
beneath its sculpted tailpiece. It had performance,
handling, and a fascinating history. MV Agusta,
one of the world's most famous marques, was back
– in style.

The old MV firm from Gallarate, north of
Milan, had won 17 consecutive 500cc world
championships and built some of the world's fastest
and most exotic roadgoing superbikes before
production ended in the early 1980s. The marque
appeared dead until revived by Cagiva boss
Claudio Castiglioni. After almost a decade of
intermittent development, design genius Massimo
Tamburini completed a bike to rank with the
mighty Ducati 916, his previous creation.

The F4's innovative chassis combined a ladder-
like tubular steel main frame with cast swingarm
pivots. On the limited-edition Serie Oro (Gold
Series) F4, of which only 300 units were built,
these cast parts were made from magnesium instead
of the aluminium used for the mass-produced F4 S.
The forks, especially developed by Japanese
specialist Showa, were of an unprecedented 49mm
diameter. The six-piston brake calipers were

developed with Nissin; the tyres specially created by Pirelli. Tamburini's Cagiva Research Centre (CRC) designed the bodywork, which was made from lightweight carbon-fibre.

Ferrari engineers collaborated in the early design of the F4's 749cc engine, a liquid-cooled, 16-valve inline four that differed from Japanese rivals by having radial valves, which MV's engineers said gave better breathing. The F4 was also the only roadgoing bike to have a racebike-style removable 'cassette' gearbox. Tamburini designed the complex exhaust system after dismantling and studying the exhaust of Castiglioni's Ferrari F40.

Glorious exhaust note

The fuel-injected motor's peak output was 126bhp, so the 750cc F4 did not match open-class superbikes for outright speed. But the bike revved to 13,300rpm, made an improbably glorious exhaust note, and was seriously fast. The four-cylinder unit was smooth and sophisticated, too. It pulled crisply at low revs, and its six-speed gearbox was slick. There was no great step to the power delivery, just a steady increase as the yellow-faced rev-counter's needle swept round the dial and the F4 headed for its top speed of over 160mph (257km/h).

Handling was superb. At 406lb (184kg) dry the Serie Oro was very light. Its short wheelbase and racy steering geometry combined with the top-quality frame and suspension to make the bike wonderfully agile yet also very stable. At high speed in a straight line the bike was unshakeable, yet it could also be snapped into slow turns with the lightest of pressure, and was easy to flick from side to side. The brakes were very powerful, too, needing just a gentle squeeze of the lever to make the bike stop with massive force.

Specification	MV Agusta 750 F4 Serie Oro (1999)
Engine	Liquid-cooled dohc 16-valve four
Capacity	749cc (73.8 x 43.8mm)
Maximum power	126bhp @ 12,500rpm
Transmission	Six-speed, chain final drive
Frame	Tubular steel and cast magnesium
Suspension	Telescopic front; single shock rear
Brakes	Twin discs front; disc rear
Weight	406lb (184kg)
Top speed	165mph (266km/h)

Left: MV Agusta's enviable reputation was forged by the marque's 38 grand prix championships, including 18 in the 500cc class, and by fire-breathing four-cylinder superbikes of the 1970s.

Below left: The first 300 F4s were in exotic Serie Oro specification, with magnesium swingarm, frame castings and wheels, where the mass-produced F4 S used aluminium.

Below: Straight-line performance of the 749cc F4 could not quite match that of open-class sports machines, but the F4's stability and handling poise were exceptional.

For all its stunning looks and innovative technology, some cynics argued that the F4, even the ultra-expensive Serie Oro version, was no lighter or more powerful than Suzuki's much cheaper GSX-R750. But to assess the F4 in such terms was to miss the point – this was a bike that was one of the most stylish and immaculately detailed ever built, as well as one that will be forever remembered as the machine with which one of the great marques made its return. For the all-new F4 to be so beautiful, so fast and so very special was an achievement to match any in the long and glorious history of MV Agusta.

Buell Lightning X1

**Top speed
140mph**
225km/h

*Below: The X1 was much
more refined than previous
models but it was still very
much a Buell, complete
with trademark features
including a big airbox
sticking out on the right
side, plus the rear shock
unit and silencer sitting
horizontally beneath an air-
cooled Harley-Davidson
V-twin engine.*

 By late 1998, Erik Buell's lively and distinctive sports bikes had come a long way since the Wisconsin-based engineer and former racer's first model, more than ten years earlier. With their distinctive styling, upright riding position, tuned Harley V-twin motors and agile chassis, Buells had provided plenty of speed and handling along with more fun than just about anything else on two wheels.

But Buells had suffered some problems, too. Models such as the S1 Lightning had been rather eccentric, with their big, ugly air filter, truck-like exhaust, uncomfortably tiny seat, soft Harley footrests and tendency to overheat their rear cylinder. That was until late 1998, when Buell introduced the X1 Lightning.

The X1 proved that founder Erik Buell and his colleagues at Harley-Davidson, which by this time owned most of the company, listened to criticism. It combined typical Buell aggression with fresh styling, a smaller air filter, a belly pan to cover the silencer, a larger seat, normal footrests, and better cooling to engine parts including the rear cylinder. It also had a stiffer steel frame, new aluminium rear subframe and swingarm, plus uprated Showa suspension at front and rear.

Like other Buells the X1 was powered by an air-cooled, 45-degree pushrod V-twin that was intended for Harley's 1200 Sportster. Here it was hotted-up with Buell's 'Thunderstorm' cylinder heads, incorporating bigger valves, reworked ports and reshaped combustion chambers. A new fuel-injection system helped give a best yet peak output of 95bhp at 6200rpm. This was a pretty remarkable achievement given that a standard Sportster produced less than 60bhp.

Specification	**Buell** Lightning X1 (1999)
Engine	Air-cooled ohv pushrod four-valve 45-degree V-twin (Harley Sportster)
Capacity	1200cc (88.8 x 98.8mm)
Maximum power	95bhp at 6200rpm
Transmission	Five-speed, chain final drive
Frame	Tubular steel ladder
Suspension	Telescopic front; single shock rear
Brakes	Single disc front and rear
Weight	440lb (200kg)
Top speed	140mph (225km/h)

New Generation: the Firebolt XB9R

Further proof of Buell's forward-thinking approach came in the 2002 model year, when the firm unleashed its best and most competitive model yet: the Firebolt XB9R. This was one of the most innovative bikes that any firm had produced for years. Fuel was held in the huge twin-spar aluminium frame; and oil in the swingarm. Other distinctive features included a sharp nose fairing and a single perimeter front brake disc with six-piston caliper. Buell's development team completely reworked Harley's Sportster engine to produce a fuel-injected, 984cc air-cooled V-twin that produced 92bhp with a fairly broad spread of torque. That gave the light, ultra-short Buell lively straight-line performance to complement its brilliantly agile handling.

That meant the X1 was good for a genuine 140mph (225km/h), and the cleverly rubber-mounted motor felt amazingly smooth, too. There was a generous amount of mid-range torque, and the bike sat effortlessly at 70mph (113km/h) with instant acceleration on tap.

Sharpened geometry

The chassis was also impressive. Steering was light enough to allow rapid direction changes, due to the X1's sharpened geometry. Showa suspension parts worked well at the front and also at the rear, where the X1 retained the traditionally quirky Buell set-up with its under-slung shock working in tension rather than the normal compression.

The X1's front brake combination of six-piston caliper and huge single disc gave powerful stopping, though it was prone to fade when very hot. Detail work was improved from previous models, with generous steering lock, dashboard-mounted ignition switch, easily adjustable mirrors, under-seat storage, and other useful details.

Anyone wondering whether these civilizing touches disguised the fact that the X1 lacked Buell's traditional raw appeal had no need to worry – the X1 still felt suitably crazy. It was a more sophisticated, up-to-date machine whose old-style Buell fun factor was very much intact. Equally importantly, the X1 was confirmation that Harley-Davidson, Buell's new owner, intended to inject the effort and investment needed for success.

Above left: Buells had a liking for wheelies and the X1 was no different. The fuel-injected Lightning motor's throttle response was slightly less immediate than that of previous models, but its 95bhp output was the highest yet.

Honda X-11

**Top speed
160mph**
257km/h

The concept of a naked bike powered by Honda's Super Blackbird engine had seemed enticing ever since the ultra-fast 1137cc four's release in 1996. When the X-11 finally arrived three years later, it did so at considerable speed, if not quite with the style that had done so much to popularize unfaired machines from firms such as Ducati and Harley-Davidson.

Plain but entertaining

In contrast to the best of those bikes, the X-11 was rather a plain-looking creation. Its liquid-cooled engine was partially obscured by a large grey plastic radiator shroud that had been added in an attempt to make the X-11 more stable than the average naked bike at high speed. But if the big Honda lacked a little in visual appeal, it certainly was fun to ride.

This bike was much more than simply a stripped-down Super Blackbird. Honda detuned the 16-valve engine with revised fuel-injection and a new exhaust, reducing peak output from 150bhp to a still impressive 134bhp at 9000rpm. Other changes include a single instead of twin balancer shafts, and a five- instead of six-speed gearbox.

The frame combined the Blackbird's twin aluminium main spars with a new cast central section at the rear. This was used to mount the swingarm, and was designed to introduce a small amount of flex into the frame. According to Honda, this gave the rider 'more of a feeling of slowly settling into corners'.

Honda also claimed that the radiator shroud not only helped feed the airbox but also created

Above: The X-11 was too bulky to match the visual appeal of models such as Ducati's Monster, but its power and practicality provided compensation. The instrument cover diverted some of the wind from the rider's chest, and the plastic radiator shroud helped stability at high speed.

Right: The Honda's main frame spars were borrowed from the Super Blackbird but the cast central rear section was new, designed to introduce an amount of flex under cornering. Cynics were unconvinced, but the X-11 handled well for such a big bike.

CB1000: the Big One

The X-11 was not the first big naked bike that Honda had created by removing the fairing from a four-cylinder superbike. Several years earlier the CB1000, based on a detuned 16-valve powerplant from the CBR1000F sports-tourer, had combined a 97bhp output with neat styling inspired by the legendary CB1100R production racer. The CB1000, known as the Big One, was softly tuned and heavy, but had plenty of mid-range torque and a top speed of 140mph (225km/h). A few years later Honda revamped it to create the CB1300, which had an even torquier engine as well as better handling due to a comprehensively uprated chassis.

downforce on the front wheel, increasing high-speed stability. The small plastic instrument surround was also intended to divert wind from the rider at speed. All of which sounded improbable… until you actually rode the X-11.

There was enough top-end power for a maximum speed of 160mph (257km/h), and by naked bike standards the X-11 was superbly efficient at such velocities. Perhaps partly due to its radiator's downforce, the Honda remained rock solid when most unfaired bikes would have been verging on instability. Even the little instrument cover diverted enough wind to allow fast cruising in more comfort than on most unfaired machines.

Despite its size and weight, the bike was reasonably low, as refined as any Honda and really quite manageable at slow speeds. Its big four-cylinder engine was notably torquier and more responsive than the Super Blackbird's. Inevitably the X-11 didn't have the faired bike's thrilling top-end power rush, but in most situations the smooth surge of acceleration from low revs was very ample consolation.

For a big bike the Honda handled very well. Its steering was reasonably light, and the fairly basic suspension gave a firm ride while soaking up most bumps. The linked brake system, a tuned version of the Super Blackbird's Dual-CBS set-up, combined plenty of power with a reassuringly normal feel. Most people who rode the Honda loved it. The X-11 might have lacked the style of some naked rivals, but it was as fast and exciting as any of them.

Above left: When you're riding a naked bike that produces 134bhp, the occasional burn-out is almost impossible to resist.

Left: Detuning the Super Blackbird's 1137cc engine gave an even stronger mid-range response – ideal for an unfaired machine.

Specification	Honda X-11 (1999)
Engine	Liquid-cooled dohc 16-valve four
Capacity	1137cc (79 x 54mm)
Maximum power	134bhp at 9000rpm
Transmission	Five-speed, chain final drive
Frame	Aluminium twin beam
Suspension	Telescopic front; monoshock rear
Brakes	Twin discs front; disc rear
Weight	489lb (222kg)
Top speed	160mph (257km/h)

Harley-Davidson Dyna Super Glide Sport

**Top speed
110mph**
177km/h

Below: Only Harley-Davidson would call a bike like this the 'Sport', but by cruiser standards the model whose official name was FXDX was quick and handled well. The Twin Cam 88 motor's most obvious feature was its oval air-filter cover – and its extra power.

When Harley-Davidson introduced its Twin Cam 88 engine for the 1999 model year, the result was a range of bikes designed to take the old firm into the 21st century. The new powerplant was more powerful, stronger, and more refined. Seven models were fitted with the Twin Cam motor in its first year. The quickest and arguably the most impressive was the new Dyna Super Glide Sport.

By Harley standards the lean and basic Sport with its near-flat handlebars, black-finished Twin Cam 88 engine and relatively sporty chassis was light, agile and powerful. Its new Twin Cam 88 motor was the star of the show, retaining the look, sound and feel of a traditional Harley but putting out enough extra power and torque to make the new bike feel distinctly more lively.

Twin-cam engine

The Twin Cam 88 got its name from its twin camshafts – which still operated pushrods – and capacity of 88 cubic inches, or 1450cc; up from the 1340cc, 80-cube Evolution engine. Apart from its larger, oval-shaped air filter cover the new motor looked much like the Evolution unit. But besides its revised cam system and extra capacity, the 88 was strengthened throughout with larger bearings and better lubrication.

Demands for retained identity convinced Harley to persist with the traditional air-cooled, pushrod-operated, 45-degree V-twin layout. The knife-and-fork conrod arrangement, which allows cylinders to remain in line, also stayed – but within that format almost everything was changed. Just 18 of the 450 parts in the Evolution engine were retained.

Specification	Harley-Davidson Dyna Super Glide Sport (1999)
Engine	Air-cooled ohv four-valve pushrod 45-degree V-twin
Capacity	1450cc (95.3 x 101.6mm)
Maximum power	68bhp @ 5400rpm
Transmission	Five-speed, belt final drive
Frame	Steel twin downtube
Suspension	Telescopic front; twin shocks rear
Brakes	Twin discs front; disc rear
Weight	661lb (300kg)
Top speed	110mph (177km/h)

Above left: Wide handlebars gave a riding position that was fine for moderate cruising speeds, but soon got tiring at 100mph (161km/h).

Left: The slim Super Glide Sport was one of seven models fitted with the Twin Cam motor in 1999.

A new oval air-cleaner cover held an airbox that was 70 per cent larger. Breathing was also improved by the engine's higher compression ratio and reshaped combustion chambers. Harley insisted that performance gains were not simply due to the new twin-camshaft layout, but the overall increase was impressive. Peak power was 68bhp at 5400rpm, compared to nearer 50bhp for the Evolution engine.

From the rider's seat, the 88 motor's big advantage was its improved throttle response. The Sport was very lively both at low revs, where it pulled cleanly from below 2000rpm, and at higher speeds, where it accelerated from 70mph (113km/h) or more with an urgency that no previous standard Harley could approach – all the way to a genuine top speed of about 110mph (177km/h).

And the Sport's handling was good too. Chassis rigidity was increased by the design of the new engine, whose gearbox was more solidly bolted on. At 661lb (300kg) the Sport was no lightweight, but it felt reasonably agile and handled fairly well, aided by soft but well-controlled suspension. Its twin front discs gave a reasonable amount of braking power, too, despite their relatively low-tech caliper design.

The Super Glide Sport was an impressive departure for Harley, and not only for its new engine. It combined long-legged cruising ability with a fair turn of speed; stable handling with surprising agility; and simple, understated looks with the trademark Harley image and quality of finish. It was a fine bike that proved the Milwaukee firm was serious about performance as well as style.

The success of the Super Glide Sport, particularly in export markets, inspired Harley to take things a stage further just 12 months later. While the 1450cc Twin Cam motor was unchanged, the chassis was uprated with fully adjustable cartridge forks, sportier geometry, more sophisticated rear shocks, new brakes with four-piston calipers, plus a fatter, soft-compound rear tyre. The result was a bike that looked almost identical, but cornered and braked notably better not just than its predecessor, but than any previous Harley cruiser.

Above: This bike is a 2000 model Super Glide Sport, complete with uprated chassis. Its powerful four-piston front brake calipers, made by Harley's traditional supplier Hayes, were later fitted to other models too. The rear tyre was a wider, 150-section Dunlop in softer sport compound for extra grip.

Yamaha YZF-R6

**Top speed
165mph**
266km/h

More even than its rivals in the fiercely contested middleweight super-sports class, Yamaha's YZF-R6 was a fast and frenetic machine that thrived on high revs and dizzy cornering angles. On a twisty road or racetrack, very few bikes of any capacity were quicker or more fun to ride. The R6's peak output of 120bhp at 13,000rpm was a record for the 600cc class, making this the first production motorcycle ever to produce 200bhp per litre. And its chassis was just as good as its engine.

Essentially the 599cc motor was a smaller version of the YZF-R1's 998cc unit, with 16 valves instead of 20, and with a forced induction system fed via a duct between the headlights. The R1's compact stacked gearbox arrangement was also used on the smaller bike, as was the technique of casting barrels and crankcase as one piece, adding rigidity and allowing the engine to be used as a stressed member of the chassis.

This Yamaha's lightweight aluminium frame helped reduce total weight to a class-leading 373lb (169kg). The R6's aggressive styling was based on that of the bigger machine, and so was the racy riding position, which cramped legs and put a lot of weight on the rider's wrists. But the YZF-R6's even more extreme personality was hinted at by the rev-counter with its 15,500rpm redline. Yamaha billed the R6 as a no-compromise sportster that delivered an extreme riding experience, and one ride confirmed that this was no exaggeration.

Above: Light weight, radical geometry and compact size combined to make the YZF-R6 arguably the finest-handling production bike of all, although the ultra-racy Yamaha was sensitive to rider weight and suspension set-up. Few bikes were as demanding or as much fun for hard riding on road or track.

Right: The YZF-R6's family resemblance to the R1 and R7 models is clear at a glance. Like the bigger models, the middleweight had a top-class chassis incorporating twin-spar aluminium frame, multi-adjustable suspension and four-piston front brake calipers.

High-rev Heritage: the FZR600

Yamaha had a history of rev-happy middleweight fours even before the YZF-R6 was launched. Its predecessor, the FZR600, had a similarly uncompromising personality, and was itself based on the air-cooled FZ600 four that had been one of the revviest, sharpest-handling bikes of the 1980s. Like the R6, the FZR held a 599cc liquid-cooled, 16-valve engine in a twin-spar frame, in this case made from steel instead of aluminium. The FZR was light, at 395lb (179kg), and handled well. Its 90bhp output gave a very competitive top speed of 140mph (225km/h).

Specification	Yamaha YZF-R6 (1999)
Engine	Liquid-cooled dohc 16-valve four
Capacity	599cc (65.5 x 44.5mm)
Maximum power	120bhp @ 13,000rpm
Transmission	Six-speed, chain final drive
Frame	Aluminium twin spar
Suspension	Telescopic front; single shock rear
Brakes	Twin discs front; disc rear
Weight	373lb (169kg)
Top speed	165mph (266km/h)

The revvy, ultra-manoeuvrable little machine was great fun provided its rider was in the mood and on the right road. It responded best to frantic flicking up and down through the six-speed gearbox to keep the revs above 12,000rpm. In town or traffic, though, the Yamaha's peakiness made life difficult. Its motor was smooth at low revs but lacked punch until the rev-counter needle was in the top half of the dial, so overtaking often required a couple of down-changes.

At home on the track

On the other hand the R6 was arguably even more satisfying than torquier large-capacity bikes when its rider encountered a series of bends and got everything just right. That was even more true on a racetrack, where the Yamaha howled out of bends with amazing speed for a 600, heading towards a top speed of 165mph (266km/h).

On road or track the Yamaha was impressively stable at very high speed, yet it was also supremely agile and easy to steer. The blend of chassis rigidity, light weight and firm, well-damped suspension gave handling that few bikes of any capacity could better. Braking power was even more outstanding, thanks to twin front discs and calipers borrowed from the R1.

Practicality was not the lean and racy R6's strong suit, although it offset its hunched-forward riding position, firm suspension, lack of centrestand and thin seat by at least having pillion grab-handles as an optional accessory. For commuting or touring there were plenty of better middleweights. But for high-revving thrills on road or track, the R6 set the middleweight standard.

Above left: Unlike the YZF-R1, the R6 benefited from a ram-air induction system, fed via a slot between the headlights. As well as being widely regarded as the fastest and best-handling of the middleweight fours in standard form, the Yamaha confirmed its top-level performance potential when German star Jörg Teuchert won the Supersport world championship in 2000.

Suzuki Hayabusa

**Top speed
190mph**
306km/h

*Below: The Hayabusa was
far from the world's most
attractive superbike, but it
was almost certainly the
most aerodynamically
efficient. Suzuki's engineers
spent hours in the wind
tunnel fine-tuning not only
its fairing, but also the
mirrors, front mudguard
and seat hump. The GSX's
slippery shape made a vital
contribution to its amazing
straight-line speed.*

With its drooping fairing nose, large front
mudguard and bulbous tail section,
Suzuki's Hayabusa was by common
consent one of the least attractive superbikes ever
launched by a major manufacturer. Yet the bike was
a big success, and few riders who bought one had a
bad word to say about its looks. There was a simple
reason for that: the Hayabusa was designed this
way to make it fast – and the result was a
phenomenal top speed of 190mph (306km/h).

Suzuki's objective had been to create the fastest
bike in the world, which meant beating Honda's
Super Blackbird. That they succeeded was due in
no small part to the ugly but aerodynamically
efficient bodywork of the model known as the
GSX1300R. To celebrate, Suzuki named the bike
Hayabusa after an aggressive, fast-flying Japanese
peregrine falcon whose prey just happened to
include blackbirds.

Record-breaking horsepower

Beneath the bodywork the GSX was not especially
hi-tech. Its 1298cc motor was essentially a larger,
revamped version of the twin-cam, 16-valve unit
from Suzuki's GSX-R1100. The new unit had
bigger valves and a reshaped combustion chamber.
A gear-driven counterbalancer allowed it to be
solidly mounted, increasing chassis rigidity. Fuel-
injection and a ram-air system – which forced cool
air into the engine via the slots in the fairing nose –
helped produce 173bhp at 9800rpm, a record for a
production streetbike.

Chassis layout was conventional, with a twin-
beam aluminium frame, upside-down front forks,
and six-piston front brake calipers squeezing large
12.6in (320mm) discs. Other notable features were
the vertically stacked twin headlights, which
allowed the fairing nose to be narrow, and the ultra-
thin, lightweight instrument panel.

The Hayabusa's speed-influenced styling was much criticized, but to Suzuki's credit there was much more to the bike than pure performance. For such a powerful machine it was versatile and easy to ride. At 473lb (215kg) the GSX was reasonably light, and its riding position was roomy and comfortable. Despite having a steering damper to aid stability, its steering was effortless and precise.

Even so, the main impression was one of outrageous power and speed. The big motor delivered instant, supremely strong acceleration throughout the rev range. Whether its tachometer needle was indicating 4000rpm or 9000rpm, the Hayabusa blasted forward like a guided missile. Provided its rider could keep the front wheel on the ground, it stormed through a standing quarter-mile in just ten seconds, reaching 60mph (97km/h) in under three. Even at 150mph (241km/h) there was strong acceleration on tap. The bike was capable of showing more than 200mph (322km/h) on its slightly optimistic speedometer.

All that straight-line performance would have been a liability if the Hayabusa had not handled well, but Suzuki had put as much effort into the chassis as the engine. The frame was very rigid, and suspension at front and rear was excellent, giving a firm ride, yet soaking up most bumps. The brakes were very powerful, the specially developed Bridgestone tyres were grippy, and ground clearance was good. Some riders complained that the low, wind-cheating screen gave inadequate protection. But few had any serious complaints, especially in 2000 when the Hayabusa fought off Kawasaki's ZX-12R to retain its unofficial 'world's fastest bike' title.

Some politicians and bureaucrats were less impressed, however. The following year, in response to a voluntary agreement between the major manufacturers (who were worried about future legal problems), Suzuki fitted the GSX with an electronic device that prevented it from reaching maximum revs in top gear, limiting top speed to 186mph (300km/h). The Hayabusa's wings had been clipped – but its status as the fastest bike on the road looked safe for some time to come.

Above: At high speed the Hayabusa's ram-air system, fed via slots in the fairing nose, provided even more power.

Below left: The view from the front was shaped almost entirely by scientific testing in the wind tunnel.

Specification	Suzuki GSX1300R Hayabusa (1999)
Engine	Liquid-cooled dohc 16-valve four
Capacity	1298cc (81 x 63mm)
Maximum power	173bhp @ 9800rpm
Transmission	Six-speed, chain final drive
Frame	Aluminium twin spar
Suspension	Telescopic front; single shock rear
Brakes	Twin discs front; disc rear
Weight	473lb (215kg)
Top speed	190mph (306km/h)

The 21st Century
Faster, Lighter, Stronger

The two-wheeled trend in the early years of the new millennium was towards specialization. Super-sports bikes became even more powerful, light and fast; typified by Suzuki's 185mph (298km/h) GSX-R1000. This development was inspired partly by the use of bikes on circuit 'track days', the popularity of which had grown rapidly in many countries in response to the difficulty of unleashing such fearsome performance on public roads.

Another machine that said much about superbiking in the early 21st century was Kawasaki's ultra-powerful ZX-12R, which was restricted to a 186mph (300km/h) top speed. This limit was agreed by the major manufacturers to avoid lower, government-imposed speeds being forced upon them.

Honda FireBlade

**Top speed
170mph**
274km/h

*Right: The fifth generation
FireBlade was the most
comprehensively modified
version yet, combining an
uprated engine with new
frame, bodywork, upside-
down forks and a 17-inch
front wheel.*

*Below: Honda's 'pivotless'
frame was designed to allow
a limited amount of flex,
although its main spars were
stiffer than the old model's.
The aluminium swingarm
pivoted in the engine.*

Honda's stunningly fast and light
CBR900RR had taken the superbike
world by storm back in 1992, establishing
an unmatched reputation for performance and agile
handling. But although the FireBlade remained
very popular through the 1990s and was updated
several times, subsequent models were notable
more for their refinement than for the raw
excitement of the original.

Then, in 2000, Honda struck back with a much
modified new generation 'Blade, known as the
CBR929RR in the States. The new machine's vital
statistics alone were enough to prove just how
serious Honda was. The CBR produced 150bhp and
weighed just 375lb (170kg), making it 22bhp more
powerful and 22lb (10kg) lighter than the previous
year's version – and giving it a small but distinct
advantage, at least on paper, over its arch rival,
Yamaha's YZF-R1.

Honda's engineers, led by 'father of the
FireBlade' Tadao Baba, threw everything at this
model, which held a much-modified engine,
enlarged from 918 to 929cc, in a completely new
chassis. The liquid-cooled motor's new capacity
was achieved by using shorter-stroke dimensions,
which allowed larger valves. Reshaped, forged
pistons, a narrower valve angle and more compact
combustion chamber also contributed to the
increased power.

Pivotless frame design

A digital fuel-injection system replaced the previous carburettors. The partly titanium exhaust system incorporated a Yamaha-style valve, and there were numerous changes in the chassis. Frame design was a variant of Honda's 'pivotless' layout, designed to permit a controlled amount of flex near the centre of gravity. For the first time the RR's front wheel was 17 inches in diameter. Upside-down forks also made a first appearance.

The Honda also looked different when viewed from the saddle, thanks to its slimmer fuel tank plus a new digital speedometer in the cockpit. More importantly, it was distinctly livelier too. The previous CBR had been fast and agile, but this bike was in a different league thanks to its ultra-light weight and added power. It responded to a sub-5000rpm tweak of the throttle in top gear by accelerating crisply and hard, charging smoothly and with no real power step towards the 11,500rpm redline. The 16-valve motor was hugely strong at the top end, too, sending the CBR storming towards a top speed of about 170mph (274km/h).

Handling was magical, thanks to the blend of frame rigidity, excellent suspension and light weight. The suspension required careful fine-tuning, but once set up correctly the Honda steered quickly, yet stayed stable despite the lack of a steering damper. An uprated front brake combination of four-piston calipers and huge discs supplied phenomenal stopping power.

Honda's revisions had not only produced the best FireBlade ever, they had put the CBR right back in contention for the unofficial title of world's fastest and best sports bike. In many respects the CBR and its YZF-R1 rival were too closely matched to split. For street riding the CBR's sophistication and reliability record counted in its favour. One thing was beyond doubt: on road and track, the FireBlade was right back on the pace.

Sharper Still: the 2002 CBR

For 2002 Honda revamped the FireBlade once again, with an enlarged, 954cc engine that earned it the name CBR954RR in the States. A revised fuel-injection system plus the extra 25cc of capacity increased peak power by 3bhp (claimed output remained 150bhp due to a different method of measurement). More aggressively shaped bodywork, a frame stiffened at the steering head, a new swingarm and titanium exhaust muffler combined to reduce weight to 370lb (168kg) – and to produce the fastest, lightest and most outrageously rapid FireBlade yet.

Above left: This FireBlade – or CBR929RR in America, where the 'Blade name was not officially used – had a reshaped fairing plus slimmer tank and seat.

Left: Honda's aim of achieving 'total control' had paid off. When correctly set up, the CBR was arguably the best-handling open-class superbike of all.

Specification	Honda CBR929RR FireBlade (2000)
Engine	Liquid-cooled dohc 16-valve four
Capacity	929cc (74 x 54mm)
Maximum power	150bhp @ 11,000rpm
Transmission	Six-speed, chain final drive
Frame	Aluminium twin spar
Suspension	Telescopic front; single shock rear
Brakes	Twin discs front; disc rear
Weight	375lb (170kg)
Top speed	170mph (274km/h)

Aprilia Mille R

**Top speed
170mph**
274km/h

*Below: With its black
paintwork and single seat
the Mille R resembled both
Aprilia's full factory
Superbike racer and the
RSV Mille SP that was
intended strictly for
professional racers. In
contrast to the expensive
and exotic SP model, the R
shared the basic Mille's
engine and frame, and had
a more affordable price.*

 Just a year after entering the superbike
market with the RSV Mille, Aprilia made
an impressive World Superbike debut
when Australian ace Peter Goddard rode the V-twin
to 12th place in the 1999 championship. For the
following year Aprilia introduced an uprated
roadster, the Mille R. With its black paintwork and
single seat, the R resembled the works Superbike.
And although designed primarily for the street, it
had some of the feel, as well as the look, of the
factory machine.

The 998cc, liquid-cooled, 60-degree V-twin
motor had a few new features. Its fuel-injection
mapping was tuned to improve low-rev output and
smoothness, and the clutch was revised with
braided hose plus internal changes. The dohc eight-
valve motor's claimed peak output of 128bhp at
9500rpm matched that of the standard Mille, whose
engine was similarly uprated.

Although the R's aluminium twin-spar main
frame sections were identical to those of the
standard RSV, the single-seat model saved weight
with a smaller aluminium rear subframe.
Elsewhere, the R's chassis was uprated. Front
suspension comprised 43mm upside-down racing
forks from Öhlins, complete with anti-friction
titanium nitride coating on the sliders. The Swedish
firm also provided the rear shock unit, plus the
transversely mounted steering damper.

Aprilia's engineers made much effort to cut
weight. Both mudguards were made from carbon-
fibre. Further savings came from a lighter battery
and from the fuel tank, which was made from a
lightweight resin. Wheels were made from forged,
rather than the normal cast, aluminium. These and
other weight-saving efforts reduced dry weight to
407lb (185kg), which was 9lb (4kg) down on the
standard Mille.

Smooth and flexible motor

The big V-twin engine was hugely impressive: smooth, flexible, and very powerful too. The Mille R thundered out of turns with a lazy feel and an impressively high rate of acceleration, heading for a top speed of 170mph (274km/h). It revved hard enough to hit the 10,500rpm limiter unless its rider flicked rapidly through the smooth six-speed gearbox, in response to the flash of red warning light in the Aprilia's sophisticated electronic instrument console.

Handling was the Mille R's forte, which was no surprise given the quality of its chassis. The Aprilia snapped into the turns with minimal effort at the handlebars, helped by the lightweight front end's reduced inertia. It steered with a superbly neutral feel, and was unshakeable through fast curves and slow, bumpy bends alike. Stopping power was exceptional, too, thanks to an uprated Brembo front brake system that improved on the original RSV's rather disappointing set-up.

Despite its race-derived look, most people bought the Mille R mainly for riding on the road, where its blend of effortless power, light yet stable handling and excellent build quality made for a very impressive sports bike. On the racetrack, too, the Mille R was impressive. Encouragingly for Aprilia, the same thing was increasingly true of the similarly styled works racer, as the booming black V-twin became established as a major force in the World Superbike series.

Sports-touring RSV: the Futura

Aprilia's plan to create a family of superbikes around its 60-degree V-twin engine led in 2001 to the Futura. Beneath the sports-tourer's angular bodywork, the fuel-injection and intake systems were modified to give extra low-rev torque, a more refined feel and reduced output of 113bhp. The aluminium frame was modified for a more upright riding position and less racy geometry. A new exhaust system with single silencer beneath the seat allowed room for panniers. The Futura was a refined and comfortable bike with excellent handling, plenty of smooth acceleration and a top speed of over 150mph (241km/h).

Above left: The Mille R's front end combined classy titanium nitride-coated Öhlins upside-down forks with a triple-lens headlamp like that of the standard RSV.

Left: Light weight, an ultra-rigid frame plus top class suspension components gave the Mille R superb handling on road or track.

Specification	Aprilia RSV Mille R (2000)
Engine	Liquid-cooled dohc eight-valve 60-degree V-twin
Capacity	998cc (97 x 67.5mm)
Maximum power	128bhp @ 9500rpm
Transmission	Six-speed, chain final drive
Frame	Aluminium twin spar
Suspension	Telescopic front; single shock rear
Brakes	Twin discs front; disc rear
Weight	407lb (185kg)
Top speed	170mph (274km/h)

Kawasaki ZX-12R

**Top speed
186mph**
300km/h

*Below: With more than
170bhp on tap, a flick of the
throttle in first gear was all
it took to get the ZX-12R's
front wheel lifting. The
Kawasaki's performance
was even more impressive
at high speed due to its
ram-air induction system.
Its intake slot protruded
from the fairing, below the
headlights, to an area of
undisturbed high air
pressure.*

The mean and rapid ZX-12R with which
Kawasaki entered the new millennium
was a potent reminder that the firm that
had made its name with big, four-cylinder
superbikes was still a major force. With its rocket-
like acceleration and top speed of almost 190mph
(307km/h), the ZX-12R challenged Suzuki's
Hayabusa for the title of world's fastest superbike.
Yet amid confusion regarding its precise power
output came reports that the ZX-12R had become
the first bike to be affected by the manufacturers'
agreement to limit top speed to 186mph (300km/h),
for fear of more drastic government-imposed
restrictions.

In the real world, away from deserted airstrips
and electronic timing lights, such figures mattered
little. What was certain was that the ZX-12R, like
its main rival, was very, very fast. Equally
importantly, it soon became apparent that Kawasaki
had not fallen into the trap of concentrating on pure
speed to the detriment of all else. The ZX-12R also

worked well at more normal velocities, and was a
good looking and technically interesting bike.

Ironically the 1199cc, liquid-cooled engine was
not the bike's outstanding feature. The dohc 16-
valve unit was essentially an enlarged version of
the motor from Kawasaki's 900cc ZX-9R, with
fuel-injection instead of carburettors. A ram-air
induction system supplied the engine from the duct
that stuck out below the twin headlights, helping
boost peak output to a heady 176bhp at 11,000rpm.

The most innovative part of the Kawasaki was
its monocoque (one-piece) hollow aluminium
frame. This was like nothing previously seen on a
production motorcycle, although the firm had used
something similar on its KR500 grand prix racer in
the 1980s. By dispensing with the normal beams
running outside the motor, Kawasaki had been able
to design a stiff structure that allowed the machine
to be narrower, improving aerodynamics. The
hollow frame also formed the large airbox. Fuel
lived under the seat, lowering the centre of gravity.

Other chassis parts were conventional. However the ZX-12R benefited from the work of engineers from the giant Kawasaki corporation's aircraft division, whose input resulted in the small wings on each side of the fairing. These were not for downforce but to prevent turbulent air off the front wheel from disturbing flow along the bike. Such things were important at the high speeds that the ZX-12R reached with tempting ease.

Violent yet docile

This deceptively ordinary looking bike was capable of tearing from a standstill to 140mph (225km/h) in just ten seconds and a quarter of a mile. Even at that speed the ZX-12R still had plenty of acceleration in hand. Yet this most violent of machines was also very docile. Peak power arrived close to the 11,500rpm redline, but the Kawasaki pulled crisply from 2000rpm. This made for easy town riding, plus effortless travel with minimal use of the six-speed gearbox.

The motor was smooth, too, although annoyingly its main patch of vibration arrived at a common top-gear cruising speed of 80mph (129km/h). Comfort was good in other respects, thanks to a roomy riding position and reasonable wind protection. And the ZX handled well for a bike weighing 462lb (210kg). Its geometry was fairly sporty and its suspension firm. The 12R was a reasonably agile yet stable bike that encouraged spirited cornering, and its six-piston front brake calipers gave plenty of power and feel.

Despite all the speculation before its launch, the ZX-12R proved slightly slower than the Hayabusa in most independent tests. But it was an impressive machine, even so – a stunningly fast, pleasantly flexible, stylish, comfortable and versatile bike that brought Kawasaki's reputation for four-cylinder performance hurtling into the 21st century.

Above left: Straights were the ZX-12R's speciality, but it was very happy in corners too.

Above: The small wing below the fairing logo was to prevent airflow being disturbed by turbulence from the front wheel.

Left: Although shaped for aerodynamics, the ZX-12R was handsome – especially in Kawasaki green.

Specification	Kawasaki ZX-12R (2000)
Engine	Liquid-cooled dohc 16-valve four
Capacity	1199cc (83 x 55.4mm)
Maximum power	176bhp @ 11,000rpm
Transmission	Six-speed, chain final drive
Frame	Aluminium monocoque
Suspension	Telescopic front; single shock rear
Brakes	Twin discs front; disc rear
Weight	462lb (210kg)
Top speed	186mph (300km/h)

Bimota SB8K

**Top speed
165mph**
266km/h

*Right: The SB8K's engine
was the powerful 996cc
V-twin from Suzuki's
TL1000, modified with a
new Weber Marelli fuel-
injection system and a high-
level exhaust.*

*Below: The sleek SB8K
shared the previous SB8R's
aluminium and carbon-fibre
frame, but not its air
intakes leading into the top
of the fuel tank.*

 Bimota caused a sensation at the start of the 2000 World Superbike season when the small and financially troubled Italian firm's rider, Australian Anthony Gobert, won a race at only the team's second ever meeting. Gobert's machine was Bimota's new SB8K, powered by Suzuki's TL1000R V-twin engine. Although the win owed much to an inspired tyre choice on a damp Philip Island track, it gave Bimota a huge boost and focused attention on the SB8K.

The production SB8K roadster on which Gobert's racer was closely based was essentially a homologation special: a redesigned, more aerodynamic and slightly more powerful version of the previous SB8R model, which used the same 996cc engine. Bimota planned to build only 150 units in 2000; the minimum number required by World Superbike rules.

Like the SB8R, the K model was an exotic machine that combined the TL's liquid-cooled, 90-degree V-twin engine with a frame whose twin aluminium main spars incorporated carbon-fibre sections at the swingarm pivot. In Bimota tradition the eight-valve motor remained internally standard, though the SB8K gained a little power from a new Weber Marelli unit with larger, 59mm throttle bodies for improved high-speed flow.

The new bike's larger airbox was fed by a conventional system from the fairing nose, rather

than the SB8R's more flamboyant arrangement of large ducts running up over the fuel tank. Bimota optimistically claimed that the SB8K, which was also modified with revised injection mapping and a new high-level exhaust, produced 149bhp, fully 15bhp more than the standard Suzuki.

There was no change to the SB8R's composite main frame or the suspension: thick 46mm Paioli upside-down forks plus a horizontally mounted Öhlins shock, situated inside the right frame spar and worked by an aluminium rod from the swingarm. But the race-ready SB8K incorporated some extra details including adjustable swingarm pivot points for tuning racetrack handling.

Thunder and aggression

At 379lb (172kg) the SB8K was slightly lighter than the SB8R and a substantial 55lb (25kg) down on the TL1000R. This combined with the extra power to give storming straight-line performance. The Bimota's big V-twin power pulses sent the bike thundering forward with even more force and aggression than riders of the ultra-torquey Suzuki had come to expect.

The SB8K was wonderfully responsive in the lower gears, although it had a stiffer throttle action than the TL, which made accelerating smoothly while leant over in mid-corner more difficult. At higher revs the Bimota really started making use of it big throttle bodies, as it charged towards it top speed of over 160mph (257km/h).

Although the blend of potent V-twin motor, light weight, short wheelbase and racy geometry could have made the bike a real handful, the

Specification	Bimota SB8K (2000)
Engine	Liquid-cooled dohc eight-valve 90-degree V-twin (Suzuki TL1000R)
Capacity	996cc (98 x 66mm)
Maximum power	149bhp @ 8500rpm
Transmission	Six-speed, chain final drive
Frame	Aluminium and carbon-fibre twin spar
Suspension	Telescopic front; monoshock rear
Brakes	Twin discs front; disc rear
Weight	379lb (172kg)
Top speed	165mph (266km/h)

SB8K's rigid frame and top-quality suspension ensured otherwise. It steered quickly and easily, yet stayed stable even under hard acceleration. Fat radial tyres gave typically high levels of grip, and Brembo's front brake set-up was powerful.

Demand for the SB8K was strong and took off following Gobert's remarkable victory at his home round in Philip Island, but things went downhill fast for Bimota. Firstly the racebike suffered a string of mechanical problems, one of which caused Gobert to crash heavily. Then the race team was disbanded in mid-season, after a main sponsor disappeared owing a large amount of money.

Finally Bimota, already in severe financial trouble following the disastrous introduction of the 500 V-due, with it clean-burning but unreliable two-stroke engine, found itself in a worse financial position than ever before. Production ceased completely before most of the SB8Ks had been completed, and the future looked bleak for the famous and forward-thinking Rimini firm which, for almost 30 years, had built some of the world's fastest and finest superbikes.

Above: The factory SB8K scored a surprise victory at rider Anthony Gobert's home round in Australia, but then suffered a series of mechanical problems, one of which resulted in a high-speed crash in Japan. Bimota's race team lacked development budget even before the troubled Italian firm's sponsor disappeared.

Left: Few SB8Ks were produced before Bimota ceased production, but nobody who rode the V-twin could fail to be impressed by it power, flexibility and light weight. Ironically demand for the SB8K was strong when Bimota ceased production due to debt.

Marine Turbine Technologies Y2K

**Top speed
250mph***
402km/h
*estimated

*Below: With its fairing
fitted the Y2K looked long
and slightly unusual but
gave few clues about the
unique nature of its
powerplant. Front
suspension was by upside-
down forks, which held a
17-inch carbon-fibre Dymag
wheel. The turbine's lack of
engine braking meant extra
work for the six-piston front
brake calipers.*

With a power output of 286bhp and a top speed of well over 200mph (322km/h), the bike that was named Y2K and produced by Louisiana firm Marine Turbine Technologies was almost certainly the most powerful and fastest motorcycle ever to go into series production. Given that Y2K was powered by a gas turbine engine previously used in a helicopter, its performance was hardly surprising.

Jet engines had been used to power drag-racing bikes and a few one-off creations before, but this was the first time that such a machine was produced for roadgoing use. Despite Y2K's price of US $150,000, there was enough demand for Marine Turbine to build and sell a small series of machines over the next few years.

Jet aero engine

With a Rolls-Royce badge on its nose – the turbine was Rolls' Allison 250 as used in the Bell JetRanger – and emitting a high-pitched whine of a kind normally heard on an airport runway, Y2K seemed the most improbable of bikes. But in one way, it made perfect sense. Marine Turbine Technologies (MTT) specialized in taking 'timed-out' jet aero engines – units that had reached the strict limits on running hours, imposed for safety reasons – and using them in new applications, from boats to fire pumps plus the occasional four-wheeled vehicle.

When MTT president Ted McIntyre decided to add a motorcycle to his firm's range, he appointed Christian Travert, a former bike racer and custom

builder, to head the project. Jet engines run best at a constant speed, and in helicopter use the turbine's compressor spun at over 50,000rpm. For motorcycle use, Travert added a gearbox and clutch to take drive through 90 degrees to a sprocket, and from there by chain to the rear wheel.

The motor ran on diesel. 'It can use anything from normal pump gas to tequila or even Chanel perfume,' said Travert. 'But diesel burns most efficiently, so that's what makes most power.' Travert also designed and built the chassis, which was similar in layout to that of a normal superbike – but much larger and stronger. A twin-beam aluminium frame held conventional Öhlins front forks and rear shock.

If that sounded almost normal, riding the Y2K was anything but. The bike had a small TV screen in the cockpit (connected to a rear-facing camera) instead of mirrors. When the starter button was pressed the turbine picked up speed, its whine rising to a shriek, until the rev-counter showed 20,000rpm, from which point ignition occurred spontaneously and the bike was ready to go.

Low-speed acceleration was unexceptional due to the tall gearing dictated by a two-speed gearbox with automatic transmission. Then the bike came alive, accelerating from 50mph (80km/h) with thrilling force and a smoothness that was almost eerie. Given the engine's power and the way that Y2K scorched from a standstill to an independently recorded 227mph (365km/h) in just 15 seconds, MTT's claims of 250mph (402km/h) performance were entirely believable.

The turbine-powered machine was too long to handle like a sports bike, and required plenty of effort from its rider on a twisty road. But it was impressively stable both in a straight line and through fast curves. Its disc brakes were powerful, too, and

were needed often because shutting the throttle did not make the turbine slow in the normal way.

Despite Y2K's high price, MTT found a steady demand for what had to be the world's most outrageous production superbike. One bonus was that the gas turbine-powered machine came with an engine warranty for the life of the original owner. As Ted McIntyre put it, 'Anyone who blows up one of these and lives deserves a new engine.'

Specification	Marine Turbine Technologies Y2K (2000)
Engine	Rolls-Royce Allison 250 gas turbine
Capacity	N/a
Maximum power	286bhp @ 52,000rpm (compressor rpm)
Transmission	Two-speed automatic, chain final drive
Frame	Aluminium twin spar
Suspension	Telescopic front; single shock rear
Brakes	Twin discs front; disc rear
Weight	418lb (190kg)
Top speed	250mph (402km/h) estimated

Cagiva V-Raptor

**Top speed
150mph**
241km/h

Right: The Suzuki V-twin engine's abundance of mid-range torque, well controlled by Cagiva's new fuel-injection system, made the V-Raptor ideal for wheelies.

Below: The V-Raptor's sharp styling had little practical value but succeeded in giving the Cagiva a distinctive look, despite its familiar format of V-twin engine and tubular steel ladder frame.

 Cagiva made a high-profile debut as a superbike manufacturer with the Raptor and V-Raptor, a pair of fast and eye-catching machines powered by the 996cc V-twin engine from Suzuki's TL1000S. The Italian firm owned MV Agusta and had already begun production of that marque's 750 F4, but the Raptors were the first superbikes to be sold under Cagiva's own name, previously best known for small bikes.

With their unfaired V-twin engines, aggressive styling and Italian origin, the Raptors had obvious similarities with Ducati's Monster, which had rejuvenated the naked bike market following its launch in 1993. That connection was no coincidence, because the Raptors' designer, Argentinean-born Miguel Galluzzi, was also the creator of the original naked Ducati V-twin.

The V-Raptor, in particular, looked very striking, with its sharp beak from which dramatic fake air-scoops led back to the fuel tank. Its style matched its name, too: Raptor is a Latin word for

bird of prey. Like the basic Raptor, which looked rather Monster-like, the V-Raptor incorporated some neat details, including the centrally placed triangular tachometer (with digital speedometer underneath) and the claw-like castings below the rear footrests.

Smoother low-rev delivery

Cagiva's development team kept the TL's 90-degree, eight-valve, liquid-cooled engine internally standard, but reprogrammed the fuel-injection system, and fitted new intake and exhaust systems with the aim of smoothing out low- and medium-rev power delivery. The engine lost a few horsepower in the process, but Cagiva's claimed output of 105bhp at 8500rpm, well down on the TL1000S's 123bhp, was misleading because the Italian firm took its measurement at the rear wheel, not at the crankshaft like most other manufacturers.

Cagiva's intake and exhaust tuning succeeded in making the low-rev delivery slightly more user-friendly, and its mid-range output remained thrillingly strong. Whether it was accelerating crisply from as little as 2000rpm, or charging forward as the tachometer needle flicked towards the 10,300rpm redline, the V-Raptor's engine delivered torque on demand. Top speed was 150mph (241km/h), vibration was minimal, and the six-speed gearbox was slick.

Chassis design was based on a Ducati-style tubular steel frame, and generally did a very good job of coping with the big V-twin unit's output. A semi-elliptical steel swingarm worked the vertically mounted Sachs shock; front suspension was by Marzocchi upside-down forks. Both ends were well-damped but fairly soft, giving a ride that was comfortable in town and also worked reasonably well at higher speeds.

At 434lb (197kg) the V-Raptor was respectably light (the standard model was slightly lighter). Although steering geometry was not particularly sporty, the V-Raptor, in particular, had wide handlebars that gave enough leverage to allow quick, neutral steering. The Brembo front brake did not quite have the power of some systems, but was adequate for the V-Raptor's roadster role.

Predictably the basic Raptor was very similar to ride although it drew much less attention when parked. Its slightly higher and less pulled-back handlebars gave a more upright riding position than that of the V-Raptor, which also benefited from a small amount of wind protection from its nose fairing. Both models confirmed that Galluzzi had succeeded in his aim of evolving the naked bike concept. They were striking, fast and agile, and were proof that Cagiva had arrived as a serious superbike manufacturer.

A year later Cagiva broadened the Raptor range by introducing both a Raptor 650, powered by the V-twin engine from Suzuki's SV650, and a limited-edition Xtra-Raptor that combined the 996cc engine with carbon-fibre bodywork, racier steering geometry and firmer, multi-adjustable suspension. But although demand for the smaller model, in particular, was very strong, Cagiva hit financial problems that severely disrupted production and cost many sales.

Left: Cagiva's frame was based on 40mm diameter steel tubes, and used the 996cc 90-degree Suzuki V-twin engine as a stressed member of the chassis. The Italian firm left Suzuki's liquid-cooled engine internally standard, but fine-tuned its output with intake and exhaust modifications designed to improve low-rev response.

Below: The V-Raptor and the more conventional Raptor model (left) were launched simultaneously, sharing the majority of components. The standard bike had a slightly more upright riding position and sold at a cheaper price.

Specification	**Cagiva** V-Raptor (2000)
Engine	Liquid-cooled dohc eight-valve 90-degree V-twin
	(Suzuki TL1000S)
Capacity	996cc (98 x 66mm)
Maximum power	105bhp @ 8500rpm
Transmission	Six-speed, chain final drive
Frame	Tubular steel ladder
Suspension	Telescopic front; monoshock rear
Brakes	Twin discs front; disc rear
Weight	434lb (197kg)
Top speed	150mph (241km/h)

Honda SP-1

**Top speed
165mph**
266km/h

*Below: With its lean and
aggressive look, the SP-1
was a very different
machine to the VTR1000F
roadster from which it was
derived. Low handlebars,
rearset footrests and a racy
seat revealed serious
sporting intent. A seat-pad
could be clipped to the
tailpiece for a pillion, but
this motorcycle was
designed to be ridden
alone – and fast.*

 After spending many seasons struggling
to keep up with Ducati in the World
Superbike championship, whose rules
gave twin-cylinder bikes a weight advantage,
Honda finally abandoned its traditional V4 engine
layout to develop a V-twin of its own. The
VTR1000 SP-1, launched in 2000, proved doubly
successful. American ace Colin Edwards rode a
twin to the Superbike world title in its debut
season, and Honda's roadgoing range was enhanced
by the arrival of a superb sports machine.

Despite its powerful 999cc, 90-degree V-twin
motor, high-quality chassis, race-derived styling
and some neat technical features, the SP-1 was not
a limited-edition machine intended solely as the
basis for Honda's Superbike challenger. The model
known as the RC51 in the United States was built
in large numbers and priced closer to a normal
sports machine than to its exotic V4 predecessor
the RC45.

Honda's line-up already contained a big V-twin,
but the SP-1 shared fewer than ten per cent of
components with the VTR1000F Firestorm. Its
motor differed in having higher compression ratio,
gear instead of chain drive to its cams, and a close-
ratio gearbox. In place of the Firestorm's
carburettors the SP-1 used fuel-injection, fed by an
innovative intake system whose central main duct
ran from a fairing slot between the twin headlights,
through the special aluminium steering head
casting to the airbox, reducing the turbulence
generated by normal intakes. Peak output was
136bhp at 9500rpm.

In contrast to the Firestorm's pivotless frame,
the SP-1 had conventional twin aluminium main
spars. The frame used the engine as a stressed
member, and mounted its rear shock on a large
aluminium lower cross-member. Front forks were
upside-down 43mm units and, like the rear shock,
were multi-adjustable.

Compact and eager to rev

The SP-1 was compact, its clip-ons low, footrests high, and seat thinly padded. The finish was basic by Honda standards, with unlacquered stickers, and wiring visible inside the fairing. Equally racy was the tall first gear, good for 70mph (113km/h). But the motor's flexibility helped make the bike fast and easy to ride. And the engine loved to rev, rocketing towards the 10,000rpm redline with such enthusiasm that the rider's left foot had to flick rapidly through the gearbox, as the bike headed for a top speed of 165mph (266km/h).

The SP-1 was not particularly light, at 431lb (196kg), but it handled very well. Its rigid twin-spar frame combined with high-quality cycle parts to make for precise control. Suspension at both ends was firm, ideal for racetrack or smooth road (though harsh on a bumpy one). And the front brake set-up of large twin discs and four-piston Nissin calipers gave real bite plus just the right amount of feel.

There was no doubt that the SP-1 had been designed primarily for the track, to recapture Honda's reputation for building the world's fastest four-stroke motorcycles. Edwards' title in the bike's first season was vindication of Honda's approach. Equally importantly, in designing the street-legal machine on which the racer was based, Honda had produced an outstanding roadster that blended the firm's traditional sophistication and engineering quality with V-twin feel and character.

Edwards' Superbike Winner

Even Honda could not have expected that its new V-twin would win the coveted World Superbike title in its first year, but Colin Edwards did just that on the Castrol-backed works machine. The Texan's bike produced 180bhp with plenty of mid-range torque, weighed just 356lb (161kg), and proved reliable as well as fast. To add to Honda's delight, a similar SP-1 ridden by Japanese grand prix stars Daijiro Katoh and Tohru Ukawa won the prestigious Eight-hour endurance race at the firm's home circuit of Suzuka.

Left: Firm, well-damped suspension made the SP-1 great for hard cornering on a smooth road or racetrack, but gave a less than comfortable ride the rest of the time.

Below left: Air was fed to the V-twin's fuel-injection system via a slot between the headlights, and through a specially shaped steering head casting.

Specification	Honda VTR1000 SP-1 (RC51) (2000)
Engine	Liquid-cooled dohc eight-valve 90-degree V-twin
Capacity	999cc (100 x 63.6mm)
Maximum power	136bhp @ 9500rpm
Transmission	Six-speed, chain final drive
Frame	Aluminium twin spar
Suspension	Telescopic front; single shock rear
Brakes	Twin discs front; disc rear
Weight	431lb (196kg)
Top speed	165mph (266km/h)

Kawasaki ZX-6R

**Top speed
160mph**
257km/h

Kawasaki had effectively invented the 600cc super-sports class back in 1985 with the GPZ600R, which featured a liquid-cooled 16-valve engine, perimeter frame and full fairing. Fifteen years later, an updated version of that model's replacement, the ZX-6R, proved that the Big K was still right on the pace in what had become motorcycling's most competitive class.

Faster, lighter, sharper...

One glance at the ZX-6R's vital statistics confirmed that despite its modest capacity this bike, like its rival fours from Honda, Suzuki, Yamaha and Triumph, was a serious high-performance superbike. The Kawasaki produced 109bhp, weighed just 379lb (172kg), and had a top speed of 160mph (257km/h). Five years after the launch of the original ZX-6R model, the challenger from the green corner was faster, lighter, sharper and better in almost every respect.

Visually the most obvious difference from the previous ZX-6R was at the front, where twin headlights sat above a larger ram-air intake mouth. Despite new paintwork the rest of the ZX-6R looked familiar, but its engine, suspension and brakes were all new, or at least substantially modified. Such was the fiercely competitive nature of the middleweight super-sports category that continual development was essential if a bike was to remain in contention for long.

Changes to the 599cc powerplant centred on a revised ram-air system, increased compression ratio and new all-aluminium cylinder barrels, plus various weight-reducing work. The valve and clutch covers joined the list of parts, including alternator and countershaft covers, that were

Above: The ZX-6R had much in common with the original model from 1995, but a succession of updates had honed its performance to good effect. A twin-spar aluminium frame, four-into-one exhaust system and green paint option remained on the specification sheet.

Right: Twin headlights gave Kawasaki's revamped ZX-6R a subtly updated look. But the more important change in the bike's fairing nose was to its ram-air scoop, which protruded slightly further to improve air flow into the engine.

Specification	Kawasaki ZX-6R (2000)
Engine	Liquid-cooled dohc 16-valve four
Capacity	599cc (66 x 43.8mm)
Maximum power	109bhp @ 12,500rpm
Transmission	Six-speed, chain final drive
Frame	Aluminium twin spar
Suspension	Telescopic front; single shock rear
Brakes	Twin discs front; disc rear
Weight	379lb (172kg)
Top speed	160mph (257km/h)

already cast in lightweight magnesium. The crankshaft, ignition coils, cams and clutch were also redesigned to save weight.

There was no change to the 6R's twin-beam aluminium frame but the swingarm, rear shock and its linkage were revised. Front and rear suspension springs were stiffer, and the fork legs were slightly wider-spaced. Other modifications included new front brake calipers plus a new instrument panel that saved a little more weight.

What all that added up to was a ZX-6R that produced 3bhp more than the previous model, and which was 11lb (5kg) lighter – improvements that were enough to put it right back in contention with the class leaders. Like any sporty middleweight, the ZX-6R's performance was concentrated at the upper end of the rev range. With its rev-counter needle nudging the 14,000rpm redline, the 6R accelerated at a blistering rate, its induction system emitting a spine-tingling howl in the process.

Kawasaki's challenger had traditionally been stronger than most of its rivals in the mid-range, and that remained true despite the engine's extra top-end performance. The 6R still pulled smoothly and, by 600cc standards, strongly from low revs. It was also reasonably roomy and comfortable, at least compared to its main rivals, with good wind protection and a roomy dual-seat.

Fine handling had been part of the ZX-6R package since the first model in 1995, and the 2000 edition was the best yet. Its stiffer suspension worked superbly on bumpy backroads and smooth racetracks alike. The Kawasaki was slightly tauter and sharper than its predecessor, yet remained very

stable even under hard acceleration. Its front brake was improved and excellent, and sticky radial tyres gave a generous level of grip.

However closely the ZX-6R was examined, very few complaints could be levelled at a superbly agile, rapid and versatile bike which, in middleweight tradition, was also competitively priced. The ZX-6R was every bit as exciting as its main rivals, more practical than most, and was many pundits' pick for top spot in the middleweight super-sports division. Not that the rival factories' unceasing development work would allow it to remain that way for long.

Left: The Kawasaki's twin-spar aluminium frame was unchanged, unlike the swingarm and both front and rear suspension. The revised 599cc, 16-valve liquid-cooled engine revved to a heady 14,000rpm.

Below left: This model's ZX-6R stickers would be replaced in 2002, when the engine was bored-out to 636cc to provide a small increase in mid-range performance.

Below: British ace Iain MacPherson's ZX-6R carried the Supersport world championship's No.2 plate in 2000, and Australian Andrew Pitt went one better to win the title for Kawasaki in 2001.

Ducati MH900e

**Top speed
130mph**
209km/h

*Right: Traditional styling
touches such as the round
headlight, half fairing and
the V-twin engine's finned
dummy sump combined with
modern features to give the
MH900e a unique look.*

*Below: Ducati's 904cc
air/oil-cooled V-twin engine
added to the visual appeal,
as did the single-sided
swingarm, made from
tubular steel instead of the
normal aluminium.*

The bike that Ducati called the Mike
Hailwood Evoluzione was proof that
sometimes even the most improbable of
ideas was worth pursuing. This unique blend of old
and new superbike began as a sketch by Pierre
Terblanche, Ducati's design chief, who was
inspired by Hailwood's heroics at the Isle of Man
TT in 1978, when 'Mike the Bike' returned from
retirement to ride a Ducati to a memorable win.

Terblanche devised a tribute in the form of a
V-twin that combined striking, 1970s type styling –
including a chrome-rimmed headlight, old-style
graphics, and a dummy sump beneath the engine –
with modern touches. He convinced Ducati's
bosses to build a concept bike, complete with
futuristic details including a rear-facing camera
instead of mirrors, and rear indicators mounted in
sticking-out exhaust pipes.

When the MH900e, as it was named, was
unveiled, the response was so positive that Ducati
decided to put the bike into limited production. The

Evoluzione was deemed ideal for Ducati's first
serious attempt at e-commerce. One thousand units
of the MH900e went on sale on the ducati.com web
site on the first day of the new millennium, and a
few hours later had sold out. Double the originally
planned number were eventually built, in a corner
of the factory in Bologna.

Stylish and beautifully detailed

One glance explained the high level of demand, especially to those old enough to remember 1978. The Evoluzione was stylish, beautifully detailed, and blended old and new with unique flair. The prototype's camera and exhaust-mounted indicators did not make it into production, but bits that did included a stylish white-faced rev-counter with digital speedo beneath, and a single-sided swingarm made from tubular steel instead of the familiar aluminium.

The basis of the Evoluzione was Ducati's 900SS, which donated its 904cc air/oil-cooled V-twin engine. The sohc motor produced a modest 75bhp, and was held in a traditional Ducati steel ladder frame. This meant that the MH900e was far from a cutting-edge sports bike, but it had a suitably raw, old-fashioned character despite the muted sound from the long silencers beneath the seat.

There was plenty of acceleration, too, thanks to the fuel-injected V-twin's generous mid-range torque, combined with slightly lower gearing from the Monster 900. Winding back the throttle from below 5000rpm was enough to get the Ducati rumbling forward, with no need for a downchange. With the rider's head behind the screen and chin on the fuel tank's neat alloy cover, the MH900e stretched its legs towards a top speed of about 130mph (209km/h).

Handling was good, too, combining reasonably light steering with the high-speed stability for which Ducatis had been known in the 1970s. The Evoluzione was not the quickest-steering machine on the block, but it had good suspension and was light enough to make good use of its abundant ground clearance and sticky radial tyres. Brembo's triple-disc brake system gave plenty of modern-day power, too. Less welcome were the poor mirrors, illegible warning lights, tall seat, and the small fuel range dictated by the tiny tank.

Such idiosyncrasies ensured that the MH900e was not the bike for every motorcyclist or even every Ducati fan. Terblanche did not mind that not every rider appreciated a machine that was never intended to be produced in large numbers. 'The people it's aimed at understand it, and I don't care about the ones who don't,' he said. For those who did, the MH900e's traditional Ducati virtues of torque, handling ability and character ensured that it was a very enjoyable motorbike as well as an outstanding piece of design.

Below left: The Evoluzione's 1970s style Ducati logo and traditional red and silver factory racing colours helped give the bike a period look without actually resembling Mike Hailwood's TT-winning racer, which had a full fairing in sponsor Castrol's red, white and green paint scheme.

Below right: The 75bhp MH900e was not particularly fast in a straight line, but its flexible V-twin motor and light weight made for plenty of entertainment.

Specification	Ducati MH900e (2000)
Engine	Air/oil-cooled sohc four-valve 90-degree V-twin
Capacity	904cc (92 x 68mm)
Maximum power	75bhp @ 8000rpm
Transmission	Six-speed, chain final drive
Frame	Tubular steel ladder
Suspension	Telescopic front; single shock rear
Brakes	Twin discs front; disc rear
Weight	410lb (186kg)
Top speed	130mph (209km/h)

Yamaha FJR1300

**Top speed
160mph**
257km/h

*Right: Styling was clearly
influenced by the YZF-R1,
but the adjustable screen
confirmed that the FJR's
emphasis was on comfort as
well as speed.*

*Below: The FJR's big
fairing, broad seat and
panniers were all features
that would be near the top
of a typical sports-touring
rider's list of essentials.*

Yamaha's old FJ1100 and 1200 models
were fondly remembered by many riders
for their powerful straight-four engines,
sound handling and long-distance ability. So it was
only natural that, in planning a return to the sports-
tourer market with a new four-cylinder superbike,
Yamaha should attempt to recreate the FJ models'
assets – while moving performance forward in all
directions with a much more modern design.

The FJR certainly did not suffer from a
shortage of speed. With a maximum output of
145bhp, its all-new 1298cc, liquid-cooled engine
had almost as much top-end power as Yamaha's
YZF-R1 super-sports unit. The new 16-valve motor
also produced more peak torque than the R1
engine, as well as having a near-flat torque curve
that guaranteed strong low-rev performance.

Unlike its FJ1100 forebear, which had
originally been designed as a sports bike before
adopting a long-distance role, the FJR was created

as a sports-tourer. It featured an electronically
adjustable windscreen, shaft final drive, a built-in
luggage rack, and purpose-designed panniers. It
also had a fairly upright riding position, much like
that of the old FJ, instead of a streamlined super-
sports crouch.

Seriously rapid

In conjunction with the low seat and footrests, it gave the FJR a relaxed feel at low speeds. But a twist of the throttle at almost any revs was enough to confirm that this was one seriously rapid motorbike. The Yamaha delivered stumble-free acceleration from as low as 2000rpm in top gear, with an arm-wrenching surge from 3000rpm that almost made the efficient five-speed gearbox an optional extra.

The FJR engine was far too civilized to have something as crude as a power step, but it pulled even harder through the mid-range and on towards the 9000rpm redline. At most revs the Yamaha was very smooth, too, thanks to twin balancer shafts. Most of the time there was just enough of a typical high-frequency tingle to confirm that the motor was a straight four.

Ironically the one period of slightly higher vibration came at the 5000rpm mark that equated to a typical fast cruising speed of about 90mph (145km/h). Some riders regarded this as all the excuse they needed to wind the FJR up towards its top speed, which was roughly 150mph (241km/h) with the screen up, and 160mph (257km/h) with panniers removed.

With luggage or without, the FJR handled very well. It was rock solid in a straight line, and stable in high-speed curves. At 522lb (237kg) the bike was respectably light, partly due to Yamaha's use of aluminium instead of steel for its frame and swingarm. Despite its size the FJR was

manoeuvrable enough to be fun rather than a handful on a twisty road.

That was partly due to the excellent suspension, which gave a comfortable ride but was firm enough for fast cornering. The front forks, in particular, did a good job of resisting the forces generated by the FJR's powerful R1-derived front brake blend of twin discs and four-piston calipers. Other touring-oriented features included a broad dual-seat and the large, flat-topped fuel tank that was ideal for fitment of a tank bag.

The adjustable screen lacked sufficient range to suit very tall riders, but in most respects the FJR was a very capable and well detailed all-rounder. Yamaha had set out to build a new machine that would fulfil the same role as the old FJ1200, but would be superior in every way. This was achieved, and the FJR1300 was arguably better than any of its modern rivals at combining long-distance comfort with much of the speed and style of a sports bike.

Above: The Yamaha backed up its straight-line speed with impressive performance on a winding road. The bike was quite light for a sports-tourer and its suspension was well controlled.

Left: Unlike previous sports-tourers, the FRJ had an aluminium twin-spar frame, complete with distinctive side sections stretching down outside the engine's cylinder head. The 1298cc four-cylinder powerplant formed a stressed member of the chassis, and aided rigidity with its one-piece cylinder/crankcase design.

Specification	Yamaha FJR1300 (2001)
Engine	Liquid-cooled dohc 16-valve four
Capacity	1298cc (79 x 66.2mm)
Maximum power	145bhp @ 8500rpm
Transmission	Five-speed, shaft final drive
Frame	Aluminium twin spar
Suspension	Telescopic front; single shock rear
Brakes	Twin discs front; disc rear
Weight	522lb (237kg)
Top speed	160mph (257km/h)

Suzuki GSX-R1000

**Top speed
185mph**
298km/h

*Below: The GSX-R1000
was distinguishable from its
lookalike 750 and 600cc
siblings by six-piston front
brake calipers and gold-
coated fork sliders. And, of
course, by the way it tried
to tear its rider's arms off
when the throttle was
opened.*

At the start of the new millennium, many sport bike enthusiasts accepted that the era of dramatic performance increases from production machines was over. After the big gains made by Honda's CBR900RR in 1992 and Yamaha's R1 six years later, they felt it would not be possible for a mass-produced bike to make such a leap again. Then Suzuki's GSX-R1000 burst onto the scene, with a devastating combination of speed and agility that left the opposition reeling and proved that the performance race was by no means over yet.

There was nothing revolutionary about this latest GSX-R, which looked so like its 750 and 600cc siblings that all three were difficult to distinguish at a glance. But there was simply no other bike on the road that came close to matching the big Suzuki's blend of monstrously powerful engine, razor-sharp handling, fierce braking and light weight.

The GSX-R1000 was the end product of all the research and development expertise that Suzuki had acquired since the original GSX-R750's launch 16 years earlier. Its 998cc engine was essentially a bored and stroked version of the most recent GSX-R750 unit, and shared some parts including much of its cylinder head with the smaller motor. Even the valves and their angles were identical, though the 1000's camshafts gave revised lift and duration.

The bottom-end layout was also similar, although the 1000 had a balancer shaft plus larger bearings. Its clutch and oil cooler were also bigger.

Specification	Suzuki GSX-R1000 (2001)
Engine	Liquid-cooled dohc 16-valve four
Capacity	998cc (73 x 59mm)
Maximum power	161bhp @ 11,000rpm
Transmission	Six-speed, chain final drive
Frame	Aluminium twin spar
Suspension	Telescopic front; single shock rear
Brakes	Twin discs front; disc rear
Weight	375lb (170kg)
Top speed	185mph (298km/h)

The four-into-one exhaust system featured downpipes made from lightweight titanium, plus a Yamaha-style exhaust valve for added mid-range performance. Peak output was 161bhp at 11,000rpm, giving the Suzuki a 10bhp advantage over its closest rivals, Honda's FireBlade and Yamaha's R1.

Frame geometry and riding position were unchanged from the 750, but the 1000's aluminium frame beams had slightly thicker outside walls, plus an extra engine mount. Even the fairing was almost identical to the 750's, but the new bike was distinguishable by its gold-finished, titanium nitride-coated upside-down forks and its six-piston front brake calipers. The bigger bike also had a larger, six-inch wide rear wheel and 190-section tyre.

Awe-inspiring performance

From the moment that the GSX-R1000 was unleashed, there was little doubt that the superbike balance of power had shifted again. The engine's performance was awe-inspiring, with a blend of savage top-end power, strong mid-range and precise throttle control that made the Suzuki not only fast but also remarkably easy to ride. There was no step or dip in its power delivery; just massive torque everywhere between 3000rpm and the 12,500rpm redline, accompanied by a vicious snarl from the ram-air fed airbox. In the right conditions the GSX-R was capable of a genuine 185mph (298km/h), and it got there mighty quickly.

And the Suzuki's chassis was every bit as impressive as its engine. At 375lb (170kg) it was only 9lb (4kg) heavier than the GSX-R750, and gained an advantage thanks to superior suspension and brakes. Both front and rear units were very progressive, soaking up small bumps and giving precise feedback, yet also coped superbly with the forces of hard cornering. The six-piston front brake

calipers delivered massive stopping power with good feel and minimal fork dive.

In typical GSX-R fashion, the new bike was unashamedly racy and single-minded. It was uncomfortable at slow speed, and so fast that much of its potential was wasted on the road. That was hardly a fair criticism; a more valid one was that this largest GSX-R, although by no means unattractive, looked rather ordinary. But the bottom line was that for pure performance, the GSX-R1000 was the best standard production bike in the world.

Above left: With its 16-valve four-cylinder engine, aluminium frame and uncompromising attitude, the GSX-R1000 was a worthy successor to the original GSX-R750 that had revolutionized super-sports motorcycling in 1985.

Left: This GSX-R is fitted with the pillion pad instead of the seat cover. Its exhaust is the standard system instead of the aftermarket pipe pictured opposite.

Below: Suzuki's 1993 500cc world champion Kevin Schwantz makes the most of the GSX-R's cornering ability during a GSX-R festival day at Brands Hatch.

Triumph Daytona 955i

**Top speed
170mph**
274km/h

*Right: Triumph tuned the
Daytona's 955cc three-
cylinder engine with new
valves, increased
compression ratio and a
revised intake system.*

*Below: The Daytona was a
good-looking bike, and
retained Triumph's unique
frame design of twin
aluminium tubes, but was
visually less distinctive than
its predecessor.*

Ever since its launch in 1997, Triumph's
three-cylinder Daytona had earned a
reputation as a fast and stylish sports bike.
But the British triple had always been slightly more
of an all-rounder than a cutting-edge super-sports
machine, and the pace of superbike development
made this even more the case by the end of the
decade. Triumph's response was a new Daytona
955i: more powerful, lighter and more competitive
than ever before.

This was Triumph's best sportster yet, but it
was not as distinctive as the old model because, in
being revamped to meet the challenge from Japan
and Italy, the triple became a little more
conventional. Its bodywork was reshaped and the
original model's single-sided swingarm was
missing. The new bike's twin-sided replacement
was lighter and allowed a shorter wheelbase, but
lacked the style of its predecessor.

The Daytona's 955cc, 12-valve motor was
tuned with new valves, reshaped ports, higher
compression, lighter conrods, revised fuel-injection
and a bigger airbox. Cooling and lubrication
systems were more efficient, and noise was

Sports-touring Triple: the Sprint ST

Triumph used its 955cc three-cylinder engine as the basis for several other models, the best of which was arguably the Sprint ST sports-tourer. This was introduced in 1999 with a detuned 110bhp version of the 12-valve engine, plus a new twin-spar aluminium frame, and was competitive with the world's best sports-tourers. Three years later, the ST was fitted with Triumph's uprated 118bhp powerplant. This resulted in an even more refined roadburner that combined 150mph (241km/h) performance with fine handling and impressive long-distance comfort.

reduced. Peak output was an impressive 147bhp at 10,700bhp. That was 19bhp more than the old model, and made this triple Europe's most powerful production motorcycle.

The tubular aluminium frame was one of few parts that was retained, and even that was fitted with a new subframe and was raised at the back to steepen geometry and improve ground clearance. Showa of Japan provided suspension, as before: the forks' internals were revised, and the shock unit was slimmer and lighter. Fitting the TT600 model's lightweight front wheel helped reduce dry weight to a very respectable 414lb (188kg).

Throaty intake howl

From the Daytona's saddle the view was of a modern instrument console also borrowed from the TT600, containing a digital speedometer and analogue rev-counter. Those new dials came alive when the Daytona's rider wound back the throttle to send the triple leaping forward with a violent burst of acceleration and a throaty intake howl.

The revitalized Daytona was a very rapid motorbike, and one that revved right to its 11,000rpm limiter in the lower gears, heading for a top speed of 170mph (274km/h). The fuel-injection's throttle response was very direct, there was plenty of mid-range torque, and the engine was pleasantly smooth. The six-speed gearbox was rather notchy, but in every other respect this was a superb powerplant.

And the Daytona's chassis was every bit as good. Although even this tweaked Triumph was still slightly more of an all-rounder than a pure

race-replica, it was very much an agile, quick-steering and impressively stable sports machine. Firm, well-controlled suspension added to the triple's pace, as did its generous ground clearance. And the Daytona also upheld Triumph's reputation for superbly powerful brakes.

When the stop-watch was running, even this revamped Daytona did not quite match the fastest of its four-cylinder rivals for pure speed. But the British bike was close enough to be in contention on road and track. And for many riders its distinctive style and three-cylinder character made the Daytona a very appealing alternative.

Above left: The Daytona's reduced weight, sportier chassis geometry and uprated suspension combined with its rigid frame to give excellent handling. Triumph insisted that the Daytona was built for the road and not the racetrack, but the triple acquitted itself very well on a track. It was agile, yet also very stable at speed.

Specification	Triumph Daytona 955i (2001)
Engine	Liquid-cooled dohc 12-valve triple
Capacity	955cc (79 x 65mm)
Maximum power	147bhp @ 10,700rpm
Transmission	Six-speed, chain final drive
Frame	Tubular aluminium perimeter
Suspension	Telescopic front; single shock rear
Brakes	Twin discs front; disc rear
Weight	414lb (188kg)
Top speed	170mph (274km/h)

Honda CBR600F Sport

**Top speed
160mph**
257km/h

*Right: Ironically the Sport
model's new engine parts,
intended to improve tuning
potential, did not increase
performance in the bike's
standard form.*

*Below: The Sport was the
most aggressive version yet
of the phenomenally
successful 599cc Honda
four, traditionally known as
the F4 in the US market.*

By 2001 the CBR600F had been one of
the world's best-selling bikes for 14 years,
its success maintained by regular
improvements since the model's launch in 1987.
But Honda faced a dilemma due to the increasing
specialization of the middleweight super-sports
division. How could the CBR remain competitive
with race-replicas such as Suzuki's GSX-R600 and
Yamaha's R6, on the road and World Supersport
racetrack, while maintaining the all-round
excellence for which it had long been renowned?

Honda's conclusion was that a single bike could
not continue to compete in all areas. So in 2001 the
firm introduced two distinct CBRs, backing-up the
revamped standard 600F with a new Sport model.
Designed primarily as a basis for Supersport racing,
the Sport incorporated a selection of tuning parts in
place of some of the more practical features with
which the CBR had traditionally been fitted.

Aggressive styling

Most of the changes were common to both models.
More aggressive styling was the most obvious, with
twin headlamps set above a reshaped pair of air
intakes. The ducts fed a new fuel-injection system,
based on that of the FireBlade. Other modifications

included a stiffened aluminium frame, digital speedometer with clock and fuel gauge, retuned suspension, plus lighter wheels and brakes.

Power output of both models was an unchanged 108bhp at 12,500rpm, as the Sport's new engine parts were aimed at making it more competitive when tuned for racing, rather than in standard form. Valvegear was revised, the flywheel lightened and the clutch strengthened. The Sport, which had a black finished frame, also had a single seat with pillion pad instead of a dual seat, and no centre-stand or grabrail.

The Sport's engine came into its own in Supersport racing, where with careful tuning the top teams were able to coax as much as 125bhp from the 599cc four, despite strict limitations on what could be changed. A flowed cylinder head, new camshafts, increased compression and a special ignition system combined to allow the CBR to rev to 16,000rpm, almost 2000rpm higher than standard, giving a top speed of over 175mph (282km/h). Despite this, Kawasaki's slower ZX-6R went on to win the 2001 championship ridden by Australian Andrew Pitt.

Ironically the Sport's engine changes made little difference to its performance in standard form. But few owners complained about that because, predictably, both versions of the new CBR6 were rapid and handled very well. Despite its more aggressive look, the Honda's famed all-round ability was very much intact. Its 16-valve motor still worked best at high revs, but there was lots of power from 9000rpm and useful torque from way down low.

Another boost was the motor's snarl through its airbox under acceleration. Although even this CBR

did not stir the senses quite like some of its harder-edged rivals, the slightly racier feel provided some welcome extra personality. Yet predictably the CBR was just as refined and well behaved as ever, striking its traditional balance between performance and practicality.

The standard 600F's revised suspension, slightly reduced weight and sticky radial tyres made it more agile than the previous CBR, though the difference was small. On a racetrack the Sport was better still, though only just. Even this Honda was not quite as sharp as its most aggressive race-replica rivals, but it was the fastest CBR600F yet. And crucially the Sport's extra pace and racy image did not spoil the all-round ability that had long made Honda's middleweight four so popular.

Left: Reshaped air intakes helped give a sharp look to the Sport and to this standard CBR, which in most respects was identical.

Below: Despite remaining more of an all-rounder than some of its race-replica rivals, the Sport handled superbly. Both CBR models were uprated with a strengthened aluminium frame, revised suspension, plus the addition of lighter wheels and brakes.

Specification	Honda CBR600F Sport (2001)
Engine	Liquid-cooled dohc 16-valve four
Capacity	599cc (67 x 42.5mm)
Maximum power	108bhp at 12,500rpm
Transmission	Six-speed, chain final drive
Frame	Aluminium twin spar
Suspension	Telescopic front; single shock rear
Brakes	Twin discs front; disc rear
Weight	372lb (169kg)
Top speed	160mph (257km/h)

Ducati ST4S

**Top speed
160mph**
257km/h

Ducati's tradition of building racy red superbikes means that the term 'sports-tourer' has a distinctly different slant in Bologna. Not for Ducati the classical balance between long-distance comfort and speed. The Italian firm's idea of a sports-tourer is a fast, light V-twin… just softened slightly with higher handlebars plus room for a pillion.

Head of the family

That approach was exemplified by the ST4S, which was introduced in 2001 to head the Italian marque's growing family of sports-tourers. The ST2, with its 944cc liquid-cooled, sohc two-valves-per-cylinder V-twin engine, had been introduced in 1997. Two years later it had been joined by the ST4, powered by a modified version of the more powerful dohc eight-valve engine from the 916 sportster.

Essentially the ST4S was a sportier version of the ST4, complete with larger capacity engine and revamped chassis. Although the S model looked restrained, there was a heart of fire beneath its grey bodywork. This sports-tourer was slightly more powerful and not much heavier than the iconic original 916, with which the Italian firm had stepped up its bid for road and race glory in 1994.

Ducati did not need to look far to find a powerplant for the ST4S. At the same time as the 916cc ST4 had been launched, the 916 sportster had been upgraded with a bigger, more powerful 996cc engine. To create truly rapid sports-tourer it was a simple task to bolt the 996 model's desmodromic V-twin motor into the ST4 chassis, after first fitting more compact cylinder heads, plus new intake camshafts that improved low-rev

Above: The ST4S's shape was identical to that of the ST2 and ST4 with which it formed a three-bike family, but the S model had higher performance and was in many ways closer to a full-blown sports bike than to a sports-tourer.

Right: Superior chassis components included Showa upside-down forks with titanium nitride coating, and an Öhlins shock with remote preload adjuster. The ST4S also incorporated improvements including lightweight wheels and a swingarm made from aluminium instead of steel.

Specification	Ducati ST4S (2001)
Engine	Liquid-cooled dohc eight-valve 90-degree V-twin
Capacity	996cc (98 x 66mm)
Maximum power	117bhp at 8750rpm
Transmission	Six-speed, chain final drive
Frame	Tubular steel ladder
Suspension	Telescopic front; monoshock rear
Brakes	Twin discs front; disc rear
Weight	467lb (212kg)
Top speed	160mph (257km/h)

Above left: The Ducati combined thunderous V-twin performance with sports-touring features including a fairly upright riding position.

Left: With its rear shock adjusted to maximize ground clearance, the ST4S could be cornered almost as hard as the super-sports 996.

performance. Peak power was 117bhp, and the ST4S was at least 10bhp stronger than the ST4 everywhere above 4000rpm.

Ducati's intention was to give the ST4S a torquey V-twin feel, plus plenty of high-rev speed and acceleration – and that's just how the bike performed. The S model didn't really start charging until about 6000rpm, by which time it was travelling at about 100mph (161km/h) in top gear on the way to a maximum speed of 160mph (257km/h). But there was smooth torque on tap from as low as 3000rpm, and a slick six-speed gearbox to help out.

Handling was excellent too. The basic ST4 was no slouch, but the S-bike combined an identical tubular steel frame with superior titanium-coated fork sliders (for reduced friction), an Öhlins rear shock with hand-adjustable preload, lighter wheels, an aluminium swingarm and stickier rear tyre. On standard settings the bike was comfortable but fairly soft. Given some suspension fine-tuning it became superbly taut, its pace on a racetrack limited mainly by the centre-stand's tendency to dig in at extreme angles.

That centre-stand confirmed that Ducati's sports-tourer did have a few compromises to comfort and practicality. Other civilizing touches included a fuel gauge and clock in the cockpit, ignition immobilizer, reasonable wind protection and fuel range, large dual-seat and plenty of leg room. For riders looking for all-round ability plus performance and agility that would have been cutting edge just a few years earlier, the ST4S was a tempting combination.

Naked V-twin: the Monster S4

Shortly before starting production of the ST4S, Ducati introduced another exciting eight-valve V-twin: the Monster S4. This was the most powerful member of the naked Monster family, which dated back to 1993. The Monster S4 combined a 916cc engine, as used in the ST4 and producing 101bhp, with an upmarket chassis whose steel ladder frame also came from the sports-tourer. The result was a wonderfully entertaining roadster, with breathtaking acceleration, a top speed of 150mph (241km/h), excellent handling, a great liking for wheelies, and even more streetwise V-twin charm than the traditional Monster.

Yamaha Fazer 1000

**Top speed
160mph**
257km/h

*Right: Although the Fazer's
998cc, 20-valve motor was
detuned from its
specification in Yamaha's
super-sports YZF-R1, it still
produced a fearsome
143bhp at 10,000rpm.*

*Below: The steel-framed
model that the Americans
called the FZ1 owed a debt
to the R1 for the sharp
styling of its half-fairing, as
well as for its engine.*

As the performance of Japanese race-
replicas increased to a remarkably high
level through the 1990s, a new class of
slightly less focused superbikes became popular.
Large capacity naked fours with detuned super-
sports engines and steel-framed chassis provided
plenty of speed and excitement, at considerably
lower cost than their fully faired, highly tuned and
aluminium-framed relations.

Suzuki's Bandit 1200, powered by a modified
GSX-R1100 engine, led the way, and was followed
by rivals including Kawasaki's ZRX1200S and
Honda's Hornet 900, with its FireBlade-based
engine. But the fastest and arguably most stylish of
the crowd was Yamaha's FZS1000 Fazer, called the
FZ1 in the States, which was powered by a detuned
version of the YZF-R1's 998cc motor.

The big Fazer was one of the most logical new
models Yamaha had ever built, because the firm's
range already included not only the R1, which
donated its engine, but also the FZS600 Fazer, a

quick and versatile middleweight sportster. Putting
the two models together to make a bike called the
FZS1000 Fazer required very little imagination.

Impressive peak output

The R1's dohc, 20-valve liquid-cooled motor was deemed excessive for Fazer duty, so was detuned – but only slightly. Smaller carburettors, a revised intake system and a new four-into-one exhaust, complete with EXUP valve, combined to reduce peak output from 150bhp to a still impressive 143bhp at 10,000rpm.

Like the Fazer 600, the new bike had a frame made from tubular steel rather than R1-style aluminium beams. Chassis dimensions were slightly longer and less steep than the R1's, and at 459lb (208kg) dry this bike weighed 73lb (33kg) more than its racier cousin. But the family resemblance was clear in the FZS1000's styling which, thanks to a sleek twin-headlamp half-fairing, was much more aggressive than that of its 600cc namesake.

Riding the big Fazer was similar to being aboard the smaller model – until the throttle was opened, when it ripped forward at what felt like twice the rate. The FZS1000's roomy, almost-upright riding position was similar to that of the smaller model, and so was the overall feel of a machine that combined speed and agility with a fair amount of comfort and practicality.

The big difference was that this big Fazer's performance was litre-bike strong, with a superbly smooth, torquey feel from well below 3000rpm – and the bonus of a thrilling kick at about 7500rpm, as the big four breathed harder and headed for its 11,500rpm redline. Given the space, an indicated 150mph (241km/h) came up on the analogue speedo in no time, provided the rider's neck muscles could take it. But the Fazer's real strength was that no matter what the revs, or which of its six gears was selected, arm-wrenching acceleration was always on tap.

Fortunately the chassis was excellent too. The tubular steel frame was rigid, and the suspension combined good control with a more comfortable, stable and relaxed (if inevitably slightly less sharp and precise) ride than that of the R1. The sleek half-fairing and small screen diverted some wind from the rider's chest, the R1-replica brakes were superbly powerful, and practical features included a centre-stand, fuel gauge and pillion grips.

The FZS1000 Fazer had always seemed destined to be a star, given the quality of the two bikes that were combined to produce it, and it was arguably the pick of the open-class 'budget' fours. Ironically its one drawback was that this description barely applied, as the FZS was considerably more expensive than its main rivals. Yamaha had given the big Fazer style, performance and practicality, but not the low price that would have ensured its success.

Left: The Yamaha's tubular steel cradle frame gave a very different look from the typical twin-spar aluminium used by the R1. Less obvious differences between the two were the Fazer's longer wheelbase, less racy steering geometry and longer-travel suspension.

Below: As well as more top-end horsepower than its naked rivals, the Yamaha had a smooth throttle response and huge reserves of mid-range torque. This made wheelies temptingly all too easy.

Specification	Yamaha FZS1000 Fazer (2001)
Engine	Liquid-cooled dohc 20-valve four
Capacity	998cc (74 x 58mm)
Maximum power	143bhp @ 10,000rpm
Transmission	Six-speed, chain final drive
Frame	Steel twin downtube
Suspension	Telescopic front; single shock rear
Brakes	Twin discs front; disc rear
Weight	459lb (208kg)
Top speed	160mph (257km/h)

MV Agusta Brutale

**Top speed
155mph**
249km/h

*Right: The Brutale's twin
silencers were angled
upwards to reveal the five-
spoke rear wheel, giving the
rear of the bike a unique
appearance.*

*Below: Compact, barrel-
chested, and eye-catching
from its headlight to its
tailpiece, the Brutale lived
up to its name even at a
standstill.*

 MV Agusta's dramatic rebirth with the
750 F4 sportster had been one of the great
motorcycling stories of the 1990s. But the
firm's boss Claudio Castiglioni knew that to make
revitalized MV successful, he needed to create a
range of bikes that would exploit the F4's
technology and image to the full. Enter the next
stage in MV's revival: the Brutale.

The naked model shared the F4's 749cc, liquid-
cooled, straight four engine layout, with its radial
four-valves-per-cylinder head design; and also the
sports machine's frame with its distinctive
combination of cast sections and steel tubes. But
one glance at the Brutale confirmed that there was
a whole lot more to this bike than an F4 with its
fairing removed.

Like the F4, the Brutale was created by
Massimo Tamburini, the former Bimota co-founder,
creator of the Ducati 916 and godfather of modern
motorcycle design. Despite its commonplace

unfaired straight four layout, the MV resembled
nothing else on two wheels. It was unique from its
drooping headlight to its pair of side-by-side
silencers on the right.

In typical Tamburini fashion the Brutale was
crammed with neat touches, such as its carbon-
fibre-rimmed instrument console (digital

Sports-bike sharp

Handling was excellent, as was to be expected of a bike so closely related to the F4. The Brutale was light, and its geometry was sports-bike sharp. Suspension at both ends was soft enough for a relaxed ride, but firm enough for precise cornering. The MV could be flicked about easily with its broad handlebars, yet was stable at speed. The F4-style six-piston Nissin front brake calipers gave powerful stopping, too. And at slower speeds in town, the bike's upright riding position made it reasonably comfortable.

MV originally announced that, as with the F4, the first 300 units of the Brutale would come in Serie Oro (Gold Series) specification, with magnesium frame castings, swingarm and wheels. But the MV Group's financial problems delayed production of those hand-built bikes and instead it was the slightly heavier and much cheaper standard Brutale, with aluminium chassis castings, that reached production first. Either way, the owners of an MV Agusta Brutale enjoyed plenty of raw performance and naked Italian style.

Left: MV detuned the 749cc four-cylinder motor slightly from its F4 specification, which combined with the crisp fuel-injection system to give very lively throttle response. The Brutale's short wheelbase and light weight also contributed to its front wheel's inability to remain on the road for long.

Below: This Brutale's gold frame casting, wheels and swingarm signified that it was a Serie Oro bike that used magnesium instead of aluminium for those parts. This saved a little weight and added considerably to the price. The two Brutale models' engines and other parts were identical.

speedometer, white-faced analogue rev-counter), adjustable footrests, intricate single-sided cast alloy swingarm, and the subtly blended-in red pillion seat. The view from the low rider's seat was dominated by the tapered, slightly raised one-piece handlebar.

The upright riding position gave the Brutale some of the aggressive feel of an old-style superbike racer. That feeling was reinforced by the bike's spine-tingling sound: a mix of intake gulping, through vents in the front of the fuel tank, and burble from the shotgun silencers. Although the Brutale engine was mechanically very similar to that of the F4, even retaining the removable cassette gearbox, it was detuned by these new intake and exhaust systems.

The result was a boost in low-rev performance, while peak output was reduced slightly from that of the latest specification F4 to 127bhp at 12,500rpm. Those changes were worthwhile, too, because the Brutale was impressively flexible for a bike with such a sporty pedigree. Its Weber-Marelli fuel injection system gave clean running from low revs, with strong acceleration above 5000rpm.

Inevitably, to reveal the bike's full performance its rider had to keep the revs up, preferably above the 9000rpm mark at which the Brutale breathed deeper and howled louder as it headed for the 13,000rpm rev-limiter and a top speed of 155mph (249km/h). That was fun in short bursts although, with such an exposed riding position, fast cruising quickly became tiring. Most riders preferred to short-shift through the six-speed gearbox and make use of the mid-range torque.

Specification	MV Agusta Brutale Serie Oro (2001)
Engine	Liquid-cooled dohc 16-valve four
Capacity	749cc (73.8 x 43.8mm)
Maximum power	127bhp @ 12,500rpm
Transmission	Six-speed, chain final drive
Frame	Tubular steel and cast magnesium
Suspension	Telescopic front; single shock rear
Brakes	Twin discs front; disc rear
Weight	395lb (179kg)
Top speed	155mph (249km/h)

Harley-Davidson V-Rod

**Top speed
140mph**
225km/h

*Right: Although the V-Rod
was very much a cruiser, it
handled well enough to
encourage enthusiastic
cornering.*

*Below: With its aluminium
finish, innovative
instrument cluster, kicked-
out front forks and many
clever details, the V-Rod
looked fresh and interesting
from every angle.*

 The VRSCA V-Rod that Harley-Davidson
unveiled in mid-2001 was far more than
simply the first of a new family of
V-twins. It was a stunningly stylish, original and
powerful machine that looked like no other
production bike ever built, and which confirmed
that the Milwaukee firm had bold and ambitious
plans for the 21st century.

It was clear at a glance that the V-Rod, long,
low, and seemingly carved from a solid block of
aluminium, was no ordinary motorcycle. Visually it
had more in common with a custom machine than
with a normal production bike, yet mechanically
the V-Rod was even more remarkable. It abandoned
Harley's traditional air-cooled V-twin engine for a
more potent and sophisticated liquid-cooled motor,
based on that of the firm's VR1000 Superbike racer
and developed with the help of Porsche
Engineering in Stuttgart, Germany.

'Revolution' engine

Until the V-Rod, Harleys had relied on pushrods to
open their valves, but the new bike's 1130cc
'Revolution' engine retained the layout of the VR
racer. That meant a 60-degree cylinder angle
(instead of the traditional 45 degrees), and twin
overhead cams opening four valves per cylinder.
Peak power output was 115bhp at 8500rpm, almost
double that of the existing Twin Cam 88 V-twin.

What looked like the fuel tank was a large
airbox, which fed the fuel-injection system via a
downdraft intake. Fuel lived under the seat. The
radiator and oil cooler were hidden by a curvaceous
aluminium shroud that ducted air onto them in a
swirling motion to improve efficiency. The tubular
steel frame was created using a hydroforming
process (involving high-pressure water) to give
smooth curves. A long aluminium swingarm
contributed to the V-Rod's lengthy wheelbase.

One brief burst of V-Rod acceleration
confirmed that this was like no other cruiser from
Milwaukee. The way the silver machine charged
away from a standstill, revving to its 9000rpm
redline through the five-speed gearbox, was
exhilarating. And the motor was also very torquey
and refined. The bike accelerated cleanly from as
low as 2000rpm and 30mph (48km/h) in top gear.
At anything above about 3000rpm it leapt forward

with real enthusiasm towards a top speed of 140mph (225km/h), and simply feeling stronger as the revs rose.

The V-Rod also handled well by cruiser standards. Its frame was strong, and suspension at both ends gave a reasonably firm yet comfortable ride. The bike was stable at speed and steered easily, while other chassis parts showed further evidence of Harley's improvements in recent years. Brakes were powerful, not surprisingly given that the front one comprised a large pair of discs gripped by four-piston calipers. Broad radial tyres gave plenty of grip.

Inevitably the radical V-Rod did not appeal to some traditional Harley riders, but it attracted many more to the marque. This was an outstanding machine that pushed two-wheeled style to new heights, and showed the firm was very serious about combining its traditional strengths with modern technology. A new era had begun at Harley-Davidson. On the evidence of the V-Rod it was going to be just as cool as the old one – and considerably more exciting.

The VR1000 – Harley's Road Racer

Harley based the V-Rod's 'Revolution' engine on the 60-degree, liquid-cooled unit of the VR1000 road racer. Introduced in 1994, the distinctive half-orange, half-black VR was designed to bring Harley glory in the AMA Superbike series, and eventually the world championship. But although Miguel Duhamel scored a second place in its debut season, the VR1000 was never truly competitive. At the V-Rod's launch in June 2001, Harley confirmed the firm's commitment to the VR project – only to announce, shortly afterwards, that the factory was quitting racing at the end of the season.

Specification	Harley-Davidson VRSCA V-Rod (2002)
Engine	Liquid-cooled dohc eight-valve 60-degree V-twin
Capacity	1130cc (100 x 72mm)
Maximum power	115bhp @ 8500rpm
Transmission	Five-speed, belt final drive
Frame	Tubular steel
Suspension	Telescopic front; twin shocks rear
Brakes	Twin discs front; disc rear
Weight	594lb (269kg)
Top speed	140mph (225km/h)

Above left: Although the V-Rod's 115bhp output far outstripped that of its previous cruisers, Harley relied on a familiar toothed belt to take drive to the fat rear radial.

Left: Solid disc wheels, a large aluminium radiator shroud and an intricately curved twin-pipe exhaust system give the V-Rod the hand-crafted look of a show-winning custom bike.

Honda VFR VTEC

**Top speed
155mph**
249km/h

Honda's 1980s dream of dominating the superbike world with V4 engines had faded and died in subsequent years. Gradually, most of the numerous V4 models of that decade had been replaced by straight fours that were cheaper and more profitable to produce. But the jewel in Honda's crown remained the VFR, the uniquely refined, liquid-cooled, 16-valve V4 sports-tourer that was known as the Interceptor in the United States.

Far from being abandoned, the original VFR750F of 1986 was reshaped and polished over the years, becoming sharper and faster without losing the sophistication and all-round ability that made it special. Substantial changes came in 1990, with sportier styling, a race-derived twin-spar aluminium frame and single-sided swingarm; and in 1998, when the engine was enlarged from 748 to 782cc, increasing peak output to 108bhp.

VTEC technology

Given the VFR's reputation for quality and high technology, it was no surprise when the comprehensively revamped 2002 model became Honda's first mainstream bike to feature VTEC variable valve technology, as used for some time in the firm's cars. VTEC, which used hydraulics to prevent half of the 16 valves from opening until 7000rpm, was designed to give the low-rev torque of a two-valves-per-cylinder engine plus the high-rev performance of a four-valver.

Rather than attempt to increase output at both ends of the rev range, Honda's engineers opted to leave the old VFR's maximum of 108bhp untouched, and use VTEC to boost the mid-range output that was more important for a sports-tourer. Ironically the VFR's most obvious change was in the other direction. Aggressive new styling combined sharper bodywork, a four-lens headlamp

Below: This was the sportiest looking VFR in the model's 16-year history, thanks largely to its distinctive new fairing. The headlamp incorporated four lenses, the top two for main beam and the lower pair for dip.

Right: Beneath the sharp new bodywork, the VFR's 782cc V4 engine incorporated some significant refinements aimed mainly at improving low-rev performance. As well as the introduction of the VTEC variable valve system, the fuel-injection was revised, and there was the inclusion of a new high-level exhaust system.

and a new exhaust system with triangular-section silencers under the seat.

At a standstill the VFR felt little changed from the old model, with the same roomy riding position and a slightly taller screen. But the VTEC motor's two-valve mode made the V4 quieter and more refined at low revs, as well as more responsive. When the throttle was wound back at 5000rpm, the VFR responded with much more urgency than its predecessor, whose torque curve dipped annoyingly at that point.

Then, as the VTEC was activated at 7000rpm, came an abrupt and thrilling burst of power and noise that seemed improbable from such a refined motorcycle. Far from working quietly and unobtrusively in the background, VTEC announced its arrival very clearly. The V4 engine's note suddenly changed from a purr to a snarl, and the bike leapt forward with new-found aggression. From that point on the VFR tore towards the 11,700rpm redline through its six-speed gearbox, heading for a top speed of over 150mph (241km/h).

Chassis performance was little changed, although the aluminium beam frame was reinforced slightly, especially around the pivot for the single-sided swingarm. Suspension was excellent, giving a softer ride than that of a true sports bike, but with enough control for fine handling on road or racetrack. This VFR featured a revised, essentially diluted version of its predecessor's Dual-CBS linked brake system. The result was superbly powerful and very stable braking with reduced chance of locking the rear wheel.

Specification	Honda VFR/Interceptor (2002)
Engine	Liquid-cooled dohc 16-valve 90-degree V4
Capacity	782cc (72 x 48mm)
Maximum power	108bhp @ 10,500rpm
Transmission	Six-speed, chain final drive
Frame	Aluminium twin spar
Suspension	Telescopic front; single shock rear
Brakes	Twin discs front; disc rear
Weight	469lb (213kg)
Top speed	155mph (249km/h)

Left: Honda no longer claimed that the VFR's single-sided swingarm was lighter than a twin-sided one of similar strength, but the VFR's clean rear end contributed to its style. The quality of finish was very high, as it had been throughout the VFR's model life.

The letters VFR had long stood for all-round excellence, and this model had plenty of high quality details to maintain that reputation. Its finish was sublime; its fairing protective. Improved fuel economy and a larger tank gave increased range. The concept of a sports-tourer inevitably involves compromise, and the VFR had long been the master of that. With the addition of VTEC, Honda's V4 was more capable than ever of providing the best of both worlds.

Left: Despite having reasonably compliant suspension, the Honda handled superbly and was very much at home being cornered with its footrest tips on the road. The 'pivotless' twin-spar aluminium frame was reinforced with stiffer main spars and extra bracing at the steering head. The VFR version with ABS also had a remote preload adjuster for the rear shock.

Ducati 998

**Top speed
170mph**
274km/h

Right: Along with the
narrow valve angle that
gave it its name, Ducati's
998cc Testastretta V-twin
engine featured oversquare
dimensions and peak output
of 123bhp.

Below: Few Ducati fans
minded that the 998's look
was almost identical to that
of the 916 that had been
launched back in 1994.

Such had been the visual impact of
Ducati's 916 that the eight-valve V-twin
remained in production for many years
with barely a change to its shape, despite being in
the fashion-conscious super-sports sector of the
market. Even in 2002, when Ducati launched a new
superbike with the number 998 on its fairing, the
sleek red machine looked almost identical to that
original 916 of eight years earlier.

But beneath those familiar curves the famous
eight-valve V-twin desmo engine, already enlarged
and modified several times since the 916's debut in
1994, had received its most important update yet.
The 998 name was one clue, although Ducati could
not be trusted that the number corresponded with
the actual capacity. In this case it did. Not only was
the liquid-cooled V-twin a 998cc unit, it had the
new generation Testastretta or 'narrow head' layout,
as pioneered on the previous year's expensive
limited-edition 996R model.

Improved engine breathing

The 996R had been launched in 2001 to form the
basis of Ducati's World Superbike racer, on which
Australian Troy Bayliss had brought another world
title back to Bologna. The Testastretta's main
benefit was the narrow valve angle that gave the
engine its name. Other changes included more
oversquare dimensions, larger valves, flatter
combustion chamber, revised intake valve timing,

the single-seat version, which had a slightly softer spring. Either way, the near limitless ground clearance, sticky radial tyres and ultra-powerful brakes combined to make the 998 an exhilarating ride as well as a rapid one.

Inevitably, the rider of a 998 needed to be on the right road, or better still a racetrack, to appreciate its performance fully. This was a supremely fast and focused machine with an ultra-sporty riding position, a thin seat, and few concessions to comfort. All of which was precisely as it should have been for this very worthy successor to the all-conquering 916.

Left: The 998's cornering performance was superb, thanks to the Ducati's blend of ultra-rigid steel frame and top class suspension.

Below: Ducati's twin-headlamp look had become familiar over the years, as had the 998's classy front end combination of Showa upside-down forks and Brembo brake.

plus a sophisticated new Marelli fuel-injection system with larger throttle bodies.

Essentially, the 998 was a Testastretta Ducati for the masses, or at least those with money to spare for a glamorous, mass-produced Italian motorcycle. It had a maximum output of 123bhp, which was a substantial 11bhp up on the previous year's 996 model, and equal to that of the exotic, limited edition 916 SPS of just four years earlier. Ducati's line-up also included a tuned, 136bhp 998S model, plus a limited-edition 998R flagship that produced 139bhp.

Chassis changes were less dramatic, not that anyone was likely to complain because even the basic 998 was very well equipped. Like the more expensive S and R models, the standard 998 had a 996R-style frame whose wider top tubes allowed a larger airbox. All three models used Öhlins rear suspension, which in the base-model 998's case was teamed with 43mm upside-down Showa forks. Brakes were also uprated with thinner front discs than the 996, still gripped by four-piston Brembo calipers. A close look confirmed that the fairing was in the subtly reshaped style of the 996R.

Ducati's eight-valve engine had always been a wonderfully powerful and torquey device, but the Testastretta motor's extra performance really was noticeable. Given enough space the 998 was good for 170mph (274km/h), and it got there at a thrilling rate. The bike tore forward from almost any engine speed, its injection system delivering a flawlessly precise, linear throttle response that made the V-twin very fast and enjoyable to ride.

The Ducati was magnificent in the bends, too. Its rigid frame and firm, well-controlled suspension ensured that handling was pin-sharp. The dual-seat Biposto model's shock worked superbly for most riders, although lighter pilots were better suited to

Specification	Ducati 998 (2002)
Engine	Liquid-cooled dohc eight-valve 90-degree V-twin
Capacity	998cc (100 x 63.5mm)
Maximum power	123bhp @ 9750rpm
Transmission	Six-speed, chain final drive
Frame	Tubular steel ladder
Suspension	Telescopic front; monoshock rear
Brakes	Twin discs front; disc rear
Weight	437lb (198kg) semi-wet
Top speed	170mph (274km/h)

Index

SALVAGE STYLE IN YOUR GARDEN

Moira and Nicholas Hankinson

Kyle Cathie Limited

To Mary Ironside McDonald Gwillim

First published in Great Britain 2001 by

Kyle Cathie Limited
122 Arlington Road
London NW1 7HP

general.enquiries@kyle-cathie.com

ISBN 1 85626 376 2

Text and designs © **Moira and Nicholas Hankinson**
Photography © **Tim Winter** except those listed below.

Senior Editor: **Helen Woodhall**
Editorial Assistant: **Andrie Morris**
Copy Editor: **Tim Jollands**
Designer: **Kevin Knight**
Production: **Lorraine Baird and Sha Huxtable**

Moira and Nicholas Hankinson are hereby identified as the authors of this work in accordance with Section 77 of the Copyright, Designs and Patents Act 1988.

A Cataloguing In Publication record for this title is available from the British Library.

Colour separations by Colourscan, Singapore
Printed and bound in Spain by Artes Gráficas Toledo S.A.U.
D.L. TO: 53-2001

PICTURE ACKNOWLEDGEMENTS

8 *right* **1** Roger Raiche, Planet Horticulture; **28, 33** *bottom left* **34** *left* **50, 55, 59, 63, 64, 67, 75, 85, 86, 112, 131, 132. 135** *bottom* and **144** Nicholas and Moira Hankinson.

Contents

An old Gothic-pattern painted iron bench and an occasionally used iron garden roller nestle below an ivy-clad stone wall and a disused telephone box from the nearby village.

INTRODUCTION

In an increasingly affluent society, reclaiming or salvaging redundant objects or discarded materials such as wood, metal or any other kind of waste material just isn't part of today's busy lifestyle.

As the greedy era of the latter half of the twentieth century turns into a less selfish, more caring society, we realise that we cannot 'have it all'. We and many others feel a strong need to preserve our architectural heritage and *Salvage Style in your Garden* presents reclaimed materials in this positive light.

RIGHT 1

This mixed urn planting features the venerable garden shovel. After years of hard work, it's retired as a sculptural artefact in this Californian garden.

RIGHT 2

A simple wooden seat constructed from a massive plank cut from a hefty wind-blown Cypress tree and placed on granite stone supports.

RIGHT 3

Detail of a table by mosaic artist Candace Bahouth, made from a glorious mixture of seashells, slate, broken tiles and laboriously collected coloured stones.

At the start of a new millennium, salvage seems to make sense and is ecologically sound. Too often in the past, proud old timbers were burnt, mellow bricks were crushed for rubble and weathered roofing slates, battered doors and ancient windows removed from buildings being refurbished or demolished were discarded as useless, not worth the effort and expense of salvaging and restoring. With no second-hand value, huge quantities of waste material were sent to landfill. Many buildings of architectural merit were destroyed and with them so much of our past which has sadly gone forever.

Change came slowly, fuelled by public interest in restoration and the realisation that there were commercial opportunities, indeed large profits to be made, in conserving much of what had previously been rejected or destroyed. Hence the gathering together of traditional building materials and decorative architectural features to form a unique resource and the stock in trade of what we know as salvage or reclamation yards.

It is in these yards that so many glories from our past can still be tracked down – chimneypots and garden statuary, beams, bricks, cast-iron grills and columns, floorboards, flagstones, millstones, panelling and stained glass, and architectural ironmongery of every description. This vast range of salvaged materials, with its character and colour, patination and texture, reflects the skilled craftsmanship, quality and attention to detail of artisans from a bygone age.

But back to the present. When the warmer weather arrives, there is a temptation to rush to the local garden centre and fill the trolley with purchases. Such places have proliferated in recent years in response to the seemingly insatiable demand for both garden products and plants. There you will see an abundance of standardised stock and rows of concrete reproductions. Some of these you may want but much of it is best left on the shelf – chances are it is poorly designed, badly made and not inexpensive. Alternatively, for someone prepared to invest time and effort, a search through reclamation or salvage yards, builders' skips or rubbish tips will reveal a cornucopia of fascinating, unusual, sometimes ugly objects, which with a little imagination can be used to great effect within the garden.

We are passionate about our subject. The aim of this book is to show how salvage can be successfully incorporated into garden schemes and if it leaves you with a more charged imagination, it will have done what was intended. We provide a framework within which to be inventive, based on an awareness of what is available, keeping component costs low and using tools you already own, or that are easily obtainable. There are numerous inspirational photographs and thirty two different projects grouped together in chapters: Seating and Retreating, Plants, Planters and Planting, A Garden Reclaimed, The Themed Garden, Elements and Ambiance, and Inventive Ideas. The projects and practical ideas are suitable for all levels of ability, whether you are a keen beginner or dedicated to handicraft.

We very much hope that through *Salvage Style in your Garden* you will discover the joy of working with materials others have discarded. When you find yourself hooked on handmade bricks or fall in love with an elegant fountain figure; when your weekends and even your holidays are spent searching the salvage yards and builders' skips for bits of masonry and snips of metal; when you have a desire to reinvent a use for damaged doors; when your choice is an expression of your taste, you forge a link with the past that still aspires to the future.

RIGHT

The shell house in the Mediterranean garden on Tresco designed as part of a competition by readers of a glossy magazine and built from reclaimed materials salvaged both from the mainland and the island. Lucy Dorrien Smith decorated the interior of this hexagonal building with mosaic images of flowers, plants and monograms of the family.

When the sun shines, the birds sing and the flora is sweetly fragrant, it is time to retreat to the garden inviting family and friends to join in long, lazy lunches that last the whole afternoon or

cast-iron sewing machine base to form one of those tables so popular in cafés and pub gardens; or even convert huge wooden cable drums into tables.

Alternatively, why not create an

SEATING AND RETREATING

romantic, moonlit supper parties that finish well into the night.

Create a romantic arbour using telegraph poles as supports in a shaded, secret area, somewhere to eat not too far from the house, and build a barbecue of bricks reclaimed from a storage heater.

As the focal point of the dining area, you could construct a table from enormous stones or boulders topped with a slab of slate or flagstone; rejuvenate a sturdy old wooden table by giving it a metal top; adapt a

eye-catching garden feature by making a mosaic-covered table out of shells collected when combing the beach or broken tiles and china unearthed while digging the garden? We show old wooden cheese presses placed on top of slender tree trunks which have a certain rustic charm. In complete contrast, a concrete slab, once the side of a coal bunker but now a table surface on a base of built-up breeze blocks, has more the look of semi-industrial chic!

NEAR RIGHT

An abandoned old blue lias stone flagstone has been installed to make a charming garden seat beneath an arch covered in clematis.

CENTRE LEFT

This glorious garden playhouse, beautifully proportioned and made of salvaged corrugated iron with cut tin embellishments, has been erected in a city garden.

CENTRE RIGHT

'The Seat of Conversion' made by sculptor Paul Grellier from an rescued wayside cross and a variety of salvaged metal and wooden components.

FAR RIGHT

The miniature 'Little House' in the grounds of Nigel and Rosalie Dawes' thirteenth-century moated manor house, Birtsmorton Court. Built of reclaimed timber at Ronsons Reclamation by David Jones, Nigel had it re-erected in the grounds of his mediaeval house, now open as a corporate hospitality centre.

ABOVE

Detail of a garden seat 'In Suspension' by sculptor Paul Grellier, showing some of the character and coloration of corroded ancient iron and weathered elm timber.

LEFT

This quiet patio area sitting high up on a slope and overlooking the garden has been floored with old clay roofing tiles retained behind a railway sleeper.

Different areas of a garden, or rooms, should have different feels. Strategically placed seating provides places to retreat to according to one's mood and adds character to a garden. Make unusual garden seats from sections of cast-iron grills salvaged from an old greenhouse. Use old scaffold boards or pallets or even timber salvaged from trees blown over in the gales to make benches, swing seats, or oversized bench/tables. Seats can be cut from the stump of an old tree. Saw up old wooden ladders no longer considered safe to make authentic ladderback chairs. Cut in half old oak whisky barrels for tub seats or take a disused dining chair and plant the seat with camomile or your favourite herb. Furnish a sunny arbour with a pine chapel bench. Someone even thought to make a seat out of an old cast-iron bath cut in half! Why not make yourself comfortable in the garden shed and make a wooden bench on which to perch when busy at the potting stand?

Visit historic houses and gardens in order to see for yourself fine architectural gems and gain ideas. You might be inspired to design

and build a folly or temple from period salvage, using old floorboards, doors, windows and shutters to create a glorious hideaway, installing a wood-burning stove for warmth. If building is beyond your budget, let loose your imagination and transform an old tool shed, privy or henhouse, giving yourself somewhere to sit quietly and contemplate. Take your inspiration from nature and make a den, shelter or a simple retreat.

Inspired by the Romans, grottos were a feature of many landscaped gardens of the eighteenth century and these in turn might inspire you to create a grotto of your own. Whatever the size of your garden, a magical space decorated with beautiful shells, planted with shade-loving, large-leaved plants, and enhanced by the soothing sound of trickling water can only add to the atmosphere. The Lost Gardens of Heligan, in Cornwall, houses a grotto lined with rock crystal which reflects candlelight beautifully, adding to its drama. In stark contrast, a mysterious cave we know is lined with prehistoric animal bones, just to put a shiver down the spine!

SCAFFOLD BENCH

EQUIPMENT

Paintbrush
Tape measure
Try-square
Pencil or marker pen
Hand saw
Hammer
Wood chisel
Electric (or hand) screwdriver
Electric (or hand) drill
Selection wood drill bits
Spanner
Mitre saw (optional)
Orbital sander (or rough grade glasspaper)

MATERIALS

Exterior-grade transparent wood
    preservative
Seven lengths 193 cm (76 in) scaffold board
Four 64 cm (25¼ in) lengths 75 mm (3 in)
    square sawn timber (legs)
Two 23 cm (9 in) lengths 50 mm (2 in)
    square sawn timber (seat supports)
Selection 75 mm (3 in) wood screws
Two 150 cm (60 in) lengths 75 mm (3 in)
    square sawn timber (top supports)
Four 10 cm (4 in) coach screws
Two pieces 20 cm x 20 cm x 5 cm
    (8 in x 8 in x 2 in) sawn timber
White emulsion paint (or selected colour
    multi-surface paint or stain)

The inspiration for this bench came from our stay at a holiday villa in Italy. Dug into the patio gravel, the legs were extended to support a pergola on which grew a glorious shading vine. The bench, far longer than the example in this project, soon became the the focal point for lazy lunches and long balmy evenings. A memorable holiday.

Tired of most of the benches so often seen in pubs and picnic areas, we decided to construct a scaled-down version of the Italian original without its roof, large enough to seat eight people, but just light enough to be moved around if wanted. The bench can be made to almost any size, its length extended by joining boards together and adding further support frames as required.

If you choose to make a static bench, the measurement of the legs should be extended to allow at least 20 cm (8 in) to be inserted in the ground. We used old fencing posts for the frame construction of this bench but rough sawn timber can be used instead. Before you start the construction of your bench, measure and record the width and thickness of the boards you will be using – we used scaffold boards which measured 23 cm x 45 mm (9 x 1¾ in). This measurement will be useful when calculating table top and seat heights, normally 76 cm (30 in) and 45 cm (18 in) respectively, and how many boards will be required for its top.

SCAFFOLD BENCH

METHOD

Treat all the wood used to make the bench with outdoor transparent wood preservative. Any cut surfaces should be similarly treated as the construction proceeds.

1 Mark a point 45 cm (18 in) from the bottom of one of the legs to represent the eventual height of the seat off the ground. Mark a second point the thickness of the scaffold board down from the first point, and a third point 50 mm (2 in) further down from the second point. Use the try-square and pencil or marker pen to draw horizontal lines across one face at the second and third points. Extend each line by 25 mm (1 in) across the two adjacent faces of the leg. Join the ends of the two 25 mm (1 in) lines to mark out the area of the leg to be cut out to create a rebate for the seat support. Use the hand saw to cut along the marked sides of the rebate then remove the wood with a hammer and wood chisel. Repeat the process for the other three legs.

2 Mark the centre of one of the seat supports and insert the support into the rebate of a leg. Make sure the support is placed centrally and the joint fits tightly. Check the joint is square and secure the support in place with two 75 mm (3 in) wood screws. Repeat with the remaining three legs and seat supports.

3 It may be a good idea before proceeding further to lay out the four legs and two frame cross-members on a level surface to familiarise yourself with the construction sequence. Take one of the top supports and using the try-square draw a line 75 mm (3 in) from one end. Mark a point centred between the line and the end of the top support and pre-

drill a hole for a coach screw. Repeat for the other end of the top support. Place one end of the top support over the top of a leg, insert a coach screw into the pre-drilled hole, and secure it to the leg using the spanner. Secure the other end of the top support to a second leg to complete assembly of the first frame. Make up the second frame with the remaining top support and two legs.

4 Use the hand saw (or mitre saw) to cut the two 20 cm x 20 cm x 5 cm (8 in x 8 in x 2 in) pieces of sawn timber in half diagonally to create four triangular corner braces. Check the assembled frames are square and fit the corner braces into position with 75 mm (3 in) wood screws. If you cannot find 20 cm x 20 cm x 5 cm (8 in x 8 in x 2 in) timber, you can use a brace made from 50 mm (2 in) or 75 mm (3 in) square timber with the ends cut at 45 degrees as an alternative.

5 Mark the central point of one end of one of the scaffold boards and a further two points 38 mm (1½ in) either side of the central point. Using the try-square, draw lines through the second and third points, continuing them around the end onto the bottom of the board to a depth of 75 mm (3 in) on each surface. Join the ends of the 75 cm (3 in) lines to create the outline of a 75 mm (3 in) square rebate which will fit tightly over the leg. Cut out the marked rebate with the saw, hammer and chisel. Repeat for the other end of the board and both ends of a second board to create the two bench seats. Place the seats over the seat supports attached to the legs with the rebate fitted over the leg and fix in place with 75 mm (3 in) wood screws.

6 The bench frame should now be self-supporting. Place it on a level surface and mark the centres of the two top supports and the centre of both ends of a scaffold board. Use the marked points to locate the scaffold board centrally on the top supports and fix in place with one 75 mm (3 in) wood screw at each end. Double-check the angles with the try-square and secure in place with two further screws at each end. Fit the remaining four boards into place butted either side of the central board and the structure of your bench is complete. Tighten all screws to make sure the bench is rigid.

7 Paint the entire bench with a coat of white emulsion paint diluted to half strength with water and leave to dry. (Multi-surface garden paint or stain can be used instead of emulsion depending on the colour finish you want. The Italian bench we so admired was stained black.)

8 When the paint is completely dry, sand with the orbital sander or glasspaper to remove the surface of the paint and reveal some of the underlying timber. Smooth off any rough timber or splinters, paying particular attention to sharp edges and areas where natural wear would occur. The bench is now ready to use.

CHEESE PRESS TABLE

EQUIPMENT

Wire brush
Rubber gloves
Stiff-bristled paintbrush
Small discardable paintbrush
Tape measure
Wood saw
Garden spade
Hand trowel
Metal or wooden rammer
Hammer

MATERIALS

Wooden cheese-press followers
Exterior-grade transparent wood
preservative
Wood hardener
Logs
A number of 15 cm (6 in) galvanised
  round head nails

METHOD

1 Take the wooden cheese-press followers and remove any very soft or extraneous rotten wood using the wire brush. Place the followers on a flat surface and saturate them with transparent wood preservative using the stiff-bristled paintbrush. Make sure the entire surface of the wood is treated and allow the preservative to soak into the wood. Leave to dry. Apply a generous coating of wood hardener with the disposable paintbrush, ensuring that any particularly soft areas are saturated. Again, leave to dry.

2 Select the logs you will be using for the furniture stands, which should be at least 20 cm (8 in) longer than the desired table or seat height. Saw one end of each log straight across. Decide on the position for the furniture. For each table or seat, dig a hole at least 20 cm (8 in) deep where the stand will be inserted and remove any remaining soil with the hand trowel. Place the post into the hole with the cut end uppermost and horizontal and replace the soil, firming it with the metal or wooden rammer until the post is firmly held in position.

3 Place each cheese-press follower on the cut end of a post, making sure it is supported at its centre and secure in place with at least three 15 cm (6 in) galvanised nails. We selected 'green' or newly cut willow logs for the table supports and there is every chance that the willow will 'strike' and sprout new growth in years to come.

Safety note

We advise that rubber or protective gloves are used when applying timber preservative or hardener. Some formulations can be harmful: follow the manufacturers' instructions for application.

Cheesemaking was once an important rural industry. Surplus summer milk was turned into cheese as food for winter and as a vital source of income.

Slow-maturing Cheddar, named after the north Somerset village, was the best known of the local cheeses. Although still made locally, Cheddar has become the generic name of what are often sad mimicries of the original farmhouse product.

Today, cheesemaking is no longer part of twenty-first century farm life and old fancifully embellished cast-iron cheese presses can still be snapped up in farm sales by collectors. The circular wooden press followers ('vollows' in local dialect), usually made of elm, are much more common. Made in different dimensions to suit the size of cheese being pressed, these wooden discs can often be found discarded, their origin unrecognised.

Over the years we have accumulated a number of wooden followers and have been seeking a practical use for some of the more worm-eaten and less well-preserved examples. Offcuts left from the pollarding of willow trees gave us the timber to convert our cheese press followers into garden seats and tables.

CHAIR PLANTER

EQUIPMENT

Pliers
Screwdriver
Marker pen
Metal or tin snips
Metal rule or straight edge
Heavy-duty craft knife
Electric drill and small metal bit

MATERIALS

Chair with seat rebate
Sheet zinc
25 mm (1 in) woodscrews

Almost any household will have one or two odd or mismatched unwanted chairs – if not, you will probably discover one in the first skip you see. Seats of many woven or upholstered chairs are removable and such chairs are ideal for this project. In our furniture design work we make a number of prototype chairs and the one used for this project is a beech chair which never went into production.

Chairs make effective and attractive planters which can be easily moved around the garden or patio. The one we made for this project is decorative, but we have made others with a more robust tray support, planted them with fragrant herbs such as thyme or camomile, and used them as practical occasional seats in the garden. Any shallow-rooted herb which is suitable for planting in a path or patio can be used but, because of the planter's shallow tray, frequent watering is essential.

We settled on a simple one-colour display for our planter but a striking effect can be achieved by using plants of different size and colour and embellishing the chair with planted flower pots hung from its back. We decided to make a shallow frame for our chair planter which would be concealed within the seat frame. If you choose to construct yours with a deeper tray to hold a greater reserve of soil or planting medium, you could plant it with hanging plants to conceal its base.

CHAIR PLANTER

METHOD

The chair we selected for this project was neither painted nor treated and since we designed it for only occasional outside use we decided to leave it that way. If you propose to leave your planter outside, treat the chair with a timber preservative or exterior-grade timber paint before use. There are a number of attractively coloured paints and preservatives now on the market, ideal for this purpose.

1 Remove the seat from the chair frame and take off any wooden supports with the pliers or screwdriver. Place the chair upside down on top of the zinc sheet on the edge of a work surface and draw around the inside of the seat with the marker pen.

2 Measure the depth of the seat rebate and add to this an extra 50 mm (2 in). Draw a second line, to the distance of this combined measurement, around the marked shape on the zinc sheet. Turn the sheet over and transfer this line to that side. Cut to size with the metal snips. Cut a rectangle from each corner from the marked seat size to the outside with the metal snips to allow the zinc sheet to be bent into a tray shape. Use the heavy-duty craft knife and metal rule or straight edge to lightly score along the marked lines outlining the shape of the seat. Turn the sheet over and score along the second and outside marked lines.

3 Place the zinc sheet on the work surface, with the scored lines of the seat shape uppermost. Gently bend each side of the sheet over the work surface edge to form a tray shape to fit inside the seat rebate. Use the work surface edge to gently bend the outside scored lines to a right-angle to create a lip around the tray to hold it securely within the seat rebate.

4 Place the completed tray on a piece of scrap timber and use the electric drill and metal drill bit to drill a series of drainage holes in the base. Drill a further two holes in each flap to allow the tray to be securely screwed into position within the seat rebate.

5 Place the tray into the seat rebate and secure in place with two 25 mm (1 in) screws driven through each flap into the seat surround. Fill the tray within the assembled chair planter with soil or planting medium and plant with your selected flowers or herbs. Press down the soil around the plants and thoroughly water before placing the planter in position. You may prefer not to plant inside the zinc tray, but construct a versatile planter which can be used to hold temporary displays of plants in pots. If this is your plan, the zinc tray will need to be made sufficiently deep to hold the selected pots.

POTTING STAND

EQUIPMENT

Paintbrush
Tape measure
Try-square
Pencil or marker
Hand saw
Electric drill and wood bit
Electric (or hand) screwdriver

MATERIALS

Colourless timber preservative
Selection 30 mm (1¼ in) wood screws
Selection 50 mm (2 in) wood screws

TIMBER

For the base:

75 mm (3 in) square softwood timber
   cut into:
   Two front legs approx. 71 cm (28 in)
   Two rear legs approx. 112 cm (44 in)
10 cm x 2 cm (4 in x ³/₄ in) softwood timber
   cut into:
   Two side stretchers approx. 60 cm
   (23¹/₂ in)
   One rear stretcher approx. 93 cm
   (36¹/₂ in)
22 cm x 2 cm (9 in x ³/₄ in) softwood timber
   cut into:
   Two bin sides approx. 60 cm (23¹/₂ in)
   One bin front approx. 97 cm (38 in)
Quantity approx. 25 mm (1 in) square
   softwood (support battens)
15 cm x 12 mm (6 in x ¹/₂ in) softwood
   timber cut into:
   Two pot boards approx. 93 cm (36¹/₂ in)
One piece 12 mm (¹/₂ in) waterproof
   plywood or particle board approx.
   93 cm x 60 cm (36¹/₂ in x 23³/₄ in)
   (bin base)

For the top:

20 cm x 2 cm (8 in x ³/₄ in) softwood timber
   cut into:
   Two side pieces approx. 89 cm (35 in)
   One bottom shelf approx. 93 cm
   (36¹/₂ in)
   One vertical divider approx. 60 cm
   (23⁵/₈ in)
   One long shelf approx. 61 cm (24 in)
   One short shelf approx. 30 cm (11³/₄ in)
One approx. 98 cm (38¹/₂ in) length 22 cm
   x 2 cm (9 in x ³/₄ in) softwood timber
   (top piece)
Seven approx. 112 cm (44 in) lengths 15 cm
   x 2 cm (6 in x ³/₄ in) softwood timber
   (back boards)

A potting shed is not only the focus of propagating activities necessary for the cultivation of a well managed garden, but if insulated and properly equipped can also be a cool retreat in summer and a cosy refuge in winter. Away from the accusing eyes of neglected roses and a vista of unmown grass, it can become a comfortable bolt hole for all but the most conscientious of gardeners – a private sanctuary where peace and quiet reign, the demanding shrill of the telephone remains unheard, and the mindless chatter of television and the clamour of much-loved children can be ignored. The perfect environment for indulgence in slow, deep and somnolent thought.

Unfortunately, such escapism demands a price. A potting shed needs a potting stand to justify your time spent in it, and ours is ideal. The bin holds sufficient compost for almost every job, the shelved back accommodates pots, packets of seed and other miscellanea, and the pot board underneath provides extra vital storage space. If desired, a plank or board can be laid over the compost bin to make a surface perfect for those other gardening necessities – a book, a cup of tea, or perhaps a glass of whisky!

Made from salvaged fence posts and reclaimed roofing softwood, the stand can be simply disassembled for installation where there is restricted access, or should you need to move it at a later date.

POTTING STAND

METHOD

Before assembling the potting stand, paint all the timber you will be using for this project with colourless timber preservative. Pay particular attention to sawn ends and end grain.

1 Lay one front and one rear leg on a flat surface, the front on the left and the rear on the right. On the uppermost faces of each leg, measure two points 20 cm (8 in) and 63 cm (24¾ in) from the bottom of the leg. Use the try-square and pencil to draw horizontal lines at each of these points. Place a side stretcher across the bottom line of both legs and a bin side on the top line and secure in place with 50 mm (2 in) wood screws. Repeat with the other two legs, but this time place the front leg on the right and the rear leg on the left to create the two opposing side frames.

2 Turn the side frames over and fit a length of batten to the inside of each bin side, one end flush with and butted against the top of the front leg the other approximately 25 mm (1 in) short of the rear leg. Place the two sides upright with their rear legs flat on the surface and the side stretchers and bin sides on the outside. Fit the rear stretcher across the rear legs inside the bin sides, its top level with the top of the battens. Screw securely in place with 50 mm (2 in) wood screws.

3 Place the bin front over the front legs, its ends flush with the outside faces of the bin sides, and secure in place with 50 mm (2 in) wood screws. Turn the base over onto its front and fit a length of batten to the rear of the bin front between and flush with the tops of the front legs. You have now made the basic structure of the potting stand base.

4 Stand the base upright on its legs and, checking the frame is square, fit the two pot boards over the side stretchers, butting them against the back legs. Fix in place with 50 mm (2 in) screws.

5 Carefully measure the inside dimensions of the open backed bin you have made and cut the waterproof plywood or particle board to that size, removing a notch from each back corner to fit over the rear legs. Drop into place so that it rests on the battens, the front legs and the top of the rear stretcher, and secure in place with 30 mm (1¼ in) wood screws. The potting stand base in now complete.

6 You are now ready to start construction of the potting stand top. First check the measurement between the outsides of the rear legs of the base. Depending on the thickness of the timber you have used for the base construction, this should be approximately 93 cm (36½ in). This measurement is important as the top is designed to fit snugly over the rear legs (which are raised above the top of the base) and rest on the bin sides. Measure a point 26 cm (10¼ in) from the bottom of each side piece and draw across with the pencil and try-square. Fit the bottom shelf between the two side pieces level with that marked point and secure it to them with 50 mm (2 in) wood screws. Take the top piece and place it on top of the side pieces with an overhang at the sides and front and fit it in place with 50 mm (2 in) wood screws. You have now constructed the basic frame of the top. Mark a point 30 cm (11¾ in) from one end on both the top piece and the bottom shelf. Fit the vertical divider at that point with 5 cm (2 in)

screws to divide the frame into two unequal sections. Mark points just above halfway on the inside of the vertical divider and side piece within the wider section and fit the long shelf in position. Finally mark points approximately 4 cm (1½ in) above the long shelf on the inside of the remaining smaller section and fit the short shelf at that position.

7 Place the assembled top structure face down on the surface, check it is square and starting at one side with the edge of the first back board flush with the outside face of the side piece, proceed to attach the remaining back boards to the rear, secured with 50 mm (2 in) screws. It may be necessary to cut the final board down to fit. Carefully lift the completed top section onto the base so that it fits over the extended back legs and the side pieces rest on the bin sides. Secure with screws driven through the back boards into the legs and rear edge of the bin sides. Place in position, fill the bin with potting compost and your potting stand is ready for use.

CONCRETE TABLE

EQUIPMENT

Pointing trowel
Shovel
Cement-mixing board or wheelbarrow
Club hammer
Spirit level
Tape measure
Soft hand brush
Paintbrush (optional)

MATERIALS

Soft building sand
Cement
Mortar plasticiser (optional)
Approximately ten 15 cm (6 in)
   concrete blocks
Concrete slab top
Multi-surface garden or masonry paint
   (optional)

METHOD

If the garden table is to be built on a solid surface, clean it of any lichen or other growth. On a new site, it must be laid on a concrete foundation (one part cement to two parts soft sand and four parts aggregate) at least 30 cm (12 in) deep. The base should be allowed to harden before the plinth is installed. Calculate how many blocks will be required to construct a plinth of the right height for the table. Table tops are normally approximately 76 cm (30 in) high. Remember to allow for the thickness of the top and each layer of mortar.

1 Place two concrete blocks approximately 20 mm (³/₄ in) apart on the ground where the table plinth will be built. Draw around them with the point of your trowel and put the blocks to one side. Make up a workable mortar mix of five parts soft building sand to one part cement and water and place a thick layer of the mix inside the trowel marks. Replace the two blocks in position on the mortar and tap into place with the handle of the trowel or club hammer, periodically checking the spirit level. Clean off excess mortar from around the base and use it to fill the joint between the two blocks. Do not fill the gap completely as this may cause them to splay.

2 Place the next two blocks at right-angles to the first course. Apply mortar across one end of both blocks sufficient for one of the blocks on the second course. Tap the block into place, checking that it is level and that the sides are vertical. Place mortar on the remainder of the first course and lay the fourth block alongside the one you have just laid. Fill the outside of the vertical joint and smooth to a good finish.

3 Continue building up the plinth to the desired height, checking the levels as you go. To fit the top, place mortar around the edge of the top course and a trowelful in the centre. Fit the top carefully on the mortar, and when centred make sure it is entirely level. Tap it firmly in place with the handle of the club hammer. Remove excess mortar from around the top of the plinth. After about four hours, brush over joints with a soft brush to give a smooth finish and remove any loose material. Keep new blockwork moist in hot weather and protect from sun, wind, rain or frost with a sheet of polythene. Allow one week for the mortar to fully cure before using the table. If desired, the plinth can be painted with two coats of multi-surface garden paint or masonry paint applied with a stiff brush.

Alfresco dining is one of life's great pleasures. Whilst any number of portable tables can be taken into the garden for an impromptu occasion, a properly designed and constructed table, erected where it will be constantly used, is very convenient. Before you build a permanent table in your garden or on your patio, we suggest you erect a temporary mock-up in the proposed position to make sure the site is suitable. Once built, it will be a lasting feature.

During inclement weather the table can be used for arrangements of plants in pots or urns, or for an outdoor sculpture. It will become a feature of the garden, as much appreciated when not in use as when it is the venue for outdoor entertaining.

Finding a table top of a suitable size can be a problem. Surfaces can be made of timber or even heavy glass, but we made this one from the side of an old concrete coal bunker which had become redundant. The side was extremely heavy, requiring at least two people to move it, and the bolt holes in its corners required filling with a sand and cement mixture. However, it had the considerable advantage of being robust and its bevelled edge made it particularly suitable as a table top. Large stones, slate or concrete paving slabs could be used as other alternatives.

It is so easy to drive down to the local garden centre, load up the trolley and buy all the containers needed for use in the garden – as easy, in fact, as going to the supermarket for the weekly food

Check in the garden shed, look at the back of the garage or investigate the unsightly pile at the front of the house awaiting a trip to the rubbish dump. Put aside old terracotta piping, metal

PLANTS, PLANTERS AND PLANTING

shopping. Although there is always a good selection of mass-produced pots and troughs to choose from, at varying price levels, the one thing they lack is individuality. So next time you are tempted to jump in the car en route to the garden centre, just stop for a moment and think about what you may already have lying around that could so easily be recycled.

buckets of differing sizes, concrete blocks and wooden packing cases, in fact anything which looks as if it could contain plants or shrubs and withstand having holes drilled in it for drainage. You will be astonished at just how much can be 'repurposed' to become something both useful and decorative, giving new colour, texture and shape to a garden.

Container gardening has many advantages, particularly where restricted space limits the number of plants that can be accommodated. Planters can be easily moved around, repositioned if the plants need more light or shade, or built up on supports to give the display height and structure. Planting in containers allows for a garden to be changed with the seasons, species intolerant of cold can be grown outside to give colour through the summer, then brought inside with the approach of colder weather.

Raised beds are often used to grow neat rows of green cabbages, lettuce, chard and other vegetables together with swirls of sage, parsley and camomile. They answer the problems posed by limited space and are useful if you want to grow acid-loving plants in a lime-rich garden. Raised beds allow the soil to heat up faster, are easily maintained and can be constructed from a wide choice of materials. Railway sleepers look informal and can be found via the classified section of the local newspaper or reclamation dealers.

A disused and bottomless metal dustbin or old tyres piled on top of one another to contain the growth of rhubarb need not look unsightly if painted in an old-fashioned dark green or other subdued colour to blend with the planting. Why not choose primary colours of red, blue and yellow, just for a bit of fun! Transform salvaged oil drums, large wooden litter bins, metal feed troughs, cans and cast-iron guttering with bright paint colours. Painting gives an instant, easy and inexpensive effect which will lift the spirits and introduce life to a boring back yard.

Create wooden tubs from whisky and sherry barrels, attach shapely legs from ancient roll-top baths to the base of an old boiler or copper – even the wire baskets from a redundant freezer make ideal planters. Transforming these essentially utilitarian, sometimes ugly objects into eye-catching containers can be quite a challenge but with some thought and a little effort there is much lying around that can be turned into interesting and unusual planters.

FAR LEFT

A carved stone feeding trough in the garden of a retired farming couple was once in use in the cattle yard of their former farm. Eight men were needed to carry it to the garden of their present home. Old stone troughs are much in demand and fetch high prices at garden antique auctions.

BELOW LEFT

Tripod legs have been secured to a weathered log to make a rustic plant-stand used to conceal an unsightly drain cover in this urban garden.

CENTRE LEFT

Ancient brick door leading from the walled White Garden to the productive kitchen gardens at Birtsmorton Court. The terracotta urns and plinths blend with the old mellow brick wall perfectly.

BELOW RIGHT

Old slate used as edging to retain a bed of flowering culinary herbs beside the kitchen garden at the retreat, Emmaus House.

NEAR LEFT

An established wisteria has been trained to grow on supports made from timber salvaged from disused wooden pallets and mounted on a stone wall facing the kitchen window of garden enthusiasts Ron and Judy Mathews.

LEFT

A typical wooden-framed farmhouse in Normandy, France, its thatched roof capped with a traditional mixture of succulents, lilies and grasses and its gable end adorned with a glorious miscellany of summer flowers in a variety of salvaged containers.

LATRINE BUCKET

EQUIPMENT

Scrubbing brush
Bucket
Electric drill
Wire wheel or sanding flap disc

MATERIALS

Galvanised metal container
Liquid soap
Two wooden wedges
Liquid metal polish
Medium-grade wire wool
Soft cotton rag

METHOD

1 Remove all wrapping and any string or labels attached to the bucket.

2 Wash thoroughly with a scrubbing brush and hot soapy water to remove surface dirt and grime. Leave to dry.

3 Place the bucket on its side on a work surface and wedge it with two wood blocks to stop it moving when you are working on it. Use the electric drill and wire wheel and/or the sanding flap disc to remove the surface oxidation and discolouration. Inevitably the galvanised coating will show evidence of the wheel or disc's action but it is important not to cut through this coating to the underlying steel.

4 Work over the surface of the bucket in a circular motion with a wad of wire wool dipped in liquid metal polish as a lubricant. Keep the wire wool saturated with polish and change it when it shows signs of breaking down and starts to lose its ability to cut into the surface. Work on a small area at a time, periodically wiping the surface clean with a cotton rag to inspect the finish until all the scratch marks produced by the wire wheel or sanding flap disc have been removed and the bucket is bright and clean.

As this planter is not perforated for drainage it is shown under the shelter of the linhay by the back door, where it is protected from the rain but can be watered as and when necessary. It is important not to over water – many plants can suffer damage from water saturation as much as from drought. Our galvanised metal planter looks particularly effective set off by the blue lias paving on which it stands.

PACKING CASE PLANTER

EQUIPMENT

Claw hammer
Pliers
Wood saw
Scissors
Staple gun
Craft knife

MATERIALS

Wooden packing case
Scrap timber or plywood
25 mm (1 in) panel pins or thin nails
Quantity of fine-mesh garden netting
    or hessian
Heavy duty staples to fit staple gun

PACKING CASE PLANTER

METHOD

1 Place the packing case on a convenient surface and remove any lid or protruding nails or staples with the claw hammer and pliers.

2 Turn the case upside down. Cut pieces of scrap timber or plywood to fill any gaps in the base of the case. Secure with panel pins or nails to make a solid floor to the planter.

3 Cut the fine-mesh garden netting, or hessian, into four pieces to match the shapes of the sides of the box. Use these to line the interior of the planter, fixing them in place with the staple gun and staples.

4 Fill the planter halfway with planting medium. Using the scissors or craft knife, cut crosses through the garden netting at places where you want plants to grow sideways through the planter. Gently insert the plants through the netting into the medium. Complete the planting from the top of the case. We used a selection of culinary herbs for this planter but almost any plants can be used. Water well and, when drained, place the planter in its selected position. If you wish, you can convert this planter into a hanging basket by attaching screw eyes and chain to each corner.

CAST-IRON BOILER PLANTER

EQUIPMENT

Wire brush
Electric drill and high-speed drill bit
(optional)

MATERIALS

Copper or cast-iron boiler
Chimneypot

METHOD

1 Clean the boiler with the wire brush to remove any extraneous rust. Similarly clean the chimneypot of any cement or mortar and unsightly stains. Should you wish to plant directly into the boiler you will at this stage have to drill a drainage hole in the boiler's base, but as we chose to use an already planted pot for our display, this was unnecessary.

2 Place the chimneypot in position, making sure it is vertical and the top level. Carefully place the boiler on top of the chimneypot, taking care not to chip the top of the pot while centering the boiler and making it secure. Check that you are happy with the final height of the planter – we decided to put an extra piece of stone under the chimneypot to give the planter additional height. Plant as desired, or place an already planted arrangement in a plastic or similar container inside the boiler.

There are many locations within almost any garden where a fixed planter can be placed to advantage. An old well in front of our house, now long disused, has been covered with a stark and unsightly stone slab which dominates what was once a vegetable garden but is now laid to lawn. We have long been looking for a simple 'architectural' planter which could mask this stone and add a touch of drama to the garden. We experimented with a sundial but decided the area needed something else. A simple yet striking tall planter seemed to be the perfect solution and, having no better ideas, we decided to visit a local reclamation yard to seek inspiration.

Copper boilers are much sought after and expensive to buy if you are fortunate to find one, but the much more common cast-iron boiler was once a feature in almost every home and the focus for the thriving domestic activity which surrounded the weekly family wash. We found our boiler among a number of others in the yard, and nearby there were some ancient chimneypots, any one of which could have been used for this project.

WASTE BIN PLANTER

EQUIPMENT

Tape measure
Pencil
Ruler or straight edge
Wood saw
Hammer
Electric drill with small wood bit
Screwdriver
50 mm (2 in) paintbrush

MATERIALS

Quantity of marine or exterior-grade
  plywood
25 mm (1 in) panel pins or thin round
  head nails
Quantity of approximately 25 mm
  (1 in) square softwood timber
40 mm (1½ in) wood screws
Dark brown timber preservative

METHOD

Our waste bin was constructed of slatted wood fixed to a rigid timber framework and had been designed to hold a removable metal or plastic inner container which had long disappeared. Otherwise the bin was in an excellent state of preservation.

1 Measure the inside dimensions of the four sides of the bin and use the pencil and straight edge to draw out their shapes on the marine or exterior-grade plywood. Cut to shape with the wood saw and nail into place with the panel pins or round head nails.

2 Measure the depth of the plant container you will be placing in the bin and add approximately 50 mm (2 in) to give you the depth at which to fix the battens inside the bin. Measure across the inside of the bin at that length and cut two battens to that length from the 25 mm (1 in) square timber. Use the wood screws to fit the two battens on opposite sides to each other in the bin.

3 Measure the width across the newly fitted battens and cut three or four slats from the 25 mm (1 in) square timber to fit. Start holes with the electric drill and wood bit and secure slats in place with the 40 mm (1½ in) wood screws. Paint the whole planter with a liberal application of preservative, allow to dry and place your selected plant container on the slatted support.

We discovered this wooden bin in our local waste and recycling depot. The bin had been discarded and its metal liner had long gone missing but its shape suggested a new life as an imposing planter. We soon discovered a second matching waste bin, this one complete with a plaque proclaiming 'Place Litter Inside', which we speedily removed and installed on the outside of our teenage daughter's bedroom.

Large planters are essential for some plants and planting schemes and these waste bins were perfect for the site and plants we had selected, requiring very little conversion. Their construction is so simple that we have subsequently made up several more in different sizes for a patio town garden.

The original waste bin was aged and very faded and we decided to smarten it with a coat of dark brown wood preservative to give it a new lease of life. There is no reason why such bins cannot be finished with a transparent timber preservative if the original look is to be maintained, or transformed with a coat of one of the many coloured wood paints and preservatives now commercially available.

TYRE PLANTER

EQUIPMENT

Wire brush
Garden spade

MATERIALS

Old car tyre
Can of multi-surface garden spray paint

METHOD

We selected a fairly small car tyre for this project as we wanted to restrict the rhubarb's growth. We knew that it would be easy to return to the source for more tyres of a similar size if we wanted to build a forcing tower of stacked tyres.

1 Use the wire brush to clean the outside surface of the tyre. Removing any mildew, dirt or fungal growth and loose or flaked tyre material will provide a sound surface for the paint.

2 Lay the tyre flat and spray the outside and top of the tyre with multi-surface garden spray paint. We recommend using a spray paint rather than painting with a brush as it is easier to achieve complete coverage, particularly inside the tyre tread.

3 Place the tyre on the ground in the position it will be installed and mark the position of the hole to be dug. Remove the tyre and dig or loosen the soil to a depth of at least 30 cm (12 in). Add manure or fertiliser, plant the rhubarb root at a good depth, and return the tyre to its position, over the plant.

Finding uses for old and discarded tyres is an increasing environmental problem. As the number of cars rises, the tyres they consume become an ever greater concern. Burning tyres in incinerators provides something of an answer as power can be generated as a by-product of this process; less acceptable is the production of carbon dioxide gas and the inevitable release of carbon particles into the atmosphere.

In country areas old tyres are frequently used to weigh down the plastic-sheeting covers of silage clamps, in which grass cut in early summer is mixed with molasses and allowed to ferment to provide a nutritious winter feed for cattle.

We have seen old tyres used in numerous inventive ways in gardens both in Britain and abroad and one of their most appealing uses is as planters for potatoes and rhubarb in kitchen gardens. While few would consider tyres an attractive addition to a garden, they can offer practical solutions where space is at a premium.

We have successfully planted potatoes in old tyres filled with soil. As the plants grow, further tyres and soil are added until a stack of up to six tyres produces a bumper crop of home grown tubers. In the past we have used old milk churns and chimneypots as improvised rhubarb forcers to provide us with an early crop of succulent blanched stalks. For this project, we decided to plant a rhubarb root inside an old tyre to restrict its invasive growth.

It is said that gardens and gardening are good for the soul and many a city dweller craves their own piece of private, outdoor space. However small — whether it is a roof terrace, or a our television screens in recent times. As a result, instant gardens fashionably furnished with wooden decking, terracotta pots and architectural, foreign plants have become top of the

A GARDEN RECLAIMED

patio just big enough for a barbecue, or a balcony decked with pot plants — it is somewhere to potter with a trowel in the open air, an essential sanctuary in which to just sit and think. This trend towards outdoor living has been fed by plethora of garden make-over programmes seen on must-have list for many people. In reality gardens are not instant but evolve over time and need some looking after, however low-maintenance the design may be. If at any stage it is redesigned, the plan will usually incorporate many of the existing plants, shrubs and trees.

ABOVE

An informal arrangement of nineteenth-century damaged terracotta pots almost overwhelmed by succulents in the Abbey Gardens, Tresco.

RIGHT

A superb example of an original Victorian greenhouse, rescued from dereliction by John Nelson and re-erected at The Lost Gardens of Heligan in Cornwall.

In this chapter we have taken a small garden which had fallen into neglect and transformed it, working as much as possible with what was already there. As lovage, fennel and a border of piercing, purplish-blue catmint were already there, they made an obvious starting point in the plan to establish a fragrant herb garden which would be sweetly scented on summer evenings, give some greenery all year round and provide delicious herbs for culinary use. The herb garden would enclose a crazy-paved area using stones salvaged from the garden and softened by more herbs growing between the slabs. Yet more herbs were planted into a few clay drainage pipes (pots could be used) to achieve extra height and structure. Reached by four stone steps edged with wooden railway sleepers, the design incorporated various edgings of terracotta and slate tiles, railway sleeper blocks and old mellow bricks, with slate chippings and tiny pebbles used as mulches, all suited to small areas.

Two other features were deemed essential: the soothing sound of water and a table for alfresco dining. An old cattle water trough was bought which made an ideal container,

NEAR LEFT

Gravel steps leading from the patio area through a rose-covered pergola to the garden beyond have been constructed from crushed stone gravel behind salvaged slate and treated timber log retainers.

BOTTOM LEFT

The interior of the orange house in the Lost Gardens of Heligan, showing detail of the restored timber framing and beaver-tail glass, some rescued from collapsed buildings on the site and some made to the original pattern.

BOTTOM RIGHT

Steps lead from the patio outside garden designer Sarah Giddens' house in a small market town and up to a pathway constructed of reclaimed bricks and salvaged pavement stone. The central feature was rescued in pieces by Sarah's antique dealer husband and carefully reinstalled to create a focal point to this garden 'room'.

painted a dark green colour to blend in with the planting. An inexpensive fountain pump was fitted in the water and the trough planted with striking yellow irises found abandoned on the roadside after ditches had been cleared. The table was constructed, its top made of the concrete side of a coal bunker and the base from breeze blocks.

Before the garden came to fruition much groundwork needed to be done. The soil had to be excavated and several loads disposed of, revealing a stony sub-structure and quite a lot of rubbish. This was nothing compared to the garden we had acquired with our rundown farmhouse which, once rotavated, produced enough stones, flint, broken terracotta, baling twine, coloured plastic, polystyrene, old bones, rusty metal, decomposing leather, shards of glass and china chips to fill a disused quarry.

It was the bits of broken china that first caught the eye. Blue and white seemed to predominate, especially willow pattern which was commonly used for everyday ware. A fascination, or perhaps one should say obsession, began to gain a grip, making a journey to the compost heap or washing line impossible without eyes glued to the ground in search of treasure. And then the joy of finding some in shades of blue ranging from pale pastels through bright cobalt to inky blacks; large pieces and small, all caked in grime, until the collection filled three empty shoe boxes. One day in the dim and distant future, when leisure allows, they will be used to cover the concrete table, making a magnificent mosaic.

EDGING BRICKS

EQUIPMENT

Pointing trowel
Garden spade
Shovel
Cement-mixing board or wheelbarrow
String line and pegs
Spirit level
Hand brush

MATERIALS

Quantity old bricks
Broken stone
Cement
Sharp builders' sand
Aggregate

METHOD

Carefully select the bricks you will use for this project. As they will be laid on edge, ensure that at least one edge is sound and remove any extraneous mortar with the trowel. If you are using different coloured bricks or the sizes vary slightly, mix them well before laying in order to achieve a uniform appearance. Put aside any mortar removed from the bricks and add it to the broken stone to be laid in the base of the trench.

1 Excavate a trench 25 cm (10 in) deep the entire length of the proposed edging border. Fill the trench with a 10 cm (4 in) layer of compacted broken stone. On the mixing board or wheelbarrow, use the shovel to make a dry mixture of one part cement to three parts sharp sand and six parts aggregate. Cover the stone base with the dry mix to a depth of about 10 cm (4 in). Using the string and pegs to give you a straight line, lay the bricks on their edges on the dry mix, each approximately 12 mm ($\frac{1}{2}$ in) apart. Tap the bricks into the bed of dry mix with the handle of the trowel, checking the level with the spirit level.

2 Make another dry mix, this time with one part cement to four parts dry soft sand, and use it to fill the joints between the laid bricks, removing any excess mortar with the brush.

3 Try to compact the mortar with the trowel and brush when the bricks are being laid. Cover with plastic sacks or a waterproof cover to protect from rain and leave for at least seven days for the mix to take up moisture from the soil and atmosphere until it completely hardens. By using a dry mix to lay the edging bricks, you will minimise any cement staining or unsightly spillage.

SLEEPER AND STONE STEPS

EQUIPMENT

Tape measure
Chain saw or cross-cut saw
Garden spade
Shovel
Wheelbarrow
Cement-mixing board
Club hammer
Bolster or stone chisel
Spirit level
Pointing trowel
Hand brush
Watering can

MATERIALS

Quantity paving stone
Quantity railway sleepers
Large quantity of broken stone
    or rubble
Cement
Sharp builders' sand
Aggregate
Selection scrap wood

Safety note

As using a chain saw is dangerous, it is advised that eye protection and a dust mask are worn. Eye protection should always be used if stone is being cut with a club hammer and bolster.

SLEEPER AND STONE STEPS

METHOD

Select the stone you will be using for this project. Look for stones of a similar size and depth and make sure each stone has at least one good surface. Reject any which are flaking or crumbling. Measure the width of the steps you will be building and cut the sleepers to that length with the chain saw.

1 Select a quantity of paving stones of approximately equal size and depth sufficient to cover the proposed tread area of the steps and put to one side. The height (rise) and depth (tread) of the step will be dependent on whether you propose to use the sleepers on edge or flat. Normally the rise should be 15 to 20 cm (6 to 8 in) and the tread should be twice that measurement. Calculate how many steps will be required by dividing the height of the slope where the steps are to be built by the measurement of a single riser. Dig out the first step to the dimension of the tread but excavate a further 15 cm (6 in) at the front, as a footing on which the sleeper riser will be laid.

2 Fill the bottom 10 cm (4 in) of the footing with compacted broken stone or rubble. On the mixing board or in the wheelbarrow, make a mortar mix of one part cement to four parts sharp sand and sufficient water to make a firm mix and use it cover the broken stone in the footing to a further depth of about 5 cm (2 in). Lay a cut sleeper on the mix, tap it into place with the club hammer and checking the level with the spirit level. Cover against rain and leave to dry for at least twenty-four hours. When dry, fill

the excavated space behind the riser with more compacted stone and rubble up to approximately 10 cm (4 in) of its top. Make up a further mortar mix, but this time dry (without water), place over the compacted stone, and bed your paving stones into it so that their surface is level with the top of the sleeper riser.

3 Lay each paving stone down with a screwing motion to ensure that it is securely bedded and will not rock or move, adding or removing dry mix as required. Try to keep the gaps between stones as small as possible – if necessary, the paving stones can be cut to size with the club hammer and bolster. Use the hammer cushioned with a scrap of waste timber to tap the stones into place. When the paving is laid and levelled to your satisfaction, use more of the dry mortar mix to fill the joints. Press down the mixture between the joints with a scrap of wood to compact it and use the brush to clean off any debris and surplus dry mortar mix from the paving surface. The dry mix will normally take up moisture from the soil and atmosphere but in dry weather curing will be aided by sprinkling water from a watering can fitted with a fine rose over the pointing. Cover and leave to set.

4 Repeat the above for each step, ensure that the level of the top of the last riser is finished flush with the proposed level of any new paving or surface. To construct the steps for our raised garden, we built a retaining side wall of reclaimed walling stone. We used a mortar mix of one part cement to one part soft sand and four parts stone dust. We use the stone dust in order to match the mortar used on the existing walls. The appearance of newly constructed steps can be softened by planting a few lime tolerant, low growing plants in soil-filled crevices left during construction.

STONE CRAZY PAVING

EQUIPMENT

Garden spade
Shovel
Wheelbarrow
Spirit level
Scaffold board or plank
String and pegs
Cement-mixing board
Club hammer
Bolster or stone chisel
Medium-bristled broom
Hand brush
Watering can (optional)

MATERIALS

Quantity paving stone
Large quantity of broken stone
    or rubble
Cement
Sharp builders' sand
Selection scrap wood

Safety note

Eye protection should always be used if stone is
being cut with a club hammer and bolster.

Our raised garden is the result of generations of former occupiers depositing their household rubbish and farming miscellanea. For the first few years after we bought the farmhouse we used the garden for growing vegetables and in the course of digging found fascinating evidence of the past. Shards of blue-and-white willow pattern crockery are now stored for future mosaics; remnants of salt-glazed pots and buckles from discarded harnesses told of earlier times; and on one occasion we even unearthed a brass cartridge case. Although it was fertile we felt this area was wasted and since it had been made redundant by a new kitchen garden we decided to create a paved sitting area where its west-facing aspect would allow us to enjoy the last evening light.

We live in an area where most houses are built of stone and the Draycott conglomerate used widely throughout the locality for pillars and gateposts and local blue lias used for flagstone floors are particularly in demand. Built on the site of a considerably older farmhouse, many of our outbuildings predate the house and a consequence of such extended occupation is the quantity of stone and other building materials to be found all over our garden hidden just under the soil. A useful building resource if not always an encouragement to cultivation.

Among the stone we have recovered from our garden is a considerable quantity of paving stone, some of which has been used for this project.

STONE CRAZY PAVING

METHOD

First make sure you have an adequate supply of reasonably large paving stones to cover the area you propose to pave. As far as possible select stones of an equal depth and make sure that one face of each stone is smooth and sound. Put aside stones with one straight edge as they will prove particularly useful as edging pieces.

1 Remove any weeds and debris from the area to be excavated, taking particular care to remove any roots.

2 Excavate the whole area with the garden spade and shovel to a depth of approximately 15 cm (6 in) plus the average depth of your selected paving below the final decided level. Compact loose soil and check that the area is almost level with the board and spirit level. Allow for a slight slope for drainage run-off.

3 If you have decided to border the paved area with beds or to create a complex shape, mark out the edges with string tied to pegs driven into the ground. Remove the soil excavated from the area. Some may usefully be retained for adding to the borders.

4 Fill the bottom 10 cm (4 in) of the excavated area with compacted broken stone or rubble. On the mixing board or in the wheelbarrow, use the shovel to make a dry mortar mix of one part cement to four parts sharp sand. Spread the dry mix over the broken stone to a depth of about 5 cm (2 in). Starting from one corner, lay the edging pieces first with the straight edge outwards adding further paving stones until the area is covered. Make sure all stones are securely bedded, adding or removing dry mix as required. Gaps between the stones should be small, and If necessary, cut paving stones to fit with the club hammer and bolster.

5 When the paving is laid to your satisfaction, sprinkle dry mortar mix over the area and use the broom to brush it into the joints. Compact the mortar between the joints with a scrap of wood and use the hand brush to clean off any surplus from the surface. In wet weather the dry mix will normally take up moisture from the soil and air but in dry conditions curing will be aided by sprinkling water from a watering can over the pointing. Cover the area to protect it from rain and leave to set.

EDGING SLATE & TILES

EQUIPMENT

Electric slate and tile cutter or disc cutter
Garden spade
String line and pegs
Shovel
Cement-mixing board or wheelbarrow
Hand brush
Pointing trowel
Spirit level
Club hammer

MATERIALS

Quantity broken slates and tiles
Broken stone
Cement
Sharp builders' sand
Aggregate
Length of scrap wood

Safety note

It is advised that eye protection and a dust mask
are worn if electrical cutting equipment is used.

Old tiles and slates together with reclaimed bricks are the life blood of most salvage yards. The variety of colour found in native and imported slate is almost bewildering and the range of sizes and patterns in which tiles were made in the past means that matching old tiles can be quite difficult and time-consuming.

We have used slates and tiles in our garden for all sorts of purposes and have seen them used in numerous inventive ways in other gardens, both here and abroad. Old slates are an obvious choice for the roofing of garden structures, but they can also be used to cap a wall or to act as a hard-wearing flooring material. We use them buried deep into the soil to contain invasive plants in a border, and laid on edge, as we show in this project, they have a particularly attractive appearance. Tiles are just as useful. We know of one enterprising gardener who has built an entire garden bench from stacked Double Roman tiles. In the same garden, tiles have been laid to delineate paths and different beds.

In almost any reclamation yard, you will find discarded and broken tiles or slates which can very often be had for the asking. There is something particularly satisfying in securing a useful material for nothing! We decided to make a border of mixed edging for our raised herb patio garden and managed to construct it entirely from old and broken slates and tiles from a local reclamation yard, had just for the cost of collection.

EDGING SLATE & TILES

METHOD

As the slates and tiles will be laid on edge make sure you have enough for the job. You will need approximately eight tiles or sixteen slates for each 15 cm (6 in) length of edging. Select slates and tiles at least 15 cm (6 in) long by at least 10 cm (4 in) wide. Use the slate and tile cutter to trim the pieces to a uniform length; the width can vary between 10 cm (4 in) and 15 cm (6 in) as this edge will be hidden below the surface.

1 Dig a trench approximately 25 cm (10 in) deep the entire length of the proposed edging. Insert the pegs at each end with the string stretched between them to act as a guide for laying the slates and tiles. Fill the trench with broken stone to a depth of approximately 10 cm (4 in) and compact it down to form a firm base.

2 On the mixing board or in the wheelbarrow, use the shovel to make a dry mixture of one part cement to three parts dry sharp sand and six parts dry aggregate. Spread the dry mix over the broken stone to a depth of about 10 cm (4 in). Make sure you have enough tiles for the job put to one side. We laid the tiles in alternate blocks of eight laid at right-angles to each other, first a block of eight across the trench, then a block laid lengthways – and so on.

3 Make up a second dry mix, this time of one part cement to three parts dry soft sand and one part dry sharp sand. Lay the tiles on edge and about 12 mm (½ in) apart in the dry mix already in the trench. Use the second dry mix to fill the gaps between the tiles, removing any excess mortar with the hand brush. Tap the tiles level with the handle of the trowel, using the spirit level to ensure accuracy.

4 Repeat the above two stages to lay the slates in the trench where required. The gap between the slates will be less than that used for the tiles and it will prove far simpler to lay them across the width of the trench rather than lengthways. Slates are quite fragile: if you need to tap them into the dry mix, use the handle of the trowel or the club hammer cushioned by a piece of wood.

5 When the edging is completed, check it with the spirit level. Ideally the surface of the edging should be just above that of the earth to be retained behind it and flush with any paved or other surface abutting it. While the concrete and mortar mixes are still dry, use the club hammer with a cushion of wood to gently tap the slates and tiles into their final position.

6 Cover the newly laid edging with sacks or another waterproof material to protect it from rain and leave for at least two days to take up moisture from the soil and harden. In particularly dry weather, sprinkle water over the finished edging with a watering can fitted with a fine rose. Finish by laying any paving or other surface up to the edging.

OFFCUT SLEEPERS EDGING

EQUIPMENT

Chain saw or cross-cut saw
Old paintbrush or household brush
String and pegs
Shovel
Cement mixing board or wheelbarrow
Club hammer
Cement trowel
Spirit level

MATERIALS

Selection of railway sleeper offcuts
Creosote or spirit-based wood preservative
Quantity broken stone
Cement
Sharp builders' sand
Aggregate
Water

Safety note

It is advised that protective clothing and full face protection are worn when using a chain saw and that eye protection and rubber or protective gloves are used when applying creosote.

Railway sleepers have become the ubiquitous yet essential raw material for almost every television garden make-over programme or newspaper article on restoring a garden produced or written over the last few years. Invaluable for constructing 'lazy' or raised beds, for building casual steps, or for terracing a sloping garden, we have used railway sleepers for innumerable purposes within our garden and have accumulated a store of offcuts from them, too short for use or too saturated with tar for burning in an open fire.

We wanted to find a practical use for the accumulated offcuts. Some we have used on end as 'paving' in a patio and others as stepping stones in a wild area of the garden. We decided that a number of them could be usefully incorporated as one of the variety of different edging materials we planned to use in our new raised patio herb garden.

The railway sleepers used for different parts of our garden had been secured from a variety of sources and some, particularly those salvaged from the restoration of our farming neighbour's new silage clamp, were quite rotten. We had trimmed the sleepers to size and some of the offcuts would require preservation before being used.

OFFCUT SLEEPERS EDGING

METHOD

1 Use the chain saw or cross-cut saw to cut the railway sleeper offcuts into blocks of uniform length, approximately 25 cm (10 in) long. Make sure that at least one end of each block is relatively sound and square.

2 Lay the blocks on a disposable surface. Using the old paintbrush or household brush, saturate the blocks with creosote or another spirit-based preservative, making sure in particular that the newly cut ends are covered. Leave to dry completely before continuing.

3 Mark out the proposed position of the edging with the string and pegs and dig a trench along it at least 25 cm (10 in) deep. Line the base to a depth of approximately 75 mm (3 in) with loose stone. Make a dry mixture on the mixing board or in the wheelbarrow of one part cement to three parts sharp sand and six parts aggregate. Lay this mixture in the trench to within approximately 75 mm (3 in) of the ground surface.

4 Make a further but wet mix of one part cement to four parts soft sand and lay it on the dry concrete mix. Place the blocks in position on a layer of the wet mortar mix approximately 12 mm ($^1/_2$ in) apart, leaving the tops approximately 75 to 100 mm (3 to 4 in) above ground level. Fill the gaps between the blocks with further wet mortar, smoothed to shape with the trowel. Use the string and pegs to check the alignment of the blocks and the spirit level to check that they are level, making any necessary adjustments with the club hammer or handle of the trowel.

Vita Sackville-West's White Garden at Sissinghurst Castle, in Kent, is perhaps the most famous, the most documented and the most copied themed garden. Using colour as a theme

Visit any of the major garden shows in London or elsewhere and you will find unexpected pleasure in discovering Japanese, African or Australian gardens right in the heart of

THE THEMED GARDEN

on which to base a garden design – whether it is in the hot spectrum of reds, yellows, oranges and pinks, or the cool blues, greens, purples and violets – is certain to draw the eye and make an impact, bringing colour to a garden from spring through late summer to autumn.

Chelsea! In the subtropical atmosphere of Tresco Abbey Gardens on the Isles of Scilly (known as England's Island of Flowers) the visitor can wander at will through lines of soaring palm trees, past a rocky Mexican garden to the terraces of the Mediterranean garden.

ABOVE

'In Memory of Everlasting Soles'. An unfinished garden sculpture by Paul Grellier which has used old iron shoe lasts and a salvaged churchyard plaque mounted on a stone plinth.

TOP RIGHT

The refurbished White Garden at Birtsmorton Court showing the specially commissioned lead fountain and impressive iron arches and pergolas. Reclaimed bricks and stone were used throughout this beautiful garden.

BOTTOM RIGHT

A timber seat hidden in a secluded corner of Tresco Abbey Gardens on the Isles of Scilly. The stone supports were rescued from the twelfth-century abbey ruins and the pots are original nineteenth-century terracotta pots.

OPPOSITE LEFT

The formality of this garden pool edged with reclaimed and mellow stone pavers is offset by the simplicity of the lawned surround and the yellow flag irises in designer Sarah Giddens' walled garden.

OPPOSITE CENTRE

Ancient quern stones once used to grind corn, make an interesting detail in a hidden corner of Tresco Abbey Gardens.

OPPOSITE RIGHT

The shallow, lichen covered steps leading down to this pond were made from old coping stones rescued from a demolished garden wall.

Other themes which make a strong statement are herb, rock, water and wild gardens. The last are important natural habitats for birds, animals and insect life and if they include woodlands can be home to masses of wild flowers and lush ferns. Take it one step further and a woodland garden can become a jungle, overflowing with palms, giant gunnera, bamboo thickets and numerous exotic trees, shrubs and marsh plants, as in the Jungle Garden at the Lost Gardens of Heligan in Cornwall.

Moving from natural wilderness to more formal gardens, props can be used to great effect as decoration. Place statuary stone lions, dogs and deer alongside ornate urns and vessels on plinths to create a 'gallery', adding a touch of grandeur to even the most modest of outdoor rooms.

Containers provide an instant effect, whether they are wooden tubs on a terrace or terracotta pots on a patio. Metal tubs, dustbins and old galvanised florists' buckets look particularly striking when planted with clipped trees or topiary shrubs and silvery

foliage. If this somewhat contrived look is not to everyone's taste, old-fashioned metal buckets can be planted with a variety of plants for a more informal appearance. Enjoy the richly aromatic fragrances of herbs in the warmth of sunlight by planting rosemary, thyme, parsley, sage, chives, marjoram, bay, basil, coriander and mint in buckets outside the back door.

The sensuous sounds of water in the garden trickling, rushing, gushing and cascading, bring about a feeling of calm, soothing away the tension and anxiety that builds up in our daily lives. Electricity, which we take so much for granted, allows power to be taken to the most far-flung parts of the garden for artificial waterfalls and fountains. A geometric rectangular, square or circular pool which may be home to koi carp or goldfish can be quite a formal feature in the garden, whereas a wildlife pond, a home for flora and fauna such as water lilies, dragonflies, frogs and toads, has a more informal, natural appearance.

Whichever theme or combination of themes is chosen for a garden, wood will play its part. Contrasting superbly with natural foliage and materials like stone, slate, brick and terracotta, it can be used in many ways both structurally and decoratively. Create boundaries with attractive picket fencing made from redundant pallets, or transform railway sleepers into sweeping steps leading to borders flanked by heavenly scented lavender bushes, or a froth of *Alchemilla mollis*, to soften the hard edges. In kitchen gardens, railway sleepers make hugely practical lazy beds containing succulent beans, courgettes and spinach.

Teak is a hardwood that is very popular for garden furniture as it is long lasting and fades to a glorious grey colour. A softwood hexagonal table which we found in a garden nursery and was once used to display stock has been reborn in a buttercup meadow, its surface planted with turf in readiness for a summer picnic, where it looks romantically ephemeral and wonderfully surreal!

SLEEPER STEPS

EQUIPMENT

String and pegs
Tape measure
Chainsaw or cross-cut saw
Garden spade
Shovel
Pickaxe
Spirit level
Club hammer
Hand saw
Hammer
Electric drill and drill bit
Board for levelling
Wheelbarrow
Garden rake
Paint brush

MATERIALS

Selection wooden railway sleepers
Lengths tanilised timber approx.
　20 cm x 25 mm (8 in x 1 in)
Dark brown timber preservative
75 mm (3 in) galvanised nails
75 mm (3 in) galvanised screws
Total weedkiller
Quantity 10 mm ($\frac{1}{2}$ in) screened and
　washed paving gravel

Note

Tanilised timber is generally softwood which has
been treated with timber preservative applied
under pressure. It is formulated especially for
timber which will be used out of doors. If it, or an
equivalent, is not available, all timber which will be
in contact with the ground should be saturated
with preservative before being put to use.

Safety note

Chain saws are potentially extremely dangerous. If
you are unfamiliar with their use, seek professional
help. In any event, always use a powerbreaker
plug and wear full protective clothing and eye
protection when using a chain saw.

Ever since the introduction of
concrete railway sleepers,
hardwood sleepers have been a
valued resource for garden
designers wanting a long lasting
raw material for construction
work. Thousands of Australian
hardwood sleepers were imported
into Europe and Africa as the
railway networks expanded.
Curiously, some African
hardwoods were exported
to make sleepers for the
Australian railways.

Sleepers can be bought at
almost any reclamation yard or
garden centre but many of those
we have used have been 'double
reclaimed', first from the railways
and subsequently from a local
farmer who had used them to line
a silage clamp. Whilst not in
perfect condition, the sleepers
were so saturated with oil and
preservative that large parts of
them could be salvaged, certainly
enough for our purposes.

There are many different ways
of building steps within a garden.
For this gentle slope, alongside
a converted pigsty finished in
reclaimed timber cladding, we
chose to use crushed stone gravel
retained behind a step made from
the base of a demolished old
stone wall already on the site and
hardwood railway sleepers.

SLEEPER STEPS

METHOD

Mark out the area to be excavated for the steps with the string and pegs. Bearing in mind that the level of the gravel will be flush with the top of the retaining sleepers, work out how many steps are required by measuring the drop from the top to the bottom of the slope and dividing this by the height of a single step – each step should be no higher than approximately 20 cm (8 in). (We decided to lay our sleepers on edge rather than flat in order to match the height of an old stone wall base we were incorporating as one of the steps and to limit the number of sleepers required.) Cut the sleepers with the chain saw or cross-cut saw to the proposed width of the steps. Treat the cut ends with timber preservative.

1 Steps look better and are easier to climb when constructed an equal distance apart. Starting at the top of the steps, use the spade (and, if necessary, a pickaxe) to excavate a trench for the first sleeper. Lay the sleeper in the trench, checking its alignment with the spirit level and making sure that it is bedded at least 75 mm (3 in) into the ground for stability.

2 Continue excavating and laying the sleeper steps until all are in place. Make sure that their ends are in line so that when the timber edging is fitted a neat appearance is achieved. Use the club hammer to bed the sleepers firmly and secure them in place with compacted soil and stones, checking the horizontal and vertical alignments periodically with the spirit level.

3 For the edging, saw pieces of the 20 cm x 25 mm (8 in x 1 in) tanilsed timber (or softwood saturated with timber preservative) to the distance between each step, making sure that each piece is long enough for its ends, when fixed, to fall in the centre of the sleepers. Apply timber preservative to the cut ends and, if desired, paint with coloured timber stain. Using the spirit level to check the alignment, fix the edging in position between each step with galvanised nails or screws, taking care when nailing near the end of a cut edge to pre-drill the nail hole in order to prevent the timber from splitting.

4 When the steps and their edging pieces have been completed, excavate the soil from the area to be covered by gravel to at least 5 cm (2 in) below the top of the retaining sleeper. Having removed the soil, compact the excavated area to form a level surface on which to place the gravel, using the spirit level and a board to check for accuracy. We treated the compacted soil with a total weedkiller to ensure that the gravel remained weed free, but this problem may be minimised by excavating a bit deeper and adding a layer of compacted hardcore on top of the earth. Add the gravel, using a garden rake to spread it level and flush with the top of the retaining sleeper. The gravel will settle over time so ensure you have a sufficient quantity in reserve to top it up at a later date.

WATER FEATURE

EQUIPMENT

Wire brush
Paint brush
Face mask
Spirit level
Paint scraper or hook

MATERIALS

Old steel cattle trough (or other suitable
   water tank)
Bitumen paint (check it is safe for
   pond use)
Red oxide metal primer paint
Spray can of multi-surface outdoor paint
Electric fountain (or water pump)

Safety note

Electricity is extremely dangerous, especially if
used in or close to water. Only use safety-checked
equipment specifically manufactured for outdoor
and underwater use and get expert advice before
connecting it to mains power. Special outdoor
fittings and wiring are essential for outdoor use or
damp conditions. Electric shocks received from
incorrectly fitted or inappropriate equipment,
particularly when used in the presence of water,
can cause serious injury or even kill, so don't take
chances: seek advice from a qualified electrician.

A great deal has been written about water features in gardens, with good reason. Running water adds the dimensions of sound and movement to a garden, and the presence of water – whether running or still – will enrich the wildlife in a garden, attracting to it numerous birds, animals and insects requiring a year-round supply of drinking water.

Water can give a focal point to a garden as well as offering the opportunity to grow a whole new range of plants. Whatever your choice of water feature, it is well worth reading up on the subject and consulting a local expert retailer about the various marginal and other suitable plants you can use and which, if any, fish to stock it with. As fish need oxygen to survive, it is most important that the feature is planted with oxygenating plants or some mechanical means is used to keep the oxygen level of the water at the correct balance.

Farmers often stock the cattle troughs in their fields with goldfish, perhaps won at the annual village fair, but they serve a useful function in helping to keep the troughs clean of insect larvae and other impurities. Our old but serviceable cattle trough, purchased at a farm sale, was incorporated into our paved garden using a small and inexpensive fountain to aerate the water and provide the attractions of sound and movement.

WATER FEATURE

METHOD

When choosing a trough or tank for this project make sure that the steel is sound, without holes or perforations. Troughs which have a hole or fitting near the top for the old water supply are ideal as the hole will provide a concealed access for the fountain's power cable.

1 Scrub the trough vigorously with a stiff wire brush to remove any rust or loose and flaking material. Clean the trough both inside and out, paying particular attention to the base which might be in contact with the ground when installed and therefore especially prone to rust.

2 Turn the trough onto its side and brush out any remaining loose material or rust debris. Apply two coats of black bitumen paint to the inside of the trough up to the level of any access hole or, if none exists, to within approximately 5 cm (2 in) of the top. Make sure the entire surface is well covered. Leave to dry.

3 Apply a coat of red oxide metal primer paint to those parts of the trough, inside and out, not covered by the bitumen paint. Leave to dry completely, then apply a second coat and leave to dry.

4 Apply one or two finishing coasts of multi-surface outdoor paint over the red oxide primer. We chose to use a purpose-made spray paint to give an even finish, but similar paints can be applied by brush. Always use a face mask if spray painting and follow the manufacturer's recommendations on the tin.

5 Install the painted trough in position. Once it is filled with water it will be extremely heavy so make sure it is exactly where you want it to be, checking its alignment with a spirit level. (We chose to raise our trough onto four bricks rather than have it sitting on the ground which can encourage rust.) Fill the trough with water to the top of the bitumen, ideally using rainwater though tap water can be used.

6 Read thoroughly the installation instructions which accompany the fountain. Feed its electric cable through the trough's access hole, if one exists, or pass it over the top of the tank into the water and place the fountain in position. It may be necessary to raise the fountain onto stones or bricks so that it is at the correct level in the water. If desired you can drill a hole into the tank just above the water level to take the electrical supply and seal the hole with waterproof mastic. Please see the safety note on the previous page. It is most important that the equipment and the power supply is checked before the power is turned on. Once this is done, plant your trough with water plants, turn on the fountain and enjoy the ambiance that trickling water creates.

Please see the safety note on page 76. It is most important that the equipment and the power supply is checked before the power is turned on. Once this is done, plant your trough with water plants, turn on the fountain and enjoy the ambiance that trickling water creates.

METAL BUCKET PLANTING

EQUIPMENT

Electric drill and 6 mm ($\frac{1}{4}$ in) metal drill bit
Paintbrush (optional)

MATERIALS

Old metal bucket
Black bitumen paint (optional)
Metal lacquer (optional)
Selection of stones or broken
   terracotta pots

METHOD

1 If the bucket being used as a planter has no perforations in its base, drill a number of holes to provide drainage to prevent the soil becoming saturated and the plants overwatered.

2 If desired, paint the inside of the bucket with black butumen paint and the outside with a coat of protective metal lacquer to preserve the appearance of the metal and help prevent further corrosion. Fill the bottom 5 to 10 cm (2 to 4 in) of the bucket with broken pot shards or stones to allow free drainage to the drilled holes in the base. Add soil or planting mixture and place your selected plant in position, firming the soil around it.

Zinc and other metal planters and containers are enjoying a resurgence in popularity in garden fashion. Our commitment to the reuse of old materials has led to the making of planters from old bread tins and dustbins, garden edging from corrugated-iron strips, arbours from metal reinforcement rods, and numerous garden arches from offcuts of steel concrete-reinforcement sheets.

Planters created from rusty, old, battered and sometimes perforated metal buckets can be far cheaper than modern metal containers, and very effective they look too. Old or discarded buckets when grouped together and well planted make an attractive display on wide steps or a patio.

Many of the buckets we have used had rusted to such an extent that no drainage holes were necessary. Should this not be the case, it is important to perforate the base to provide adequate drainage.

LAZY BED

EQUIPMENT

Tape measure
Chain saw or cross-cut saw
Four scaffold boards or planks
Garden spade
Spirit level
Board for levelling
Club hammer
Hammer

MATERIALS

Two 3 m (10 ft) railway sleepers
Quantity 15 cm (6 in) galvanised
    round head nails
Quantity sieved garden soil or
    growing medium/compost
Timber preservative or creosote

Safety note

Chain saws are potentially extremely dangerous. If
you are unfamiliar with their use, seek professional
help. In any event, always use a powerbreaker
plug and wear full protective clothing and eye
protection when using a chain saw.

Railway sleepers are extremely heavy. Do not
attempt to lift them on your own.

A 'lazy' or raised bed is one of the most productive uses of a small growing space. Ideally the bed should be constructed to a size that can be worked on without the need to walk on it. Once established, the raised bed should never again require deep digging; all cultivation, manuring, planting, weeding and harvesting can be carried out from the sides and ends; and because it is never compacted, the soil will remain friable and easily worked. No wonder it is commonly known as a 'lazy' bed.

A properly established and managed lazy bed allows closer planting than is normal and will produce an appreciably greater yield than can be obtained in most ordinary beds. The lazy bed in this project was constructed from 3 m (10 ft) railway sleepers and in order to minimise wastage it was decided to lay the sleepers on edge and cut them into 180 cm (6 ft) and 120 cm (4 ft) lengths with the shorter lengths laid outside the longer ones to create a bed approximately 220 cm (7 ft 3 in) long by 120 cm (4 ft) wide, an ideal size to allow easy access to any point within it.

Raised beds can be constructed from many different materials. We have seen them made from brick, stone, concrete blocks, old wooden palettes and even raised earth banks, but railway sleepers are ideal for this particular application.

LAZY BED

METHOD

1 Cut the sleepers into 180 cm (6 ft) and 120 cm (4 ft) lengths with the chain saw or cross-cut saw. Treat the cut ends with timber preservative or creosote and roughly assemble them on some flat ground in the shape of the proposed bed. Measure the outside dimensions (i.e. including the sleepers) of the assembled bed. Lay the four scaffold boards or planks on the ground where the bed will be dug to enclose a space of the measured dimensions.

2 Using the garden spade, dig a trench the width of a sleeper around the perimeter of the space enclosed by the boards to a depth of at least one third of the height of a sleeper, which will be set below the surface of the surrounding soil. Use the spirit level and a board to check that the base of the trench is level.

3 Lay one of the longer sleepers in position in the trench. Tap it into place with the club hammer, making sure it is securely bedded, and check it is level with the spirit level. Carefully lay at right-angles to it one of the shorter endpiece sleepers. Bed down the endpiece, ensuring that the tops of both sleepers are level and that their ends are butted tightly together. Nail the sleepers together with two 15 cm (6 in) galvanised round head nails driven in at an angle from the top of the sleepers at each side of the joint.

Repeat the process with the two remaining sleepers, making sure that the corners are square and the tops of the sleepers level. When the sleepers are fitted, dig the soil inside the newly created bed to at least one and preferably two spade's depths, incorporating manure, compost or sieved garden soil to bring the final soil level up to just under the top of the sleepers. This is the perfect opportunity to remove any stones or weeds. When the bed is dug for a final time, try not to walk on or compact the turned earth as this is when you will create the loose, friable soil structure which is the feature of a lazy bed.

GRASS TOP TABLE

EQUIPMENT

Old paintbrush for preservative
Pliers, wire cutters or heavy-duty scissors
Staple gun and staples
Sharp knife or craft knife
Garden sieve (optional)

MATERIALS

Old slatted wooden table
Timber preservative
Wire netting
Plastic sheeting
Quantity garden turf
Quantity sieved soil (optional)

METHOD

Any slatted table can be used for this project. Alternatively, a solid table would do if perforated with sufficient holes to provide adequate drainage. If the table selected has no retaining surround, construct one out of tanilised or preservative-treated softwood timber, fixed to the edge of the table to provide a rebate of at least 10 cm (4 in).

1 Treat the whole of the table with a timber preservative, paying particular attention to end-grain timber, the legs where they will be in contact with the ground, and the table top and surround into which the soil and turf will be placed.

2 When the preservative is completely dry, cut the wire netting with the pliers, wire cutters or heavy-duty scissors to the shape of the table top and fix it in place with the staple gun.

3 Cut the plastic sheeting (we used an old tarpaulin) to fit the table top and perforate it for drainage. If the rebate is sufficiently deep, spread a layer of approximately 10 cm (4 in) of sieved soil over the entire surface. Lay the turfs on the soil or plastic liner, cut them to shape with the knife, and press firmly into place making sure the joints between the turfs are tight to allow for shrinkage. Water the feature thoroughly and keep it moist otherwise the turf will dry out. In autumn, spring bulbs can be planted between the turf and the underlying soil to provide a stunning spring flower display.

Every so often you come across something which you know is just too good to miss! Such was the case with this wooden plant display table which was bought 'for a song' as the first lot in the closing down sale of a garden nursery. Once home, the table sat outside, adding to the detritus of what has become our very own reclamation yard. We knew that one day we would find a use for it.

Events have a way of precipitating action. Early one morning, we awoke to the sound of what we thought was thunder until, looking out of the window, we saw a herd of cattle gambolling like overgrown lambs on our lawn. After five months of being penned in during winter, smelling the lush green grass of our precious lawn, they had broken out and proceeded to turn the lawn into what looked like a tank training ground or the aftermath of a pop festival.

After several weeks and a few visits from grim-faced insurance assessors, the turfing contractors came to re-lay the lawn. One week later we had a new expanse of bowling-green quality lawn and several turfs left over from the job. Inspiration struck. Why not plant our table with turf and create a year-round feature, even if as a table it would be somewhat impractical?

We planted the turfs straight into the existing shallow rebate of the table. For a lasting effect, the turf should be laid onto a base of compacted soil at least 10 cm (4 in) deep.

Long ago, the elements were thought to be earth, water, air and fire. Here, the elements are the structures, textures, colours, planting, props and light that help to create an ambiance topiary established. Lakes and follies were designed to blend into the part-constructed countryside, interrupted only by a hidden ha-ha. Today few of us can change the physical

ELEMENTS AND AMBIANCE

and make a garden personal.

The great landscape designers of the past created amazing vistas by altering the natural landscape to fit an invented plan or scheme. Tree planting was undertaken on a massive scale, formal structures with large sweeps of manicured, terraced and walled gardens were formed, and parterres and characteristics of our gardens. We have to live with and work around what is already there, usually on a minute scale compared with the great estates. With monotonous regularity we clip the hedges, mow the lawns to perfection, weed the borders, and deadhead the roses in an effort to achieve a neat, tidy and well managed garden.

ABOVE

Water pours from an old brass faucet into a reclaimed stone trough in Chrissy Price's water garden.

RIGHT

Massive stone pillars support timbers cut from storm blown trees felled during the great storm of 1990 which destroyed so much of Tresco Abbey Gardens, make an oversized pergola supporting long established kiwi fruits and passion flowers.

There is a body of people who have become bored with rows of box balls, who are reacting against symmetry, who no longer want to force flowers and plants to grow in conditions which are the very opposite of their natural habitat; who, in short, feel we should all stop fighting nature and, instead, work with it. These same people find the smoke, petrol fumes and noise pollution of the lawn mower antisocial and consider that conventional gardening involves too much destruction of the natural environment. This movement favours a looser style of lush planting for the twenty-first century, accidental-looking drifts or expanses of shape, colour and texture. Emulating nature, they advocate mixes of grasses, perennials, herbs, self-seeding annuals even fruits grown at random, spontaneous mixes of wild flower meadows emerging under the title of 'new perennial planting'. Of course, nothing is ever quite that easy. This style of planting requires skill to make it look as if it has just happened, and it needs a degree of control, otherwise it looks a mess. But the timing is right for it; it is part of the organic, environmentally friendly trend we feel comfortable with.

LEFT

View from the stone bridge across the moat of thirteenth-century Birtsmorton Court to an entrance to the walled garden. The wrought iron gates, lead planter and staddle-stones were installed during restoration work on the property.

BELOW LEFT

Old stone slabs salvaged from a farmhouse are surrounded by ancient cobbles and then bordered with an edging of reclaimed clay roof tiles to make a path through this kiwi-fruit-shaded pergola.

BELOW RIGHT

An informal pond – a haven for wildlife – has been bridged by an old railway sleeper, entirely in keeping with the mood and colours of this part of an exciting garden.

Hankering after the flower-filled fields and meadows of our childhood, so much of it now swallowed up for development, may sound fine to those who have the rolling acres, but what about the rest of us? Do not despair – there is no reason why a scaled-down wildlife reserve cannot be planted in a back yard or clumps of graceful grasses freely cultivated on a balcony or even in a window box.

This freedom of expression is at odds with those designers who fill show gardens with bold concepts in concrete, metal and glass with only the occasional nod towards the token plant. If you find this controlled style both ugly and brutal, look to where your pleasure lies.

Perhaps you have a fleeting image of an evolving space whose structures are a succession of mellow brickwork walls,

gentrified cobbles, gnarled and knobbly wooden fences, glorious slate terraces in greys, blues, blacks and heathers; summer houses laced with an air of mystery, their ancient windows of uneven glass and pathways of muddy brown stone and shingle. Linked by a natural theme of scents from flowers and herbs, sounds from birds and insects with the distant gurgle of water, it is a haven of refuge offering a kind of spiritualism which seems to be missing in many of our daily lives.

GLOVE STAND

EQUIPMENT

Craft knife
Electric drill
Selection of spade bits

MATERIALS

Selection of firewood offcuts
Glasspaper
Waterproof wood glue

METHOD

Choose the timber you will use for this project carefully, ensuring it is dry and well seasoned. You will need to select a larger heavy piece with one flat surface for the base and a number of fairly thin, similarly sized straight branches for the uprights.

1 Use the craft knife and glasspaper to remove any bark from the timber and sand to a smooth finish. Cut the branches to an equal length to form the uprights. Round off the top or smaller end of each upright with glasspaper.

2 Trim the bottom or larger end of each upright with the craft knife and glasspaper into a uniform tapered shape.

3 Using the drill and spade bit, cut a hole for each upright in the base piece. Drill each hole at a slight angle from the vertical so that when the uprights are fitted into place they will splay at a consistent angle.

4 Apply waterproof wood glue to each hole and fit the uprights firmly into position. Check the splay and put the completed stand to one side to dry. You might wish to finish the stand with an application of wood preservative or furniture wax.

What to do with the perishable rubber gloves used for outdoor painting when they are not in use? Where to keep the leather pruning gauntlets when they are damp? And anyway, where are they? However neat the garden room or potting shed, the multitude of gloves needed for the various jobs around the garden have a habit of getting mislaid or obdurately secreting themselves in some dark and dusty corner.

In an attempt to tackle this problem, we have come up with a storage stand for the many different garden gloves that we all seem to own. A simple stand which will store damp gloves allowing them to dry properly, an object both functional and pleasing to look at.

Our view is over a Site of Special Scientific Interest and a European Heritage Area. In other words we live in an area where English Nature and the Department of the Environment closely control the management of the countryside. Willow trees (locally known as 'withies') line every rhine and ditch and farmers must pollard them (known as 'shading') on a regular basis. As well as delighting in a constantly changing landscape, we therefore enjoy an abundance of firewood, the perfect resource for our project.

GARDEN LIGHT

EQUIPMENT

Orbital sander or glasspaper
Tape measure
Hand saw
Electric drill and wood drill bits
Electric (or hand) screwdriver
Pencil or marker pen
Straight edge
Paintbrush

MATERIALS

Wooden framed stained-glass window
Glazing putty (if necessary)
Length 25 mm (1 in) square timber (battens)
Quantity 50 mm (2 in) wood screws
Length 20 cm x 25 mm (8 in x 1 in) planed
    timber (sides and base)
Multi-surface outdoor paint

When daylight has dwindled, night-time dining outdoors by the soft light of candles is particularly pleasurable. A bewildering selection of electrical outdoor lights can be purchased but we prefer the glow from lamps and the flickering light of flares. For different occasions we have glass candle lights on tall metal spikes that we insert in the grass and borders, nightlights in antique Victorian glass containers, and others in small faceted tumblers. We own several old paraffin lamps bought at farm auctions and have made numerous candle holders from old farm and garden tools, staircase spindles and clay ink bottles found at car-boot sales.

When asking reclamation dealers what they find difficult to sell, one answer is the small stained-glass windows removed from late-nineteenth and early-twentieth century houses, for which there seems to be little alternative use. Easy to find and inexpensive to buy, we thought they could be simply converted into garden lights which, standing on a low wall or table, cast an attractive diffused glow through their patterned glass. We have made many of these lights and others have been used to cover recessed wall lights. One we have inserted into the gable end of a garden shed to cast patterned shafts of coloured light onto an otherwise boring interior.

GARDEN LIGHT

METHOD

1 Use the orbital sander or glasspaper to remove any loose or flaking paint from the window frame. It is not essential to remove all the paint but important to provide a sound surface for subsequent painting. Make good any putty missing from the front of the window.

2 Turn the frame onto its front, the back uppermost, and measure its height. Cut the 25 mm (1 in) square timber into two battens, each approximately 4 cm (1½ in) less than the height of the frame. Pre-drill screw holes along the length of each batten and attach to the rear of the frame 25 mm (1 in) from each outside edge with 50 mm (2 in) screws. (The distance the battens are fitted inside the edges of the frame will depend on the thickness of timber you are using for the sides. Measure your timber and adjust this dimension accordingly.) The battens should be attached approximately 25 mm (1 in) from the bottom and 15 mm (½ in) from the top of the frame.

3 Place the 20 cm (8 in) x 25 mm (1 in) planed timber on the work surface and make sure its end is square. (If you are using timber such as an old floorboard, you will probably need to cut the end off in order to discard damaged wood.) Mark a point the distance of the height of the frame along one edge of the plank. Mark a second point approximately 25 mm (1 in) less on the opposite edge of the plank. Join the points with a pencil or marker pen and straight edge and saw along the line. Using this sloping cut end as a pattern, cut a second identical piece from the remainder of the plank.

4 Place one of the cut sides onto the back of the frame and butted against the batten with the sloping end towards the top and the taller edge to the front. Pre-drill screw holes and fix to the batten with at least three 50 mm (2 in) wood screws, making sure not to insert any screw within 25 mm (1 in) of the bottom. Repeat with the other side piece.

5 Measure the distance between the side pieces assembled on the frame and cut another piece of the 20 cm x 25 mm (8 in x 1 in) planed timber to that measurement to form the base. Attach the base to the frame using 50 mm (2 in) wood screws driven through pre-drilled holes in the side pieces. Your assembled sloping-sided light should now be able to stand in position without additional support.

6 Paint all the wood surfaces with multi-surface garden paint, place a candle inside a secure metal or other fire-resistant container behind the stained glass, and the garden light is ready to use.

SLATE BOARD

EQUIPMENT

Slate cutter
Palette knife or paint scraper
Selection of different grades
    glasspaper or emery paper
Electric drill and 6 mm ($^1/_4$ in) bit
Block of scrap wood
Paintbrush (optional)

MATERIALS

Selection old roofing slates
20 cm (8 in) length of leather
    bootlace for each slate
Matt or satin finish exterior-grade
    varnish (optional)

METHOD

1 The size of the slate board will depend on the slate available but this is a very useful way of using smaller or broken slates. Slates are normally hand split and cut to create one bevelled edge and one flat edge. The slate cutter is designed to produce a similar cut edge and we recommend you experiment with it on scrap slate to familiarise yourself with how it cuts before cutting your project slates to size.

2 Use the paint scraper or palette knife to remove any flaking or delamination to reveal the sound surface underneath. Use glasspaper or emery paper to sand the slate smooth, starting with course grade and finishing with fine grade paper to achieve the best finish. Place the slate on a piece of waste timber and with the electric drill and 6 mm ($^1/_4$ in) bit drill a hole through from the top (i.e. the side with the bevelled edge), centred about 25 mm (1 in) from the top of the slate. Drilling through the slate into scrap timber will minimise any risk of the slate breaking while the hole is being cut.

3 Feed the leather bootlace or strips cut from scrap leather through the hole, tie into a simple knot and the slate board is ready for hanging from a hook or nail, the perfect aide-mémoire for the garden room or potting shed. If desired, the slate surface can be sealed with a coat of matt or satin exterior-grade varnish.

Slate is lovely to look at, has an interesting texture, and is one of the most versatile of salvaged materials with a multiplicity of uses throughout the home and garden. We show how salvaged slate can be used to make garden markers (page 116) and edging (page 60), and in the chapter 'A Garden Reclaimed' we illustrate how broken and chipped slate, collected from slate cutting at a reclamation yard, can be used as a very effective and attractive garden mulch. Old slates can be used to isolate invasive plants such as mint in a herb bed and as tiles on the surface of a stone or wooden table. The offcuts from thick slate which has been cut down to make flooring slabs and kitchen work surfaces can be obtained from flooring contractors to make an imposing path edge.

Reclaimed roof slates are easily cut and even when heavily delaminated or flaking through exposure to air, rain and weather, can be simply converted into invaluable place mats, memo boards and clipboards for the home and garden. In this project we show how to make a stylish slate memo board but the project can be easily adapted to create a clipboard by fitting a bulldog clip to the top to hold a paper pad.

When writing with chalk on a slate board, wet the chalk first. This simple hint will ensure that your writing stands out effectively when the chalk has dried.

TOOL RACK

EQUIPMENT

Tape measure
Carpenter's square
Pencil
Hand saw
Straight edge
Jig saw (optional)
Electric drill
38 mm (1 ¹/₂ in) hole cutter bit
25 mm (1 in) wood chisel
Wood drill bits to fit screws
Electric (or hand) screwdriver

MATERIALS

Selection timber:
2 pieces approx. 40 cm x 90 cm x 25 mm
   (16 in x 36 in x 1 in) (sides)
2 pieces approx. 25 cm x 110 cm x 25 mm
   (10 in x 43 in x 1 in) (top and base)
1 piece approx. 15 cm x 110cm x 25 mm
   (6 in x 43 in x 1 in) (rear)
Selection approx. 65 mm (2¹/₂ in) screws

METHOD

1 Take the two pieces of 25 cm x 90 cm x 25 mm (10 in x 36 in x 1 in) timber and mark two lines approximately 5 cm (2 in) inside from each edge with the pencil and straight edge along the length of one face of each piece. Starting 5 cm (2 in) from one end, mark points at 20 cm (8 in) intervals on each line to give two rows of five marks. Select one board as the top and drill holes through at the marked points with the electric drill and hole cutter. On the second board which will form the base, drill holes with the hole cutter at the marked points but only to a depth of approximately 12 mm (¹/₂ in). Remove the cut wood with the wood chisel to give a rebated hole into which the tool handles will eventually sit.

2 Mark a point 25 cm (10 in) on one face at one end of each of the two pieces of 40 cm x 90 cm x 25 mm (16 in x 36 in x 1 in) timber and with the pencil and straight edge draw a line from these points to the full 40 cm (16 in) width of the timber at the opposite end. Use the hand saw or jig saw to cut along the drawn lines to make the two sides measuring 90 cm x 40 cm (36 in x 16 in) (base) and 25 cm (10 in) (top).

3 Measure a point 5 cm (2 in) from the base of both side pieces and use the carpenters square and straight edge to draw a line across each piece. Fit the top piece of drilled 25 cm x 110 cm x 25 mm (10 in x 43 in x 1 in) timber inside and flush with the 25 cm (10 in) end of both cut side pieces with screws. Pre-drill screwholes before assembling to prevent the timber splitting. Fit the base piece of 25 cm x 110 cm x 25 mm (10 in x 43 in x 1 in) timber, with the half drilled holes facing up and inside the 40 cm (16 in) ends of the side pieces at the line drawn 5 cm (2 in) up from the base so that the base will be raised 5 cm (2 in) off the ground when the rack is placed in position.

4 To reinforce the structure and stop the construction 'racking', screw the 15 cm x 110 cm x 25 mm ((6 in x 43 in x 1 in) rear piece inside the back of the tool rack so that it fits under the top piece. Tighten all screws to secure the construction, place on a flat surface and the tool rack is ready for use.

Two things with irresistible appeal for us are interesting old tools and reclaimed timber. Finds from sources ranging from skips to garage sales have included some superb lengths of figured antique elm which now form the head and foot boards of a four poster bed, massive moulded cornices which when stripped of layers of white paint were revealed to be carved from solid oak, and large quantities of both painted and unpainted softwood which we have used for numerous projects saving considerable expenditure on new wood. We have a store stacked from floor to ceiling with reclaimed timber and some of this was used to construct the tool rack.

Garden tool storage is a constant problem. Our accumulation of old and modern tools and garden equipment makes a considerable inroad into already limited space and although we have fitted a tool shed with a peg board round the walls from which to hang many of the tools, some inevitably end up in a corner of the room. To store some of our numerous straight-handled tools, we decided to construct a simple free-standing rack to keep them in order. The project shows how a modestly sized rack can be constructed but the design can of course be adjusted to be larger or smaller to suit your own particular needs.

TRELLIS WALL RACK

EQUIPMENT

Pencil
Spirit level
Hand saw
Electric drill
Wood drill bit (to fit screws)
Bradawl
Masonry bit (for solid walls)
Screwdriver

MATERIALS

Old trellis
Two lengths waste timber batten
Selection wall plugs (for solid walls)
Selection screws
Metal cup hooks

METHOD

1 Place the trellis against the wall in the selected position with the horizontal bars facing out and mark on the wall the positions of the second bar from the top and the second bar from the bottom. Cut two lengths of batten to the width of the trellis. Using the electric drill and wood bit, drill fixing holes in the battens approximately 20 cm (8 in) from each end. Align the top batten with the positional marks on the wall, mark the position of the fixing holes on the wall using the bradawl, then repeat for the bottom batten. Drill holes into the wall with the electric drill and masonry bit, fill the holes with wall plugs, and screw the battens to the wall.

2 Using the wood bit, drill fixing holes through two thicknesses of trellis where the vertical bars cross the second horizontal bar from the top and bottom. Offer the trellis up against the wall so that the battens are hidden by the horizontal bars of the trellis. Secure in place with screws driven through the fixing holes into the battens behind, using the spirit level to check for accuracy. Fit cup hooks to the horizontal bars as required.

As the plans for our garden change or evolve, we are often left with redundant trellis. Much we cut down or adapt for a different location but, when we decided to refurnish our garden room, we reserved one piece as a wall storage rack on which to keep all those notes, packets of seed and other miscellanea which would otherwise create clutter.

Nothing could be simpler, yet – properly secured to a wall – a trellis rack is an invaluable addition to a practical work area or potting shed. We have also used old trellis fixed to the ceiling of a tool store. Using metal 'S' hooks, we hang from it such things as garden umbrellas over winter, terracotta wall pots to protect them from the frost, string bags of bulbs awaiting planting, and even bunches of flowers left to dry.

Although garden trellis is readily available and inexpensive, we dislike the colours commercially available trellis is stained. We prefer to make most of our own from offcut softwood waste timber, protecting it with outdoor preservative stained with various pigments to achieve a subdued shade to merge with the background against which the trellis is erected.

INVENTIVE IDEAS

Before disposing of items or relics that appear to be past their useful life, exercise a little lateral thinking as almost anything can be reused.

Over the past twenty-five years we have greatly increased our consumption of wine which means the task of recycling our empty wine bottles is done with a sense of duty rather than enthusiasm. Having downed the last drop of Chardonnay, the empty container gets slung onto a mounting pile before being transported to the local bottle bank, from where it is collected for recycling. We visited a garden where empty bottles had been saved and used to create a garden feature. Rows of neatly arranged green wine bottles were stacked from floor to ceiling in the alcove of a high, old stone wall. With sunlight bouncing off their bases, this exciting creation resembled a huge honeycomb.

Empty wine bottles can also be used to make idiosyncratic garden sculptures, their necks wedged randomly into the stump of a decaying tree. Colourful recycled glass chippings, purchased from garden supply stores can be used to great effect to create paths, make a mulch or in a water feature.

NEAR RIGHT

A mirror, framed by a mosaic of pebbles, stones and broken coloured china in garden designer Sue Berger's town centre garden, leads the visitor towards an imaginary doorway into another secret garden.

CENTRE LEFT

A scarecrow constructed mainly of old clay flower pots with flowering chives growing from its head. A light-hearted flight of fancy in the garden of Emmaus House, a retreat and conference centre.

CENTRE RIGHT

Weathered coping stones laid in a broken line and overgrown with a profusion of verdant plants in a wild flower bed at Emmaus House give the appearance of a fallen and half-buried stone column.

FAR RIGHT

This galvanised steel bird table made from a variety of rescued components by an enthusiast who spends much of his leisure time scavenging for the raw materials for his imaginative constructions.

BOTTOM LEFT

This ancient oak gate post, complete with its original iron latch stop has been left in position in the garden of a village house to make an unusual feature.

BOTTOM RIGHT

Empty wine bottles from the restaurant at Emmaus House stacked from floor to ceiling in a garden wall alcove make an eye-catching feature when illuminated by the sun.

Another garden we visited was stuffed with practical and inventive recycling ideas. It sported wine corks on spikes to support fruit netting without causing damage to the net, or indeed a poke in the eye; telephone wires fixed against the walls for training roses and other climbers; large terracotta pots turned upside down and topped with wooden slats to form a potting surface; and even a horse's saddle rest attached to an outside wall housing a garden hose. (The hose reel in this chapter was made from an abandoned electric cable drum.) An old window frame, complete with glass, was put to good use as the lid on a cold frame and generous sized garden markers were cut from salvaged timber and roofing slate.

On an agricultural note, old farm equipment can be put to good use in gardens. Stable hay feeders make good planters for a colourful flower display and old harrows can be fixed to a wall and used as supports for climbing plants. A retired farmer used timber from a disused calf pen and salvaged telegraph poles to make a pool-side bench and table, while the cart shafts featured in this chapter were decoratively installed to emphasise a view. Even the peeling white painted wall within a linhay has been cleverly adorned with a collection of salvaged artefacts, including rusty tools, a battered wooden shelf, assorted implements, ancient horseshoes and an antlered skull!

Less unusual but not to be dismissed are cast-iron gutter hoppers which can be fixed to a wall or cartwheel and planted with summer blooms. Likewise, old clay roof hip tiles and flowerpots attached to ridge tiles and filled with colourful flowers provide a vibrant display from spring through to autumn. A simple oak whisky barrel cut in half and planted is another sight seen almost everywhere.

The average garden may not have room for a gargantuan stone fallen 'column', cleverly contrived from salvaged coping stones, creating an informal moss-covered border lying strewn on the earth like some prehistoric reptile. We came across just this in Emmaus House, a conference centre and retreat run by nuns. In the same garden we turned a corner and to our surprise encountered the figure of a man, made entirely out of old flowerpots, sitting with hoe in hand and chives for hair – a bit of light-hearted fun to frighten off the birds!

Mirrors used on a garden wall are a clever trick when attempting to make a space seem larger, which is particularly useful in small town gardens. An artist friend attached a bamboo-framed mirror, painted soft lavender blue, to a patio wall and allowed ivy and other creepers to spread and drape themselves around it. They blended so well with the frame that the mirror was at first glance disguised, giving the illusion of light in an enlarged area. Garden designer Sue Berger created a handsome Gothic arch from stones, pebbles, shells and broken china on the ivy-clad wall of her metropolitan garden, fooling the visitor into believing that it leads to another secret enclosure. She also welded together old steel reinforcement rods (usually used to support concrete frame buildings) to form a rusty, barley-twist pergola which in the height of summer is covered in roses, clematis and a rampant golden leaf vine.

HOSE REEL

EQUIPMENT

Hand saw
Electric or hand screwdriver
Electric jigsaw
Electric orbital sander or glasspaper
Paintbrush

MATERIALS

Empty plywood cable drum
Selection tongue-and-groove cladding
Selection 20 mm (³/₄ in) wood screws
Multi-surface garden paint
Four 60 mm (2¹/₂ in) wood screws

A garden hose is essential in any well managed garden, but its storage can be a nightmare. Hoses seem to have a life of their own. Wound up in a coil, they always seem to develop tangles; when unwound, the flow of water is prevented by mysteriously appearing kinks and bends. To prolong the life of a hose and prevent accidental damage, it should always be housed on a reel when not in use. Hose reels are readily available from shops and garden centres and most do a good job – but at a cost. Here we show how an effective wall-mounted hose reel can be simply constructed from a discarded cable drum with only basic tools and a little patience.

Cable drums come in many sizes, from gigantic wooden drums unreeled from the back of a cable-laying vehicle to cardboard drums on which domestic electric cable is sold. Most larger drums are recycled, returned to the cable manufacture for reuse, but if you can secure one it can be transformed into a practical garden table. For this hose-reel project, we used a plywood electric-cable drum which we found abandoned on an industrial building site, a source of numerous useful finds.

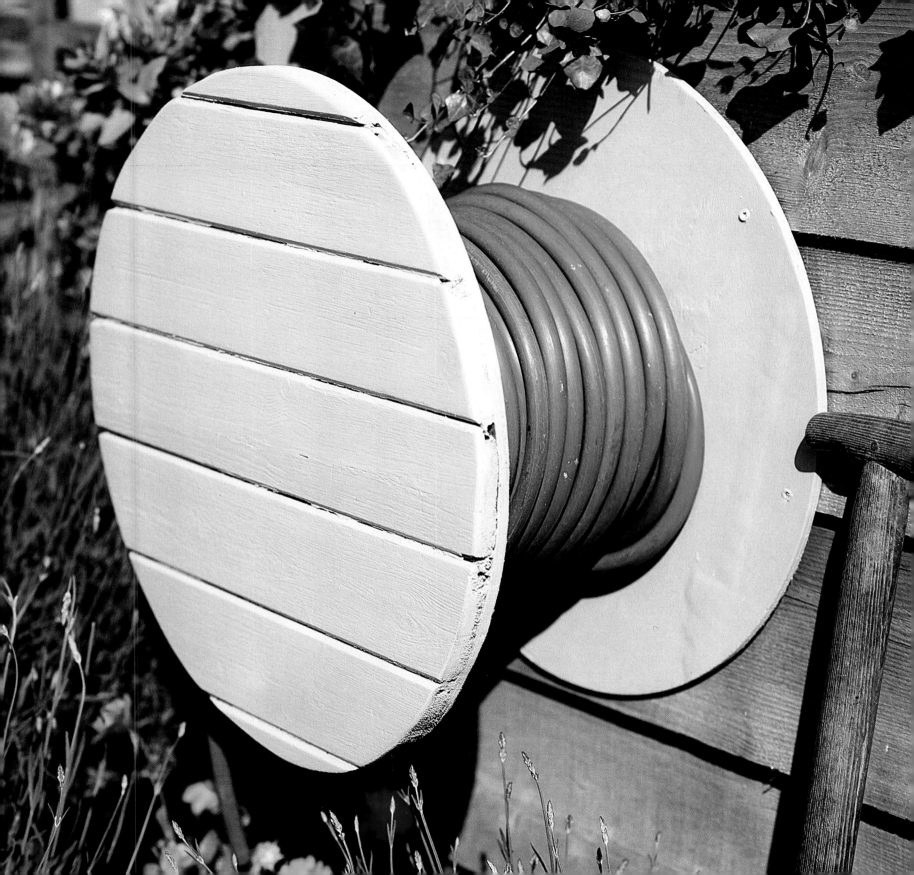

HOSE REEL

METHOD

1 Saw the tongue-and-groove cladding into lengths roughly the diameter of the cable drum, join the boards together and lay them face down on the work surface. Lay the drum on top and fix it to the tongue-and-groove using two 18 mm ($^3/_4$ in) wood screws to fasten each board.

2 Place the drum and fitted boards onto a block of wood raised above the work surface and cut the boards to shape with the jigsaw, using the circular drum base as a guide.

3 Turn the drum over and use the orbital sander or glasspaper to give a smooth and rounded finish to the newly cut edge.

4 Apply at least two coats of multi-surface garden paint of your chosen colour to the whole of the hose reel, remembering to paint the rear to protect it from water and decay.

5 When the paint is dry, the hose reel can be secured in position with the four 60 mm ($2^1/_2$ in) wood screws driven through its base into the wall behind. (If secured to a solid wall, the screws should be driven into wall plugs inserted into previously made holes drilled with a masonry bit.) Touch up exposed screw heads with a dab of paint. The reel is now ready for use.

CLAY PIPE PLANTERS

EQUIPMENT

Garden spade
Garden trowel

MATERIALS

Selection clay drainage pipes
Quantity broken stone or pot shards
Sieved soil, compost or
    growing medium

METHOD

1 Decide where the pipes are to be positioned then dig a trench slightly deeper than the depth you propose to sink the deepest pipe. Place a layer of stone or broken potshards in the base of the trench to provide a firm footing for the pipes.

2 Place the deepest pipe into position and then add the others, supporting their bases by building up the foundation of stone and broken pots under them. Fill around the base of each pipe with soil, firming into place to secure it properly.

3 Fill the pipes with growing mixture, compost or sieved soil, leaving a bit of space between the soil and the top of the pipes in order to make watering easier. Water thoroughly and plant. It can be quite difficult to control the growth of weeds around grouped pipe planters, so it is worth mulching around their bases.

Terracotta drainage and soil pipes are readily available and can be found in numerous lengths, gauges and finishes. Some are now being replaced with plastic but the traditional clay pipe is still widely used.

Many clay pipes would seem to be broken either in transit or during installation and damaged ones are a familiar sight around most building developments. Broken pipes are of little or no use to the builder or contractor and they can often be rescued before they are broken up to make hardcore, their otherwise inevitable end.

Clay pipes can be used to construct effective garden features. Pipes inserted into the ground at different depths, or a combination of pipes of varying lengths, add height, texture and an almost architectural quality to a garden, border or bed. The fact that most pipes are made with one flush and one ferruled end offers further opportunities to vary the appearance of a feature.

Short lengths of pipe can be most attractive when used as containers inserted into the soil to control the otherwise rampant growth of certain invasive plants. They can also be most attractive when installed flush with the surface of paved areas to contain low-growing herbs or sweet-smelling plants.

GARDEN MARKERS

Serried ranks of twigs and sticks surmounted by tatty seed packets placed in the garden to identify rows of seedlings or emerging plants can be a bit of an eyesore.

Slugs attack most of the packets, the writing fades and becomes illegible, and anyway, half go missing, blown or washed away. Plastic markers do an excellent job and can be used to mark repotted plants or cuttings to record species and dates, but the gardener with an eye to combining practicality and aesthetics will always find a use for robust and attractive garden markers which are easily read and can be used time and time again.

Slate is an obvious choice of material for making garden markers: strong and almost impervious to decay or degradation, its colour is perfect for writing on in chalk or white paint. We demonstrate how to transform redundant roofing slates into simple and long-lasting garden markers.

Wood is another excellent material from which to make garden markers and we show how softwood timber rescued from a broken picket fence can be transformed into highly individual markers. Almost any wood can be utilised and should you have access to a ripsaw or saw bench, it is simple to cut down waste softwood or hardwood timber to a suitable size.

SLATE MARKERS

EQUIPMENT

Tape measure
Straight edge
Marker point or nail
Slate cutter
Palette knife or paint scraper
Electric orbital sander
   (or various grades of glasspaper
   and emery paper)
Paintbrush

MATERIALS

Selection roofing slates
Matt or satin finish
   exterior-grade varnish

METHOD

All slate has a grain and roofing slates are generally cut with the grain running along the length of the slate. A slate cutter will make a better job cutting across the grain. This project requires the markers to be cut into strips along the grain, so particular care should be taken.

1 Use the tape measure, straight edge and marker point or nail to divide the width of the slate into strips approximately 6 cm (2¹/₄ in) wide. Cut the strips with the slate cutter. As the action of the slate cutter will produce one bevelled edge and one flat edge, always cut the slate from the same face in order to produce a matching cut.

2 Cut each strip of slate to the desired length and create a point at one end by cutting from both edges at an angle of approximately 45°. This can be quite tricky and may result in a number of broken points before you master the technique. (Keep pieces of broken and chipped slate for use as a garden bedding mulch.)

3 Lay the completed markers on a flat surface and remove any delamination or flaked material with the palette knife or scraper. Use the orbital sander (or varying grades of glasspaper and emery paper) to sand to a smooth finish.

4 Wipe clean of any dust and debris and apply two coats of matt or satin outdoor varnish with the paintbrush, leaving to dry between coats. When the second coat of varnish is completely dry, the garden markers are ready for use.

WOOD MARKERS

EQUIPMENT

Carpenters saw or mitre saw
Paintbrush

MATERIALS

Lengths of approx. 65 mm x 12 mm
    (2¹/₂ in x ¹/₂ in) sawn softwood timber
White or light colour multi-surface
    garden paint

METHOD

1 Cut the strips of 65 mm x 12 mm (2¹/₂ in x
¹/₂ in) sawn softwood timber into lengths of
approximately 30 cm (12 in). Cut one end into a
point with a hand saw or mitre saw.

2 Apply at least two coats of multi-surface
garden paint to all faces of the strips, paying
particular attention to the point and end grain.
When dry, a felt-tip pen or pencil can be used on
the markers. After some use, it is a simple job to
renew the finish with a further coat of paint.

CART SHAFT FEATURE

EQUIPMENT

Paintbrush
Hammer
Sledgehammer
Spirit level
Spanner

MATERIALS

Selection cart shafts
Exterior-grade transparent wood
preservative
Waste timber for props
Selection nails
2 metal fence spikes per shaft
Waste block of wood to fit
    inside metal spikes
Selection wooden wedges

Safety note

We advise that rubber or protective gloves are
used when applying wood preservative.

The cart shafts used for this project were bought at auction. In the lot were also a selection of harness, some old brasses and a number of mysterious iron and wooden objects, the purposes of which we only found out later from a farmer who had spent his early life with working horses.

Made redundant by modern farming methods, much early working horse harness and tools is now rusting and rotting away on farms, a fast disappearing resource of functional artifacts largely ignored by collectors and museums which will soon be lost for all time. We used some of the metal traces and harness as decorations but the heavy shafts sat ignored for months.

When a herd of cattle almost totally destroyed our garden, the only answer was to rotavate the entire lawn and lay new turf. Three months later, we had a new lawn which stretched down to our small orchard and the open countryside beyond. We wanted to emphasise the view and decided to erect three of the shafts to frame the longest vista. Another shaft has been used as an archway leading to a garden seating area and we have plans to erect more as objets d'art.

CART SHAFT FEATURE

METHOD

1 Before you start constructing the feature, saturate the shafts with exterior-grade transparent wood preservative to treat any rot or worm and protect the timber from further deterioration. Pay particular attention to end grain and any timber that will be below the ground.

2 Nail a piece of wood to each shaft to form temporary props. Erect the shafts in the garden, moving them around until you have found the best position for each shaft. Stand back and view them from a distance, fine-tuning their positions until you have achieved the effect you want.

3 Lay the shafts on the ground just behind their proposed positions and remove the temporary props. For each shaft, use the sledgehammer cushioned by a block of wood to drive a metal fence spike for each upright into the ground. Start by driving the spike halfway, check it is upright with the spirit level, then continue to drive the spike into the ground until only its socket is visible, making sure the integral tightening bolt is still accessible.

4 You will need assistance for the final part of the job. Place the uprights of the shaft into the metal spikes and, while someone holds the shaft vertical, anchor the uprights by means of wooden wedges. Use the spirit level to check the shaft is vertical and finally tighten the integral bolt on each spike with a spanner to ensure the shaft is secure.

LOG BIRD FEEDER

EQUIPMENT

Electric drill and 32 mm (1¼ in) hole cutter
25 mm (1 in) wood chisel

MATERIALS

Wooden log
Empty metal tea light candle bases
Three 38 mm (1½ in) galvanised screw eyes
Light chain
Three small key ring or snap hooks
Large key rings or snap hook

METHOD

An old but lightweight log was selected for this project in order to make a feeder which would be large enough to hold a reasonable quantity of bird food but light enough to hang from a slight branch to discourage visits from larger birds.

1 Place the log on a flat surface and drill several holes in the top surface to make a depth of approximately 36 mm (1½ in) with the electric drill and 32 mm (1¼ in) holecutter.

2 Remove the cores of cut wood from the drilled holes with a chisel and scrape the base of the holes level.

3 Screw the three galvanised screw eyes into the extremities of the log to provide secure anchorage points for the hanging chain. Cut the chain (salvaged if possible) into three equal lengths, join one end of each to each of the screw eyes with a small key ring or snap hook and the join the remaining ends with a larger key ring or snap hook.

4 Place an empty tea light candle base into each drilled hole in the top surface of the log and fill with a mixture of melted fat and chopped peanuts or birdseed. Leave the fat to set. Hang the bird feeder from the outer branch of a convenient tree and leave for the wild birds to discover and enjoy. Keep a number of spare empty metal tea light candle bases filled with more of the fat and seed mixture, and refill the feeder with them when the first containers have been exhausted.

Everyone welcomes birds and wildlife into their gardens. Kitchen scraps, wild bird seed, a hanging coconut and string bags full of peanuts all provide vital food for birds (and the occasional squirrel) in winter months. Large numbers of the wild bird population die over winter and garden birds can come to depend on the food put out for them. If you care for wildlife, it is a good idea to provide clean food and fresh water all year round.

A regular supply of food can make all the difference to survival, particularly of fledgling birds in spring.

We enjoy watching the birdlife which surrounds our home. Three species of swan gather over winter on the fields beyond our garden, wild duck abound and the cries of curlew are a constant sound in winter. Both green and larger spotted woodpeckers are common and we keep a patch of garden wild to attract goldfinches. Recently we have seen an increasing number of buzzards but the most destructive of all our visiting birds are the myriad noisy, bullying magpies which have proliferated over recent years.

With no shortage of wood, we decided to construct a simple hanging bird feeder which would attract a cross section of the smaller species but thwart the depredations of grey squirrels and the larger jackdaws, rooks and magpies which otherwise steal the food.

WINDOW COLD FRAME

EQUIPMENT

Orbital sander or glasspaper
    and sanding block
Tape measure
Hand saw
Electric drill and wood bit
Electric screwdriver
Pencil or marker pen
Straight edge
Electric jigsaw
Electric planer
Paintbrush

MATERIALS

Old window frame
Quantity softwood planking
    approx. 15 cm x 25 mm (6 in x 1 in)
Quantity softwood approx.
    5 cm x 5 cm (2 in x 2 in)
Quantity 65 mm (2¹/₂ in)
    galvanised screws
Quantity softwood approx.
    5 cm x 25 mm (2 in x 1 in)
Length softwood approx.
    25 cm x 5 cm x 25 mm (10 in x 2 in x 1in)
Two metal washers
White or light coloured opaque
    garden wood paint

In the absence of a greenhouse, no garden should be without a cold frame, a place where plants can be started early, protected from the cold and frost. Keen gardeners, we enjoy home-grown vegetables, safe in the knowledge that they have been fed only on well-rotted farmyard manure and garden compost and are free of pesticides and sprays. Somehow they seem to taste so much better.

Unfortunately our growing season is all too short. In past years we have protected newly sown plants with glass cloches rescued from a local strawberry grower who was replacing them with plastic tunnels. The problem with cloches is that they break easily, are heavy, and are difficult to store when not in use. Luckily we had the materials from which to make a number of cold frames to replace them. For the tops we used old windows with frames and glass intact, bought at a local clearance sale. For the frames we decided to use some softwood timber planks, once used to line a roof and rescued from a local reclamation yard, just for the cost of collecting them – painted with bitumen they had so many nails in them that they were uneconomic to recycle.

Discarded windows, all too often replaced by plastic double glazing, are easy to find and should cost you little. They make a wonderful resource material and can be used as doors for wall cupboards in a kitchen, made into coffee tables, and even reused as windows in garden sheds and garages.

WINDOW COLD FRAME

METHOD

When selecting a window frame for this project, check that the putty securing the glass in place is sound and that there are no gaps or holes which will allow moisture to penetrate the wood and encourage rot. We selected a number of window frames of equal size to make several uniform cold frames.

1 Use the orbital sander or glasspaper and a sanding block to remove any residual paint from the window frame. If the paintwork is in relatively good condition, sand it to a sound surface.

2 Measure the width of the planks you will be using for the project and decide on the height of the proposed cold frame. As the frame is designed to slope from back to front, for simplicity we used three planks for the back and two for the front. Cut two lengths of the 5 cm x 5 cm (2 in x 2 in) softwood to approximately 25 mm (1 in) less than the combined width of two planks and two further pieces to approximately 25 mm (1 in) less than the combined width of three planks. This will give you two short and two long battens. Cut six lengths of the planking to approximately 5 cm (2 in) longer than the shorter side of the window frame to form the sides of the cold frame. Place three of the cut planks on a surface and join them together with a short batten at one end and a long batten at the other, pre-drilling the screwholes where they fall close to the ends of the planks in order to prevent the timber splitting. Repeat with the remaining three planks and two battens to form the second side piece, ensuring that when placed together the corresponding battens face each other.

3 Cut five lengths of planking each approximately 5cm (2 in) longer than the longer side of the window frame to form the front and back of the cold frame. Place three planks together on a surface and measure their combined width. These three pieces will form the back of the frame. Measure the combined width of the remaining two planks which will form the front of the frame. Take one of the assembled side pieces and mark a point at each end, the first at the height of the front of the frame and the second on the opposite end at a point approximately 1 cm ($^1/_2$ in) less than the height of the back of the frame. Use a pencil or marker and straight edge to draw a line from the first point to the second point and cut the side piece to shape along the marked line with a jigsaw or hand saw. Repeat with the second side piece.

4 Take the two planks cut for the frame front and pre-drill two holes at both ends of each plank approximately 25 mm (1 in) from the end, one close to the top, one close to the bottom. Fit the two planks to the sloping side pieces to form the front of the frame, screwing through the pre-drilled holes into the battens. Repeat with the three remaining planks to form the rear of the frame. The cold frame carcass is now assembled.

5 Place the assembled carcass on a level surface and use the electric plane to plane the tops of the front and back of the frame level with the slope of the side pieces. Always plane away from the ends towards the centre of the timber to minimise the risk of the planer snagging on and damaging the side pieces. Take the length of 5 cm x 25 mm (2 in x 1 in) softwood and cut to form a frame sitting on top of the carcass, the inner dimension to be just greater than the rebate size of the window and the outside to overlap the sides of the carcass. Pre-drill and fix in place with screws driven into the top of the carcass. Place the window into the rebate to check the fit. Take the piece of 25 cm x 5 cm x 25 mm (10 in x 2 in x 1 in) softwood timber and drill a screwhole in it approximately one third along its length. Using two washers behind the screw, attach the piece of wood at the top of the inside face of the cold frame and at the centre of the top plank to form a prop which can be used to keep the window open in order to provide ventilation for growing plants in warmer weather. The washers behind the screw will make it easier to move the prop. Finally, paint the completed cold frame with two coats of white or light-coloured opaque garden wood paint or multi-surface outdoor paint.

In *Salvage Style in your Garden* we give you hints and ideas about the sourcing, preservation and different uses of salvaged materials. We advise you to look about yourself, to think before

recycled and salvaged materials.

In some areas planning authorities insist on the use of vernacular materials. If working on a scheduled building it is a legal requirement that appropriate

HOW TO GET IT, HOW TO DO IT

you dispose of anything, and never to rush into buying new if there is a reclaimed material that can be used instead.

Reclamation yards are the supermarkets of salvage where a bewildering array of stacked timber, tiles, bricks and artefacts awaits the purchaser. The days in which all reclaimed materials could be purchased for less than their modern counterparts are gone but, unless you are prepared to search for yourself, reclamation yards are the ideal solution for the enthusiast wanting to enjoy the appeal of

materials are used. Remember that when a building is listed the plot on which it stands is also listed, so planning and listed building consent must be obtained before any alterations or construction work are carried out on the house or garden. In some conservation areas even the colours used for decoration are controlled. There are strict rules governing the felling and pruning of trees, particularly if they are the subject of a preservation order. A tree takes years to grow – and can be felled in an hour.

ABOVE

A selection of roof ventilators removed from old buildings await buyers in a reclamation yard. One of these verdigris copper ventilators has now been transformed into an imposing dovecote.

ABOVE RIGHT

A stunningly beautiful floor in the summer house of the Lost Gardens of Heligan, carefully restored by John Nelson using as much of the original brick and stone as possible.

OPPOSITE

An eclectic selection of architectural antiques and miscellaneous salvage lined up and labelled ready for sale at an auction held in the grounds of a country house.

Consider carefully before attempting major work in your garden. If you are in any doubt, check with your local planning office. We owe it to our predecessors, and those who will follow us, not to alter, damage or destroy something which is fundamentally irreplaceable. Every tree felled to make way for a patio or conservatory, every window replaced by an unsightly uPVC double-glazed unit, is another nail in the coffin of the diminishing resource of our historic past.

There is nothing intrinsically wrong with the new. Indeed, architects and garden designers are responsible for much of the current interest in contemporary design. Some modern materials can and do outperform their obsolescent predecessors. There is, however, a time and a place for everything and in

Salvage Style in your Garden we hope to persuade you to look again at what others have discarded and to show you how challenging and exciting working with old and discarded materials can be.

Visit gardens whenever you can. Many have used reclaimed materials and we were particularly impressed by the Lost Gardens of Heligan in Cornwall and Tresco Abbey Gardens on the Isles of Scilly. Many inspirational private gardens are open to the public through local and national garden schemes which raise funds for charity from entrance charges. Adapt the projects in this book to what you have available. Use different materials and components. Experiment with things you have discovered, some of which perhaps are peculiar to the part of the world in which you live. And if you have the space, collect and store discovered items which you may not have a current use for but are sure you will find a purpose for 'one day'.

SOURCES OF SALVAGED MATERIALS

Time and again in *Salvage Style in your Garden*, we suggest you keep your eyes open for that opportune find. Sources of discarded artefacts, timber and building materials are all around you, and should you be fortunate to see an opportunity to salvage something, never overlook it.

Reclamation yards are an invaluable source of reclaimed and salvaged materials. Most dealers specialise and a little research trying to find the expert in the field is time well spent. We are committed supporters of SALVO (see 'Useful Addresses') and its voluntary code of conduct. SALVO code dealers undertake to keep a record of the provenance of everything they sell. They agree not to buy any item if there is the slightest suspicion that it may be stolen or sell anything removed from a listed building or scheduled monument. The theft of architectural and garden antiques is growing and SALVO members have helped the police recover numerous stolen articles.

Most reclamation dealers are expert in their field and keen to impart their knowledge. If they don't know the answer to a question, they will know 'someone who does'. Dealers are extremely busy during weekends when much of their business is done. Don't cross-question otherwise helpful dealers if this prevents them from attending to other customers. Instead, return during the week when they are less busy. The yard is more likely to be frequented by trade customers then and the prices may reflect this.

Reclamation yards can be a source of materials at knockdown prices. Hidden behind the ranks of bricks on pallets, the carefully sorted tiles, or store of softwood timber may well be a treasure trove of useful materials, yours for the asking. Dealers have a problem disposing of broken items and offcuts: if you can use it, make them an offer. Most of the broken tiles and slates used for edging in 'A Garden Reclaimed' were found in a skip at a reclamation yard. At another we secured a job lot of roofing timber too full of nails to be economic for the yard to remove – no problem for us, we used the timber to make our Potting Stand in 'Seating and Retreating' and the Window Cold Frame in 'Inventive Ideas'.

Never ignore government surplus dealers. As the armed forces contract, the civil service 'downsizes' and nationalised industries are privatised, a bewildering array of equipment is disposed of to dealers who offer the items at often ludicrously cheap prices to the public. Old ammunition boxes discarded by the army are ideal for storing tools and the odds and ends which clutter up most garden rooms and potting sheds.

The Latrine Bucket we made into a planter in 'Plants, Planters and Planting' came from a government surplus yard and other finds have included redundant tent poles, used to construct a garden arbour, the buckets used as planters in 'The Themed Garden' and numerous tools we have put to good use in our own garden. Most things made for the armed forces were manufactured to exacting standards and many are ideally suited for conversion or reuse in the home or garden.

If you haven't yet visited a government surplus yard, do so: they provide a fascinating insight into government profligacy and a

BELOW

Looking through a cart shaft into a brocante in northern France, where a mouthwatering assortment of rural artefacts, bric-a-brac, salvage and antiques are offered for sale at sometimes remarkably low prices.

valuable resource for the enthusiastic salvager.

Scan the small advertisements in your local newspaper for bargains. Many newspapers run free ads for articles under a certain value, a worthwhile way of disposing of unwanted items. For the advertiser it may be unwanted, for you it could be worth a great deal.

We have secured numerous things from newspaper small ads. Timber rescued from an old greenhouse – now incorporated in a garden shelter – was one of our best finds, the wooden fencing which protects part of our garden was made from a demolished building we found advertised, and even the chickens we keep in our garden are the descendants of some battery hens we bought as the result of a small ad.

Car-boot sales are a godsend to the keen-eyed salvager. Whilst they have achieved something of a reputation as an outlet for the disposal of goods with a dubious history, car-boot sales are where unwanted house and garden items can be bought at bargain prices. Many of the plants and shrubs in our garden and the old glass garden lights and paraffin lamps we use for outdoor dining were bought at car-boot sales.

Garage sales can also be rewarding. At one of the most recent we attended the owners were emigrating and disposing of a lifetime's accumulation of house and garden tools and equipment. We bought dozens of terracotta pots and a collection of neglected but robust garden tools, now invaluably employed in our garden.

Scan the press for details of farm sales and auctions. Farm sales can be a busy social occasion where the selling of livestock and equipment accumulated sometimes over generations of farming life takes second place to meeting around the mobile catering van or discussing the woes of modern farming. The water trough used for the Water Feature in 'The Themed Garden' and the cheese presses

for the Cheese Press Table in 'Seating and Retreating' were found at farm sales. Should you live in a rural area, they can be one of the most rewarding and enjoyable hunting grounds for disregarded treasures.

Increasing in popularity are architectural and garden antiques and salvage sales. Many artefacts fetch quite staggering prices at these sales but bargains can be found. We bought the cart and carriage shafts used in 'Inventive Ideas' at such an auction and one of our most satisfying purchases – a wonderful resource of hardwood timber and mouldings – was made at a recent sale.

Never ignore builders' skips. A search through a roadside skip can reveal a cornucopia of useful things. The scaffold boards used to construct the Scaffold Bench in 'Seating and Retreating' were salvaged from a skip. (It is always worth checking with the householder or builder where possible that the material in the skip has been intended for disposal rather than storage to avoid being accused of theft!)

You may find a building being demolished where the timbers are being burnt, the bricks sent to landfill and the roofing slates being discarded. Make the builder an offer for some of the discarded materials, or better still, offer to take them off his hands. Disposing of unwanted materials is expensive and the value of much salvaged building material is outweighed by the cost of sorting it. If you see something useful to you, approach the contractor: if you don't get in the way or hold up the work you may be able to walk away with some wonderful raw materials.

We frequently stumble upon a building site where valuable materials are being thrown away. On a recent shopping trip we discovered a department store being gutted to make way for a new development. Shop fittings were being discarded, panelling destroyed and hundreds of bricks had been

dumped into a skip. After a brief chat with the site foreman we were away, the back of the car laden with bricks. An hour's work cleaning them and we had more than enough clean bricks to construct the edging used for the raised garden in 'A Garden Reclaimed'.

Development sites are another wonderful source of salvageable materials. You will be surprised by the number of old pipes which are abandoned on site, too damaged to be used by the builder, but fine for the Pipe Planter in 'Inventive Ideas'. Timber offcuts from roof trusses and floor joists, broken roof tiles and bricks abound – if you don't have them, they will be burnt or end up as rubble.

Building sites are dangerous and on most of them access is restricted. Never venture onto a site without authority and always seek permission before removing anything.

Scrap-metal yards contain a wealth of useful items. We have salvaged copper pipes to make a greenhouse sprinkler system, used scrap lead sheeting to protect the tops of fencing posts and clad an outdoor building, and even adapted discarded steel reinforcing bars to construct a light and airy garden pergola. Scrapyards can be dangerous places. Make your wishes known to the owner who will almost invariably be helpful. Your finds will be weighed and you should be asked for little more than their scrap value.

Car breakers' yards can be a source of inspiration. We have seen wonderful planters constructed from old wheel hubs and were enchanted by the centrepiece of the garden of a Citroën enthusiast, an old 2CV filled to overflowing with flowering plants.

The web is a growing source of salvaged and recycled materials and information. Websites we have found particularly useful are www.salvoweb.com which lists reclamation and salvage dealers worldwide and provides links to numerous other sites; www.recycle.net who run Recycler's World and a materials buying and selling website; and arcsal.com a simple to use and well illustrated web directory of salvage, reclaimed materials and architectural and garden antiques.

Finally, look to your own home and think first before you throw something away. Many useful items can be reincarnated in another form. Old buckets which might appear to be past their usefulness can be transformed into striking garden planters. If too far gone, use them sunk into the soil to contain invasive plants. Corrugated-iron sheets can be cut down with metal sheers to make lawn edging, even that old and broken chair can soon become a planter, overflowing with scented camomile. All too often we find ourselves searching through skips and reclamation yards to replace an item we once had but threw away. The Trellis Rack in 'Elements and Ambiance' is an example of how we put to a different use something which was surplus to requirements and could have ended up being discarded. Instead, it was given a new purpose, and very useful it is too.

HINTS & TECHNIQUES

SAFETY FIRST

Safety must come first. Before you start any project or building activity, ensure you have the correct tools, everything is in working order and take every precaution to prevent unnecessary accidents. Damaged tools are dangerous and faulty power tools deadly. Check power tools for damage and have them regularly maintained. Think through the project before you start and clear the working area of any extraneous materials or equipment.

If using sharp equipment such as chisels or power saws, always work away from yourself,

never cut towards your hand or body. A moment's inattention can result in a nasty wound. Never cut close to your hand, clamp anything you are cutting securely to a work surface, and use a scrap of timber to push timber through a planer or bench saw. Think first, cut afterwards.

Most importantly, keep all tools, equipment and substances which are likely to be dangerous out of the reach of children and animals.

TOXIC SUBSTANCES

Many projects involve the use of preservatives, stains and other potentially dangerous substances. Please read and follow the instructions on the container and make sure you have old cloths or rags to hand for wiping up spilled materials. Never casually dispose of any waste or empty containers which may cause pollution or react with other discarded substances.

Some old timber was painted with lead-based paints. This material is hazardous and you must wear a dust mask if you are sanding or planing down old paint. Dust from any substance is dangerous and if you are working without a dust-extraction system a dust mask (or even full face mask) is essential.

The dangers of asbestos are well known and it can be present in old buildings being demolished or renovated. Strict laws apply to its removal and only registered experts, properly equipped, are allowed to undertake this work. Occasionally traces of asbestos can be found on timber salvaged from old buildings. Some amateurs undertaking home improvements fail to recognise it and unthinkingly deposit it in a roadside skip. Always err on the side of caution. If in doubt, leave well alone.

PROTECTIVE CLOTHING

Wear the correct clothing for the job. Loose clothing can become entangled with moving parts of power equipment and injuries can be caused by unthinking operation. Always work with sleeves fastened. Ties or scarfs can be extremely dangerous and long hair should be tied up or a hair covering worn.

Proper protective clothing is essential. A face or dust mask, protective gloves and a coverall should be part of the workshop inventory. Eye protection is most important when using rotary sanders or other power equipment. We own a full face mask which is attached as a visor to a protective helmet. Obtained from Tools Direct (see 'Useful Addresses'), a company which helped us with this book, the visor is comfortable to use and ideal when operating a chain or power saw.

Protective padded clothing is essential if you are using a chain saw and advisable if you are working with sheet metal. Head protection is a legal requirement for most building and demolition sites and you should never venture onto one or work on something over your head without it. Safety shoes or boots incorporating a hardened toecap and protective sole are a good investment, as are strong rigger's or similar gloves.

ELECTRICITY OUTDOORS

Electricity is dangerous, and the combination of electricity and water is potentially lethal. Never use electrical equipment outdoors if it is raining and always keep leads out of the wet. Always use a circuit breaker attached to the lead of any electrical equipment used in the garden (essential for underwater equipment such as pumps and aerators) and should any

TOP

Stable bricks are made in a vast range of patterns and these examples were found in the yard at South West Reclamation.

BOTTOM

A weathered and worn oak sherry barrel, complete with its original stencil markings sits among a stack of wooden pallets.

electrical lead become damaged, replace it rather than attempt a repair.

Purpose-made electrical fittings are manufactured for outdoor electrical supply and, unless you are experienced, these should be fitted by a qualified electrician. Have all outdoor electrical installations checked by a qualified electrician before use.

Water features are increasing in popularity, many involve a pump or other electrical equipment. Ask the advice of a specialist water garden retailer before you install such equipment. OASE (see 'Useful Addresses'), the manufacturer of pumps and water garden equipment, have a helpful website which is most informative.

FIRST AID

Work involving sharp tools or power equipment entails an element of danger and a basic first-aid kit should be kept handy in case of accidents. Familiarise yourself with its contents and keep it restocked if at any time you have cause to use it.

EQUIPMENT AND TOOLS

Most projects in *Salvage Style in your Garden* require only simple tools. We have been supplied with some very useful power tools by Black and Decker (see 'Useful Addresses') to assist with this book and you will find many of these extremely helpful. A well-equipped workshop should include a number of basic tools: the better the quality of tool you purchase, the better it will perform and the longer it will last.

Maintain your tools in good condition and store them properly. Edged tools stored where

moisture is likely to affect them should be protected with a wipe or spray of oil when not is use. As far as possible, keep tools stored in a dry environment. Screws, nails and other supplies should be kept in airtight containers. We keep only a limited supply of many fixings and supplies as Tools Direct (see 'Useful Addresses'), one of the companies which helped us with this book, operates an efficient overnight delivery service obviating the need to keep large and sometimes deteriorating stocks of materials in our workshop.

We hire tools for many projects, a cement mixer for larger jobs and a diamond rotary cutter for slicing bricks and cutting slate. The hire shop will also supply the appropriate safety equipment.

USING OLD TIMBER

Both hardwood and softwood timber develop a patina and colouration over time, part of a wood's attractiveness. Salvage old timber whenever possible, remove any nails or hardware and store it in the dry where air can circulate around it. Oak, a particularly attractive hardwood, can be discoloured by iron or steel nails or screws. If metal fixings are required, these should be brass.

Salvaged woods can be used for numerous garden projects and constructions and examples of now rare woods can be found in reclamation yards and old demolished buildings. It is important to remove nails and fixings before using power equipment or serious damage to your tools can result.

Painted softwoods can be stripped at home using a paint-stripping solution (time consuming and quite unpleasant) or one of the modern paint-stripping pastes or taken to a specialist firm which will dip the wood in a hot caustic solution. (This process can loosen joints and cause some discolouration.) It is inadvisable to strip hardwoods in a caustic solution. Old paint can be removed by sanding with a machine or by hand, or by using a heat gun, but unless used very carefully the underlying wood can become scorched.

Always treat reclaimed timber with a timber preservative to prevent the spread of worm or rot. A number of coloured and colourless timber preservatives are available and Cuprinol (see 'Useful Addresses'), who helped us with this book, also produce an effective wood hardener, useful if parts of its structure have started to deteriorate.

Timber used in contact with the ground or underground should be saturated with preservative before use. Place it in a container holding the preservative and leave overnight to allow maximum take-up. If new timber is to be used in these situations, make sure it is tanilised timber – timber which has been treated with preservative applied under pressure.

BRICKS, TILES AND TERRACOTTA

Old bricks, tiles and terracotta were produced in small factories in an extraordinary variety of shapes and colours. Manufactured from local clay and distributed only within a small area they ranged in colour from pale cream to almost black. Although in later years they were made to an almost standard size, bricks can be found glazed, unglazed, perforated, high-fired for use in factories, or even patterned for stable use. Many bear the mark of their maker, testimony to a once-thriving local industry.

Handmade bricks were produced by throwing wet clay into wooden moulds before air drying and firing. Some still bear the fingerprints of their long-dead makers. When sliced in half (hire a diamond cutter to do this),

old bricks reveal stunning patterns of swirling colours. Sealed with linseed oil or tile sealant, they make very attractive conservatory flooring. Roof tiles were produced to quite individual local designs and your local reclamation yard should hold a selection of indigenous patterns.

Most old bricks will need to be cleaned of mortar, a time-consuming job requiring chipping with a bricklayer's trowel or bolster. Stained bricks can be cleaned with a proprietary brick cleaner or a solution of proprietary brick cleaner, an unpleasant job not to be lightly undertaken. Bricks can be used in their original condition for paths and edging but some types are susceptible to water penetration and frost damage. Engineering grade bricks should be used if exposed to severe conditions.

Roofing tiles make excellent pavers for patios and are also good for wall capping. In 'Seating and Retreating' we show them used as the floor in a seating area and in 'Inventive Ideas' we illustrate a garden path where clay tiles have been used to edge a garden path. Broken tiles make very effective garden edging (see 'A Garden Reclaimed') and can be used as hardcore for concrete or to provide drainage in garden pots and planters.

Damaged terracotta pots and urns can be repaired with a two-part epoxy resin glue. A specialist two-part, cold-setting, coloured epoxy putty – Milliput (see 'Useful Addresses') – is effective for both repairing and filling broken terracotta.

SLATE

Slate is one of the most versatile reclaimed materials for use in the garden. We show both whole and broken roofing slates used for edging, made into practical garden markers or

slate boards, and as an effective mulch. Large slates are ideal paving material and make perfect weatherproof tops for garden tables.

Roofing slates can be cut with a slate cutter, available from builders' merchants, or a small water-cooled, diamond-bladed, electrical tile cutter. (Ours came from Tools Direct who helped us with this book). Larger pieces of slate should be cut by a professional although a specialist rotary saw can be hired for this job. Although most old roofing slates have suffered delamination through years of exposure to the elements, we show you how to return slate to an almost pristine condition in a number of the projects using slate in this book.

RECLAIMED METALS

Reclaimed metal and metal objects have innumerable uses in the garden. Old buckets make attractive planters and reinforcing rods and sheets can be used to construct pergolas and arches for climbing plants. Some welding may be required – not a job for the amateur, so you would be well advised to employ an experienced welder.

A huge variety of salvaged metals can be found at scrap-metal yards. We have found old copper piping for garden irrigation systems and some quite unique fencing. Thin sheet steel and zinc can be pot-riveted to construct fashionable planters and scrap lead sheet is extremely useful for waterproofing gullies and the tops of posts. Molten lead can be used to fill nail holes in old roofing tiles and cast into moulds to create quite elaborate shapes for finials and wall decorations. Do not work with molten lead without assistance, wear full protective clothing and take the utmost care.

Most salvaged metals show evidence of oxidation or corrosion. At best they will have tarnished or developed a patina through exposure to the elements. Some patination can be attractive, but to prevent further degradation and potential structural damage, salvaged metals should be protected with an appropriate paint or finish. A number of single-coat metal paints are now available: ask your paint retailer for advice. To preserve the appearance of bright metals, spraying with metal lacquer can be quite effective.

CEMENT, CONCRETE AND MORTAR

Cement is the basic constituent of concrete and mortar, together with sand, gravel, ballast or aggregate – and in days gone by, lime or ash. Different mixes are required for different purposes although time and trouble can be saved by using commercially available bags of ready-mixed, general-purpose concrete and bricklaying mortars.

Sands and aggregates in general use:
SHARP SAND A course, gritty material normally used with other aggregates to make concrete.
SOFT OR BUILDERS' SAND This has finer particles and is used for bricklaying mortar.
COURSE AGGREGATE, GRAVEL OR CRUSHED STONE With particles normally between 5 mm ($1/4$ in) and 20 mm ($3/4$ in), these are used to make concrete.
BALLAST OR ALL-IN AGGREGATE A mixture of course aggregate and sharp sand used to make concrete. Normally pre-mixed in the ratio of 2 parts course aggregate to 1 part sharp sand.

For most external constructions, the usual mixtures are:
BRICKLAYING MORTAR 1 part cement to 4 parts soft sand.
BLOCKWORK OR STONE MORTAR 1 part cement to 5 parts soft sand.

CONCRETE FOR DRIVEWAYS AND HEAVY LOAD AREAS 1 part cement to 2 parts sharp sand and 4 parts course aggregate.
CONCRETE FOR PATHS, PATIOS, BASES FOR GARDEN SHEDS AND OTHER LIGHT-LOAD AREAS 1 part cement to 3 parts sharp sand and 6 parts course aggregate.
If concrete is laid to a depth of less than 75 mm (3 in), a 'stronger' mixture is required. Concrete foundations and paths require a sub-base of at least 75 mm (3 in) of broken stone, bricks or other rubble.

All the measurements are by volume – use a bucket for measuring purposes. Concrete and mortar should be mixed with a shovel on a flat surface (a sheet of waste plyboard is ideal) or in a wheelbarrow (clean thoroughly after use). Mix the dry components then add the cement, continuing to mix until an even colour is achieved. Shape the mix into a mound, make a hole in the centre and add water slowly, mixing all the time until a consistency is achieved which allows you to make with the shovel a series of ridges on the surface which hold their shape.

Newly mixed concrete and mortar should be used within two hours. It dries quite quickly but will not achieve its full strength for about seven days. Cover new work with polythene as protection from the wet and extremes of heat and cold. In very hot weather, light spraying with water once a day for a week will prevent it deteriorating. The addition of an accelerator and frost protector additives to the mixture will help drying in cold weather.

Various additives were traditionally used with mortar, particularly lime which made it easier to work and allowed some flexibility in the finished work. Lime mortars are smoother and more durable than their modern counterparts. Ask the advice of an expert restoration builder, but similar results can be

achieved by making a mixture of 1 part cement to $1/2$ part lime to 2 to 4 parts soft sand. Modern masonry mortars containing up to one third limestone filler can be bought, some containing a plasticiser. Try to match the colour of existing mortar by using the local sand (or stone dust) whenever possible. Cement colouring additives are available but they should be used with caution as the mortar will change colour when dry and over time. Some old mortars contain coal ash or cinders, not always to advantage, although industrial ash is a constituent of some modern pre-mixes.

Useful information about cement, concretes and mortars can be found on the Blue Circle Industries website, www.bluecircle.co.uk

PAINTS AND STAINS

Add interest and colour to garden timber with paints and stains. We mix our own stains with transparent wood preservative to achieve quite effective results. Many modern garden paints contain preservative and Cuprinol (see 'Useful Addresses'), who helped us with this book, make products specially formulated for garden use which are both attractive and easy to use. Their multi-surface paints are extremely practical and give an excellent result on stone, brick, blockwork, wood and even rubber and metals.

If traditional paints are being used on planed wood surfaces, the timber should be primed and undercoated before application of the final paint finish. If wood is being varnished, use a product designed for outdoor application as interior varnishes will not stand prolonged exposure to weather.

So many paints and stains are now available there should really be no limit to your garden palette.

USEFUL ADDRESSES

TOOLS & SUPPLIES

BLACK AND DECKER
210 Bath Road
Slough
Buckinghamshire
SL1 3YD
Tel: 01753 511234
Fax: 01753 551155
website:
www.blackanddecker.com
Electrical and battery
powered hand garden tools
for the professional and
hobbyist.

SCREWFIX DIRECT
Mead Avenue
Houndstone Business Park
Yeovil
Somerset
BA22 8RT
Tel: 0500 414141
Fax: 0800 0562256
email:
online@screwfix.com
website:
www.screwfix.com
Screws, nails, hardware and
tools; plumbing and
electrical supplies by mail
order – overnight.

MILLIPUT
Unit 8
The Marian
Dolgellau
Mid Wales
LL40 1UU
Tel: 01341 422562
website: www.milliput.com
Two part cold setting epoxy
putties for repair and filling
terracotta.

**BLUE CIRCLE
INDUSTRIES**
Technical Centre
305 London Road
Greenhithe
Kent
DA9 9JQ
Tel: 01322 382244
Fax: 01322 382266
email: bctc@bciplc.com

website:
www.bluecircle.co.uk
Technical department for
leading manufacturer of
cements for all applications

PAINTS, STAINS AND TIMBER TREATMENT PRODUCTS

CUPRINOL LTD
Adderwell
Frome
Somerset
BA11 1NL
Tel: 01373 475000
Fax: 01373 475050
Timber treatment products,
stains and colour washes for
internal and external use.
A useful advice line for
customer queries.

GARDEN DESIGNERS

**BERGER PHILLIPS TOWN
GARDEN DESIGN**
69 Kingsdown Parade
Bristol
BS6 5UG
Specialists in urban and
small town gardens.

SARAH GIDDENS
Tel: 01920 420459
Designer working
throughout South West
England.

**BEN PIKE GARDEN
DESIGNS**
Round Trees
Smallway
Congresbury
North Somerset
BS19 5AA
Tel: 01934 876355
Fax: 01934 835566
Garden and landscape
design. Water gardens and
features.

INFORMATION ON RECLAMATION & ARCHITECTURAL ANTIQUES, DEALERS, CRAFTSPEOPLE & SERVICES

SALVO
PO Box 333
Cornhill-upon-Tweed
Northumberland
TD12 4YJ
Tel: 01890 820333
Fax: 01890 820499
email: tk@salvoweb.com
website: salvoweb.com
Publishers of information on
architectural antiques,
reclaimed materials,
reclamation dealers and
craftspeople working with
salvage. Originators of the
SALVO code and the SALVO
Code Dealer list. The SALVO
website links many different
dealers from all over the UK
and abroad.

GARDEN ARCHITECTURAL ANTIQUES, RECLAMATION & SALVAGE DEALERS

arcsal.com
Regent House
Fore Street,
Castle Cary
Somerset.
BA7 7BG
Tel: 01963 351797
Fax: 01963 351988
email: info@arcsal.com
website:
www.arcsal.com
Simple to use and well
illustrated web directory of
salvage, reclaimed materials
and architectural and garden
antiques. All articles are sold
online and delivered to your
doorstep.

AU TEMPS PERDU
30 Midland Road
St Phillips
Bristol
BS2 0JY
Tel: 0117 929 9143
mobile: 0374 486648
Architectural and garden
antiques, 'Down to earth
materials at down to earth
prices'. SALVO Code dealer.

**BAILEYS HOME AND
GARDEN**
The Engine Shed
Station Approach
Ross-on-Wye
Herefordshire
HR9 7BW
Tel: 01989 563015
Fax: 01989 768172
Garden antiques and
accessories. Old garden
tools and equipment.

BINGLEY ANTIQUES
Springfield Farm Estate
Flappit
Haworth
West Yorkshire
BD21 5PT
Tel/Fax: 01535 646666
website:
www.bingleyantiques.com
Open Tues–Sats.

**BORDERS
ARCHITECTURAL**
2 South Road
Wooler
Northumberland
NE71 6TQ
Tel/Fax: 01668 282475

DORSET RECLAMATION
The Reclamation Yard
Cow Drove
Bere Regis
Dorset
BH20 7JZ
Tel: 01929 472200
Fax: 01929 472292
email:
tessa@dorsetrec.u-
net.com
Reclaimed traditional
building materials, garden
antiques and rural artefacts.
SALVO Code dealer.

**DRUMMONDS
ARCHITECTURAL
ANTIQUES**
The Kirkpatrick Building
25 London Road
Hindhead
Surrey
GU26 6AB
Tel: 01428 609444
Fax: 01428 609445
email:
info@drummonds-
arch.co.uk
website:
www.drummonds-
arch.co.uk
Antique garden artefacts and
reclaimed materials. SALVO
Code dealer.

**EARTHWORM
LANDSCAPING
AND CONSULTANCY**
18 Northbrook Road
Shapwick
Bridgwater
Somerset
TA7 9LM
Tel: 01458 210822
Garden design. Always a
ready supply of hard
landscaping and garden
reclamation, granite troughs,
stone rollers, driftwood and
objets d'art.

ENGLISH GARDEN ANTIQUES
The White Cottage
Church Brow
Bowdon
Cheshire
WA14 2SF
Tel: 0161 928 0854
Fax: 0161 929 8081
Reclamation dealer specialising in rare and unusual decorative garden features.

IN-SITU MANCHESTER
Talbot Mill
44 Ellesmere Street,
Hulme
Manchester
M15 4JY
Tel/Fax: 0161 839 5525
email:
info@insitumanchester.com
website:
www.insitumanchester.com
Old established company dealing in reclaimed garden materials and artefacts including flagstones, paving, edging stone, statuary and architectural items. SALVO Code dealer.

JOHN EDMONDS
Buscott Farm
Station Road,
Ashcott
Bridgwater
Somerset
TA7 9QP
Tel: 01458 210359
Fax: 01458 210096
email:
enquiries@jecm.co.uk
website: www.jecm.co.uk
Garden design and supply of garden and landscaping reclamation. Original antique Japanese garden artifacts and lighting. New World driftwood timbers.

LASSCo
St Michaels Church
Mark Street
London
EC2A 4ER
Tel: 020 7749 9944
Fax: 020 7749 9941
email:
stmichaels@lassco.co.uk
website: lassco.co.uk
Five depots in London specailising in a range of reclaimed materials for gardens. SALVO Code dealer.

MINCHINHAMPTON ARCHITECTURAL SALVAGE COMPANY
New Catbrain
Cirencester Road
Aston Down
Nr Minchinhampton
Gloucestershire
GL6 8GE
Tel: 01452 814064
Fax: 01452 813634
email:
masco@catbrain.com
website:
www.catbrain.com

MONGERS
15 Market Place
Higham
Norfolk
NR9 4AF
Tel: 01953 851868
Fax: 01953 851870
email:
mongers@ukgateway.net
Reclaimed stone and terracotta, floor bricks, York stone, stone troughs, some antique garden tools and artefacts.

ROCOCO ANTIQUES
5 New Street
Lower Weedon
Northamptonshire
NN7 4QS
Tel/Fax: 01327 341288
email:
nevillegriffiths@talk21.com
website:
www.nevillegriffiths.co.uk
Large selection of decorative architectural antiques, terracotta and stone. Staddle stones, troughs, decorative ironwork, engineering pavers and garden ornaments.

RETROUVIUS
32 York House
Upper Montagu Street
London
W1H 1FR
Tel/Fax: 020 7724 3387
Mobile: 0378 210855
email:
mail@retrouvius.com
website: retrouvius.com
Unique architectural antiques and building components nationwide. Interior and exterior design projects 'bridging the gap between destruction and construction'.

RONSONS RECLAMATION AND RESORATION
Norton Barn
Wainlodes Lane
Norton
Gloucester
GL2 9LN
Tel: 01452 731236
Fax: 01452 731888
email:
ronsons@netcomuk.co.uk
website:
ronsonsreclamation.com
Reclamation dealers with vast stock of reclaimed and salvaged materials. SALVO Code dealer.

SOLOPARK plc
Station Road
Pampisford
Cambridge
CB2 4HB
Tel: 01223 834663
Fax: 01223 834780
email: info@solopark.co.uk
website:
www.solopark.co.uk
Large stock of reclaimed building materials and decorative salvage.

SOUTH WEST RECLAMATION
Gwilliams Yard
Edington
Nr Bridgwater
Somerset
TA7 9JN
Tel: 01278 723173
Fax: 01278 722800
website:
www.southwest-rec.co.uk
Reclamation dealers specialising in flooring and Bridgwater roofing tiles. SALVO Code dealer.

TALISMAN
The Old Brewery
Wyke
Gillingham
Dorset
SP8 4NW
Tel: 01747 824423/824222
Fax: 01747 823544
email:
talisman@globalnet.co.uk
Architectural antiques for gardens and interiors.

WELLS RECLAMATION
The Old Cider Farm
Coxley
Wells
Somerset
BA5 1RQ
Tel: 01749 677087
Fax: 01749 671089
website:
www.wellsreclamation.com
Comprehensive stock of architectural and garden antiques, and reclaimed traditional building materials.

WILSONS CONSERVATION BUILDING PRODUCTS
123 Hillsborough Road
Dromore
Co. Down
Northern Ireland
BT25 1QW
Tel: 028 9269 2304
Fax: 028 9269 8322
email:
rosyw@enterprise.net
Architectural antiques and reclaimed materials. Flooring, wall cappings, setts, cobbles, bricks, beams and decorative metalwork.

GOVERNMENT SURPLUS STORE

HARPERS BAZAAR
263 Worcester Road
Malvern
Worcestershire
WR14 1AA
Tel: 01684 568723
Fax: 01684 612837
Government surplus suppliers; garden and camping supplies, storage, ex-armed forces, government and nationalised industry articles and equipment.

USEFUL ADDRESSES

WATER GARDEN SUPPLIES

BLAKEWAY FISHERIES
Blakeway Farm
Wedmore
Somerset
BS28 4UB
Tel/Fax: 01934 713833
Mobile: 0374 993013
Everything for the garden pond. Specialists in Koi carp.

OASE (UK)
PO Box 1709
Andover
Hampshire
SP10 3GW
Tel: 01264 333225
Fax: 01264 333226
email:
oase.uk@btinternet.com
website:
www.oase-pumpen.com
The world's largest manufacturer of pumps and equipment for water gardens.

ARTISTS AND CRAFTSPEOPLE

PAUL ANDERSON
104 West Street
Hartland
Devon
Tel: 01237 441645
Maker of primitive interior and garden furniture crafted from old oak or elm joists.

CANDACE BAHOUTH
The Old Ebenezer Chapel
Pilton
Somerset
BA4 4BR
Tel: 01749 890433
Mosaic artist working in a variety of reclaimed materials.

PAUL GRELLIER
Ruriculture
Westrip Farmhouse
Cherington
Tetbury
Gloucestershire
GL8 8SL
Tel/Fax: 01452 770094
email:
ruriculture@ukonline.co.uk
website:
www.nemonelight.com
Sculptor specialising in work with reclaimed and salvaged metal, stone and wood. He also incorporates old agricultural and industrial machinery and equipment into his sculptures.

PLANTS AND SHRUBS

POPLAR HERB FARM
Burtle
Bridgwater
Somerset
TA7 8NB
Tel: 01278 723170
email:
richardfish@lineone.net
website:
mikesplants@bc1.net
Organically grown culinary, medicinal and aromatic plants, unique astrological herb garden and herbal preparations.

LANDS END NURSERIES
Heath House
Wedmore
Somerset
BS28 4UQ
Tel/Fax: 01934 713234
email: landsend.bc1.net
website:
mikesplants@bc1.net
Wholesale garden nursery.

CHELSEA FARM CENTRE
Chelsea Farm
Harp Road
Brent Knoll
Nr. Bridgwater
Somerset,
TA9 4HQ
Tel: 01278 760480
Fax: 01278 760144
Garden and plant centre.

WINROW NUSERIES
Laurel Farm
Lewis Drove
Panborough
Wells Somerset
BA5 1PT
Tel: 01934 712571
Fax: 01934 713606
Nursery specialising in trees and shrubs – wholesale only.

GARDEN FURNITURE AND ACCESSORIES

SOMERSET CREATIVE PRODUCTS
Laurel Farm
Westham
Wedmore
Somerset
BS28 4UZ
Tel: 01934 712416
Fax: 01934 712210
email:
somprods@globalnet.co.uk
Authors of *Salvage Style in your Home* and *Salvage Style in your Garden*. Designers and makers of furniture and accessories using reclaimed materials.

PLACES TO VISIT

THE NATIONAL GARDENS SCHEME
Hatchlands Park
East Clandon
Guildford
Surrey
GU4 7RT
Tel: 01483 211535
Fax: 01483 211537
email: ngs@ngs.org.uk
website: www.ngs.org.uk
Charitable organisation which raises money for charities by opening private gardens to the public. Publishers of *The Yellow Book*, which details over 3,500 gardens open to the public in England and Wales.

THE LOST GARDENS OF HELIGAN
Pentewan
St Austell
Cornwall
PL26 6EN
Tel: 01726 845100
Fax: 01726 845101
email: info@heligan.com
website www.heligan.com

TRESCO ABBEY GARDENS
The Tresco Estate
Tresco
Isles of Scilly
Cornwall
TR24 0QQ
Tel: 01720 422849
Fax: 01720 422807
email:
contactus@tresco.co.uk
website: www.tresco.co.uk
The sub-tropical Tresco Abbey Gardens, The Island Hotel, The New Inn, Hell, Bay Hotel (Bryher), timeshare and holiday rental properties.

THE BONE CAVE
Banwell
North Somerset, Tel/Fax: 01934 820516
The bone cave and stalactite cave, Banwell Tower and the follies.

EMMAUS HOUSE
Clifton Hill
Clifton
Bristol,
BS8 1BN
Tel: 0117 907 9950
email:
emmaushouse@msn.com
website:
www.emmaus-house.co.uk
Conference and retreat centre. Bed and Breakfast and restaurant.

OTHER SERVICE PROVIDERS

BIRTSMORTON COURT
Birtsmorton
Malvern
Worcestershire
WR13 6JS
Tel: 01684 833424
Fax: 01684 833837
Corporate hospitality in a mediaeval moated manor house.

JON GOWAN
Aspen Cottage
Upper New Road
Cheddar
Somerset
BS27 3DW
Mobile: 0585 699540
General builder.

CANADA

ALL AROUND DEMOLITION CO.
4912 Still Creek Avenue,
Burnaby
British Columbia,
V1X 2C1
Tel: + 1 604 299 2967
Fax: + 1 604 299 1383

HAPPY HARRY'S USED BUILDING MATERIALS
4128 South Service Road,
Burlington
Ontario
L71 4X5
Tel: + 1 905 631 0990
Fax: + 1 905 631 0991
website:
www.happyharry.com
Salvaged doors, windows, plumbing supplies, staircases, spindles, architectural glass and doors, blocks and bricks.

HAPPY HARRY'S USED BUILDING MATERIALS
5044 45th Street,
Red Deer
Alberta
T4N 1K9
Tel: + 1 403 343 1818
website:
www.happyharry.com
Demolition recycling. Mainly salvaged windows and doors.

HAPPY HARRY'S USED BUILDING MATERIALS
20 Bulmer Lane
Sackville
New Brunswick
E4L 3R4
Tel: + 1 506 364 0803
Fax: + 1 506 198 5364
email:
gbeland@mailserv.mta.ca
website:
www.happyharry.com
New, second and reclamation building materials.

HAPPY HARRY'S USED BUILDING MATERIALS
140 Caledonia Road
Caledonia Industrial Park
Moncton
New Brunswick
E4L 3R4
Tel/Fax: + 1 506 855 7999
email:
gbeland@mailserv.mta.ca
website:
www.happyharry.com
Salvaged building materials.

HAPPY HARRY'S USED BUILDING MATERIALS
46 Wright Avenue
Burnside Industrial Park
Dartmouth
Nova Scotia
B3B 1G6
Tel: + 1 902 468 2319
Fax: + 1 902 468 3666
Windows, doors and plumbing particularly.

MIKE'S SALVAGE
Penetanguishene
Ontario
L9M 1R
Tel: + 1 705 533 4457
email: mikev@csolve.net
Lumber, doors, windows, trim, plumbing, electrical fixtures.

UNIQUITIES ARCHITECTURAL ANTIQUES
940 2nd Avenue NW,
Calgary
Alberta
T2N 0E6
Tel: + 1 403 228 9221
Fax: + 1 403 283 9226
email:
shantzj@cadvision.com

AUSTRALIA

AUSTRALIA'S OPEN GARDEN SCHEME
PO Box 87
Gisborne
Australia 3438
Tel: + 61 35428 4557
Fax: + 61 35428 4558
email
national@opengarden.org.au
website
www.opengarden.abc.net.au

AUSTRALIAN ARCHITECTURAL HARDWOODS
45-47 South Street,
Kempsey
Tel: + 61 2 6562 2788
Reclaimed timber including flooring and sections.

INTEXT PACIFIC PTY LTD
13 St John's Parade
Kew
Victoria 3101
Tel: + 61 3 9853 0364
Fax: + 61 3 9853 3302
email:
intex@bigpond.net.au
website:
www.intexpacific.com
Suppliers of natural landscape and garden materials including railway sleepers and large selection old bricks.

OLD RED BRICK COMPANY
16 William Street,
Beverley, South Australia
Tel: + 61 8 8347 2419
Fax: + 61 8 8347 2144
Salvaged doors, windows, bricks and timber.

QUALITY RECYCLED DEMOLITIONS
34 Woodfield Boulevard,
Caringbah 2229,
Sydney, NSW
Tel: + 61 2 9542 7203
Fax: + 61 2 9531 5762
Custom-make a huge array of items (baths, doors, windowframes etc.) with a number of materials including timber and bricks.

SECOND HAND BUILDING CENTRE
432B West Botany Street
Rockdale, NSW 2216
Tel: + 61 2 9567 1322
Fax: + 61 2 9597 1782
email: info@shbc.com.au
website:
www.shbc.com.au
Complete range of reclaimed timber, building materials, hardware, baths and sanitary fittings and architectural antiques.

SELECT SALVAGE
76 Smith Street,
Kensington
Victoria
Tel: + 61 3 9376 2543
Showroom open Mon–Sat, 10am–4pm.

THE SYDNEY SECONDHAND SANDSTONE COMPANY
Brookvale, Sydney
Tel/Fax: + 61 2 9905 7151
Mobile: 0408 259155
Based in Sydney, which was built on sandstone, this company buys and preserves old sandstone which they sell on to stone-masons, builders and homeowners.

VIC PARK SALVAGE
39 Briggs Street,
Welshpool, WA
Tel: + 61 2 9472 3316
Fax: + 61 2 9470 4615
Architectural antiques, windows, doors, de-nailed timber, flooring and lots more.

USEFUL ADDRESSES

NEW ZEALAND

EASTWOOD RECYCLED BUILDING SUPPLIES
171 Kaikorai Valley Road
Dunedin
Tel: + 64 3 476 7868

HERITAGE 100% RECYCLED
61 Ward Street
Dunedin
South Island
Tel: + 64 3 474 9405
Fax: + 64 3 474 9405
Bricks, gates, doors, paving, salvaged hardwood, sleepers etc.

KAMAPAT NEW AND RECYCLED TIMBER
7 Matai Street
Stoke Nelson
South Island
Tel: + 64 3 547 8158
Fax: + 64 3 547 8128
email:
KAPAMAK@xtra.co.nz
website:
www.skyboom/realcrafty.co.nz (look under recycled timber for details)
They sell among other things products made from 100% pure New Zealand timber.

MANAWATU HOUSE PARTS
102 Armstrong House
Palmerston North
Tel: + 64 6 355 0043

PUMP HOUSE SALVAGE YARD
Cnr Tuan & Mathesons Road
Linwood
Christchurch
Tel: + 64 3 389 6638

THE RENOVATOR'S CENTRE
40 Perry Street
Masterton
North Island
Tel: + 64 6 378 8422
Fax: + 64 6 378 8422
Kitchens, bathrooms. doors, windows etc. Furniture, French doors and windows made from recycled timber.

SOUTHERN RECYCLED TIMBER
380 Waterloo Road
Christchurch
Tel: + 64 3 349 2534

_____

EUROPE

THE ORIGINAL ARCHITECTURAL SALVAGE COMPANY
South Gloucester Street
Dublin 2
Ireland
Tel: + 353 1 677 3557
Fax: + 353 1 677 3318
email:
info@architecturalclassics.com
website:
www.architecturalclassics.com
Sanitary ware, bathroom fittings, antique lighting, door furniture, garden statuary, chimney pieces, fireplace accessories and lots more.

MARICHAEL AND MAERSCHALCK
Baarle
Oost Vlaanderen
Belgium
Tel: + 32 9282 2097
Fax: + 32 9282 9175
Antique garden statuary and ornaments

OCCOMAT BCA RECYCLAGE
49500 Hotellerie de Flee
Maine et Loire
France.
Tel: + 33 233 94 74 00
Fax: + 33 233 94 46 56
Old materials, old oak beams and flooring

QUEEN OF THE SOUTH
Haseltweg 377
3600 Genk
Belgium
Tel: + 00 89 356247
Fax: + 00 89 386333

MEDUSA
Lierse Steenweg 199
2220 Heist-op
Den Berg
Belgium
Tel: + 00 15 24 06 06
Fax: + 00 15 25 08 35
2500m^2 of architectural antiques, interior and exterior decorations, garden ornaments etc.

RIK STORMS
Aland 4
Mechelen
Leest
Belgium
Tel: + 00 15 712535
Fax: + 00 714149

TIME LESS TRADING
Biezenstraat
2470 Retie
Belgium
Tel: + 00 14 370542
Fax: + 00 14 375598

VERGRABO
Schoolebeekstraat 91
2500 Lier
Belgium
Tel: + 00 3 4802349
Fax: + 00 3 4880322

DELAIRE ORNAMENTATIE
Brugse Steenweg 395
8520 Kuurne
Belgium
Tel: + 00 56 713008
Fax: + 00 56 713008

VAN HUCLE
Grensstraat 16
8730 Beernem
Belgium
Tel: + 00 50 275001
Fax: + 00 50 27599

FRANK SCHEERLINK
Ninoofse Steenweg 86b
1760 Pamel-Roosdaal
Belgium
Tel: + 00 54 320715
Fax: + 00 54 320715

INDEX

ACKNOWLEDGEMENTS

Our thanks to all at Kyle Cathie Publishers: **Kyle Cathie, Helen Woodhall, Andrie Morris**; **Julia Barder, Melanie Beveridge**, our photographer **Tim Winter** and his assistant **Jo Fairclough**.

Our thanks also to the companies who generously helped us with equipment, materials and advice:

Black and Decker
Hand and power tools for the professional and handyman.
Cuprinol Ltd
Timber treatment products, and decorative colour stains and finishes.
Screwfix Direct
Hardware and tools by mail order – overnight.

Also to all those who kindly allowed us to photograph their gardens:

Susan Boss and **Tony Hill**
Leo and **Jilly Cooper**
Mr and **Mrs Hubert Fear**
Ron and **Judy Mathews**
Alan and **Lucy Moore**
Graham and **Chrissy Price**
John Teller and the Ashley Vale Allotments Association
Joe and **Angela Tucker**
John Woolley

And to the following people whose addresses can be found in our 'Useful Addresses' section on page 138:

Candace Bahouth: mosaic artist; **Sue Berger**: Berger Phillips Town Garden Design; **Nigel and Rosalie Dawes**: Birtsmorton Court; **Robert Dorrien-Smith, Mike Nelhams and Andrew Lawson**: Tresco Abbey Gardens; **Mike Duckett**: Lands End Nurseries; **Mark Durston-Sweet**: Blakeway Fisheries; **Richard Fish**: Poplar Herb Farm; **Sarah Giddens**: garden designer; **Jon Gowan**: builder; **Paul Grellier**: sculptor; **Lawrence Harper**: Harpers Bazaar; **Ron Jones**: Ronsons Reclamation and Restoration; **Thornton Kay** and **Hazel Matravers**: SALVO; **John Nelson** and **Tim Smit**: The Lost Gardens of Heligan; **Stephen Paul**: head gardener at Emmaus House; **Ben Pike**, garden designer; **Andrew Rowland**: Winrow Nurseries; **Sandra Spearing**: South West Reclamation; **Derek Wooton**: Chelsea Farm Centre Ltd.

Thanks also to Clive and Alex Limpkin for allowing us to use their garden props.